BLACKS AT HARVARD

BLACKS AT HARVARD

A Documentary History of African-American Experience at Harvard and Radcliffe

EDITED BY

Werner Sollors,
Caldwell Titcomb, and
Thomas A. Underwood

WITH AN INTRODUCTION BY

Randall Kennedy

NEW YORK UNIVERSITY PRESS

NEW YORK AND LONDON

NEW YORK UNIVERSITY PRESS
New York and London

Library of Congress Cataloging-in-Publication Data

Blacks at Harvard: a documentary history of African-American experience at Harvard and Radcliffe / edited by Werner Sollors, Caldwell Titcomb, and Thomas A. Underwood; with an introduction by Randall Kennedy.
       p.   cm.
   Includes bibliographical references and index.
   ISBN 0-8147-7972-7 (alk. paper) -- ISBN 0-8147-7973-5
(pbk. : alk. paper)
     1. Harvard University--History--Sources.   2. Afro-Americans--Education (Higher)--Massachusetts--History--Sources. 3. United States--Race relations--History--Sources.
4. Radcliffe College--History--Sources. I. Sollors, Werner. II. Titcomb, Caldwell.
III. Underwood, Thomas A.
LD2151.B57 1993 92-27074
378.744'4--dc20   CIP

New York University Press books are printed on acid-free paper,
and their binding materials are chosen for strength and durability.

Manufactured in the United States of America.

c 10 9 8 7 6 5 4 3 2 1
p 10 9 8 7 6 5 4 3 2 1

To the memory of Nathan Irvin Huggins
(1927–1989)

CONTENTS

LIST OF ILLUSTRATIONS

Randall Kennedy in 1990

INTRODUCTION: BLACKS AND THE RACE QUESTION AT HARVARD

RANDALL KENNEDY

The history of blacks at Harvard mirrors, for better or for worse, the history of blacks in the United States. Harvard, too, has been indelibly scarred by slavery, exclusion, segregation, and other forms of racist oppression. At the same time, the nation's oldest university has also supported and allowed itself to be influenced by the various reform movements that have dramatically changed the nature of race relations across the nation. The story of blacks at Harvard is thus inspiring but painful, instructive but ambiguous—a paradoxical episode in the most vexing controversy of American life: "the race question."

The evolution of the race question at Harvard is tellingly displayed by the documents that have been collected here by Werner Sollors, Caldwell Titcomb, and Thomas A. Underwood. Two salient characteristics distinguish the collection. The first is the rich variety of its sources. Included in this documentary history are scholarly overviews, poems, short stories, speeches, well-known memoirs by the famous, previously unpublished memoirs by the lesser known, newspaper accounts, letters, official papers of the university, and transcripts of debates. The editors bring to their compilation persons as diverse as Booker T. Washington, Monroe Trotter, William Hastie, Malcolm X, and Muriel Snowden to convey the complex and various ways in which Harvard has affected the thinking of African Americans and the ways, in turn, in which African Americans have influenced the traditions of Harvard and Radcliffe. Notable among the contributors are significant figures in African-American letters: Phillis Wheatley, Alain Locke, Sterling Brown, Countée Cullen, Marita Bonner, James Alan McPherson, and Andrea Lee. Equally salient are some of the nation's leading historians: W.E.B. Du Bois, Rayford Logan, John Hope Franklin, and Nathan I. Huggins.

The second noteworthy characteristic of the collection is its lack of sentimentality. The editors have made no attempt to hide or mini- mize embarrassments or conflicts, regardless of the actors involved. The result is a sourcebook that brings readers close—perhaps on occasion uncomfortably close—to a history that is full of painful tensions.

The documents that constitute *Blacks at Harvard* can usefully be divided into three periods: (1) the era during which Harvard excluded virtually all African Americans from participation in the intellectual life of the school; (2) the era during which Harvard admitted a small number of black students, excluded black teachers, and generally relegated "the race question" to the margins of the university's consciousness; and (3) the era during which the numbers of black students at Harvard rose dramatically, black scholars emerged as a small but discernible presence on the faculty, and the race question became not only a central and burning issue, but also an issue institutionalized to a considerable degree through the creation of an Afro-American Studies Department.

I

African Americans affected life at Harvard long before they came to the campus as students or professors. As Emory J. West notes in his essay, "Harvard and the Black Man, 1636-1850," the university reaped considerable benefits from the slave trade, which was, through- out much of the seventeenth and eighteenth centuries, a major pillar of New England's commerce. Students and professors at Harvard owned slaves (including at least two presidents of the university, Increase Mather and Benjamin Wadsworth). And students and pro- fessors helped to justify "the peculiar institution." In his essay "The Black Presence at Harvard," Caldwell Titcomb attributes to Dean Henry Eustis the statement that blacks are "little above beasts," and quotes Dean Nathaniel Shaler as declaring that blacks were "unfit for an independent place in a civilized state." Yet, it is a student who earns the dubious distinction of having uttered the most memorable example of racist, pro-slavery advocacy in the documents that follow. At "A Forensic Dispute on the Legality of Enslaving the Africans,

Held at the Public Commencement [of Harvard College] in Cambridge, New-England, (Boston, 1773)," a graduating senior, defending slavery, asked revealingly: "[W]ho I beseech you, ever thought the consent of a child, an ideot, or a madman necessary to his subordination? Every whit as immaterial, is the consent of these miserable Africans, whose real character seems to be a compound of the three last mentioned. . . . What can avail his consent, who through ignorance of the means necessary to promote his happiness, is rendered altogether incapable of choosing for himself?"

Although many members of the Harvard community either defended or tolerated slavery (with all of the damaging intellectual and moral implications flowing from such positions), some did play outstanding roles in the antislavery campaign. Latin Professor Charles Beck, for instance, aided runaway slaves, going so far as to put a trap door on the second floor of his residence (now Warren House, the home of the Harvard English Department) to help fugitives moving north on the Underground Railroad. The most prominent fact, however, about Harvard and its relationship with black Americans prior to the Civil War, is that, by and large, the university firmly shut its doors to African Americans. For a brief moment in 1850, it seemed that that tradition would change. In that year, the Harvard Medical School admitted three black students: Daniel Laing, Jr., Isaac H. Snowden, and Martin R. Delany. Yet this break with tradition was short-lived. The Medical School administration expelled the blacks at the end of their first session of classes because of pressure exerted by white students opposed to the blacks' presence. Explaining the Medical School's action, Dean Oliver Wendell Holmes (the father of Justice Holmes) maintained that "the intermixing of the white and black races in their lecture rooms is distasteful to a large portion of the class and injurious to the interests of the school."

Setting aside the Medical School's brief experiment, Harvard University shut its doors to African Americans throughout the first 229 years of its existence.

II

The origins of an African-American presence among students at Harvard dates back to the years immediately following the Civil War. In 1865, the Medical School reversed its policy prohibiting black students and admitted Edwin C.J.T. Howard. The same year, Harvard College admitted Richard T. Greener. Four years later, Howard and two other African-American students—George L. Ruffin of the Law School, and Robert Tanner Freeman of the Dental School—became the first blacks to graduate from Harvard, an accomplishment attained in 1870 by Greener.

These students and the trickle that followed them encountered a complicated set of conflicting responses at Harvard. In important respects, they found a community willing to recognize, develop, and reward their talents and achievements. W.E.B. Du Bois's memories of his Harvard years are filled with praise (as well as criticism) for the university:

Harvard University in 1888 was a great institution of learning. . . . From the beginning my relations with most of the teachers at Harvard were pleasant. They were on the whole glad to receive a serious student. . . . I was repeatedly a guest in the home of William James; he was my friend and guide to clear thinking. . . . I sat in an upper room and read Kant's *Critique* with Santayana; Shaler invited a Southerner, who objected to sitting beside me, to leave his class. . . . I became one of [Albert Bushnell] Hart's favorite pupils and was afterwards guided by him through my graduate course . . .

Other black pioneers at Harvard expressed positive sentiments. In a speech at the Harvard Club of New York, Richard Greener recalled his undergraduate years with lavish fondness, praising the university for what he viewed as its commitment to equal opportunity. At Harvard, he contended, there is "but one test for all. Ability, character, and merit—these are the sole passports to her favor."[1] Ordinary nostalgia may account, in part, for the exuberance of Greener's exaggerated praise. Probably more important, however, is the fact that, compared to the open, vicious animus with which most of white American society dealt with black Americans in the century following the Civil War, Harvard's treatment of its black students, though deficient by today's standards, constituted a welcome, and

---

[1]Several observers of life at Harvard have prematurely announced the extinction of the color line on campus; in 1960, the black senior who delivered the Latin oration at the Harvard College graduation declared that "at Harvard there are no differences between people." He seems to have confused wishful thinking with realistic description.

deeply appreciated, contrast. In an era during which most whites considered African Americans, as a race, to be mentally and morally inferior to Euro-Americans, Harvard rewarded black students who distinguished themselves academically. Greener won the Boylston Prize for Oratory and the Bowdoin Prize for his senior essay. Clement G. Morgan '90 also won the Boylston Prize, edging out Du Bois, who finished second. Monroe Trotter '95 and Leslie Pinckney Hill '03 were elected to Phi Beta Kappa. In 1890, when reaction against racial equality was reaching new heights of power and respectability, Du Bois served as the commencement speaker at the Harvard graduation ceremonies, while Morgan gave an address as class orator.

Despite their privileged positions, however, blacks at Harvard did not escape the humiliating stigma of the color bar inside and outside of their famous campus. As Du Bois put it, "[s]ometimes the shadow of insult fell": being mistaken constantly for a servant; being turned away from local barbershops on account of color; knowing better than even to ask the white families who rented lodgings to white students whether they would be willing to rent the same lodgings to blacks; suffering exclusion from various extracurricular activities because of race.

The most notorious single example of racism at Harvard in the years after the admission of black men occurred in 1922 when university president Abbott Lawrence Lowell prohibited Negro students from residing in the Freshman Dormitories, a residence that was required for all white students. The social standing of the blacks immediately affected by this policy highlighted the significance of the color bar that Lowell imposed. One was Roscoe Conkling Bruce, Jr., a graduate of Phillips Exeter Academy, the grandson of Blanche K. Bruce, the first black United States senator, and the son of a 1902 Harvard College graduate who had received his degree *magna cum laude*, been elected to Phi Beta Kappa, and been selected as class orator. Castigating Lowell's action, the *New York Amsterdam News* observed that Harvard's policy "should convince all of us that our success is not dependent upon individual attainment. . . . [T]o President Lowell and to thousands like him [Bruce's] distinguished ancestry and preparation are as nothing when placed alongside of the fact that he is a Negro."

Seeking to justify his decision, President Lowell wrote that "in Freshman Halls, where residence is compulsory, we have felt from the beginning the necessity of not including colored men." "[W]e have not thought it possible," he maintained, "to compel men of different races to reside together."

The response to Lowell's action was an extraordinary outpouring of protest from blacks and whites within and outside of the Harvard community. The elder Bruce, principal of a high school in West Virginia, observed acidly:

The policy of compulsory residence in the Freshman Halls is costly indeed if it is the thing that constrains Harvard to enter open-eyed and brusque upon a policy of racial discrimination. It ill becomes a great mother of culture avoidably to accentuate the consciousness of racial differences among Americans—that seedbed of so many strifes and griefs.

James Weldon Johnson, secretary of the National Association for the Advancement of Colored People (NAACP), maintained that "by capitulating to anti-negro prejudice in the freshman dormitories or anywhere else, Harvard University affirms that prejudice and strengthens it, and is but putting into effect the program proclaimed by the infamous Ku Klux Klan and its apologists." Moorfield Storey and several other distinguished white alumni initiated a petition condemning Lowell's action. And publications such as the *Nation* and the *New York Evening Post* editorialized against Lowell's decision. Even the *Harvard Alumni Bulletin* observed that "for Harvard to deny to colored men a privilege it accords to whites appears inevitably as a reversal of policy, if not a positive disloyalty to a principle for which the university has taken an open and unshaken stand."

The Dormitory Crisis can be looked upon as an ugly provocation that eventually mobilized the best elements in Harvard's traditions. Writing in the *Crisis*, Du Bois maintained that "[d]eep as is the shame and humiliation of Harvard's recent surrender to the Bourbon South, the spirited and whole-souled response that it has evinced is perhaps the most heartening sign of sanity on the race problem that has happened in fifty years." Not only did Harvard alumni, black and white, spark a strong protest against Lowell; they sparked a strong protest that, to an important extent, prevailed. In 1923, the Harvard Board of Overseers resoundingly overruled President Lowell, thereby allowing black students to reside in the Freshman Dormitories.

On the other hand, despite the reversal of Lowell's policy, it reflected sentiments at Harvard that had deep roots, firm backing, and a long future. Lowell certainly lost. But blacks at Harvard did not wholly triumph. The Board of Overseers decided that "all members of the freshman class shall reside and board in the Freshman Halls" and that no man shall be excluded from a dormitory "by reason of his color." But the Board of Overseers also decreed that "[i]n the application of this rule, men of the white and colored races shall not be compelled to live and eat together"—a statement at once cryptic and clear: cryptic in that it did not suggest the situation of compelled interaction that the Overseers feared, clear in that it obviously manifested a desire to mollify in some way the inflamed sensibilities of white supremacists.

Between 1865 and 1970, scores of distinguished African Americans contributed to Harvard as students or guests of one sort or another. Some thoroughly relished their involvement with Harvard. Recounting his feelings when the university conferred an honorary degree upon him in 1896, Booker T. Washington expressed a mixture of appreciation and awe: "To see over a thousand strong men, representing all that is best in State, Church, business, and education, with the glow of enthusiasm of college loyalty and college pride—which has, I think, a peculiar Harvard flavour—is a sight that does not easily fade from memory." Others experienced mixed feelings. "I was in Harvard," writes W.E.B. Du Bois, "not of it." Still, others seem to have truly suffered through their stints at the university. Keenly attuned to the myriad ways in which Harvard's caste-ridden practices routinely belied its meritocratic pretensions, John Hope Franklin recalls that when he left Harvard in the spring of 1939, "I knew that I did not wish to be in Cambridge another day."

III

A substantial number of the documents featured in *Blacks at Harvard* have to do with the black presence there since 1970. This concentration stems from two interrelated facts. First, during this period Harvard hosted more black students, professors, administrators, and guests than in all of the previous years combined. Second, during this era the nation underwent a profound change in moral, political, and intellectual consciousness because of the Civil Rights Movement, the Black Power Movement, and, most recently, the Diversity Movement, all of which have insistently focused attention upon the relevance of race in all aspects of our culture.

Ever since blacks first joined the Harvard community, they have engaged in efforts to fashion within it a suitable place for themselves. Since the early 1960s, these efforts have been marked by an increased emphasis on organized collective action, a rising militance nurtured by larger numbers, and heightened skepticism regarding the legitimacy of certain central Harvard traditions.

Various controversies, well illustrated by the documents that follow, shed light on these developments. One arose in 1963 when a group of students sought to create the Association of African and Afro-American Students (AAAAS), an organization "open to African and Afro-American students" to "promote mutual understanding between African and Afro-American students, to provide ourselves a voice in the community . . . and to develop the leadership capable of effectively coping with the various problems of our peoples." For many, the problem was that the organization's membership clause appeared implicitly to exclude non-Africans and non-blacks. Critics argued that this constituted racial discrimination and that, therefore, the University should withhold official recognition. Official recognition was important because only officially recognized groups were authorized to use Harvard buildings or to solicit new members every year at registration. In some statements, defenders of the association suggested that its membership clause did not constitute a racial exclusion. In others, defenders argued that a racially restrictive organization of black students on a predominantly white campus—at that time blacks constituted about one percent of the student body—was justifiable on the grounds that Africans and Afro-Americans share a common heritage of oppression beyond the understanding of whites and that the presence of whites in Association meetings would hinder the efforts of black members to develop what one spokesman called "a greater sense of Negro identity."

One defender of the new Association was Martin L. Kilson, a lecturer in the Department of Government who subsequently became the first tenured black member of the Harvard Faculty of Arts and Sciences. Another of the Association's backers was Archie Epps III, a first-year graduate student who later became the Dean of Students at Harvard College. One of the leading undergraduate proponents of the Association was Ayi Kwei Armah, a Ghanaian who subsequently became an important figure in African letters, writing among other things the novel *The Beautyful Ones Are Not Yet Born* (1968).

Opinion on and off campus was widely divided. A black Harvard alumnus, William Harrison '32, an editor of the *Boston Chronicle*, wrote a letter to the editor of the *Harvard Crimson* in which he called the formation of the Association "a capital idea," voiced regret at the absence of such an organization when he attended the college, and recalled the words of Harvard's famous philosopher George Santayana: "The Negro, if he is not a fool, loves his own inspiration, and expands in the society of his own people." Another commentator urged the University to recognize the Association on libertarian grounds: "A discriminatory membership policy is part of the ideology of this group; punishing it for its membership policy by withholding the privileges granted other undergraduate political groups would be punishing it for its ideology."

On the other hand, Herbert H. Denton Jr., a black member of the *Crimson*'s editorial board who went on to become a prize-winning journalist with the *Washington Post*, criticized the exclusivity of the African and Afro-American Association with elegant harshness. He challenged every aspect of the asserted rationale of the Association's membership policy, particularly the "idea that whites and Negroes are intrinsically incapable of understanding one another." He questioned the empirical soundness of this thesis—noting that it is "always assumed, never demonstrated"—as well as its political usefulness:

One thing is certain: the surest way to prevent equality is to convince everyone of such a thesis. Paranoid presuppositions rapidly become self-fulfilling prophecies. The ideal of equality is not refuted, it is merely rendered historically impossible by ideologies which generate racial distrust.

Asserting a point of view in 1963 that came under increasing pressure over the next quarter century, Denton maintained:

Negro students coming to the University are likely to be overwhelmed with the idea, promoted by the only "official" Negro organization on the campus, that even the most liberal and interesting white students they may meet cannot possibly understand them, and may even be hypocrites—that the only place they are truly among friends is in an all-Negro organization strongly influenced by Black Nationalism. Such an outcome drastically curtails their ability to benefit from the central Harvard experience of association with and exposure to the broadest possible spectrum of people, ideas and movements. One may seriously ask whether an organization which so functions is in anyway compatible with the educational ideals of this University.

Harvard's Student Council on Undergraduate Activities denied recognition to the Association, condemning its membership clause as "discriminatory." The relevant Faculty committee concurred, stating that it was "unwilling . . . to put the weight of Harvard's approval behind the principle of racial separatism and exclusion." This rebuke, however, did not extinguish the sentiments that prompted the Association's founding and the defiant defense of a membership clause that, in retrospect, appears only to have served a purely symbolic purpose.

Those sentiments grew stronger in the years to come and were undoubtedly nourished by three appearances that Malcolm X made on Harvard's campus between 1961 and 1964. On the second of these appearances, a talk given on March 18, 1964, to the Leverett House Forum, Malcolm X made a statement that continues to reverberate on Harvard's campus and throughout the nation as a whole. "What is logical to the oppressor," Malcolm X asserted, "isn't logical to the oppressed. And what is reason to the oppressor isn't reason to the oppressed. . . . There just has to be a new system of reason and logic devised by us who are on the bottom, if we want to get some results in this struggle that is called 'the Negro revolution.'"

The radicalism of Malcolm X seeped into the rhetoric of black students who expressed a profound sense of alienation from Harvard. Their very presence, however, at the nation's premier "white" university indicated, by and large, a desire to "make it" within the established framework of American institutions while simultaneously seeking to reform these institutions as much as possible for the benefit of the African-American community. Reformist aims at Harvard have centered primarily upon enlarging the numbers of blacks associated with the university as students, teachers, and administrators and, relatedly, with institutionalizing a black presence. Each of these aims was implicated in the struggle to create an Afro-American Studies Department.

A revealing reflection on the extraordinary circumstances surrounding that struggle is that many black students boycotted the official memorial service that mourned the assassination of Dr. Martin Luther King, Jr. While Harvard president Nathan Pusey led services inside Memorial Church, the largest site of religious activity on campus, eighty black students stood outside on the steps. "If they come out of [Memorial Church] with tears in their eyes," the president of the AAAAS is reported to have said, "We want it to be plain that we don't want their tears. We want black people to have a place at Harvard." Black students' successful efforts to create an Afro-

American Studies Department embodied that search for a place.

In 1968-69, against the backdrop of increasingly radical student protests against the draft, the war in Vietnam, college restrictions on personal (primarily sexual) conduct, university ties with the Central Intelligence Agency and companies doing business in South Africa, government repression of the Black Panthers and other similarly incendiary groups—in short, against the backdrop of the most tumultuous phase of "the sixties"—black students at Harvard demanded that the University create a structure for the study of Afro-American affairs. A committee chaired by Professor Henry Rosovsky addressed these demands by recommending, among other things, the building of "a social and cultural center for black students," the creation of a major in Afro-American Studies, the establishment of a Center for Afro-American Studies, and the setting aside of fifteen to twenty graduate fellowships a year for black students "who possess the potential to become scholars of the first rank." To underline the committee's commitment to fast and concrete action it wrote that while its "report—as all university committee reports—necessarily uses many unspecific terms and qualifiers typical of institutional language, it would be tragic if this obscured the sense of urgency felt by the Committee."

The report of the Rosovsky Committee and its adoption by the University indicated a level of solicitude for African-American students that was unprecedented in Harvard's history. Yet it encountered resistance from a substantial part of the organized, activist sector of the black student community. These critics articulated two principal complaints. One was that the Rosovsky Committee report envisioned Afro-American Studies as a program instead of a department. This was viewed as important because programs typically have less institutional autonomy and prestige than departments. As envisioned by the Rosovsky Committee a student or professor would be affiliated with Afro-American Studies along with some other, more established discipline. Some critics viewed this as an insulting subordination of Afro-American scholarship studies to traditional, "white" sectors of the community. The second objection was that the Rosovsky Committee did not provide for student participation in the selection of faculty for the planned Afro-American Studies Department. This was in keeping with tradition. But the AAAAS activists wanted to upset tradition. They wanted students to be able to play a significant role in choosing faculty members so that Afro-American

Studies would be more than merely another scholastic enterprise; they wanted it to embody a commitment to the empowerment of the black community. Recognizing that they viewed the purpose of the Afro-American Studies initiative in a different way than did the upper reaches of the University hierarchy, the activists also recognized that they would evaluate candidates for faculty positions differently than did the University administration. To have some influence on the constitution of Afro-American Studies faculty, the students sought a place in the choosing of their professors.

In April 1969, after anguished debate, the faculty of the Harvard College of Arts and Sciences acquiesced to the critics of the Rosovsky report. It voted to recognize Afro-American Studies as a department and to seat six students (including three chosen by Afro) as full, voting members of the body chosen to select faculty members for the new department. This vote, broadcast live on the student-run radio station, was taken soon after the traumatic "bust" in which President Pusey called on Cambridge police to remove leftist students (the great majority of whom were white) from University buildings they had occupied to protest the Vietnam War and express dissatisfaction with various policies of the University. The vote was also taken at a moment when substantial numbers of professors and administrators, taking seriously even the most heated rhetoric of campus militants, feared that at least some black students might physically damage the campus in the event of a negative vote on the part of the faculty.

Some observers hail the events of April 1969 as a significant advance in the fortunes of blacks at Harvard and beyond. Looking back with pride on the actions that he and others took, Ernest J. Wilson III, one of Harvard's leading student activists, puts the matter this way:

We had a lot of gall even to attempt such changes; we were just wet-behind-the-ears undergraduates. Part of the hubris came from our feeling that, at last, history was going our way. We knew that we were riding the crest of a wave. With Nina Simone singing that all of us were "young, gifted, and black," we felt our newly assertive blackness was not just an extra burden, as it was for many of our predecessors, but also at times a decided social benefit. And after all, cities were literally burning over the question of black equality, and the real heroes of the black revolt, courageous black students in the Deep South, were engaged in far less genteel and more dangerous battles at Ol' Miss and Texas Southern. For us, pressing for Afro-American Studies in Cambridge seemed the least we could do. And the excitement of creating something new, scholarly, and socially relevant was exhilarating.

Others are more skeptical. Martin Kilson, the only black professor on the Rosovsky Committee, voted *against* the students' demands. Recalling the episode he writes:

The militant students wanted lots of political activism in the operation of the Afro-American Studies Department and were disdainful of rigorous intellectual and scholarly values ("Whitey values," some called them). I, on the other hand, favored no ethnocentric militancy in the character of the Afro-American Studies Department and stood firm for the highest intellectual and scholarly criteria. I lost out. . . .

Similarly critical is Nathan Huggins, a distinguished African-American historian who did his graduate work at Harvard and later returned as a professor and director of the W.E.B. Du Bois Institute, a direct offshoot of the struggle for Afro-American Studies. Noting that the birth of Afro-American Studies stemmed in large part from a sense of "perceived threat," he writes that the department suffered "during its first ten years, from the lingering doubts and resentments harbored by faculty never fully convinced of Afro-America as a legitimate field of study . . . and suspicious of what often appeared to be separatist tendencies on the part of its advocates."

For all the criticisms leveled at the way in which the Harvard Afro-American Studies Department was founded, however, one thing is irrefutable: for over two decades it has provided a source of support for a broad range of scholars exploring African-American culture and established itself as a permanent part of the university community. It is worth considering whether this could ever have been accomplished without the pushing and shoving, the excesses and errors that struggles for social change always entail.

IV

African Americans have encountered, as we have seen, a wide range of reactions at Harvard. Their responses have varied greatly. Some, like Richard Greener, have expressed an unalloyed happiness with the University. For others, however, considerable pain accompanies the recollection of their experience with Harvard. Herbert W.

Nickens remembers:

Being black exacerbated the already difficult freshman adjustment in
addition to raising questions all its own. We not only had to live with
strangers, but with white strangers whose attitudes toward us were rarely
indifferent to our color. We often bore the burden of being cultural and
anthropological curiosities: inspected, sometimes devaluated, frequently
overvalued, but never regarded in absence of the black factor. We found
ourselves spread-eagled between black and white.

Ambivalence is the word that best captures the way in which most
African-American students, professors, administrators, guests, and
alumni seem to have perceived, and reacted to, Harvard. Many of the
documents that follow give voice to African Americans who feel,
simultaneously, admiration for Harvard's traditions and desire to
reform the institution, a sense of accomplishment derived from association with Harvard and a sense of sorrow or even guilt that this
privilege is beyond the circumstances of the great mass of black
Americans, a yearning for acceptance and a desire to remain rebel-
lious outsiders, recognition that Harvard has sought to make itself
more hospitable to African Americans and anger that the nation's
leading university has failed to do more.

W.E.B. Du Bois's "A Negro Student at Harvard at the End of the
Nineteenth Century" is one of several memoirs that vividly capture
these tensions. He admired the intellectual potentialities that the
University offered, but consciously embraced his status as an outsider.
"I was very happy at Harvard," he recalled, "but for unusual reasons.
One of these was my acceptance of racial segregation." Du Bois did
not see racial segregation as a "final solution." To the contrary, he
welcomed the "prospect of ultimate full human intercourse, without
reservations and annoying distinctions." But in light of the racist
humiliations that blacks constantly faced in social interactions with
whites, Du Bois concluded that, for him, the best thing to do at
Harvard was "to consort with my own and to disdain and forget as far
as possible that outer, whiter world":

I asked nothing of Harvard but the tutelage of teachers and the freedom of
the laboratory and library. I was quite voluntarily and willingly outside its
social life. . . . This cutting of myself off from my white fellows, or being cut
off, did not mean unhappiness or resentment. . . . I thoroughly enjoyed life.
I was conscious of understanding and power, and conceited enough still to

imagine . . . that they who did not know me were the losers, not I.

Du Bois suggests that he was "exceptional among Negroes at Harvard in my ideas on voluntary race segregation." His fellow blacks, he remarks with a trace of disdain, "saw salvation only in integration at the earliest possible moment and on almost any terms . . . ; I was firm in my criticism of white folk and in my dream of a self-sufficient Negro culture even in America."

"Harvard and the Small-Towner" (1986) is a more recent memoir of university life that also articulates the complicated, conflicting emotions of an African-American intellectual seeking to subvert conventions of racial dominance. In it, Martin Luther Kilson (mentioned earlier as the first tenured black professor on the Harvard Faculty of Arts and Sciences), reflects upon his long (and ongoing) association with the University. From his years as a graduate student in the 1950s, when he helped to found the Harvard Society for Minority Rights, to his years in the 1980s and 1990s as the senior black faculty member within Arts and Sciences, Kilson has been involved in all of the many racial controversies that have surfaced on campus. As was noted above, he helped to form the Harvard Afro-American Students Association and backed it during its confrontation with critics who attacked the Association's racially exclusionary membership policy. In "Harvard and the Small-Towner" Kilson continues to defend this early "bid to give vigorous intellectual formation to students' Black-ethnic awareness," contending that the Association was "Black-skewed" but "not ethno-centrically-Black-skewed." Kilson gives no hint as to how he justifies his conclusion; after all, insofar as the student group at issue did limit its membership on a racial basis, it seems that the group could appropriately be labelled as "ethnocentric." But the more significant point for present purposes is not Kilson's early defense of the Association, but rather his condemnation of it after 1968 when it was, in his words, "shanghaied" by student proponents of the Black Power Movement who, among other things, insisted upon the formation of an Afro-American Studies Department independent from other University programs and one in which students would have an important hand in governance. According to Kilson, these students—"the new Black solidarity militants"—indulged in a "dead-end cathartic ethnocentrism" that had a lingering destructive influence:

During the late 1960s to early 1970s era, something happened to the willingness of Black students to take academic and intellectual pursuits seriously. . . . What happened was in large part of Blacks' own making, or rather [the] making of Black ethnocentrists who convinced themselves and other Blacks that the catharsis associated with mau-mauing "Whitey's values" was preferable to a pragmatic employment of ethnic militancy.

For historians of ideas, the task of the future will be to identify the line separating what Kilson defends as pragmatic "ethnic militancy" on Harvard's campus from what he condemns as "ethnocentrism."

Another memoir by an African-American professor is "A Pioneer: Black and Female" by Eileen Southern, who in 1971 became the first black woman appointed to a tenured faculty position. The first black American recipient of a Ph.D. in musicology, Southern was a professor in the Music Department, a chair of the Afro-American Studies Department, and the author of numerous books and articles including *The Music of Black Americans: A History* and a *Biographical Dictionary of Afro-American and African Musicians*. Like Kilson's account, Southern's is distinguished by the openness with which she criticizes other African Americans at Harvard. Recalling her early years on campus, Southern writes, for instance, that "it seemed that the minorities already at Harvard did not welcome the idea of being joined by others. It was as if they were reluctant to lose their status of being 'the only one.'" Unlike Kilson's account, Southern's explicitly criticizes the University itself for racism and sexism, which, in her view, were an "ever-present" reality that she "gradually learned to endure." At the same time, echoing Du Bois, whom she expressly cites as her role model, Southern lavishly praises Harvard's influence on her intellectual life. "In its role as nurturer of scholars," Southern observes, "Harvard never let me down! I could feel myself growing from year to year, almost month to month. . . ." She even concedes that her minority status "at times brought special dividends":

Some honors came . . . not only because I was qualified, but also because, as a black woman, I was highly visible . . . my husband and I were invited to glamorous dinner parties and receptions, where we met the great leaders of our time, the celebrated and the obscure.

Yet another memoir that poignantly captures the characteristic duality with which many African Americans experience Harvard is "The Reform of Tradition, the Tradition of Reform" by Ernest J. Wilson III, the student dissident cited above. He is currently a professor of politics at the University of Michigan. When Wilson came to Harvard in 1966 he was no stranger to its traditions. Several of his older relatives had attended Harvard, including his maternal grandfather, T. Montgomery Gregory, who graduated alongside John Reed and Walter Lippmann in the illustrious class of 1910. Wilson freely confesses his indebtedness to Harvard, noting that, "however imperfectly, [it] showed me that the intellectual life and the life of [political] commitment can, with effort and imagination, be combined." Moreover, it is clear from Wilson's memoir that he indulged in the most mainstream and even elite activities of Harvard undergraduate life. Without embarrassment, Wilson recalls that he "joined the *Harvard Lampoon*, wrote for the *Crimson*, ate at the Signet, was elected Class Marshal, and joined one of Harvard's final clubs, well-known locally for its splendid garden parties." It should come as no surprise, then, that Wilson experienced much of his time at Harvard as "sheer delight."

On the other hand, Wilson did perceive that "more than a whiff of condescension [was aimed] toward black students":

Some whites acted as if we were a black tabula rasa ready to be filled with New England education and high culture. Others caricatured us only as the carriers of the culture of James Brown; any interest in the written word or in Beethoven was somehow disappointing and inauthentic.

More important, Wilson encountered at Harvard an oppressive absence: "the invisibility of the things that I took for granted at home—the disciplined and serious and sustained study of black culture, politics, and life." Redressing this problem became, as we have seen, a focal point of Wilson's collegiate career and the careers of many African-American students. He speaks for several generations when he asserts with pride: "[W]e changed Harvard as Harvard changed us."

V

Blacks at Harvard will certainly nourish scholarly inquiry into the social and intellectual history of African Americans in elite national institutions. One hopes that it will also spur further efforts to answer the scores of open questions: What have the quiet majority of black students thought and felt about their time at Harvard? What have been the career trajectories of African-American alumni? To what degree have they remained in touch with the University? In all of these respects, how does the experience of African Americans compare with that of people of other racial backgrounds? Further exploration of these subjects will undoubtedly lead scholars to undertake a comprehensive review of the student press and to compile oral histories. This anthology is an important and impressive first step towards documenting a fascinating aspect of African-American culture that warrants closer attention.

RANDALL KENNEDY

Randall Leroy Kennedy was born in Columbia, South Carolina, on 10 September 1954. He attended St. Albans School in Washington, D.C., and won the Freeman History Prize. Upon his graduation from Princeton University, where he was Historical Studies Editor of the *Princeton Journal of the Arts and Sciences*, he studied for two years at Oxford University as a Rhodes Scholar. In 1979 he entered Yale Law School, and served as Note and Topics Editor of the *Yale Law Journal*.

He spent the 1982-83 academic year in Washington, D.C., as law clerk to Judge J. Skelly Wright of the U.S. Court of Appeals, and the following year as law clerk for Justice Thurgood Marshall of the U.S. Supreme Court. In 1984 he joined the Harvard Law School faculty, becoming a full professor in 1989. He has written widely on civil rights and race-relations law. In 1990 he became the founding editor of the quarterly journal *Reconstruction*, devoted to African-American politics, society, and culture.

BLACKS AT HARVARD

THE BLACK PRESENCE AT HARVARD: AN OVERVIEW

CALDWELL TITCOMB

The earliest reference to a black at Harvard was the admission by the wife of the College's first head that a slave had lain on a student's bed in 1639. As the seventeenth and eighteenth centuries rolled on, the list of the leading slaveholding families in Massachusetts contained the names of numerous Harvard men, including Presidents Increase Mather (1685-1701) and Benjamin Wadsworth (1725-37). In the eighteenth century and later, blacks in and around Boston were encouraged to attend Harvard's Commencement, which became for them the most festive day of the year; in 1773 they could have heard two seniors debating the legal pros and cons of enslaving Africans.

For most of the nineteenth century, the well-to-do undergraduates each had a black servant called a "scout" (a term borrowed from Oxford). Blacks later served as janitors, laboratory custodians, and waiters in Memorial Hall, where students ate from 1874 to 1924.

If the low opinion of the black race held by Harvard's most famous nineteenth-century scientist, Louis Agassiz, was echoed by science deans Henry Eustis '38 ("little above beasts") and Nathaniel Shaler '62 ("unfit for an independent place in a civilized state"), the faculty did have its outspoken Abolitionists, such as Henry Wadsworth Longfellow and James Russell Lowell '38. Divinity School professor Henry Ware Jr. '12 was the founding president of the Cambridge Anti-Slavery Society in 1834, and the first anti-slavery novel, *The Slave* (1836)—reprinted many times under such titles as *Archy Moore, The White Slave or, Memoirs of a Fugitive*—was written by Richard Hildreth '26. Latin Professor Charles Beck (1798-1861) put in a trap door on the second floor of his Cambridge residence (now Warren House, the home of the Harvard English Department) to shelter fugitive slaves moving north on the Underground Railroad. The 1650 Charter under which Harvard still operates spoke of "the education of the English & Indian Youth of this Country," and a few Indians were enrolled between 1653 and 1715, though only one completed his degree (Caleb Cheeshahteaumuck in 1665). But the Charter said nothing about the education of blacks, and none appeared on Harvard's rolls until the middle of the nineteenth century.

The earliest baccalaureate degrees that American colleges awarded to blacks went to Alexander Twilight (Middlebury, 1823), Edward Jones (Amherst, 1826), John Russwurm (Bowdoin, 1826), and Edward Mitchell (Dartmouth, 1828).

The first black student to enter Harvard College would have been Beverly G. Williams, in 1847. He was an outstanding scholar in a preparatory-school class that included President Edward Everett's own son. Everett himself proclaimed the lad to be the best Latinist in his class, and Williams's virtues were even debated in the U.S. Congress. When grumblings were voiced about accepting a black student, Everett stated that, "as he will be very well fitted, I know of no reason why he should not be admitted." Unfortunately, a few weeks before the academic year began, Williams died of tuberculosis, two months short of the age of 18.

Consequently, the first blacks to begin studies at Harvard were not in the College but the Medical School. In 1850, the celebrated Martin R. Delany and two other blacks were briefly enrolled. Yet it was not until the 1869 Commencement that Harvard would have its first black degree recipients: Edwin C.J.T. Howard at the Medical School, George L. Ruffin at the Law School, and Robert T. Freeman at the Dental School (its first graduating class). Ruffin and Freeman were the first blacks in the country to receive their respective degrees. Ruffin became the first black judge in Massachusetts; and Freeman, though he died young, had a dental society named for him.

The first black student in the College was Richard T. Greener, who entered in 1865 and took his degree in 1870, winning the chief prizes in writing and speaking along the way. He became a philosophy professor, law school dean, and foreign diplomat, and was an acclaimed orator. Radcliffe, founded in 1879, had in 1898 its first black A.B. recipient, Alberta V. Scott.

For some time the number of black students in Harvard College remained small (including, however, descendants of some illustrious figures, such as the grandson of Frederick Douglass and the son of Charles W. Chesnutt, both in the Class of '05). But since the Class of 1899 there have been only three classes without black members. A marked surge in black enrollment occurred starting with the Class of 1963, and an enormous leap to more than 100 students a year began with the Class of 1973, the first class to be admitted following the national trauma of Dr. Martin Luther King Jr.'s assassination (Harvard and Radcliffe admissions were merged in 1975). The cumulative number of black men and women enrolled as undergraduates at Harvard and Radcliffe through the Class of 1996 comes to about 3,800.

Among the black alumni of the College are: Robert H. Terrell, A.B. 1884, the first black man to deliver a Harvard Commencement oration and the first black municipal judge in Washington, D.C.; William E. B. Du Bois '90, one of the intellectual titans of the twentieth century, and the first black to receive a Harvard A.M. (1891) and Ph.D. (1895); journalist W. Monroe Trotter '95, the first Harvard black elected to Phi Beta Kappa; Alain L. Locke '08, Ph.D. '18, the only black Rhodes Scholar in the country until the 1960s, and godfather to the Harlem Renaissance; Plenyolo Gbe Wolo '17, the first black African graduate and first member of his Liberian tribe ever to get a higher education; Robert C. Weaver '29, Ph.D. '34, the first black Cabinet member (Secretary of HUD); Clifton R. Wharton Jr. '47, first black president of a major "white" university and later chancellor of SUNY's 64 campuses; Gerald E. Thomas '51, the second black admiral in the Navy, Ambassador to Kenya, and Harvard Overseer; Clifford L. Alexander Jr. '55, president of the Student Council, who later became the first black Secretary of the Army and a Harvard overseer; J. Max Bond Jr. '55, dean of CCNY's school of architecture and environmental studies; Harold R. Scott '57, prominent in theatre as actor, director, producer and professor; Thomas Sowell '58, prolific economist and ethnologist; W. Haywood Burns '62, law professor and dean; Isaiah A. Jackson III '66, internationally active orchestral conductor; and Keith A. Saunders '75, ballet soloist.

Black alumnae of Radcliffe include: Dorothy C. Guinn '13, executive director of the National Council of Negro Women; Eva B. Dykes '17, Ph. D. '21, one of the first three black American women to receive a Ph.D. (all in 1921); Frances Olivia Grant '17, first black Radcliffe member of Phi Beta Kappa; teacher and anthropologist Caroline Bond Day '19, A.M. '30; composer and writer Marita Bonner

Occomy '22; Theodora R. Boyd '27, Ph.D. '42, chairman of the French Department at Howard University; singer Lola Wilson Hayes '27; Muriel S. Snowden '38, social worker, founder of Freedom House, and the first black woman elected to the Harvard Board of Overseers; political scientist Merze Tate, Ph.D. '41, first black American woman to study at Oxford; Elizabeth Fitzgerald Howard '48, first black to be elected president of a Radcliffe class; Lois Dickson Rice '54, senior vice-president of Control Data Corporation; sociologist Bennetta Washington Jules-Rosette '68, Ph.D. '73; and Constance B. Hilliard '71, Ph.D. '77, president of the African Development Foundation.

A surprising number of important black historians had training at Harvard. In addition to the aforementioned Du Bois and Tate, they include: Benjamin G. Brawley, A.M. '08; Carter G. Woodson, Ph.D. '12 (Harvard's second black Ph.D.); William M. Brewer '19, A.M. '29; Charles H. Wesley, Ph.D. '25; William Leo Hansberry '21, A.M. '32; Alrutheus A. Taylor, A.M. '23, Ph.D., 36; Rayford W. Logan, A.M. '32, Ph.D. '36; Clinton E. Knox, Ph.D. '40; John Hope Franklin, A.M. '36, Ph.D. '41, recent president of the American Historical Association whose standard history of Afro-Americans has gone through six editions since 1948; Robert H. Brisbane Jr., Ph.D. '49; Jerome W. Jones, A.M. '51, Ph.D. '60; Otey M. Scruggs, A.M. '52, Ph.D. '58; Nathan I. Huggins, A.M. '59, Ph.D. '62; and Kenneth R. Manning '70, A.M. '71, Ph.D. '74.

Black alumni who have made a mark in prose fiction include Cecil A. Blue '25, A.M. '26; William Melvin Kelley '60; Ayi Kwei Armah '63; John A. McCluskey '66; James Alan McPherson, LL.B. '68, winner of both the National Book Award and the Pulitzer Prize; and Andrea N. Lee '74, A.M. '78. Among the poets are Leslie Pinckney Hill '03, A.M. '04; Sterling A. Brown, A.M. '23; Countée Cullen, A.M. '26; Paul Vesey (pseudonym of Samuel W. Allen, J.D. '41); Johnie H. Scott '68; Ifeanyi Menkiti, Ph.D. '74; and Raymond R. Fleming, Ph.D. '76.

The roster of those alumni who, since the heyday of Du Bois and Trotter, have distinguished themselves in print journalism include Hallowell Bowser '44; Melvin B. Miller '56; L. Deckle McLean Jr. '63; Herbert H. Denton '65; Stephen T. Curwood '69; Marvin A. Hightower '69; Lee A. Daniels '71; Anthony C. Hill '73; Sylvester Monroe '73; Scott B. Minerbrook '74; Ronald W. Wade '76; Mark T. Whitaker '79, a *summa cum laude* graduate in social studies; Celia W. Dugger '80; Leigh A. Jackson '82; Jacob V. Lamar '83; and

Sophfronia Scott Gregory '88.

Of the professional graduate schools, none has had a more continuous and far-reaching body of black alumni than the Law School. Since the already cited Judge Ruffin, one might mention Archibald H. Grimké, LL.B. 1874, president of the American Negro Academy and U.S. consul; William H. Lewis, LL.B. '95, the first black assistant attorney general of the United States (also a football captain and coach while at Harvard); Charles H. Houston, LL.B. '22, S.J.D. '23, first black on the *Harvard Law Review* and proclaimed by Justice William O. Douglas as one of the country's ten great lawyers of the past 100 years; Judge Raymond Pace Alexander, J.D. '23; Edward O. Gourdin '21, LL.B. '24, first black on the Massachusetts Superior Court; William H. Hastie, LL.B. '30, S.J.D. '33, first black on a circuit court of appeals, and later chief justice; William T. Coleman, LL.B. '43 (received degree in '46), the top scholar in his class, first black clerk for the U.S. Supreme Court, and second black presidential Cabinet officer; Wade H. McCree Jr., J.D. '44 (received degree in '48), judge, Solicitor General, and Harvard Overseer; C. Clyde Ferguson Jr., LL.B. '51, law dean, Ambassador to Uganda, and Harvard's second tenured black law professor (after Derrick A. Bell Jr., appointed in 1971); Christopher F. Edley Sr., LL.B. '53, head of the United Negro College Fund; John H. Bustamante, LL.M. '54, founder of Ohio's only black-owned bank; Theodore Roosevelt Newman Jr., J.D. '58, first black judge to head a state-level court system (District of Columbia); law professor Anita L. Glasco, J.D. '67; Randall M. Robinson, J.D. '70, director of TransAfrica; judge Marie Oliver Jackson, J.D. '72; Margaret T. Okorodudu, LL.M. '77, in the Nigerian Ministry of Justice; and Raymond M. Burse, J.D. '78, president of Kentucky State University.

Harvard began bestowing honorary degrees in 1692. The first black recipient was Tuskegee Institute president Booker T. Washington, who made his celebrated and controversial "Atlanta Compromise" speech in 1895 and received a Master of Arts degree at the next year's Harvard Commencement (he was also made an honorary member of Harvard's Phi Beta Kappa chapter in 1904). The same degree was presented in 1929 to Washington's Tuskegee successor, Robert Russa Moton. No further honorary degrees went to blacks until after World War II.

No issue concerning Harvard's blacks comes close to matching the storm that arose all over the country in 1922-23 after President Lowell (who was also unhappy over the increased number of Jewish students in the College), acting on his own authority, barred blacks from living in the freshman dormitories (which were compulsory for whites), saying, "We have not thought it possible to compel men of different races to reside together." (At that time Harvard even had a Ku Klux Klan chapter.) Eventually the Corporation modified the policy: "Men of the white and colored races shall not be compelled to live and eat together, nor shall any man be excluded by reason of his color." In practice, Harvard did not readily integrate student housing until the 1950s.

Black students have always participated in extracurricular activities, notably athletics and musical organizations. On many occasions Southern institutions objected to their presence; Harvard's reaction was sometimes to exclude the blacks from joint events, and sometimes to stand firm against bigotry.

The first black on Harvard's staff was the professional boxing teacher A. Molyneaux Hewlett, who was appointed in 1859 to superintend the new Gymnasium (now demolished) and to teach gymnastics. Hewlett continued as athletic director until his death in 1871. In recent years, Harvard has engaged a number of black head coaches, including basketball stars K.C. Jones and Tom "Satch" Sanders.

The first black member of the Harvard faculty was George F. Grant, D.M.D. 1870, the second black graduate of the Dental School, where he taught as "demonstrator" and instructor from 1878 to 1889. President Eliot was one of his personal patients. Grant was also the inventor of the golf tee. The second black faculty member was William A. Hinton, '05, M.D. '12, who held annual appointments as instructor at the Medical School starting in 1918. A pioneering syphilologist, he was the first black American to publish a medical textbook (1936). He was promoted to professor—the first of his race to attain that rank at Harvard—in 1949, one year before retirement.

The first black person named to the Faculty of Arts and Sciences was Ralph J. Bunche, A.M. '28, Ph.D. '34, appointed a professor of government in 1950. Because of pressing obligations at the United Nations, which won him the Nobel Peace Prize, he requested a postponement of teaching duties, and finally decided to resign his professorship in 1952 without ever having taught a course (he did, however, become the first black Overseer, 1959-65). In 1961, the same department appointed as tutor Martin L. Kilson Jr., A.M. '58, Ph.D. 59, who moved up the academic ladder and received tenure in

1969. Since then Harvard has tenured a number of black faculty in Arts and Sciences. By far the most widely known black on Harvard's staff is Alvin F. Poussaint, a psychiatry professor and dean whom the Medical School wooed away from Tufts in 1969; his views on a broad range of subjects are constantly sought by the media.

The year 1969 also saw the Faculty vote to establish an Afro-American Studies Department, whose first chairman was a black alumnus, the late Ewart G. Guinier '33. Its later black chairmen were musicologist Eileen J. Southern and the aforementioned Nathan Huggins. Although the Department has not had as smooth sailing as its Yale counterpart, it is still thriving and also operates a special Afro-American Studies Reading Room and Listening Center in Lamont Library. In addition, Harvard set up the W.E.B. Du Bois Institute for black research in 1975, and the next year Radcliffe initiated its Black Women Oral History Project. In 1991 black scholar Henry Louis Gates Jr. assumed the leadership of both the Department and the Institute.

The size of the black student body has been sufficient since the 1960s to inspire a goodly number of Afro-American organizations, of which about a dozen are currently functioning. Students published a *Harvard Journal of Negro Affairs* from 1965 to 1971, and in 1976 began a black literary magazine, *Diaspora*.

In 1974 Peter J. Gomes, B.D. '68, became the first black, and at 32 the youngest person, appointed Minister in Memorial Church; since then *Time* magazine has profiled him as one of "seven star preachers" in the nation. Since the mid-1970s two black men have been serving at Harvard as Dean of Students (Archie C. Epps III, B.D. '61) and Senior Admissions Officer (David L. Evans).

From tentative beginnings and on "thro' change and thro' storm," a substantial black presence at Harvard and Radcliffe is clearly now here to stay.

PHILLIS WHEATLEY

Phillis Wheatley was born sometime in 1753 (perhaps 1754) in West Africa and brought to Boston on a slave ship in 1761. Though frail, she was bought by the well-known merchant John Wheatley and his wife Susanna, and given the name of the schooner that had borne her. Spared from hard toil, she received instruction in English, Latin, and other subjects within the family, and made such fast progress that she was writing letters and verse as early as 1765, publishing her first poem in 1767. In the same year she wrote the first version of a poem to Harvard University.

In 1772 she issued a prospectus for a book of poetry, attracting insufficient subscribers. Thereupon her mistress arranged for publication in London, where the author traveled in 1773 and oversaw the first of several printings (at least five within a year) of *Poems on Various Subjects, Religious and Moral.* She returned to Boston earlier than planned, in order to attend her ailing mistress, who gave the servant her freedom a few months before Mrs. Wheatley's death in March of 1774. After the death of Mr. Wheatley, she married John Peters in 1778 (bearing three children all of whom died in infancy), and in 1779 issued the prospectus for a second book, which came to nought. Her fortunes declined, and she was eventually obliged to resort to manual labor. Never robust, Phillis Wheatley Peters weakened, died on 5 December 1784, and was buried in an unmarked grave.

Although the Long Island slave Jupiter Hammon had issued a one-sheet poem in 1761 (and would in 1778 publish a 21-quatrain poem addressed to Phillis Wheatley), the 1773 Wheatley volume was the first book published by a black American. It contained thirty-eight of her poems, including the revision of her free-verse ode to Harvard here reprinted. The book also carried a testimonial to her precocious talents signed by eighteen prominent Bostonians (fourteen of them Harvard alumni), including the governor and lieutenant-governor. Today the Wheatley canon consists of fifty-five poems, twenty-two letters and a prose prayer, though we have the titles for dozens more poems that so far have not come to light. Her literary accomplishments were praised by Voltaire and George Washington, though curtly dismissed by Thomas Jefferson. Harvard owns several Wheatley manuscripts as well as the poet's personal copy of Milton's *Paradise Lost* presented to her by the Lord Mayor of London.

To The University of Cambridge, in New-England

WHILE an intrinsic ardor prompts to write,
The muses promise to assist my pen;
'Twas not long since I left my native shore
The land of errors, and *Egyptian* gloom:
Father of mercy, 'twas thy gracious hand
Brought me in safety from those dark abodes.

      Students, to you 'tis giv'n to scan the heights
Above, to traverse the ethereal space,
And mark the systems of revolving worlds.
Still more, ye sons of science ye receive
The blissful news by messengers from heav'n,
How *Jesus'* blood for your redemption flows.
See him with hands out-stretcht upon the cross;
Immense compassion in his bosom glows;
He hears revilers, nor resents their scorn:
What matchless mercy in the Son of God!
When the whole human race by sin had fall'n,
He deign'd to die that they might rise again,
And share with him in the sublimest skies,
Life without death, and glory without end.

      Improve your privileges while they stay,
Ye pupils, and each hour redeem, that bears
Or good or bad report of you to heav'n.
Let sin, that baneful evil to the soul,
By you be shunn'd, nor once remit your guard;
Suppress the deadly serpent in its egg.
Ye blooming plants of human race divine,
An *Ethiop* tells you 'tis your greatest foe;
Its transient sweetness turns to endless pain,
And in immense perdition sinks the soul.

                                                    (1767; pub. 1773)

A FORENSIC DISPUTE ON THE LEGALITY OF ENSLAVING THE AFRICANS, HELD AT THE PUBLIC COMMENCEMENT IN CAMBRIDGE, NEW-ENGLAND (BOSTON, 1773)

THEODORE PARSONS AND ELIPHALET PEARSON

From Harvard's very first Commencement in 1642, it was standard practice for the public exercises to include lengthy debates in which two degree candidates took opposing sides of a given topic. At the Commencement on 21 July 1773 two seniors engaged in a disputation on the legitimacy of slavery. It elicited so much comment that the debate was immediately printed and published, running to forty-eight pages. We offer some excerpts from the text to convey the tenor and flavor of the event.

Both speakers were natives of Newbury, Massachusetts, and both received an A.B. in 1773 and an A.M. in 1776. Arguing in favor of slavery was Theodore Parsons, who would shortly enter the Revolutionary War as a surgeon on the armed ship Bennington, which, immobilized by ice on the St. Lawrence River, saw all aboard perish in 1779.

Taking the anti-slavery position was Eliphalet Pearson, who was the first principal of Phillips Andover Academy from 1778 to 1786, when he returned to Harvard as the Hancock Professor of Hebrew, being also elected a Fellow in 1800 and Acting President of the University in 1804. He resigned from Harvard in 1806 and founded the Andover Theological Seminary, where he remained until his death in 1826. In 1802 he received an honorary LL.D. from both Yale and the College of New Jersey (now Princeton).

[Pearson] . . . The candor of this truly venerable, this learned and polite assembly will excuse us in attempting, in a few words, to examine, *Whether the slavery, to which Africans are in this province, by the permission of law, subjected, be agreable to the law of nature?* And since, fully persuaded of the truth of those principles, in which is founded the idea of natural equality, to the exclusion of a right in one individual of the human species to exercise any degree of authority over another without his consent, I am obliged to appear in favor of the negative of the proposition; and since, if I rightly remember, I have sometimes heard you express a very different sentiment, if you are disposed to join in the proposal, I will first attend to what may be offered on your part in support of it. And shall therefore only observe, that the strangely inconsistent conduct of mankind, respecting this matter, furnishes us with reflections upon the present state of human nature by no means the most agreable. To me, I confess, it is matter of painful astonishment, that in this enlightened age and land, where the principles of natural and civil Liberty, and consequently the natural rights of mankind are so generally understood, the case of these unhappy *Africans* should gain no more attention;—that those, who are so readily disposed to urge the principles of natural equality in defence of their own Liberties, should, with so little reluctance, continue to exert a power, by the operation of which they are so flagrantly contradicted. For what less can be said of that exercise of power, whereby such multitudes of our fellow-men, descendants, my friend, from the same common parents with you and me, and between whom and us nature has made no distinction, save what arises from the stronger influence of the sun in the climate whence they originated, are held to groan under the insupportable burden of the most abject slavery, without one chearing beam to refresh their desponding souls; and upon whose dreary path not even the feeblest ray of hope is permitted to dawn, and whose only prospect of deliverance is—in death. If indeed the law protects their lives, (which is all that can be said even here, and more—shame to mankind!—more than can be said in some of our sister colonies) the only favor these unhappy people receive, from such protection, is a continuation of their misery; the preservation of a life, every moment of which is worse than non-existence. A favor this, no doubt, that in a very special manner demands acknowledgement!

[Parsons] Though conscious, my friend, of my inability, the most advantageously to represent the arguments in favor of this proposition, especially when circumscribed within the narrow limits the present occasion will allow; yet clearly convinced of the propriety of attentively considering this question, especially at a period when persons of every denomination are so justly affected with a sense of Liberty, I readily comply; rather hoping that if any present, are in doubt respecting this matter, they will take occasion from hence, so fully to examine it, as to procure satisfaction to themselves, than expecting what shall be now offered on my part will have so desirable an effect.

I am well aware of the difficulty of his task who attempts to defend a proposition of this nature. An heart replete with benevolence and compassion will hardly admit reasoning that involves principles seemingly incompatible with the happiness of *any*. Suffer me therefore to entreat you, that every tender sentiment, that even the feelings of humanity may be suspended, while we calmly attend to the voice of reason, which is the voice of nature's alwise and benevolent Author.

That Liberty to all is sweet I freely own; but still 'tis what, in a state of society at least, all cannot equally enjoy, and what even in a *free* government can be enjoyed in the most perfect sense by none. Such is the nature of society, that it requires various degrees of authority and subordination; and while the universal rule of right, *the happiness of the whole* allows greater degrees of Liberty to some, the same immutable law suffers it to be enjoyed only in less degrees by others. And though[,] my friend, I can most cordially join with you in the benevolent wish, that it were possible that these Africans, who I am free with you to call my brethren, and to whom, it is confessed, the principles of our civil constitution allow but a small degree of liberty, might enjoy it equally with us; yet 'till I am convinced it might comport with the rule above mentioned, to allow them more I am in duty bound to appear an advocate for those principles. . . .

[Pearson] . . . I am much at a loss to conceive how your reasoning in favor of slavery *in general*, were it ever so fully conclusive, could possibly justify us in thus forcibly subjugating the *Africans*, between whom and us nature seems to have made no such difference as that, upon which you suppose the notion of *natural inequality* to be founded: For I suppose you will hardly imagine the darkness of a man's skin incapacitates him for the direction of his conduct, and authorises his neighbours, who may have the good fortune of a complexion a shade or two lighter, to exercise authority over him.

And if the important difference does not lay here, it seems not very easy to determine where it does; unless perchance, it be in the quality of their hair; and if the principle of subordination lies here, I would advise every person, whose hair is inclined to deviate from a right line, to be upon his guard. If indeed any should alledge, that they are distinguished by the flatness of their noses, I can't but think this circumstance against them, for if a man is to be led and governed by the nose, it may well be questioned, whether a nose of a different figure would not be better adapted to the purpose.

[Parsons] My friend, I am no enemy to humour, but I think it rarely serves to illustrate a logical conclusion. I confess my argument, as you have represented it, appears ridiculous enough; but if you had deferred your reply till I had made an application of the principle to the point in hand, perhaps it had saved you this needless expence of wit. I have not pretended, as a consequence from my principles, that every degree of superiority in point of discretion would warrant to any individual of a community a right to exercise authority over his neighbour: I have only contended, that the notion of *equality*, in the strict sense, had no foundation *in nature*; but as happiness is the only end of action, so superiority in wisdom, goodness, &c. is in the nature of things a proper foundation of authority. And as nature has made differences among creatures in these respects; so it is fit and proper, and agreable to nature's law, that different degrees of authority in point of direction of conduct should be exercised by them; and that in some cases, even among the human species, this difference is so important, as to render the exercise of authority justifiable, even without the consent of the governed: For this I have produced an example from fact, in the case of parents and children. All this you have implicitly allowed. I now go on to say, as a consequence from the same acknowledged principle, that whenever such a connection of things takes place, that any number of men cannot, consistently with the good of the whole, have a residence in any community but in a state of involuntary subordination, and that their residence in such community notwithstanding such subordination, be in fact best for the whole, such subordination, though involuntary, is no violation of the law of nature; but on the contrary to all intents and purposes correspondent thereto. This is a true conclusion from premises incontestible, principles universally acknowledged, and which you yourself have but now admitted. Subordination in this case comes fully within the reason of the subordination of children, rests on precisely the same foundation, and is therefore justifiable on precisely the same principles. For whether the necessity of such subordination arises from natural incapacity, or from any other quarter, it matters not, if this is in fact the case; if the interest of the whole does require it; let the causes or reasons of such requirement be what they may, such subordination is equally justifiable as in any other case whatever; not only in the case of children, but even in the case of consent; for the obligation to submission arising from consent, is founded in the general obligation to fulfil contracts; which obligation is ultimately founded in the good of society. . . .

[Pearson] . . . I am ready to allow, that was it *certain* that their condition here is happier on the whole, than in their own country, your premises, in this *independent view* of the matter, would well warrant your conclusion; but even this I apprehend is far from being true. You have represented the misery and wretchedness of these people in their native land, in a light indeed disagreeable enough: But I am still disposed from my apprehension of the dignity of the rational nature, at least to hope that your colouring is a little too strong; and that notwithstanding the unhappy state of degradation into which they are confessedly sunk, they are still some degrees above brutes. It is acknowledged that they are extremely unacquainted with the politer arts, and almost wholly ignorant of every thing belonging to science, and consequently strangers to all the pleasures of a scholar and a philosopher; they are also confessedly destitute of an acquaintance with the principles of urbanity and consequently want, in a great measure, the happiness resulting from a well regulated civil society; their condition is allowedly not greatly different from a state of nature; though it is to be remembered, that if modern writers of the best reputation are to be credited, their manners, in most parts of that extensive country, are far less savage and barbarous; their conveniences and enjoyments much more numerous, and in a word their manner of life much more agreable than has been heretofore represented. And indeed it is not to be wondered that those who have been disposed to make a gain by this iniquitous practice of enslaving their fellow men, should be careful, for their justification, to represent them as nearly upon a level with the brute creation as possible; not to mention the ridiculous attempts that have, in this view, been made to prove them actually of another species. But granting their condition to be, as in fact it is, comparatively low; that their sources of happiness, when compared with those which the members of a well-ordered civil society enjoy, are few; yet it is not to be forgotten, that their appetites and desires are in some good measure proportional. *Nemo desiderat quae ignorat* [No one craves what he knows nothing about]. The benevolent author of our being has accommodated our *natural* desires in a great measure to the *natural* means of gratification. And he who attentively considers the anxious and perplexing cares; the fatiguing and often fruitless labors; the cravings of *unnatural* appetites; the frequently disappointed views and expectations; and, in a word, the various and almost innumerable *new* sources of infelicity *naturally*, and many of them *inseparably* connected with what is commonly called a state of civilization, will perhaps perceive that the difference, in point of *real* happiness, between the scholar, the courtier, and the simple child of nature, is far from infinite. But allowing it to be very considerable, allowing that the privileges and advantages of a *free* member, of a *free society*, where useful sciences and the liberal arts are patronized and flourish, and where all those principles that beautify and adorn the rational nature are cultivated, are comparatively very great: What, I beseech you has all this to do with the present question? What advantage is all the learning of this country to those ignorant wretches, who are now practicing their ludicrous gambols on yonder common, except indeed that it generally procures them one day in the year, a dispensation from the severity of their servitude—What is all our boasted acquaintance with science and the politer arts to these miserable creatures, who, by their situation, have little more concern in these matters than their brethren in the middle regions of *Africa*; and which knowledge, could they obtain it, must serve only to increase their misery? What a blessing, for example, would a knowledge of the principles of civil Liberty be to a person perpetually doomed to a state of the most abject slavery?—In their native country, though their condition be indeed contemptible enough, they have the blessing of *Liberty* to sweeten every pleasure, and give a relish to every enjoyment: But here, though their condition were in other respects much more favourable than it is, while conscious of perpetual and absolute dependance upon the will of others, this reflection, so opposite to the strong sense of Liberty implanted in the heart of every son of Adam, must necessarily mar the happiness of every gratification, effectually chill the sense of pleasure, and stop every natural source of felicity.

A keen excruciating sense of liberty forever lost must still predominate, till, the spirit broken by the fatigue of incessant distress, they sink into a state of lifeless insensibility. And then forsooth we are presently disposed to tax them with natural stupidity; and make the very thing that our unnatural treatment has occasioned the ground of our justification.—It is well known, that stupidity is by no means the natural characteristic of these people; and when we consider the nature of their condition in this country, how miserably dejected, depressed and despised, instead of marking their want of apprehension, we ought rather to admire that there are any the least appearances of sensibility remaining in them. . . .

But we must not stop here: Upon your own principles, we must consider this practice *in all its connexions*; we must not only regard the evils of slavery in *this* country, but must take in also the miseries and calamities that are by this means brought upon *any* of the human race. Before this practice can be justified, it must appear to be productive of general happiness; it must correspond with the general good of the *whole*. Now if we consider the practice of slavery in this country, in it's tendency to countenance and encourage the same thing, as it is practiced in the southern colonies, and West-Indies, it will appear much more glaringly iniquitous and unjust. Several hundred thousands of those unhappy creatures, are, by the best information, annually exported from the various parts of *Africa* to *America*, a great proportion of whom, thro' the shocking, the unparalleled sufferings of transportation, miserably perish on the voyage, and as to those who unhappily survive, to enter upon that state of perpetual servitude, to which they are destined, it is well known, that they are treated with less humanity, more merciless severity, and savage barbarity, than reason would warrant us to exercise towards the meanest of the brute creation. It would wring drops of blood from an heart of adamant to relate the cruel sufferings of these unhappy people, in those countries, who, at the same time, have less advantages for christian knowledge, than the natives of California, or the inhabitants of the antarctic circle.

But I forbear—The person that can imagine the practice of slavery in this country, considered in all its consequences, connexions and tendencies, productive of the happiness of mankind, must, I think, allow, that the direct way to encrease their happiness is by every possible means to encrease their misery.

(1773)

Major Martin Delany in 1865

MARTIN R. DELANY AND THE HARVARD MEDICAL SCHOOL

Medical Intelligence

Trouble among the Medical Students of Harvard University—The following facts have been collected respecting some unhappy proceedings last week at the Massachusetts Medical College in this city. Among the students attending the medical lectures, are *three colored young men*. One of them is from Pittsburgh, Pa.; one belongs in this city, and we believe is a native, a son of the late Rev. Mr. Snowden, a colored preacher of much eminence for many years; the locale of the other is unknown to us. They are all, as we have understood [not Delany, however], under the immediate auspices of the American Colonization Society, and by them are to be educated as physicians for the colony at Liberia. It was understood by the students last week that a *lady* was also to be added to the class. These departures from established rule gave offence to a portion of the members. On Tuesday morning the class held a meeting, and appointed a committee to draft a set of resolutions. The meeting was adjourned to the afternoon, when the students again assembled. The resolutions, respectfully remonstrating against the admission of *colored* men and *white* women, were then taken up *seriatim*, and passed by a majority of the students *present*. We should here state, that the class attending the meeting in the morning showed a majority for sustaining the faculty in the course of admitting whom they pleased to their lectures; but not supposing any such resolutions would be presented, many of them did not attend the afternoon meeting. Those present who disapproved of the resolutions, immediately appointed a committee to present a minority report, sustaining the faculty, to be presented to the class at a future meeting. We regret exceedingly this little disturbance, and the course adopted by the class. We cannot but think that if they had any real grievances, it would have been better to have approached the faculty in some other way. It may be considered an innovation to admit colored men into our colleges; but when it is remembered for what purpose these were admitted, there really cannot be so much objection after all. But as to the propriety of admitting females to medical colleges in common with males, it is a matter in which there is a great diversity of opinion. We should most decidedly object to the adoption of the practice, preferring to have all females who wish to become disciples of the healing art, or otherwise assume the masculine professions, attend separate institutions for their education.

Since writing the above, we learn that the faculty have announced to the class, that the lady in question, on hearing that there was a feeling against her being admitted to the college, has withdrawn her application. Respecting the colored men, they declined to reject them from the college, under the circumstances—as they have purchased tickets and thereby acquired a right of attendance during the present year.

Boston Medical and Surgical Journal (1850)

Petition

To the Medical Faculty of Harvard University;
Gentlemen,

The undersigned, members of the medical class, would respectfully submit to the Medical Faculty their desire to be informed whether colored persons are to be admitted as students at another course of lectures. This request is offered not with the view of influencing any action of the Faculty, but simply that the undersigned may have opportunity to make such arrangements for the future as shall be most agreeable to their feelings in the event of negroes being allowed again to become members of the school.

(Signed)

C. A. Robertson
W. N. Lane
Joa. B. Cordeiro
Rufus A. Stockton
Jno. S. Whiting
W. A. C. Randall
Wm. Dickinson
Geo. A. Blake

E. P. Abbe
A. J. Webb
D. M. Tucker
C. Kidder
H. M. Northrup
Israel N. Smith
James Hartley

[The signatories were: Charles Archibald Robertson, A.B. 1850, M.D. (Jefferson Medical College) 1853; William Nourse Lane, M.D. 1853; Joaquim Barbosa Cordeiro, M.D. 1854; Rufus A. Stockton, no degree; John Samuel Whiting, A.B. 1850, M.D. 1853; William Allen Chipman Randall, M.D. 1852; William Dickinson, A.B. (Dartmouth) 1843, M.D. 1851; George Albert Blake, A.B. (Williams) 1849, M.D. 1853; Edward Payson Abbe, A.B. (Yale) 1848, M.D. 1852; A. J. Webb, no degree; Dexter Mills Tucker, M.D. 1852; Charles Kidder, M.D. 1852; H. M. Northrup, no degree; Israel N. Smith, no degree; James Wardlee Hartley, M.D. 1852.]

Countway Library, Dean's File, Harvard Medical Archives, November-December 1850

Pride, Prejudice, and Politics

PHILIP CASH

In social terms the academic year 1850-1851 was one of the most controversial in the Harvard Medical School's two centuries of existence. In that year one woman and three blacks, including Martin Robison Delany, "The Father of Black Nationalism" and great rival of Frederick Douglass for the leadership of the black community during the critical era of abolition, civil strife, and partial emancipation (1840-1880), applied for admission to the school. The woman was persuaded to withdraw her application while the blacks were allowed to attend for one semester and then dismissed. While from the perspective of another century and another era it is easy to condemn these actions in a self-righteous manner, it is difficult, but far more important, to understand them in their historical context.

In order to attain this historical perspective one has to have some understanding of the Boston of 1850. At that time the "hub of the universe" and "Athens of America" was growing, prosperous, and progressive. However, with this progress and prosperity came social conflict, economic dislocation, and deep anxiety. Widespread opportunity coupled with a laissez-faire social and economic system not only meant growth and mobility, but also waste, exploitation, and corruption. Furthermore, to sustain this growth, Boston, long noted for its stability and homogeneity, was forced to adjust to two new and unsettling forces: manufacturing and the Irish. This combination changed Boston from an urban community unusual in America for its social and cultural consensus to one that was uniquely polarized between WASP and Hibernian. Also, at this time antebellum reform was boiling up in New England, fueled by the ideological fires of

Transcendentalism, Unitarianism, Universalism, and Swedenborgianism. These variegated and generally desirable, yet bitterly divisive, reforms, were then further complicated by abolitionism, temperance, and black and women's rights. Of these, abolitionism was the most explosive, and Boston was on the verge of civil conflict over attempts to enforce the newly enacted Fugitive Slave Act.

As a major Boston institution, Harvard Medical School could hardly escape the force of this turmoil. What is more, the school was still traumatized by a recent scandal of its own. This was the highly controversial conviction of John White Webster, professor of chemistry at the medical school, for the murder of Dr. George Parkman, a prominent, if not universally beloved, Brahmin, who had been a major benefactor of Harvard. Most seriously affected was Oliver Wendell Holmes, dean of the medical faculty and Parkman Professor of Anatomy, who had played an important role at the trial. Webster had been sentenced on April 1 and [hanged] August 30, 1850.

Clearly, Harvard Medical School in the fall of 1850 was not in a mood for any further excitement or conflict. However, before examining the challenge offered by the application of a woman and three blacks, it might be wise to review the admission requirements and the composition of the medical faculty at this time. The criteria for acceptance were basically the same as when the school had opened in 1782; three years' training with a regular physician, evidence of good moral character, and a college degree (which only a small minority held) or a demonstration of a knowledge of Latin, mathematics, and basic science deemed satisfactory by the medical faculty. Unstated, of course, but traditionally assumed, was that acceptable candidates would also be white and male. Now these assumptions were being tested at Harvard as at a number of other medical schools.

The medical faculty in 1850 consisted of: Oliver Wendell Holmes, professor of anatomy and dean of the medical faculty; Walter Channing, professor of midwifery and medical jurisprudence; Jacob Bigelow, professor of materia medica and lecturer on clinical medicine; his son, Henry J. Bigelow, professor of surgery and clinical surgery; John B. S. Jackson, professor of pathological anatomy; John Ware, professor of the theory and practice of physic, and E. N. Horsford, newly appointed professor of chemistry—in place of Webster —and later dean of the Lawrence Scientific School. This was a medical faculty the equal of any in America at the time. These men were true Brahmins, steeped in tradition and used to success, status, and prestige. Yet, despite their considerable accomplishments and strong personalities, there is little doubt that the affable, adroit, and multi-talented Holmes, then at the height of his influence in Boston, was the dominant force in the school.

During the winter semester of 1850-1851 a number of events rocked the medical school. On October 22, a Mr. Charles Brooks sent a letter to the Harvard Medical faculty asking that one Daniel Laing, Jr., "a young man of colour," be admitted gratuitously to the winter course of lectures to prepare himself for the practice of medicine in the newly independent African state of Liberia. On November 1, the Massachusetts Colonization Society petitioned to have both Laing and Isaac H. Snowden, another black, admitted to the winter semester with the acknowledgment that they would subsequently emigrate to Liberia. Under the Society's direction, Laing and Snowden had been studying with Dr. Horace Clarke, a surgeon on the staff of the Massachusetts General Hospital. On November 4, with Horsford absent, the faculty voted four (Channing, Holmes, Jackson, and Ware) to two (the Bigelows) to accept Laing gratuitously and four to one, with only Bigelow, Jr., dissenting, to accept Snowden, whose fees would be assumed by the Colonization Society.

Laing and Snowden were native Bostonians and attractive and able young men. Both had been independent printers who despaired of getting ahead in a land of white opportunity. When they went to the Colonization Society to seek aid in getting to Liberia, the Society suggested that that country had too many printers and not enough doctors; it urged them to study medicine under the Society's auspices. Both men readily agreed to do so.

Several weeks after the acceptance of Laing and Snowden another black appeared in Dean Holmes's office to seek admission to the winter semester, then already underway. This was the formidable Martin Robison Delany, thirty-eight years old, jet black, of a squat, muscular build, and already well-known in abolitionist circles throughout the North. Delany's application was more of a challenge than those of Laing and Snowden. His intention was both to earn a medical degree and to practice in his native country. However, he possessed impressive credentials. There were strong letters of recommendation from his preceptors, Drs. Joseph Gazzam and F. Julius Le Moyne, eminent Pittsburgh physicians who also were abolitionists. In addition, there was a letter of endorsement signed by ten other members of the Pittsburgh medical fraternity and another signed by seven practitioners from neighboring Allegheny City. Lastly, three black ministers from Pittsburgh had written testimonials regarding Delany's solid moral character. Holmes was undoubtedly swayed by this support as well as by the force of Delany's personality. He may already have heard of Delany, and apparently did not anticipate any serious difficulty. Holmes admitted him the same day.

Before moving on to an account and analysis of the student reaction to the admission of these three blacks, and the consequent faculty response, a closer look at the career of Delany up until this time is in order. He was born in Charles Town (Charleston), Virginia (now West Virginia) in 1812 of a free mother and a slave father who obtained his freedom when Martin was ten. The family fled to Chambersburg, Pennsylvania in 1822 and Martin went on to Pittsburgh in 1831, at the age of nineteen. Over the next two decades Delany left a strong and favorable mark on this brawling, bustling river city. He was a leader in various black self-improvement societies, black politics, the Underground Railroad, and the abolitionist movement. His greatest influence and fame, however, came to him as the founder and editor of the excellent and pioneering black newspaper, *The Mystery*, still in print today as the *Christian Recorder*. Delany also found time to marry Kate A. Richards, the mulatto daughter of a wealthy black Pittsburgh landowner and merchant who was swindled out of his estate because white lawyers refused to take the case of a rich black against fellow whites. Martin and Kate were to have eleven children, seven of whom lived to adulthood.

In 1848, Delany left Pittsburgh to go to Rochester, New York where he joined with Frederick A. Douglass and William Nell of Boston in founding the *North Star*, the leading black newspaper of the antebellum period. After eighteen months Delany left this newspaper in the capable hands of Douglass and returned to Pittsburgh.

Throughout these intensely active years Delany also had a continuing interest in medicine. Early in his Pittsburgh days he had begun studying the medical arts with Dr. Andrew N. McDowell, but did not have the resources to complete his apprenticeship. He then earned a part of his livelihood as a cupper and bleeder for many of the doctors of the region. However, in 1849, buoyed by the fact that a few blacks were now being accepted by American medical schools (although most of them were supposed to be emigrating to Liberia), he renewed his apprenticeship, this time with Drs. Gazzam and Le Moyne.

After finishing his apprenticeship Delany began to apply to medical colleges. Since most of the doctors in and around Pittsburgh who had attended regular medical schools were from Jefferson and the University of Pennsylvania, he applied to these Philadelphia institutions, but was refused entrance. The School of Medicine at the University of Pennsylvania had a predominantly southern student population during this era. Of the 144 men who graduated there in 1838, a typical year, over half were from Dixie (see Richard H. Shryock, *Medicine in America: Historical Essays* [Baltimore, 1966], 56, fn. 19). Undaunted, Delany then applied to Geneva, where a woman, Elizabeth Blackwell, had just completed her studies, and to Albany Medical College. But again he was rejected. Following this, a Pittsburgh merchant by the name of John Cook suggested the Berkshire Medical College in Pittsfield, Massachusetts. Cook knew Dr. Henry Childs, the dean, and offered to write him a letter of introduction and recommendation. This time Delany applied in person. Berkshire had already accepted three blacks, but they were all destined for Liberia. When Delany told Dean Childs of his intention to practice in America he once more was denied admission. However, Childs did send him on to see his friend, Dean Holmes of the Harvard Medical School. With Holmes's approval, Delany's long quest seemed about to be fulfilled.

However, this dream, like so many others in his life, soon was to be shattered. On Tuesday morning, December 10, the students of Harvard Medical School, already in a state of agitation, assembled to consider the question of the three blacks in their midst and the rumor that a woman was soon to join them. At this morning session a committee was appointed to draft resolutions. This committee was headed by J. Randolph Lincoln as chairman and Edward Payson Abbe (A.B., Yale) as secretary. Both men were Bostonians. The meeting was then adjourned until the afternoon when a smaller number of students—about sixty out of a class of 116 (counting the three blacks) —reassembled. At this afternoon meeting two series of resolutions were passed and forwarded to the medical faculty. The first series expressed opposition to the admission of a woman and were passed with little or no dissent. The second series protested the admission of the three blacks. These were much more controversial and were passed over strong objection. The arguments in these resolutions have a familiar ring: the students had not been informed that such a decision had been made, the presence of blacks would cheapen the

Harvard medical degree, the quality of education would suffer, the presence of an inferior race was socially offensive.

The students who opposed the second series of resolutions were led by William Fifield of Weymouth, Richard Gundry of Simcoe, Canada West (Ontario), and Adams Wiley (A.B., Harvard) of Roxbury. They held another meeting the following day and drew up two petitions to present to the medical faculty. The twenty-six signers of the first petition, acting, they averred, as "students of science" and "candidates for the profession of medicine," solidly endorsed the decision to admit blacks. Twenty-one of these men were from Massachusetts (eleven from Boston, two from Roxbury, two from Weymouth, and one each from Cambridge, Charlton, Essex, Lowell, Salem, and Springfield). Two others were from Connecticut and Vermont. The remaining three were from outside New England (two from Canada West and one from Farmington, Iowa). Six had graduated from Harvard College and one each from Brown and Dartmouth. The students from Iowa and Vermont already held M.D. degrees, probably from rural medical schools. Four of these signers (Fifield, Gundry, Lothrop, and Waldock) were to win Foster prizes at graduation.

The second petition took a more neutral stance. It opposed the second series of resolutions (which decried the admission of the blacks), but did not support the blacks. Twenty-two students signed this. Ten were from Massachusetts (five from Boston and one each from Dorchester, Framingham, Needham, Tisbury, and Salem). Eight were from Maine. The others were from Canada West, Mississippi, New Hampshire, and Rhode Island.

In addition to these petitions there were two others—opposed to the retention of the blacks—presented to the medical faculty. One, submitted in late December or early January, contained the signatures of fourteen or fifteen students who threatened to leave Harvard should the blacks remain beyond one term. [See Petition above.] One signatory, Mr. A.J. Webb, is not to be found in either the *Matriculating Book* or the *Catalogue of Students Attending Medical Lectures, 1850-1851*. Of the rest, six were from Massachusetts (three from Boston and one each from Beverly, Charlestown, and Fall River), two were from New Hampshire, two from Canada (New Brunswick and Nova Scotia), two from the South (Kentucky and Mississippi), and one each from Brazil and Connecticut. Two of these students were from Harvard and one each from Dartmouth, Williams, and Yale. The Mississippi student, Mr. William Dickinson (A.B.,

Dartmouth), had also signed the petition that opposed the second set of resolutions but did not support the blacks.

The other petition opposing the blacks is at best insignificant. It contains only eight signatures and five of those names are in neither the *Matriculating Book* nor the *Catalogue*, while two others were on the other petition in opposition to the retention of the blacks beyond one semester. The remaining signatory was John Randolph Lincoln, who had been chairman of the committee that drafted the two series of resolutions.

These petitions seem to indicate three things. First, there clearly was a strong body of active support within the medical class for Delany, Laing, and Snowden. This was especially noticeable among those who came from eastern Massachusetts, and it was from there that Harvard Medical School drew the bulk of its students until well into the twentieth century. Secondly, another large scholastic group, probably a clear majority, were almost certain to go along with whatever decision the faculty made regarding the blacks. Lastly, while those students strongly in opposition to the retention of the blacks undoubtedly were very vocal and active, they were a distinct minority and geographically scattered.

On Thursday, December 12, the entire medical faculty met to consider the student resolutions and petitions. At this time no decisions were made, but Holmes and Jacob Bigelow were appointed to take up the question of the continued presence of Delany, Laing, and Snowden. The following evening, the faculty, with the exception of Channing, reconvened at Holmes's residence on Montgomery Place. At this meeting they quickly disposed of the student concern over the possibility of a woman being accepted into their class, noting that the female applicant had, upon the advice of the faculty, withdrawn her request for admission; therefore, no further action was necessary. A resolution, drafted by Holmes and addressing the question of the black students, was then presented to the faculty by Jacob Bigelow. It stated that since these students were already in possession of their tickets of admission to the various courses, they were entitled to complete the semester. This resolution was approved, although the votes were not recorded in the "Minutes." Possibly the vote was unanimous, but Henry J. Bigelow may well have dissented. Holmes passed these decisions on to the student body. . . .

At a meeting of the medical faculty on December 26, it was deemed "inexpedient, after the present course, to admit colored students to attendance on the medical lectures." Supporting this decision were the Bigelows, Holmes, and Jackson. Opposed were Channing and Ware. Horsford was excused from voting. Channing tried to have the question of admitting blacks to the medical lectures referred to the president and fellows of the university for a final decision, but this too was voted down. Holmes was directed to write a letter to the Colonization Society informing them that "this experiment" had satisfied the faculty "that the intermixing of the white and black races in their lecture rooms, is distasteful to a large portion of the class and injurious to the interests of the school." Curiously, there was no great outcry either among Boston's blacks or the abolitionists or other reformers over this regrettable decision. Apparently, there were at this time just too many battles being fought both internally and externally by these groups. It was not until Edwin Clarence Joseph Turpin Howard graduated in 1869 that the Harvard Medical School produced its first black doctor.

After their dismissal from Harvard Medical School, Laing and Snowden continued their struggle to complete their medical educations. Laing first went to Paris where he studied under the master surgeon [Alfred] Velpeau and then returned to receive his M.D. from Dartmouth in 1854. Snowden renewed his studies with Dr. Clarke. In November 1853, he reapplied for admission to the Harvard Medical School, indicating that he still intended to go to Liberia. His application was supported by a petition signed by seventy-five members of a medical class of 118, including Samuel Abbott Green, later president of the Massachusetts Historical Society and author of a classic history of Massachusetts medicine; Edward L. Holmes, later president (1890-1898) of Rush Medical College; Israel Tisdale Talbot, the first dean (1873-1899) of the Boston University School of Medicine, and Conrad Wesselhoeft, later a distinguished pathologist at Boston University School of Medicine. This petition supporting Snowden shows that, not only in 1850-1851 was there a strong nucleus of support for the blacks among the students then in attendance, but also among those who were soon to matriculate. Nevertheless, the medical faculty voted down Snowden's reapplication, even though only eight students were in opposition.

It is possible that both Laing and Snowden emigrated to Liberia in 1854. However, if this is true, at least Laing apparently returned to the United States, and died in Charleston in 1869.

From the time he left Harvard Medical School in March 1851

until just before the Civil War, Delany practiced medicine both in Pittsburgh, where he received a citation from the board of health and the city council for his work during the cholera epidemic of 1854, and in Chatham, Canada West (the fugitive slave capital of Canada), where he moved in 1856. However, he also worked ceaselessly for the destruction of slavery, the rights of free blacks, and voluntary black emigration (he even made an exploratory trip to the Niger Valley in 1859-1860). He also found the time to write one of the earliest black novels, called *Blake; or, The Huts of America*, which depicted a fictional general slave revolt in the south. [Reprinted below is one chapter from the novel, which was serialized in the *Anglo-African Magazine* in 1859, and in the *Weekly Anglo-African* in 1861 and 1862.]

During much of the Civil War, Delany served as a highly success-ful recruiter of blacks for the Union Army. Indeed, it is worth noting here that nearly ten percent of the Northern troops were black (see James McPherson, *The Negro's Civil War* [New York, 1965], 237). On February 18, 1865, he was commissioned as a major in the infantry, the first black field officer in the history of the United States Army. He remained in the army until 1868, serving chiefly with the freed-men's bureau in Hilton Head, South Carolina. Following his discharge he remained highly active in the politics of the Palmetto State until the collapse of Reconstruction. He then rejoined his family in Xenia, Ohio, near the campus of Wilberforce College, where, in an increas-ingly hostile society, he continued the struggle for black rights and black pride until his death in 1885.

From the vantage point of 1980 it can be maintained with consid-erable conviction that the Harvard Medical Faculty, and particularly Dean Holmes, in 1850-1851 made a wrong turn which did much to deprive the Harvard Medical School of the kind of leadership in the social dimension of the medical profession that it has enjoyed in the clinical and scientific areas. Delany, Laing, and Snowden could have been allowed to complete their medical education. Holmes was influ-ential and adroit enough to have carried the medical faculty with him had he decided in favor of the blacks. There also was enough support among the students to have kept the unrest and economic damage within reasonable bounds. The student petition of 1853 shows that there also was strong support, among those who would enroll in the school in the near future, for at least some black presence. What's more, Boston in the 1850s was moving toward greater support for black rights, as demonstrated by the admission of John V. de Grassa

(Bowdoin M.D., 1848) to the Boston Medical Society in 1854, and the desegregation of the public schools in 1857. Also, if Harvard Medical had retained the black students in 1850-1851, it probably would not have taken another century for women to be admitted.

However, from the perspective of 1850, things take on a different aspect. The medical faculty, and especially Holmes, were deeply affected by the Parkman murder case and the fact that the Fugitive Slave Act was tearing apart their beloved Brahmin class. And they were forced, all within a few months, to adjust to the idea of accepting a woman, two young blacks destined for Liberia, and a controversial mature black of strong personality who intended to take a degree and practice in America. Little wonder that a moderate amount of student discontent should have unnerved them, especially since the Bigelows already were aggressive social conservatives. Lastly, while Holmes was a man of amiable good will, he also was a dean, and deans are seldom given to prophesying or crusading. Thus, if the Harvard medical faculty made a mistake at this time, it was a very human and a very understandable one.

Harvard Medical Alumni Bulletin (1980)

The Slave Factory

MARTIN R. DELANY

"Hark!" exclaimed Angelina, unaccustomed, from her continued absence at school, to such a sound— "What is that I hear?"

"It comes, my child, from the barracoons," explained the mother, with a deep sigh.

"Do you tell me, mother, that wailings come already, since the tapping of that bell? What does it mean?"

"Preparing the slaves, my child, for packing, I suppose."

"How preparing them, mother?   What do they do to them?" anxiously inquired the girl.

"They whip and burn them, my child, to make them obey."

"And what do you mean by 'packing'?"

"Putting them down in the bottom of the ship, my child, so they can't move about."

"How can they live this way? Oh mother, they can't live!"

"They can't live long, my child; but many of them die, when that makes room, and some of them live."

"O horrible! cruel, cruel!" exclaimed the more than astonished girl. "Pardon me, mother—I cannot help it—and is this my father's business?"

"It is, my daughter," replied the mother, the brightness of whose eyes were glaring with the evidence of sympathy for the sufferings of her people.

"Then forgive me, mother, I receive nothing from this day forth from my father's hand.[1] He's cruel, and—"

---

[1]The young mulatto daughter of a slave trader on the coast peremptorily refused to leave her people and go with him to Portugal to finish an education.

"Stop, my child!" interrupted the mother. "Curse[2] not him from whose lines you came."

"Forgive me, mother, Heaven forbid! But I cannot consent to go to Madrid to obtain accomplishments at the price of blood. The Lady Superior when at Lisbon, taught me to 'love my neighbor as myself'— that all mankind was my neighbor. I thought I was educated to come home and teach my race."

"My child, you must—"

"Hark! Mother, don't you hear?" again exclaimed the young affrighted girl, when another wailing came, more terrible than the other.

"Have patience, my child."

"I can't mother—I can't! How can I have patience with such dreadful things as these?"

"God will give you patience, my child. Depend on Him."

"I will depend on Him, and go directly to the spot and beseech Him in mercy for the poor suffering ones. Come and take me to them," she concluded, calling for native servants to carry her after them, as the party had now left the receptacles for the trading posts at the landing on the lagoon, nearly a mile distant.

Soon she arrived near the dreadful scene

Where fiends incarnate—vile confederate band—
Torture with thumbscrew, lash, and fire-brand.

This most remarkable spot which for years had sent forth through the world its thousands of victims—a place repulsively noted in the history of wrong—was a dismal nook in the northeastern extremity of the lagoon, extending quite into the bush, forming a cove of complete security and quiet. In this position lay the "Vulture"; and near the barracoons, under cover of seemingly impenetrable undergrowth, sat the beautiful Angelina, the good-hearted natives who bore her there lying at her feet to protect her, as is their custom to strangers in the forest. In this position, quietly inspecting the whole proceedings, her soul became horror-stricken.

[2]The native African is very correct in speech, pronouncing very distinctly any word they learn in other languages. Curse—to speak ill of, by the native African.

"Hark!" again exclaimed Angelina in a suppressed frightened tone, unconscious, seemingly, of the half-dressed natives lying at her feet. "Don't you hear? What in God's name does it mean?"

Scarcely had the awe-stricken girl given utterance, till a heart-rending wail sent a thrill through her.

"O! O! O!" was the cry from a hundred voices, as the last torture was inflicted upon them.[3]

Again came a hissing sound, accompanied by the smell of scorched flesh, with wailing in their native tongues for mercy to God.

"Holy Madonna! Mother of God! Is this the sacrifice, or what is it?"

"Yes," replied a hidden, unknown voice, in chaste and elegant Portuguese—"a sacrifice of burnt offering to the god of Portugal and Spain."

"Good sir, pray tell me"—looking around she said—"what is this, and where am I?"

"Be patient, dear child—be patient, and you shall hear—as from the graves of our forefathers—of untold suffering from this spot—

"A place where demons daring land—
Fiends in bright noon day—and sit
A hellish conclave band to barter
The sons and daughters of our land away."

"May God protect me!" she screamed, and sunk in a swoon, when in an instant the servants bore her in the hammock away.

In parties of ten or more the branding iron was applied in such quick succession, that a sound and smell like that of broiling and scorched flesh was produced. At this last sad act of cruelty, and the voice in explanation of it, the tender and affrighted girl, yielding to frail nature, had sickened and fallen at the root of a tree where she sat, when the first impressions of consciousness found her again at the side of a devoted mother under the roof of the dwelling, fondly ministering to her relief.

---

[3]One method of torture inflicted by the foreign traders to prevent meeting, is an oblong square piece of iron in a box form, made so as to admit the ends of the middle and ring fingers, when it is driven down as far as it will go, tearing the flesh from the bone as it forces its way.

"O, mother—O, mother! What an experience have I had this day! O what my ears have heard!" were the first words of Angelina on recovering.

"Tell me, my child," with native simplicity but earnestness inquired the mother, "what is it?"

"As well may you, mother," replied the excited, intelligent girl, "go

"Ask the whirlwinds why they rove;
  The storms their raging showers:
  Ask the lightning why they move,
  The thunders whence their powers!"

"My child, your head is bad; it is hot; it is not sound. You must keep quiet, my child," anxiously admonished the mother, applying leaves taken from cold water continually to her brow.

"A cup of water, mother; I am sick. Oh, I hear it again! They are burning them alive!" continued she to talk at random, till sleep quieted her voice, whilst the mother stood over her with a calabash of leaves and water anxiously watching every breath she drew.

From *Blake; or, The Huts of America* (1859), chapter 49

Richard Greener in 1870

Richard Greener in 1895

RICHARD T. GREENER:

THE FIRST BLACK HARVARD COLLEGE GRADUATE

For Good Government & Urban Politics

Richard Theodore Greener '70 was the first Negro to graduate from Harvard College. . . . A Harvard education was by no means Greener's youthful ambition; in fact, though his grandfather had taught in a school for colored children in Baltimore, there was no college tradition in his family. His father, when Greener was born on January 30, 1844, in Philadelphia, was a steward on a Liverpool packet. A few years later the father shipped on a California packet, and in 1853 the California gold fever hit him. Successful in his mining for a while, he was taken ill and suffered losses, and shortly disappeared; his family never heard from him again, and in due time presumed him dead.

The year the father "went to digging for gold" the mother moved the family to Boston. Finding no good schools for colored children in that city she shortly moved hers across the Charles to Cambridge, so that they might attend an "unproscriptive school," and Richard secured his early education at the Broadway Grammar School under the direction of Master Roberts and Miss Lucretia Clapp.

When about fourteen years old, however, he left school to help support his mother, and worked two years in a shoe store, a year with a wood engraver, a year or more as a porter at the Pavilion Hotel on Tremont Street, Boston, briefly in the fruit business and the newspaper trade, and then for two years as a porter for Messrs. Palmer and Batchelder on Washington Street, Boston.

During these years he became convinced that his was a high destiny, that he would make something of his life. While employed by D.J. Smith & Co., wood engravers, he plunged into the intricacies of the craft, and indeed showed considerable aptitude; but one day, either in anger or under-estimating his employee's pride, the employer struck him—and Richard walked out of the plant. He seriously considered the life of an artist, on the basis of his experience with D.J. Smith, but when he "found he could not go abroad" he turned his attention to obtaining an education.

While he was at the Pavilion Hotel Richard aroused the interest of a number of the guests. A Judge Russell gave him access to his library, and a Mrs. Maria S. Cook undertook to instruct him in French. Later, when he moved on to Palmer and Batchelder's his duties included that of night-watchman, and he occupied his spare nocturnal time reading English and French books, and also familiarizing himself, from what records were available to him, with the "banking and all the other details of business." Believing he had earned a position superior to that of porter, he approached his employer and suggested promotion. When told that his employer "was afraid to attempt it," he vowed to "do nothing else but study for the next ten years if necessary." He was sure that at the end of the war opportunities never before available would open to colored people, and he determined to be in position to take advantage of them.

In the summer of 1862 he wrote Franklin B. Sanborn '55, later to become a famous teacher and reformer, who was then teaching in a private school in Concord, to ask if he might enter Mr. Sanborn's school and there prepare for college. To this Sanborn agreed; but, told of the arrangement, Batchelder suggested Oberlin as an alternate; Oberlin was cheaper, he said, and he'd help him financially. Greener deferred to his employer's suggestion, and while waiting for Oberlin to open in the fall of 1862, began reading Latin with George Herbert Palmer '64, for he knew he was ill prepared for formal education.

At that time Oberlin offered two years of pre-college work, and in the first of these, the junior preparatory class, Greener plunged with the energy and ambition that was to characterize all his career. Whether he was slighted by reason of "colorphobia," as he thought he was, or whether (as seems more likely) he was ill prepared for his studies, he did not receive "as high an appointment" as he thought he deserved, and he decided to leave Oberlin—and "carry out a latent desire to enter Harvard."

To Exeter he applied first, for admission to the senior class, but he was told he was not fitted for it and "Dr. Soule wouldn't let me try to keep up with it." (Gideon Lane Soule was Exeter's third principal.) At Andover he had better luck, and Dr. Samuel H. Taylor told him he might try, though warning him that the preparation he had at Oberlin was far below the Eastern standard. Greener found the going hard, but he tackled his studies with a will, and gained no little distinction for his declamations.

In the fall of 1865, in his twenty-first year, Richard Theodore Greener entered Harvard College, heavily conditioned. It was another year before he could fully rise to his educational challenges, and found he had best repeat his freshman year.

By his own reckoning Greener had a happy and rewarding under-graduate experience. He turned his forensic and literary propensities to good purposes when he won a Bowdoin Prize as a sophomore for elocution, and another as a senior for his English essay, "The Best Way of Crushing the Agitator is to Give him his Grievance," which criticized the system of land tenure in Ireland. He belonged to two societies and a "radical religion club." The last reflected an early disillusionment with the evangelical practices of his time. "Under the mistaken impression" that he was converted, he had joined the First Independent Baptist Church on Joy Street, Boston, when he was working for Messrs. Palmer and Batchelder, in 1861. Convinced later of "his error," he applied for and secured from the church "honorable dismissal."

Rumors inevitably sprang up among his classmates as to his background; he was variously represented as an escaped slave, a genius who had come straight from the cotton field to the College, as a Scout in the Union Army, as the son of a Rebel general, and so on. When these came to his attention, Greener was always at pains to divulge his antecedents and background unhesitatingly.

Appraising himself and his prospects at the end of his senior year, Greener admitted a great fondness for art and some aptitude towards it, and strong interests in metaphysics, general literature, and also in the Greek and Latin classics—when "divested of their grammatical pedantry." He planned to go forth in the world and get all the knowledge he could and make all the reputation he could (and as a corollary to these to make a comfortable competence). He thought he might do best in the profession of the law.

The road to admission to the bar, which he achieved seven years after, was a devious one. First of all he needed a job, and in August of 1870 he found one, as principal of the Male Department of the Institute for the Colored Youth of Philadelphia. Two years later found him principal of the Sumner High School in Washington, and a member of the staff of the *New National Era*. When that publication expanded into the *New National Era and Citizen*, he accepted the challenge of associate editorship.

Shortly he achieved a dual appointment in the Office of Public Works and in the office of the District Attorney, where he applied himself for the first time to the study of law.

Then South Carolina, in the midst of its painful reconstruction period, beckoned him, and in October, 1873, he accepted an appointment as Professor of Mental and Moral Philosophy at the University of South Carolina. And here, in academic surroundings, his immense energy and ambition found scope. In addition to teaching Philosophy, he assisted in the Departments of Latin and Greek, Mathematics, and Constitutional History.

He also acted as librarian, rearranging the university's "rare library" of 27,000 volumes and beginning the preparation of a catalogue. At the same time he studied law, was graduated from the University's Law School in 1876, was admitted to the Supreme Court of South Carolina the next year, and to practice at the bar of the District of Columbia the one after that. Greener's academic career was abruptly terminated in 1877 when the Wade Hampton legislature closed the door of the University of South Carolina to Negroes.

His career became kaleidoscopic: Board of Health of Columbia, S.C.; American Philological Association; commission to revise the school system of the State; clerkships in the Post Office Department and in the Treasury Department. In late 1877 he was appointed instructor in the Law Department of Howard University, and upon the death of the incumbent he became Dean of the Department. After a term as law clerk to the First Comptroller of the United States Treasury he resigned to enter into private practice.

Lectures now demanded much of his time, particularly in his capacity as secretary of the Exodus Committee. At the Social Science Congress at Saratoga in 1879 he debated with Frederick Douglass, who had been advising the freedmen of the the South to stay put; Greener advocated their migrating west, to Kansas. As an attorney he pleaded and won a number of cases famous in their day. Politics occupied much of his time, and he was particularly proud of his membership in the Republican conference of 1880 which united the Republican factions for Garfield.

In 1885 he was appointed secretary of the Grant Memorial Association in the State of New York. He had always admired President Grant from the time he met him on the occasion of Grant's visit to Harvard in 1865, and had led delegations of "Republicans and colored men" to wait on him in Washington in 1871, 1873, 1875, and 1876.

The next few years he "devoted himself largely to literary work," including associate editorship of the *National Encyclopedia of American Biography,* but found time to attend as delegate meetings of the Unitarian Conference at Saratoga and of the American Missionary Society. He was secretary of the Irish Parliamentary Fund, which raised $150,000 for Parnell and Gladstone. "In every reform movement in New York City since 1885 I have been active for good government and clean politics," he admitted; "but always as a Republican."

He served as consul briefly in Bombay, India, and in 1888 became Commercial Agent of the United States at Vladivostok, East Siberia. In 1892 the Chinese government conferred on him the Order of the Double Dragon, for services rendered Chinese merchants and for aid in succoring the Shansi famine sufferers.

He remained at his Vladivostok post during the Russo-Japanese War, representing officially the British and Japanese interests. Before hostilities he was instrumental in sending back some 1,500 Japanese and lent what protection he could to those who had chosen to remain in Vladivostok.

Greener retired from foreign service in 1905. The latter part of his life was spent in Chicago, where he joined the Harvard Club. He died on May 2, 1922.

Harvard Alumni Bulletin (1964)

The White Problem

If one wishes to observe eccentricity, vagary, platitude, and idiosyncrasy all combined, let him only read the literary effusions of the so-called "Caucasian" intellect from Thomas Jefferson's "Notes on Virginia," down to the recent contributions to the *Forum*, when discussing any phase of the "Negro Problem." Jefferson, fresh from Hume,[*] uttered some platitudes about the two races living together in freedom, treading very cautiously, as is his custom, when not too sure of his premises. Imlay and Abbé Grégoire routed him at once, and, as if to complete the poetic irony, the Negro almanac maker, Benjamin Banneker, who had, from 1792 until 1800, calculated alone the only almanacs printed for Maryland, Delaware, District of Columbia, and Virginia, sent him a copy, with an autograph letter, couched in as choice English as Jefferson ever penned, and of equal chirography. Nevertheless, the special negro-hate went on. Nott & Glidden, De Leon, DeBow, *alius alii*, quoting, rehashing Jefferson, supplementing him with modern discoveries.

A phase of the white problem is seen in the determination, not only to treat the Negro as a member of a child-like race, but the grim determination to keep him a child or a ward. In every advance, since emancipation, it has, with true Caucasian gall, been assumed that everything must be done for him, and under no circumstances must he be allowed to do for himself. In religion, in politics, in civil and social life, he must be developed in a pen, staked off from the rest of mankind, and nursed, coddled, fed, and trained by aid of the longest spoons, forks, and rakes obtainable. All along there has been heard the solemn, low refrain of doubt, small hope, and feeble expectation

---

[*]As was common in the nineteenth century, Greener usually cited people by last name only. Some of these are clear a century later, but many are obscure. Instead of cluttering his text with dozens of explanatory brackets, we have placed all the full identifications together at the end.—Eds.

as to the probable survival of this black infant. Indeed, nothing has so weighed upon the average American Christian heart as the precarious health of this infant, whom no one had the heart exactly to kill, were it possible, but whose noiseless and peaceful departure to a better world, would have been hailed with smothered sighs of intense relief.

This feeling obtains North as well as South: scalawag, native, carpet-bagger or sand-hiller, democrat, republican, or independent, seemed to think that for some occult reason this infant must not be allowed to grow in any one of the social, religious, or political ways, in which other American citizens grow and develop healthfully for the good of their country. All the traditions seemed against the Negro, all the arguments surely were. He was rarely given a real chance, as here, to talk freely for himself, and when such opportunity was afforded, he generally took his cue from his audience, and talked to the jury, and usually with bated breath. When he spoke humbly, apologetically, deprecatingly, he was an intelligent, sensible fellow, a milder form of "good nigger," before the war. Among the *novi homines* of the Republic it is so self-satisfying to have some one to look down upon and despise, just perhaps, as you have emerged from the mire yourself, and before, indeed, the evidence of "previous condition" has been thoroughly obliterated.

> Wut *is* there lef' I'd like to know,
> Ef't ain't the difference o' color,
> To keep up self-respec' an' show
> The human natur' of a fullah?
> Wut good in bein' white, onless
> It's fixed by law, nut lef' to guess,
> That we are smarter, an' they duller.

Another difficulty of this white problem is the universal belief that somehow the Negro race began its career with President Lincoln's proclamation. All such novices would do well to look up their old histories, newspapers, and pamphlets. Next to the Indian, he is probably of the purest racial stock in the country, and as has been stated, whatever accession has come to him, has been from the "choicest" blood of the country. He has been thoroughly identified with it from the beginning. He was the agricultural laborer and the artisan at the South, the trusted servant and companion; at the North he took part in all mechanical pursuits, helped build the houses, worked on the first newspapers, made the first wood cuts, and was the best pressman at Charleston, Philadelphia, and Boston. In every industrial, social, and political movement, as well as in the different warlike struggles, he has borne an honorable part, which to profess ignorance of, is not creditable, or, if denied, shows wilful prejudice. He was on the heights of Abraham with Wolfe; in the French and Indian wars with Braddock; the first martyr of the Revolution; is seen in Trumbull's picture retreating with the patriots from Bunker Hill, musket in hand; Washington did not disdain to share a blanket with him on the cold ground at Valley Forge; at the South with Marion and Greene; at the North with Washington and Gates, with Wayne and Allen. On account of the injury to the United States through him, the war of 1812 was begun, and his fertile brain suggested the defence of New Orleans, and, after the battle, led Andrew Jackson to say in public proclamation:

I expected much: I knew well how you loved your native country . . . You have done much more than I expected . . . The President of the United States shall hear how praiseworthy was your conduct in the hour of danger . . . The American people, I doubt not, will give you the praise your exploits entitle you to. Do we not know how they fought with Lawrence in the Chesapeake, and formed more than half of the crew of Old Ironsides, were with Scott and Taylor in Mexico, as they were with Grant and Sherman, and Sheridan and Butler, with Farragut and Foote and Porter, at Port Hudson and Battery Wagner? He who doubts the record can read it from the pen of Negro historians, from Nell or Williams or Wilson, for "of those who perform the deeds, and those who write, many such are praised."

No sneer of race, no assumption of superiority, no incrusted prejudice will ever obscure this record, much less obliterate it, and while it stands, it is the Negro's passport to every right and privilege of every other American.

Not alone a soldier and a sailor, the Negro was a citizen, under colonial and proprietary governments, under the Articles of Confederation, and in most of the original thirteen states, was an honorable part of "we people," who ordained and established this constitution for the United States of America. Long before Calhoun and Taney, he fought, lived, voted, and acted like any other citizen; and if many of his race were enslaved, he was not alone. There were "free willers," "indentured servants," and "apprentices," many of them to bear him company. Not a few of these, as records show, white men, Irishmen, Scotchmen, Englishmen, Moors, Palatines, were ruthlessly sold into slavery as the exactions of the traffic became more pressing. At the earliest period there was always a class of black freemen, and they were found at the South as well as at the North,—at New Orleans, Mobile, Charleston, and Virginia, as well as at Washington, Baltimore, Philadelphia, New York, and Boston, where in business, in social life, in church and in politics, they were active, enterprising, and respected. In rare instances, with acquired wealth, like some "free willers," and "indentured servants," they went West or North, as the case might be, and mingled and blended into the new surroundings and developed civilization, where, but for names and traditions, all traces of them would be lost. There come to mind, of such men, three United States senators of distinction, at least ten representatives in Congress before the war, five eminent officers of the United States Army, two cabinet officers, three eminent Catholic prelates, four prominent divines of the Episcopal Church, while in the other churches, in medicine and in law, the list is too long for enumeration.

But of those who were content to remain chafing under the indignities and ostracism, which increased from 1820, it is time it should be clearly, emphatically and proudly stated that instead of being a pauper pariah class as is supposed, there was no movement looking to the amelioration of their condition, from 1808 until John Brown's raid in 1859,—nothing which tended to unshackle the slave or remove the clogs from the free colored man, in which he was not the foremost, active, intelligent participant, never a suppliant, never a mere recipient. On the contrary he was first to organize for his own emancipation; among the first to speak, and write, and print in his own behalf. From Benezet and Grégoire, Condorcet, Brissot de Warville, from Franklin, Rush and Rittenhouse, and more than all, from that "glorious communion of the saints," the Friends, he had early learned the value of his own manhood, was willing to fight for it, and acquired the art of putting his complaint into pretty choice English, at a time, too, when Abbé Raynal, 1779, thought it a matter of astonishment that America had not a good poet, an able mathematician, or a man of genius, in any single art or science, and "not one of them shows any decisive talent for one in particular."

When Fisher Ames was saying, 1807, "Excepting the writers of two able books on our politics, we have no authors. . . . shall we match Joel Barlow against Homer or Hesiod? Can Tom Paine contend against Plato?"; when Sydney Smith, 1818, wrote, "There does not seem to be in America, at this moment, one man of any considerable talents," a Negro astronomer was calculating logarithms, studying all alone, in the woods of Maryland, Ferguson's Astronomy, and making valuable observations, viewing the stars, and computing his almanacs. During this period, 1780-1810, the Negro had his churches, literary societies, abolition societies, and, later on, newspapers, with educated editors, and active agents for the assertion of their rights and privileges, before Lundy and Garrison.

Mr. Howells looks up the streets of "Nigger Hill," and sees only a few straggling Negroes. They are of no interest, and of course have "no story, bless you, to tell." And yet there are many stories, many traditions, much history clustering about that hill, from Cambridge Street to the Common, from Charles to Hancock. Big Dick, the boxer, the precursor of Jackson; the Blind Preacher, Raymond, Prince Hall, and Easton, Master Paul and his church and *school*, in which the first American anti-slavery society was organized, Jan. 6, 1832.

"On that dismal night, and in the face of public opinion, fiercer far than the tempest, or wind and hail that beat upon the windows of that 'nigger school-house,' were laid the foundations of an organized movement against American slavery that at last became too mighty to be resisted." Mr. Garrison might have told Mr. Howells, he certainly could have learned that, among colored men of that dear old town, the first patrons of the *Liberator* were found, who supported it the first year, when it had not fifty white subscribers. Mr. Garrison, at Exeter Hall in London, sixty years ago said, "I am proud to say that the funds for my mission ... were principally made up by the voluntary contributions of my free colored brethren at very short notice. ... Many of their number are in the most affluent circumstances, and distinguished for their refinement, enterprise, and talents ... they have flourishing churches, temperance and other societies. ... Among them is taken a large number of daily and weekly papers, and of literary and scientific periodicals, from the popular monthlies up to the grave and erudite *North American* and *American Quarterly Reviews*. I have, at this moment, to my own paper, *'The Liberator,'* *one thousand subscribers among this people*; and from an occupancy of the editorial chair of more than seven years, I can testify that they are more punctual in their payments than any five hundred white subscribers whose names I ever placed indiscriminately in my subscription book."

Not alone Wm. Lloyd Garrison. Long before Frederick Douglass began "to pray with his legs" and look toward the "north star," the leading colored men of Washington, Carey, and Fleet, and Cook; of Philadelphia, Forten, Allen, Burr, and Purvis; of Baltimore, Grice, Greener, and Watkins; of Boston, Paul, Easton, Barbadoes, and Walker, corresponded with, aided, lodged and fed the apostle Lundy, in his mysterious journeyings through the southern states, and circulated his Genius of Universal Emancipation.

My account is from Isaac Carey, who knew "the little, pale, thin man," and he says Lundy never departed empty handed.

It was in Master Paul's Church, Belknap Street, that the abolitionists, driven from Tremont Temple, in 1860, found refuge, and preserved there free speech for Boston and America. Master Paul himself was a college graduate, accompanied Mr. Garrison to England, and won praise from Daniel O'Connell for his scholarship and eloquence.

Before emancipation in New York state, *Freedom's Journal*, edited by Cornish and Russwurm, a graduate of Bowdoin, I am told, afterwards President of Liberia, demonstrated the public spirit, intelligence, and literary character of the American Negro. If David Walker's *Appeal*, issued in 1829, had been printed in 1765 or '70, and had been about the rights of the colonies, it would long since have attracted attention. But it was written by one of the "old clo' merchants" of Brattle Street—an extinct guild—and is the voice of a black John the Baptist, crying in the wilderness. It attained the honor of legislative attention, and a reward set for the author's head; but it is an American classic, and forever answers all hints at Negro contentment under oppression. By law of heredity, thanks to Governor Butler, Walker's son became a lawyer and a municipal judge in Boston.

These facts taken at random would tend to show that the American Negro has traditions—far more, and more honorable than many of his traducers. They are of services, ancestry, interests in public affairs in his own future. Now traditions of blood and training and achievement can never be permanently repressed. Pile Etna upon them, they will break forth, no matter how long or persistently kept down. As a help to the solution of the White Problem, this article is to show that they exist, and if they have not hitherto asserted themselves, it is because they could afford to wait, not because they are not cherished and kept for inspiration. Some complacent critics of the Negro, who analyze, weigh, measure him with their little poles, discuss his removal to

Africa, debate his admission to trade unions, into the ranks of business, into the literary circle, into social life, would save themselves much unrest if they knew his motto, *J'y suis, j'y reste*.

He is a reader of the Census. He calmly contemplates either horn of the politico-economic problem—absorption, all he asks to be is an actual American citizen; repression and fifty years of race isolation, —one of the ruling forces of this Republic, the arbiter of the South. For, in fifty years, he will be nearly 100,000,000 strong, and, judging solely by the advance since 1863, in thrift, in education, in race development, in equipoise, in aspiration, all that tend to consolidate and strengthen, he will have no fear of the few white chips which will here and there attempt to stem the rush of this black Niagara. Truly he can afford to wait. One of the worst phases of the White Problem is the fatuous clinging to certain ideas, especially the good done to the Negro by bringing him to America. As well tell the descendants of Virginia convicts, the progeny of the kidnapped Irish, 1645-52; the proud descendants of Dutch, Scotch and English poor-houses, shambles and heaths, of the benefits which have accrued to them.

For the presence of all these, the Negro included, America is the gainer, humanity the debtor. The value of his contribution far outweighs any benefit he may be supposed to have received. He has reaped down the fields, developed new ideas, preserved the ark of the Nation's inheritance, and, if Fletcher of Saltoun, and Dr. Dvorak have any weight, he is to become greater than the lawgiver, he is to found the American music of the future.

"The future music of this country must be founded upon what are called negro melodies . . . They are American. They are the folk songs of America, and your composers must turn to them . . . In the negro melodies of America, I discover all that is needed for a great and noble school of music. There is nothing in the whole range of composition that cannot find a thematic source here."—*Dvorak*.

The Negro has no tears to shed over that "wonderful school of slavery, under Providence," so often quoted. He is no such hypocrite as to go through the pretense of believing that slavery is ever a good, a necessary, or beneficial school. Much less does he grant that any phase of that school, at any stage, affected him morally, socially, or physically, except adversely, while he does know from bitter experience, how utterly pharasaical, how absurdly hypocritical, and how thoroughly unchristian the entire system was in practice, example, and influence.

Whatever of intelligence, Christianity, or civilization the Negro possesses today, let it be remembered he retains in spite of slavery, and its relic, caste. Whatever of honesty or morality or thrift has survived the charnel-house, comes from that excellent stock—better than the Indian—which Galton says is now farther behind the best English brain of today than it is behind the brain of Athens! It is due to brain that slavery could not disintegrate, to a happy heart, an abiding faith.

I am at loss to observe how close the race maintains its hold on orthodox Christianity, when it is remembered how even the maxims of the common law were set aside, at its behests—*partus requitur patiem*—how Virginia (Hening, v.II, 491) declared that those imported thither, "except Turks and Moors in amity," shall be accounted slaves, "notwithstanding a conversion to Christianity after their importation." How far from solution seems the white problem, when the Negro reflects how powerless is Christianity to repress race prejudice; how often indifferent to real brotherhood, while affecting deep denominational interest. Indeed, while an emasculated religion has been preached to the Negro, each denomination has seemed to shirk the question of, Who is my Neighbor? A premium has been offered every self-respecting Negro to repudiate Christianity as it is taught. Why speak of the Christian? Take the cultured editor, the moulder of public opinion. How despairing the "white problem," when this is the high water-mark of culture:

Consider him at his best. I cite the case of a manly and accomplished gentleman of the race. His life has no background. What we mean by ancestry is lacking to him; and not only is it lacking but its lack is proclaimed by his color, and he is always reminded of it. Be who he may and do what he may, when the personal test comes he finds himself a man set apart, a marked man.

There is a difference between the discrimination against him in one part of the country (the South) and in another part (the North), but it is a difference in degree only. He is not any where in a fellowship in complete equipoise with men of the other race. Nor does this end it. The boundless sweep of opportunity which is the inheritance of every white citizen of the Republic, falls to him curtailed, hemmed in, a mere pathway to a few permissible endeavors. A sublime reliance on the ultimate coming of justice may give him the philosophic temper. But his life will bring chiefly opportunities to cultivate it. And for his children what better? To those that solve great social problems with professional ease, I commend this

remark that Mr. Lowell is said to have made, 'I am glad I was not born a
Jew; but if I had been a Jew, I should be prouder of that fact than any
other.' You can find men who are glad that they were not born Negroes;
but can you find a man, who, if he had been born a Negro, would be
prouder of that fact, than of any other? When you have found many men
of this mind, then this race problem will, owing to some change in human
nature, have become less tough, but till then, patience and tolerance.

Here is a paragraph which most people would acquiesce in; which
bears the air of hard sense, stern reality, deep philosophic insight,
keen analysis and delicate humor. It is already winging its way, and
will be quoted as a solid fact. If it were true then Schopenhauer
reigns in America; religion and culture have failed to soften the
manner but have hardened and intensified the small prejudices of two
centuries ago. If the statements were true, acquiescence in such
condition would show the utmost callousness, a more than heathen
indifference, a heartlessness, and inhumanity, unworthy of the century.
If character, reputation, manly accomplishments, the heights reached,
the palm won, still find any black hero a "marked man," because of no
fault of his own, and church and society, home and club, united in
thus ostracising him and his children, then is it not demonstrated that
it is not the Black but the White Problem, which needs most serious
attention in this country?
Mr. Lowell, as always, was wisely terse. No trace of the snob was
in him; he was no panderer to caste. Of course he was not anxious
to be born a Jew, for he knew unreasoning and unreasonable pride of
race still pecked often at its superior; but Lowell, knowing the history
of the race, and what its sons had accomplished in spite of persecution, felt he "would be prouder of that fact if he were a Jew than any
other." Nor is it true that every social avenue is closed to the aspiring
and manly Negro of today. Professor Washington, of Tuskegee, the
leader in perhaps the greatest work of the race, is received among the
best people of Boston, Philadelphia, and New York. The late Professor Price of North Carolina, was the recipient of exceptional attention
at home and abroad, on account of his talents and rare eloquence.
Professor Scarborough, the best Greek scholar of the race, meets the
members of the American Philological Association on terms of
equality, and Mr. Du Bois, who won a travelling scholarship at
Harvard, read a paper before the American Historical Society, and has
been offered a professorship in a white college. It is surely no

unusual thing in New York City to see educated colored men, at various social functions, collegiate, theological, political, literary, professional. These are sporadic cases, of course; but so are the cases of the bright farmer boys from Vermont, North Carolina, Michigan, Connecticut, and New York State, who have, by virtue of study or talent, gained entree to the same salons. The fact springs from the new ozone of equality, or better liberality, which is in the air, and is prompted and encouraged by those who have a clear notion of the fitness of things. Here at least, it is not a race, nor color, nor creed line.

Against that flippancy which draws too hasty conclusions, which cannot conquer its early prejudices, or ignore its limitations, there looms up a quiet unobtrusive but persistent force, which is determined not to give way to caste distinctions; but to see to it that there is a career open to all, despite sex, or creed, or race, in order that no atom of intellectual force shall be lost to our common country, and it is this which tends to the solution of our problem. Once in a while the great utterance of some broad-souled, warm-hearted American, determined to give his testimony, comes to us. Bishop Potter, broader than his entire church, says tersely, "What the Negro needs more than anything else is, opportunity." Or, it is Cable: "I must repeat my conviction that if the unconscious habit of oppression were not already there, a scheme so gross, irrational, unjust and inefficient as our present caste distinctions could not find a place among a people so generally intelligent and high-minded. . . . We hear much about race instinct. The most of it, I fear, is pure twaddle. It may be there is such a thing. We do not know. It is not proved. And even if it were established, it would not necessarily be a proper moral guide."

Then, it is Bishop Dudley, bravely fighting his way through traditions: "The time may come and will, when the prejudices now apparently invincible shall have been conquered. Society then as now organized upon the basis of community of interests, congeniality of tastes, and equality of position, will exclude the multitude who cannot speak its shibboleth; but there will be no color line of separation. . . . Such a social revolution as will open wide the drawing-rooms of Washington to the black men who have been honored guests in the palaces of England and France. . . . Capacity is not lacking, but help is needed, the help, I repeat, which the intelligence of the superior race must give by careful selection and personal contact with the selected. Does not our mother Nature teach us that this is the only process offering prospect of success, such being her method of procedure, working under the Creator's law?"

Not on the Protestant side alone. Here this clearer blast from the leader of the Catholic cause in the Northwest, Archbishop Ireland of Minnesota: "The right way. There is a work for us. Slavery has been abolished in America; the trail of the serpent, however, yet marks the ground. We do not accord to our black brother all the rights and privileges of freedom and of a common humanity. They are the victims of an unreasonable and unjustifiable ostracism. . . . It looks as if we had grudgingly granted to them emancipation, as if we fain still would be masters, and hold them in servitude.

"What do I claim for the black men? That which I claim for the white men, neither more nor less. I would blot out the color line. White men have their estrangements. They separate on lines of wealth, of intelligence, of culture, of ancestry. Those differences and estrangements I do not now discuss, and will not complain if the barriers they erect are placed on the pathway of the black man. But let there be no barrier against mere color. Treat Negroes who are intellectually inferior to us as we treat inferior whites, and I shall not complain. The Negro problem is upon us, and there is no other solution to it, peaceful and permanent, than to grant to our colored citizens practical and effective equality with white citizens." Here are men whose words shed some rays of light upon the solution of this terrible White Problem, which I may lay some slight claim to the distinction of having discovered, though it would be presumptuous for me to say the solution is clear to me. If it could properly be stated, perhaps, Edmund Burke's *"timid prudence with which a tame circumspection so frequently enervates the work of beneficence,"* and of all things being *"afraid of being too much in the right,"* might be found its salient point on the positive side, while, as I have hinted, the absolute ignorance about the Negro presents the negative side.

> Slaves of Gold! whose sordid dealings
> Tarnish all your boasted powers,
> Prove that you have human feelings
> Ere you proudly question ours.

We learn from the *Forum* editor that there are members of this race who are "accomplished" and "manly." He is mistaken in supposing they have "no back-ground"; some of them have several, three generations of education, sufficient, according to Emerson, to make a scholar. Some have proved their capacity, not in contests with Negroes alone, but with representatives of all races; some have, it is true, from training and heredity, the philosophic temperament. Like Hebrews, who look not back to Jerusalem, or await a Messiah; like Irishmen, who do not dream alone of a resuscitated Irish monarchy, or see visions of an Irish Parliament at Dublin, they are painfully aware what disadvantages still hedge the members of any proscribed race, in ordinary pursuits, and in daily life; but they see no reason because of this, why they should feel ashamed of the fact, seek to deny it, or attempt to ignore it. They feel that they are first of all American citizens, and secondarily Negroes. From their reading, observation, and reflection, they are not sure but that the very fact of their origin may have been the means, under God's guidance of the Universe, of saving them from illiberal prejudices, from over-weening race-pride, from utter disregard of other races' rights, feelings and privileges, and from intellectual narrowness and bigotry.

[David Hume (1711-76), Scottish philosopher; Capt. Gilbert Imlay (1754?-1828?), author of *Topographical Description of the Western Territory of North America* (1792 and later eds.); Henri Grégoire (1750-1831), bishop, author of *De la Littérature des Nègres* (1808); Josiah Nott (1804-73) and George R. Gliddon (1809-57), co-authors of *Types of Mankind* (1854) and *Indigenous Races of the Earth* (1857); Thomas Cooper De Leon (1839-1914), author of *Four Years in Rebel Capitals* (1890); James D.B. DeBow (1820-67), founder/-editor of the proslavery *DeBow's Review* (1846ff.); *alius alii*, "one to another."

Novi homines (lit. "new men"), parvenus, upstarts; verse quotation from James Russell Lowell (1819-91), *Biglow Papers*, 2nd Series, No. 11 (1867).

Abraham Lincoln issued formal "Emancipation Proclamation" 1 Jan. 1863; James Wolfe (1727-59), British general at Battle of Quebec, 13 Sept. 1759; Edward Braddock (1695-1755), commander-in-chief of British forces in America, 1754-55; "first martyr," Crispus Attucks (1723-70), fell in Boston Massacre, 5 Mar. 1770; John Trumbull (1756-1831), painter of "Battle of Bunker Hill" (1786); U.S. Revolutionary generals: George Washington (1732-99; later 1st President), Francis Marion (1732?-95), Nathanael Greene (1742-86), Horatio Gates (1728?-1806), "Mad" Anthony Wayne (1745-96), Ethan Allen (1738-89), Andrew Jackson (1767-1845; later 7th President), proclamation 18 Dec. 1814; James Lawrence (1781-1813), Naval officer, who, mortally wounded, cried, "Don't give up the ship!"; Army commanders in Mexican War: Winfield Scott (1786-1866), Zachary Taylor (1784-1850; later 12th President); Civil War generals: Ulysses S. Grant (1822-85; later 18th

President), William Tecumseh Sherman (1820-91), Philip Henry Sheridan (1831-88), Benjamin Franklin Butler (1818-93); Civil War admirals: David Glasgow Farragut (1801-70), Andrew Hull Foote (1806-63); Fitz-John Porter (1822-1901), Civil War brigadier-general; black historians: William C. Nell (1816-74), author of *The Colored Patriots of the American Revolution* (1855), George W. Williams (1849-91), author of *History of the Negro Race in America* (1882) and *History of the Negro Troops in the War of the Rebellion* (1887), Joseph T. Wilson (1836-91), author of *The Black Phalanx* (1888).

John C. Calhoun (1782-1850), Vice-President and U.S. Senator, champion of slavery; Robert B. Taney (1777-1864), Chief Justice, responsible for notorious Dred Scott decision (1857).

Anthony Benezet (1713-84), antislavery activist; Antoine de Caritat, Marquis de Condorcet (1743-94), author of *Esquisse d'un Tableau Historique des Progrès de l'Esprit Humain* (1794), propounder of theory of "infinite perfectibility of man"; Jacques Pierre Brissot de Warville (1754-93), French journalist, founder of abolitionist Société des Amis des Noirs; Benjamin Franklin (1706-90), statesman, signer of antislavery petition (1790); Benjamin Rush (1745-1813), physician, cofounder of first U.S. antislavery society (1774); David Rittenhouse (1732-96), astronomer, president of American Philosophical Society (1790), attacked slavery; Guillaume T.F. Raynal (1713-96), author of *A Philosophical and Political History of the Settlements and Trade in North America* (1779; French original 1770).

Fisher Ames (1758-1808), U.S. statesman; quotation from essay "American Literature"; Joel Barlow (1754-1812), poet/diplomat, author of two epics, "The Vision of Columbus" (1787) and "The Columbiad" (1807); Thomas Paine (1737-1809), political philosopher and author; Sydney Smith (1771-1845), English clergyman and essayist, cofounder of *Edinburgh Review* (1802ff.), denouncer of most things American; "a Negro astronomer," Benjamin Banneker (1731-1806); James Ferguson (1710-76), Scottish scientist, author of *Astronomy Explained Upon Newton's Principles* (1756); abolitionists: Benjamin Lundy (1789-1839), William Lloyd Garrison (1805-79), founder/editor of *The Liberator* (1831-65).

William Dean Howells (1837-1920), novelist, editor, critic, long-time Boston resident; "Big Dick," Richard Seavers (c.1794-c.1830), who stood 6 feet 5 inches; Peter Jackson (1861-1901), heavyweight boxer, "Black Prince of the Ring"; John T. Raymond (fl. 1830-50), Baptist clergyman; Prince Hall (1735?-1807), Masonic organizer and abolitionist; Rev. Hosea Easton (c.1799-1837), author of *A Treatise on the Intellectual Character . . . of the Colored People* (1837); Rev. Thomas Paul (1773-1831), pioneer of independent black Baptist churches; the New England Anti-Slavery Society.

Garrison's Exeter Hall speech: 13 July 1833.

Washingtonians: Isaac Carey (fl.1830-40), successful challenger of law forbidding Negroes to sell merchandise; Dr. James H. Fleet (d.1861), founder of Negro schools; Rev. John Francis Cook, Sr. (d.1855), Presbyterian, head of Negro school in Washington; Philadelphians: James Forten (1766-1842), abolitionist; Richard Allen (1760-1831), abolitionist, founder of African Methodist Episcopal Church; John P. Burr (fl.1830-40), official of Colored Convention and of Moral Reform Society; Robert Purvis, Sr. (1810-98), abolitionist; Baltimoreans: Hezekiah Grice (1801-c.1870), leader of black activists, later émigré to Haiti; Richard T. Greener (1844-1922), the present author; Rev. William James Watkins (1801-58), antislavery writer, vice-president of Moral Reform Society; Bostonians: Revs. Paul and Easton (v. above); James G. Barbadoes (d.1841), abolitionist; David Walker (1785-1830), abolitionist, author of famous *Appeal . . . to the Colored Citizens of the World* (1829).

Greener understandably confused three members of the Paul family. The Baptist church on Belknap St. was served by the aforementioned Thomas Paul. It was one of six brothers (all clergymen), the Rev. Nathaniel Paul (1775-1839), who accompanied Garrison to England. And it was his schoolteacher son, Thomas Paul, Jr. (1812-85), who graduated from college (Dartmouth, class of 1841). Daniel O'Connell (1775-1847), a lawyer, was the dominant force in Irish politics, and an ardent antislavery fighter.

Samuel E. Cornish (1795-1858) and John Russwurm (1799-1851), abolitionists and co-editors of the first black U.S. newspaper (1827). Benjamin F. Butler (1818-93), Massachusetts governor (1882-84), did indeed nominate David Walker's son, Edward Garrison Walker (1830?-1901), to a municipal judgeship; but the nominee was thrice rejected, and the post went to the first black graduate of Harvard Law School, George L. Ruffin (1834-86), LL.B. 1869.

J'y suis, j'y reste: "Here I am and here I stay," attributed to French marshal Marie Edmé Patrice Maurice de MacMahon (1808-93) on finally capturing the Malakoff in the Crimean War (8 Sept. 1855).

Andrew Fletcher of Saltoun (1655-1716), Scottish politician and writer; Antonin Dvořák (1841-1904), famous Czech composer, director of the National Conservatory of Music in New York City, 1892-95, during which time he made the quoted statement in an interview with the *New York Herald* (25 May 1893).

Sir Francis Galton (1822-1911), English anthropologist, founder of eugenics.

Partus requitur patiem: a linotypist's garbling of some such phrase as *partus requirit patientem*, "Giving birth calls for a patient person." William Waller Hening, ed., *The Statutes at Large Being a Collection of All the Laws of Virginia*, 13 vols. (1809-23); the statute quoted is dated 10 Nov. 1682. The "cultured editor" is Walter Hines Page (1855-1918), and the long passage quoted comes from his essay "The Last Hold of the Southern Bully," *Forum*, Nov. 1893, 311-12; the Lowell cited is James Russell Lowell.

Arthur Schopenhauer (1788-1860), German philosopher, expounder of pessimism.

Booker T. Washington (1856-1915), educator, principal of Tuskegee Institute; Joseph C. Price (1854-93), clergyman, orator, founding head of Livingstone College (1882); William S. Scarborough (1852-1926), philologist, Wilberforce University professor and later president (1876-1920); William E.B. Du Bois (1868-1963), scholar, who read a paper, "The Enforcement of the Slave-Trade Laws," before the American Historical Association, Dec. 1891.

Henry C. Potter (1835-1908), Episcopal bishop of New York, 1887ff.; George Washington Cable (1844-1925), writer, whose quotation comes from "The Freedman's Case in Equity," *Century Magazine*, Jan. 1885, 416 & 418.

Thomas U. Dudley (1837-1904), Episcopal bishop of Kentucky; the quotation is from "How Shall We Help the Negro?" *Century Magazine*, June 1885, 277-78.

John Ireland (1838-1918), Roman Catholic rector of the cathedral, St. Paul, Minnesota (1867), bishop of St. Paul (1884), archbishop (1888), major force in founding Catholic University in Washington (1889); Edmund Burke (1729-97), British statesman and author; "Slaves of Gold!" quatrain unidentified; "the *Forum* editor" is again Walter Page, in the essay cited above; Ralph Waldo Emerson (1803-82), essayist, deliverer of many anti-slavery speeches, famous especially for his oration, "The American Scholar," presented before the Harvard chapter of Phi Beta Kappa (31 Aug. 1837).]

Lend a Hand: A Record of Progress (1894)

Speech at the Harvard Club of New York

What Sir John Coleridge in his 'Life of [John] Keble' says of the traditions and influences of Oxford, each son of Harvard must feel is true also of Cambridge. The traditions, the patriotic record, and the scholarly attainments of her alumni are the pride of the College. Her contribution to letters, to statesmanship, and to active business life, will keep her memory perennially green. Not one of the humblest of her children, who has felt the touch of her pure spirit, or enjoyed the benefits of her culture, can fail to remember what she expects of her sons wherever they may be: to stand fast for good government, to maintain the right, to uphold honesty and character, to be, if nothing else, good citizens, to perform, to the extent of their ability, every duty assumed or imposed upon them,—democratic in their aristocracy, catholic in their liberality, impartial in judgment, and uncompromising in their convictions of duty. [Cheers and applause.]

Harvard's impartiality was not demonstrated solely by my admission to the College. In 1770, when Crispus Attucks died a patriot martyr on State Street, she answered the rising of independence and liberty by abolishing all distinctions founded upon color, blood, and rank. Since that day, there has been but one test for all. Ability, character, and merit,—these are the sole passports to her favor. [Applause.]

When, in my adopted State, I stood on the battered ramparts of Wagner, and recalled the fair-haired son of Harvard who died there with his brave black troops of Massachusetts,—

> him who, deadly hurt, agen
> Flashed on afore the charge's thunder,
> Tippin' with fire the bolt of men,
> Thet rived the Rebel line assunder,[*]

---

[*]James Russell Lowell, *Biglow Papers*, second series, No. 10.—Eds.

I thanked God, with patriotic pleasure, that the first contingent of negro troops from the North should have been led to death and fame by an alumnus of Harvard [Robert Gould Shaw '60]; and I remembered, with additional pride of race and college, that the first regiment of black troops raised on South Carolina soil were taught to drill, to fight, to plough, and to read by a brave, eloquent, and scholarly descendant of the Puritans and of Harvard, Thomas Wentworth Higginson ['41]. [Great applause and cheers.]

Is it strange, then, brothers, that I there resolved for myself to maintain the standard of the College, so far as I was able, in public and in private life? I am honored by the invitation to be present here tonight. Around me I see faces I have not looked upon for a decade. Many are the intimacies of the College, the society, the buskin, and the oar which they bring up, from classmates and college friends. I miss, as all Harvard men must miss to-night, the venerable and kindly figure of Andrew Preston Peabody ['26], the student's friend, the consoler of the plucked, the encourager of the strong, Maecenas's benign almoner, the felicitous exponent of Harvard's Congregational Unitarianism. I miss, too, another of high scholarship, of rare poetic taste, of broad liberality—my personal friend, Elbridge Jefferson Cutler ['53], loved alike by students and his fellow-members of the Faculty for his conscientious performance of duty and his genial nature.

Mr. President and brothers, my time is up. I give you 'Fair Harvard,' the exemplar, the prototype of that ideal America, of which the greatest American poet has written,

> Thou, taught by Fate to know Jehovah's plan,
> Thet man's devices can't unmake a man,
> An' whose free latch-string never was drawed in
> Against the poorest child of Adam's kin.[*]

[Great applause.]

G.W. Williams, *A History of the Negro Race in America* (1883)

---

[*]Ibid., No. 2, "Mason & Slidell" [6 Jan. 1862].—Eds.

CLEMENT G. MORGAN

Clement Garnett Morgan was born in Stafford County, Virginia, on 9 January 1859. His slave parents, on being emancipated, moved to Washington, where their son attended high school. Morgan then worked as a barber and went to St. Louis to teach school for four years. Craving a college education, he spent two years at Boston Latin School as preparation for entering Harvard at the age of 27. Barbering and substantial scholarships covered most of his expenses. As a junior he won first prize in the annual Boylston oratory contest (the second prize going to his black classmate W.E.B. Du Bois). He received his bachelor's degree in 1890, proceeding directly to Harvard Law School, from which he was graduated in 1893—the school's third black graduate and the first of his race to hold degrees from both the College and Law School.

For the rest of his life he resided in Cambridge and maintained a law practice in the same Boston office at 39 Court Street. He was active in Republican politics and, elected from an almost all-white ward, served on the Cambridge Common Council in 1895 and 1896 and on the Board of Aldermen in 1898 and 1899, but thrice was an unsuccessful aspirant to the state legislature. Ever the agitator, he was in 1903 largely responsible for the closing of a segregated school for 33 colored children in the western Massachusetts town of Sheffield, and in 1905 joined Du Bois as a founding member of the Niagara Movement and its successor, the NAACP. He died in Cambridge on 1 June 1929.

Clement Morgan in 1890

Harvard's Negro Orator

CHOSEN BY THE SENIOR CLASS
IN PREFERENCE TO AN "ARISTOCRAT"

HIGH HONORS FOR THE BARBER STUDENT,
SON OF AN EX-SLAVE

Clement Garnett Morgan Has Striven Diligently for an Education and His Classmates in the University Confer Unique Distinction Upon Him—Elected by a Bare Majority of One Vote in a Hot Contest.

[Special to the *World*]

Boston, Oct. 20—It is learned on good authority that the color line was drawn in the case of the colored student, Clement Garnett Morgan, who was chosen class orator at Harvard, as told in to-day's *World*. The members of the class, many of whom were seen to-night, positively refuse to talk about the proceedings of the meeting [16 Oct.] at which the colored student was elected. The meeting was secret and only the bare result of the election, without any statement as to the number of votes cast for either candidate, was given to the press. However, it is certain that Morgan was elected by a majority of one vote in a total vote cast of over 250.

The other officers were elected on a larger margin, but the real excitement and the cause of the prolongation of the meeting until the hour of midnight was the question whether Harvard would choose the colored man. When the vote was announced it is understood there was a call for a recount, which was made amid intense excitement. The opponents of Morgan were crestfallen when the tellers made the announcement that Morgan had just one vote over his competitor. The colored man, on the other hand, received the warm congratulations of his supporters. His following did not include the wealthy and aristocratic element which was represented by a candidate of their own, whose identity, owing to the peculiar circumstances of the case, is one of the things to be kept from publication. The supporters of this candidate made a great effort prior to the meeting to beat the colored man, although it is only just to say that not all of them objected to Morgan on account of his color so much as because they wanted their man to win.

Morgan's antecedents and the fact that he had in his first year and previous to his entrance made money as a barber served to set some of the aristocratic students against him. Up to within a few days of the election Morgan had not been seriously thought of for the honor, because of the feeling that he could not win. But his supporters considered that the election of a colored man would be a handsome way of showing Harvard's friendship for the race, especially in view of the notable part filled by such Harvard men as [Charles] Sumner, [Wendell] Phillips and others in the abolition movement. These young men put their heads together and organized a movement to place the colored classmate in the honored office, and the vote they rolled up was the big surprise of the meeting.

Heretofore the Bloods and the Sevells have run the election, and up to last year the rest of the class had submitted. Last year the rule was broken in the election as class orator of young [Walker Warren] Magee ['89]. A good deal of feeling has cropped out over Morgan's success, but the chances are it will die a natural death before commencement, by which time it is hoped the unceasing kickers will come to their senses.

Morgan is the son of a former slave now living in West Washington, D.C., where the young man was born and attended and graduated from the High School. In Washington he learned his trade as a barber and worked in a barber shop there. Later he taught school in St. Louis. His ultimate object being the earning of money enough to go to Harvard. He came to Boston in 1884, entered the Latin school and graduated in 1886 with honorable rank. He entered Harvard in the Fall of 1886 and during his vacation worked in a Saratoga hotel. He also earned money delivering lectures in New England on the colored problem. He won the prize for oratory last year by reciting Carl Schurz's oration on "The Emancipation Proclamation." It is not generally known to the class and this fact is the chief reason why he was not regarded as a formidable competitor for class orator.

New York World (1889)

Class Day Oration

Ladies and Gentlemen,

Classmates,

"Help them who cannot help again."

Keen joy or grief we must often bear alone, whether we will or not. So, on this our Class Day, we, knowing joys which others may not share, come yet with sorrows which they can scarcely be expected to feel or even understand. Still we can spend but a moment sighing, since Alma Mater knows, as every mother will tell you, that the strength or tenderness of filial affection is measured, not by sighs and tears at parting, but by strictness in keeping precepts. So, in these days we live in thought of those teachings which have for us been the same as for all Harvard men, whether expressed in "piety, morality and learning," in "knowledge and godliness," in "Truth for Christ and the Church," or in simple Truth, embracing all: for it is by truth, which, as an active living principle, becomes our "ought," our "must," that we answer the questions which each of us puts to himself to-day, "What is my relation to the world about me?" and "Where can I help?" Every son of Harvard imbued with this principle, going forth "with freedom to think," "with patience to bear,"and "for right ever bravely to live," has been aptly described in the words of Browning:

One who never turned his back but marched breast forward,
Never doubted clouds would break,
Never dreamed, though right were worsted, wrong would
            triumph,
Held we fall to rise, are baffled to fight better,
Sleep to wake. [*Asolando*, 'Epilogue' (1889)]

And is not the example of every one of them acting upon us, as it has acted upon no class before? Let two instances at the beginning of our university life assure us that it is:

You remember that to us entering college there was entrusted the keeping of that which is ever held dearest here—of worship. It was because the strength of character of those preceding us warranted the belief that voluntary devotion, "a thing unique in university training in the world," would not suffer at our hands; that there might be written over our chapel doors, "not compulsion, but invitation." How glad we were last fall to hear that the departure had more than met expectations! And yet, let us not forget, its continued success rests largely on you and on me,—the first ripe fruits of it; for our new system is after all an old one. We saw its complete foreshadowing in the thought out of the "Upanishads" which to-day in the midst of our questioning seems to say, "Worship and despair not; if not on a high plane, give lower service, seek to reach men; if thou canst not worship meaningly, toil; in work is the blessing of man."

The second instance:—We had had about a month to set up our ideals, when the day of our quarter millennial celebration came. What an impressive sight was the line of procession past the buildings, through the Yard, here into the theatre! And then the meaning of it all! You will recall how, in the evening, we, with an enthusiasm which modesty could not check, did not forbear boasting that "these two hundred fifty years are for Ninety." You doubtless see the transparency now. A jest do you say? I am sure it was, but that jest today becomes our earnest. Those years were for us, and bringing with them great privileges, put upon us like obligations and responsibilities.

There occurs to me a case from history where a memorable victory was won under the influence of the spell of mere antiquity. When Napoleon, on the plains of Egypt, pointing to those monuments of human endeavor and of human achievement, said to his soldiers, "Remember that from the top of those pyramids forty centuries look down upon you," those few simple words carried with them the inspiration which won the "Battle of the Pyramids." In the years which we claimed, and which now in their turn claim us, there is no such charm, but holding you and me there is a greater power—the spirit of plain, zealous, single-minded men, who, preferring the hardships of the wilderness to beds of ease under tyranny, among their first acts set up in this place on the basis of sound learning, civil and religious liberty; of men, who in the hour of their country's need, leaving home, friends, social position, worldly honor, all that could make life worth living, gave themselves a willing sacrifice, if only they might make way for liberty, for truth and for humanity. This is the power holding you and me, making those two hundred fifty years ours.

The example of these men shows clearly that the true road to success, to any excellence, is that of plain, genuine simplicity, sincerity and unselfishness; for this, and this alone, leads to the culture, the character and the civilization which stand the test of time.

Their example shows, too, that the man for any great work in any age must be earnest, faithful, patient, the man who can wait, if need be;—not, bear in mind, he who stands idly waiting, but he who, while waiting, works, with the earnestness of life, with the faithfulness of industry, and with the patience of heroism, of farsightedness, and of unshaken confidence in that "Force always at work to make the best better, the worst good." To him, biding his time, the bitterest tear becomes as sweet spring water.

Their example shows also, in the words of him who once chid us for indifference here, that "power, ability, influence, character and virtue are only trusts with which to serve our time." The purposes of an education are but two: (1) adding, by diligence, discovery and invention, to the thought and to the material development of the world; and (2) informing, moving, directing, uplifting men. Both of these have one end, the well-being of mankind. Then he serves his time best who serves humanity best; and who does so serves best his country and his Alma Mater.

From the oration of the two hundred and fiftieth anniversary you will, I am sure, remember this thought: "The only way in which our civilization can be maintained, even at the level it has reached, the only way in which that level can be made more general and be raised higher, is by bringing the influence of the more cultivated to bear with more energy and directness on the less cultivated, and by opening more inlets to those indirect influences which make for refinement of mind and body. Democracy must show its capacity for producing, not a higher average man, but the highest possible types of manhood in all its manifold varieties, or it is a failure." It is not, I think, assuming too much to say that in seeking to bring "the influence of the more cultivated to bear with energy and directness on the less cultivated," to make it impossible for democracy to be a failure, is your duty and mine,—a duty from which the only escape is performance.

Public speakers say that they make it a point to hit in their audience the man farthest off, assured that if he hear, all others must.

Do you then in your relation with the world, in your service to humanity, make it your business to reach the lowest man? I use the word in no vulgar sense; for we here scarcely need the aid of any philosopher to know that the great thing in the world is Man. I know, like travelers up a mountain side, looking back, our heads may grow giddy with the heights we have reached, but looking beyond and seeing the summit so far off it seems we have not begun to climb and our foolish pride goes. I mean him who has not like advantages with you, the man struggling against odds, who in the depths of ignorance, rudeness and wretchedness, it may be, is longing and striving, in his imperfect human way, for something higher, better, nobler, truer,— reach him; for to him making a fight in the face of difficulties, there are two spurs: one, opposition, developing strength; the other a cheering word from those who in nobleness of heart do, by their sympathy, make the fight with him. Of the first he will always have enough; alas, if you withhold from him the second! No evil is greater or farther reaching in its consequences than that of disregard for the dictates and demands of humanity. Then make him feel the possibilities within him and help him to develop those possibilities.

There are ways to that above and beyond Sir Launfal's,—giving from a sense of duty, but insulting to the dignity of human nature,—ways, too, which never descend to patronage, hurting alike to helper and to helped. These will suggest themselves in obedience to will. A striking case, lately brought to our notice by the newspapers, is that of the college settlement in New York, where a few heroic women, with brave heart and a purpose, carry on successfully a plan for helping others in a real human way. As we read of them we could scarcely help thinking that Brook Farms may fail but Rivington Settlements must persist. You will remember that here a few years ago we were told by the Scotch scholar visiting us of a similar plan in operation among university men in his country. The same thing you will find, too, among students in London. We know of something of the kind here in a modest way. What an advance since the days of Horace Greeley if men are to be saved by the college graduate and not from him!

There is no intention of making missionaries of you except in that larger sense in which every man is a missionary, but prominent in our college conference this year has been this thought: "What the world needs is what Margaret Fuller calls the spiritual man of the world." Now we do not think the world scandalous, skeptical, or epicurean, nor do we believe nothing remains but hunger and cant, still it is in some respects a queer world, for with it you are at once "the fast set" and expected leaders of a great moral movement. However, you must fill the bill. There is abundant need for giving the world the assurance which Goethe gave Carlyle: "It is still possible that man be a man." Indeed, from one act here, small in and of itself, the world expects, nay, demands of us that assurance. When, conscious of a possible taunt of writhing under defeat, we took a stand against professionalism in college athletics, we put ourselves on record, virtually saying that the winning or losing of a game, a match, or a race, is one matter, but the means of gain or loss is a far different thing; the principles underlying sports, as those governing conduct, reconcile means with ends only when both are honorable. The protest, though ill-received, was nevertheless right, and will, I believe, lead to fairer and better athletics; at any rate, having taken high ground, we have no retreat which is not disgraceful.

Looking from our college world to the great world outside University gate, we cannot fail to see a great moral movement going on; it leads a Russian count from the court to a bench with the cobblers, it dismisses in Germany a "man of iron will" and teaches him that the revolutionary minority which he feared must not stand in the way of the greatest good to the greatest number and of right and fair play for all; it acts on the brain of an unpretentious man, and sets a-going the thought of the whole country. You may not agree with Tolstoi in some of his theories, though take him for all in all, he is one of the grand examples of our time; for from the day on which the first rude savage freely gave his life for the advancement of his tribe, down to the day of John Brown of Ossawattomie at Harper's Ferry, men have seen that the noblest thing on earth, that which most surely touches the heart, is vicarious suffering, human self-sacrifice; you may question the outcome of the efforts of William of Germany and of the Berlin Conference; you may find fault with the methods of the nationalists; but you cannot deny that the purpose of all of these is not only to help men to a comfortable living, but to add to their intellectual and moral welfare.

This movement, not yet developed into widespread enthusiasm for humanity, waits "men of thought and men of action to clear the way," and looks with anxious eyes on you. Believing with Emerson that the test of civilization is not in the census, nor in the size of cities, nor in the crops, but in the kind of man the country turns out, see to it that our civilization stand the test by taking the Calibans of our soil and making Prosperos of them, by making the peasant brain wise. Intelligence is virtue's own handmaid, labor's helpmeet; if the one have not her aid, nor the other her companionship, vice and misery result. You have in that truth the strongest argument for developing and stimulating the intellectual faculties of every human being. Here in America, where the humblest man counts one, and where however much some may look down, their neighbor will not be found looking up, it is especially imperative that every man be a thinker.

Classmates of Ninety, looking over our number here I find we touch by actual residence, extreme points, East and West, North and South, in our country; we cannot go away rightly impressed with the deepest meanings of this place without feeling impelled to add somewhat to its greatness. To do that, what you and I must take account of is, not success, but that which alone deserves it, endeavor. "The measure of a nation's true success," says Mr. Lowell, "is the amount it has contributed to the thought, the moral energy, the spiritual hope and consolation of mankind." So then it must be our endeavor to open to every man, woman and child in this land every door leading to intelligence and virtue. The time has come when honorable men disdain to be guilty of accusing their fellows of ignorance and vice while they either deliberately dam up the "inlets to the influences which make for refinement of mind and body," or else in their indifference turn not a hand to give free passage to them. The case before us requires not so much words, as work with might and main. Let each of us do his duty and in that find our relation to the world about us; there, see where we may help. So, and only so, were those two hundred fifty years ours, and we in our turn theirs.

Class of 1890 (1890)

W.E.B. DU BOIS

William Edward Burghardt Du Bois was born on 23 February 1868 in Great Barrington, Massachusetts, where he was the only black member of his high-school graduating class in 1884. After a year's mill job and a scholarship offer, he had the wherewithal to go to all-black Fisk University in Tennessee, where he was granted sophomore standing, edited the school paper, and received his A.B. in 1888. Entering Harvard (a longtime goal) as a junior, he took another A.B. in 1890, an A.M. in 1891, and—after studying in Berlin—in 1895 became the first black to receive a Harvard Ph.D. His dissertation, *The Suppression of the African Slave-Trade*, was published in 1896 as the first book in the Harvard Historical Series.

Short stints teaching Classics and sociology at Wilberforce University and the University of Pennsylvania led to a professorship in the social sciences at Atlanta University from 1897 to 1910. He helped to found the National Association for the Advancement of Colored People, and conceived and edited its monthly organ, *The Crisis*, from 1910 until 1934, when disagreements led to his resignation and a return to Atlanta University, from which he was forcibly retired in 1944.

Throughout his life, Du Bois produced a torrent of words—not just speeches and works of scholarship and opinion, but even poetry, fiction, and drama. His *The Souls of Black Folk* (1903) remains one of the supreme pieces of American writing. Du Bois received the Spingarn Medal in 1920, and more than a half dozen honorary degrees here and abroad. His increasing left-wing activity in later years resulted in indictment, trial, and acquittal. At the age of 93 he joined the Communist Party and moved to Ghana, where he died on 27 August 1963.

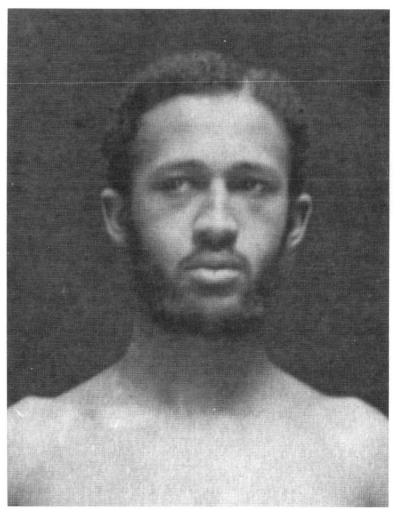

W.E.B. Du Bois on arriving at Harvard in 1888 (previously unpublished)

W.E.B. Du Bois in 1915

A Negro Student at Harvard

at the End of the Nineteenth Century[1]

Harvard University in 1888 was a great institution of learning. It was two hundred and [fifty-two] years old and on its governing board were Alexander Agassiz, Phillips Brooks, Henry Cabot Lodge, and Charles Francis Adams; and a John Quincy Adams, but not the ex-President. Charles William Eliot, a gentleman by training and a scholar by broad study and travel, was president. Among its teachers emeriti were Oliver Wendell Holmes and James Russell Lowell. Among the active teachers were Francis Child, Charles Eliot Norton, Justin Winsor, and John Trowbridge; Frank Taussig, Nathaniel Shaler, George Palmer, William James, Francis Peabody, Josiah Royce, Barrett Wendell, Edward Channing, and Albert Bushnell Hart. In 1890 arrived a young instructor, George Santayana. Seldom, if ever, has any American university had such a galaxy of great men and fine teachers as Harvard in the decade between 1885 and 1895.

To make my own attitude toward the Harvard of that day clear, it must be remembered that I went to Harvard as a Negro, not simply by birth, but recognizing myself as a member of a segregated caste whose situation I accepted. But I was determined to work from within that caste to find my way out.

The Harvard of which most white students conceived I knew little. I had not even heard of Phi Beta Kappa, and of such important social organizations as the Hasty Pudding Club, I knew nothing. I was in Harvard for education and not for high marks, except as marks would insure my staying. I did not pick out "snap" courses. I was there to enlarge my grasp of the meaning of the universe. We had had, for

[1]W.E.B. Du Bois recorded a variant version of this memoir; the tape is in the Harvard Archives.

instance, no chemical laboratory at Fisk; our mathematics courses were limited. Above all I wanted to study philosophy! I wanted to get hold of the bases of knowledge, and explore foundations and beginnings. I chose, therefore, Palmer's course in ethics, but since Palmer was on sabbatical that year, William James replaced him, and I became a devoted follower of James at the time he was developing his pragmatic philosophy.

Fortunately I did not fall into the mistake of regarding Harvard as the beginning rather than the continuing of my college training. I did not find better teachers at Harvard, but teachers better known, who had had wider facilities for gaining knowledge and lived in a broader atmosphere for approaching truth.

I hoped to pursue philosophy as my life career, with teaching for support. With this program I studied at Harvard from the fall of 1888 to 1890, as an undergraduate. I took a varied course in chemistry, geology, social science, and philosophy. My salvation here was the type of teacher I met rather than the content of the courses. William James guided me out of the sterilities of scholastic philosophy to realist pragmatism; from Peabody's social reform with a religious tinge I turned to Albert Bushnell Hart to study history with documentary research; and from Taussig, with his reactionary British economics of the Ricardo school, I approached what was later to become sociology. Meantime Karl Marx was mentioned, but only incidentally and as one whose doubtful theories had long since been refuted. Socialism was dismissed as unimportant, as a dream of philanthropy or as a will-o-wisp of hotheads.

When I arrived at Harvard, the question of board and lodging was of first importance. Naturally, I could not afford a room in the college yard in the old and venerable buildings which housed most of the well-to-do students under the magnificent elms. Neither did I think of looking for lodgings among white families, where numbers of the ordinary students lived. I tried to find a colored home, and finally at 20 Flagg Street I came upon the neat home of a colored woman from Nova Scotia, a descendant of those black Jamaican Maroons whom Britain had deported after solemnly promising them peace if they would surrender. For a very reasonable sum I rented the second story front room and for four years this was my home. I wrote of this abode at the time: "My room is, for a college man's abode, very ordinary indeed. It is quite pleasantly situated—second floor, front, with a bay window and one other window . . . As you enter you will perceive the bed in the opposite corner, small and decorated with floral designs calculated to puzzle a botanist . . . On the left hand is a bureau with a mirror of doubtful accuracy. In front of the bay window is a stand with three shelves of books, and on the left of the bureau is an improvised bookcase made of unpainted boards and uprights, containing most of my library of which I am growing quite proud. Over the heat register, near the door, is a mantel with a plaster of Paris pug-dog and a calendar, and the usual array of odds and ends . . . On the wall are a few quite ordinary pictures. In this commonplace den I am quite content."

Following the attitudes which I had adopted in the South, I sought no friendships among my white fellow students, nor even acquaintanceships. Of course I wanted friends, but I could not seek them. My class was large—some three hundred students. I doubt if I knew a dozen of them. I did not seek them, and naturally they did not seek me. I made no attempt to contribute to the college periodicals since the editors were not interested in my major interests. But I did have a good singing voice and loved music, so I entered the competition for the Glee Club. I ought to have known that Harvard could not afford to have a Negro on its Glee Club travelling about the country. Quite naturally I was rejected.

I was happy at Harvard, but for unusual reasons. One of these was my acceptance of racial segregation. Had I gone from Great Barrington High School directly to Harvard, I would have sought companionship with my white fellows and been disappointed and embittered by a discovery of social limitations to which I had not been used. But I came by way of Fisk and the South and there I had accepted color caste and embraced eagerly the companionship of those of my own color. This was of course no final solution. Eventually, in mass assault, led by culture, we Negroes were going to break down the boundaries of race; but at present we were banded together in a great crusade, and happily so. Indeed, I suspect that the prospect of ultimate full human intercourse, without reservations and annoying distinctions, made me all too willing to consort with my own and to disdain and forget as far as was possible that outer, whiter world.

In general, I asked nothing of Harvard but the tutelage of teachers and the freedom of the laboratory and library. I was quite voluntarily and willingly outside its social life. I sought only such contacts with white teachers as lay directly in the line of my work. I joined certain clubs, like the Philosophical Club; I was a member of the Foxcroft Dining Club because it was cheap. James and one or two other teachers had me at their homes at meal and reception. I escorted colored girls to various gatherings, and as pretty ones as I could find to the vesper exercises, and later to the class day and commencement social functions. Naturally we attracted attention and the *Crimson* noted my girl friends. Sometimes the shadow of insult fell, as when at one reception a white woman seemed determined to mistake me for a waiter.

In general, I was encased in a completely colored world, self-sufficient and provincial, and ignoring just as far as possible the white world which conditioned it. This was self-protective coloration, with perhaps an inferiority complex, but with belief in the ability and future of black folk.

My friends and companions were drawn mainly from the colored students of Harvard and neighboring institutions, and the colored folk of Boston and surrounding towns. With them I led a happy and inspiring life. There were among them many educated and well-to-do folk, many young people studying or planning to study, many charming young women. We met and ate, danced and argued, and planned a new world.

Towards whites I was not arrogant; I was simply not obsequious, and to a white Harvard student of my day a Negro student who did not seek recognition was trying to be more than a Negro. The same Harvard man had much the same attitude toward Jews and Irishmen.

I was, however, exceptional among Negroes at Harvard in my ideas on voluntary race segregation. They for the most part saw salvation only in integration at the earliest moment and on almost any terms in white culture; I was firm in my criticism of white folk and in my dream of a self-sufficient Negro culture even in America.

This cutting of myself off from my white fellows, or being cut off, did not mean unhappiness or resentment. I was in my early manhood, unusually full of high spirits and humor. I thoroughly enjoyed life. I was conscious of understanding and power, and conceited enough still to imagine, as in high school, that they who did not know me were the losers, not I. On the other hand, I do not think that my white classmates found me personally objectionable. I was clean, not well-dressed but decently clothed. Manners I regarded as more or less superfluous and deliberately cultivated a certain brusquerie. Personal adornment I regarded as pleasant but not important. I was in

Harvard, but not of it, and realized all the irony of my singing "Fair Harvard." I sang it because I liked the music, and not from any pride in the Pilgrims.

With my colored friends I carried on lively social intercourse, but necessarily one which involved little expenditure of money. I called at their homes and ate at their tables. We danced at private parties. We went on excursions down the Bay. Once, with a group of colored students gathered from surrounding institutions, we gave Aristophanes' *The Birds* in a Boston colored church. The rendition was good, but not outstanding, not quite appreciated by the colored audience, but well worth doing. Even though it worked me near to death, I was proud of it.

Thus the group of professional men, students, white-collar workers, and upper servants, whose common bond was color of skin in themselves or in their fathers, together with a common history and current experience of discrimination, formed a unit that, like many tens of thousands of like units across the nation, had or were getting to have a common culture pattern which made them an interlocking mass, so that increasingly a colored person in Boston was more neighbor to a colored person in Chicago than to a white person across the street.

Mrs. Ruffin of Charles Street, Boston, and her daughter, Birdie, were often hostesses to this colored group. She was widow of the first colored judge appointed in Massachusetts, an aristocratic lady, with olive skin and high-piled masses of white hair. Once a Boston white lady said to Mrs. Ruffin ingratiatingly: "I have always been interested in your race." Mrs. Ruffin flared: "Which race?" She began a national organization of colored women and published the *Courant*, a type of small colored weekly paper which was then spreading over the nation. In this I published many of my Harvard daily themes.

Naturally in this close group there grew up among the young people friendships ending in marriages. I myself, outgrowing the youthful attractions of Fisk, began serious dreams of love and marriage. There were, however, still my study plans to hold me back and there were curious other reasons. For instance, it happened that two of the girls whom I particularly liked had what was to me then the insuperable handicap of looking like whites, while they had enough black ancestry to make them "Negroes" in America. I could not let the world even imagine that I had married a white wife. Yet these girls were intelligent and companionable. One went to Vassar

College, which then refused entrance to Negroes. Years later when I went there to lecture I remember disagreeing violently with a teacher who thought the girl ought not to have "deceived" the college by graduating before it knew of her Negro descent! Another favorite of mine was Deenie Pindell. She was a fine, forthright woman, blonde, blue-eyed and fragile. In the end I had no chance to choose her, for she married Monroe Trotter.

Trotter was the son of a well-to-do colored father and entered Harvard in my first year in the Graduate School. He was thick-set, yellow, with close-cut dark hair. He was stubborn and strait-laced and an influential member of his class. He organized the first Total Abstinence Club in the Yard. I came to know him and joined the company when he and other colored students took in a trip to Amherst to see our friends Forbes and Lewis graduate in the class with Calvin Coolidge.

Lewis afterward entered Harvard Law School and became the celebrated center rush of the Harvard football team. He married the beautiful Bessie Baker, who had been with us on that Amherst trip. Forbes, a brilliant, cynical dark man, later joined with Trotter in publishing the *Guardian*, the first Negro paper to attack Booker T. Washington openly. Washington's friends retorted by sending Trotter to jail when he dared to heckle Washington in a public Boston meeting on his political views. I was not present nor privy to this occurrence, but the unfairness of the jail sentence led me eventually to form the Niagara movement, which later became the NAACP.

Thus I lived near to life, love, and tragedy; and when I met Maud Cuney, I became doubly interested. She was a tall, imperious brunette with gold-bronze skin, brilliant eyes, and coils of black hair, daughter of the Collector of Customs at Galveston, Texas. She had come to study music and was a skilled performer. When the New England Conservatory of Music tried to "jim-crow" her in the dormitory, we students rushed to her defense and we won. I fell deeply in love with her, and we were engaged.

Thus it is clear how in the general social intercourse on the campus I consciously missed nothing. Some white students made themselves known to me and a few, a very few, became life-long friends. Most of my classmates I knew neither by sight nor name. Among them many made their mark in life: Norman Hapgood, Robert Herrick, Herbert Croly, George Dorsey, Homer Folks, Augustus Hand, James Brown Scott, and others. I knew none of these intimately. For the most part I do not doubt that I was voted a somewhat selfish and self-centered "grind" with a chip on my shoulder and a sharp tongue.

Only once or twice did I come to the surface of college life. First I found by careful calculation that I needed the cash of one of the Boylston prizes in oratory to piece out my year's expenses. I got it through winning a second oratorical prize. The occasion was noteworthy by the fact that another black student, Clement Morgan, got first prize at the same contest.

With the increase at Harvard of students who had grown up outside New England, there arose at this time a certain resentment at the way New England students were dominating and conducting college affairs. The class marshal on commencement day was always a Saltonstall, a Cabot, a Lowell, or from some such New England family. The crew and most of the heads of other athletic teams were selected from similarly limited social groups. The class poet, class orator, and other commencement officials invariably were selected because of family and not for merit. It so happened that when the officials of the class of 1890 were being selected in early spring, a plot ripened. Personally, I knew nothing of it and was not greatly interested. But in Boston and in the Harvard Yard the result of the elections was of tremendous significance, for this conspiratorial clique selected Clement Morgan as class orator. New England and indeed the whole country reverberated.

Morgan was a black man. He had been working in a barber shop in St. Louis at the time when he ought to have been in school. With the encouragement and help of a colored teacher, whom he later married, he came to Boston and entered the Latin School. This meant that when he finally entered Harvard, he entered as freshman in the orthodox way and was well acquainted with his classmates. He was fairly well received, considering his color. He was a pleasant unassuming person and one of the best speakers of clearly enunciated English on the campus. In his junior year he had earned the first Boylston prize for oratory in the same contest where I won second prize. It was, then, logical for him to become class orator, and yet this was against all the traditions of America. There were editorials in the leading newspapers, and the South especially raged and sneered at the audience of "black washer-women" who would replace Boston society at the next Harvard commencement.

Morgan's success was contagious, and that year and the next, in several leading Northern colleges, colored students became the class orators. Ex-President Hayes, as I shall relate later, sneered at this fact. While, as I have said, I had nothing to do with the plot, and was not even present at the election which chose Morgan, I was greatly pleased at this breaking of the color line. Morgan and I became fast friends and spent a summer giving readings along the North Shore to defray our college costs.

Harvard of this day was a great opportunity for a young man and a young American Negro and I realized it. I formed habits of work rather different from those of most of the other students. I burned no midnight oil. I did my studying in the daytime and had my day parceled out almost to the minute. I spent a great deal of time in the library and did my assignments with thoroughness and with prevision of the kind of work I wanted to do later. From the beginning my relations with most of the teachers at Harvard were pleasant. They were on the whole glad to receive a serious student, to whom extra-curricular activities were not of paramount importance, and one who in a general way knew what he wanted.

Harvard had in the social sciences no such leadership of thought and breadth of learning as in philosophy, literature, and physical science. She was then groping and is still groping toward a scientific treatment of human action. She was facing at the end of the century a tremendous economic era. In the United States, finance was succeeding in monopolizing transportation and raw materials like sugar, coal, and oil. The power of the trust and combine was so great that the Sherman Act was passed in 1890. On the other hand, the tariff, at the demand of manufacturers, continued to rise in height from the McKinley to the indefensible Wilson tariff, making that domination easier. The understanding between the Industrial North and the New South was being perfected and, beginning in 1890, a series of disfranchising laws was enacted by the Southern states that was destined in the next sixteen years to make voting by Southern Negroes practically impossible. A financial crisis shook the land in 1893, and popular discontent showed itself in the Populist movement and Coxey's Army. The whole question of the burden of taxation began to be discussed.

These things we discussed with some clearness and factual understanding at Harvard. The tendency was toward English free trade and against the American tariff policy. We reverenced Ricardo and wasted long hours on the "Wages-fund." I remember Taussig's course

supporting dying Ricardean economics.   Wages came from what
employers had left for labor after they had subtracted their own
reward.   Suppose that this profit was too small to attract the
employer, what would the poor worker do but starve!   The trusts and
monopolies were viewed frankly as dangerous enemies of democracies,
but at the same time as inevitable methods of industry.   We were
strong for the gold standard and fearful of silver.   On the other hand,
the attitude of Harvard toward labor was on the whole contemptuous
and condemnatory.   Strikes like that of the anarchists in Chicago and
the railway strikes of 1886, the terrible Homestead strike of 1892 and
Coxey's Army of 1894, were pictured as ignorant lawlessness, lurching
against conditions largely inevitable.

It was not until I was long out of college and had finished my first
Karl Marx was mentioned only to point out how thoroughly his
theses had been disproven; of the theory itself almost nothing was
said.   Henry George was given but tolerant notice.   The anarchists of
Spain, the Nihilists of Russia, the British miners—all these were viewed
not as part of political and economic development but as a sporadic
evil.   This was natural.   Harvard was the child of its era.   The
intellectual freedom and flowering of the late eighteenth and early
nineteenth centuries were yielding to the deadening economic
pressure which would make Harvard rich but reactionary.   This
defender of wealth and capital, already half ashamed of Sumner and
Phillips, was willing finally to replace an Eliot with a manufacturer and
a nervous war-monger.   The social community that mobbed Garrison
easily electrocuted Sacco and Vanzetti.

It was not until I was long out of college and had finished my first
studies of economics and politics that I realized the fundamental
influence man's efforts to earn a living had upon all his other efforts.
The politics which we studied in college were conventional, especially
when it came to describing and elucidating the current scene in
Europe.   The Queen's Jubilee in June, 1887, while I was still at Fisk,
set the pattern of our thinking.   The little old woman at Windsor
became a magnificent symbol of Empire.   Here was England with her
flag draped around the world, ruling more black folk than white and
leading the colored peoples of the earth to Christian baptism, and, as
we assumed, to civilization and eventual self-rule.   In 1885, Stanley,
the traveling American reporter, became a hero and symbol of white
world leadership in Africa.   The wild, fierce fight of the Mahdi and
the driving of the English out of the Sudan for thirteen years did not
reveal their inner truth to me.   I heard only of the martyrdom of the

drunken Bible-reader and freebooter, Chinese Gordon.

After the Congo Free State was established, the Berlin Conference of 1885 was reported to be an act of civilization against the slave trade and liquor. French, English, and Germans pushed on in Africa, but I did not question the interpretation which pictured this as the advance of civilization and the benevolent tutelage of barbarians. I read of the confirmation of the Triple Alliance in 1891. Later I saw the celebration of the renewed Triple Alliance on the Tempelhofer Feld, with the new, young Emperor Wilhelm II, who, fresh from his dismissal of Bismarck, led the splendid pageantry; and, finally, the year I left Germany, Nicholas II became Czar of all the Russias. In all this I had not yet linked the political development of Europe with the race problem in America.

I was repeatedly a guest in the home of William James; he was my friend and guide to clear thinking; as a member of the Philosophical Club I talked with Royce and Palmer; I remember vividly once standing beside Mrs. Royce at a small reception. We ceased conversation for a moment and both glanced across the room. Professor Royce was opposite talking excitedly. He was an extraordinary sight: a little body, indifferently clothed; a big, red-thatched head and blazing blue eyes. Mrs. Royce put my thoughts into words: "Funny-looking man, isn't he?" I nearly fainted! Yet I knew how she worshipped him.

I sat in an upper room and read Kant's *Critique* with Santayana; Shaler invited a Southerner, who objected to sitting beside me, to leave his class; he said he wasn't doing very well, anyway. I became one of Hart's favorite pupils and was afterwards guided by him through my graduate course and started on my work in Germany. Most of my courses of study went well. It was in English that I came nearest my Waterloo at Harvard. I had unwittingly arrived at Harvard in the midst of a violent controversy about poor English among students. A number of fastidious scholars like Barrett Wendell, the great pundit of Harvard English, had come to the campus about this time; moreover, New England itself was getting sensitive over Western slang and Southern drawls and general ignorance of grammar. Freshmen at this time could elect nearly all their courses except English; that was compulsory, with daily themes, theses, and tough examinations. But I was at the point in my intellectual development when the content rather than the form of my writing was to me of prime importance. Words and ideas surged in my mind and spilled out with disregard of exact accuracy in grammar, taste in word, or restraint in style. I knew the Negro problem and this was more important to me than literary form. I knew grammar fairly well, and I had a pretty wide vocabulary; but I was bitter, angry, and intemperate in my first thesis. Naturally my English instructors had no idea of, nor interest in, the way in which Southern attacks on the Negro were scratching me on the raw flesh. Tillman was raging like a beast in the Senate, and literary clubs, especially those of rich and well-dressed women, engaged his services eagerly and listened avidly. Senator Morgan of Alabama had just published a scathing attack on "niggers" in a leading magazine, when my first Harvard thesis was due. I let go at him with no holds barred. My long and blazing effort came back marked "E"—not passed!

It was the first time in my scholastic career that I had encountered such a failure. I was aghast, but I was not a fool. I did not doubt but that my instructors were fair in judging my English technically even if they did not understand the Negro problem. I went to work at my English and by the end of that term had raised it to a "C." I realized that while style is subordinate to content, and that no real literature can be composed simply of meticulous and fastidious phrases, nevertheless, solid content with literary style carries a message further than poor grammar and muddled syntax. I elected the best course on the campus for English composition—English 12.

I have before me a theme which I submitted on October 3, 1890, to Barrett Wendell. I wrote: "Spurred by my circumstances, I have always been given to systematically planning my future, not indeed without many mistakes and frequent alterations, but always with what I now conceive to have been a strangely early and deep appreciation of the fact that to live is a serious thing. I determined while in high school to go to college—partly because other men did, partly because I foresaw that such discipline would best fit me for life . . . I believe, foolishly perhaps, but sincerely, that I have something to say to the world, and I have taken English 12 in order to say it well." Barrett Wendell liked that last sentence. Out of fifty essays, he picked this out to read to the class.

Commencement was approaching, when, one day, I found myself at midnight on one of the swaggering streetcars that used to roll out from Boston on its way to Cambridge. It was in the spring of 1890, and quite accidentally I was sitting by a classmate who would graduate with me in June. As I dimly remember, he was a nice-looking young man; well-dressed, almost dapper, charming in manner. Probably he was rich or at least well-to-do, and doubtless belonged to an exclusive fraternity, although that did not interest me. Indeed I have even forgotten his name. But one thing I shall never forget and that was his rather regretful admission (which slipped out as we gossiped) that he had no idea as to what his life work would be, because, as he added, "There's nothing in which I am particularly interested!"

I was more than astonished—I was almost outraged to meet any human being of the mature age of twenty-one who did not have his life all planned before him, at least in general outline, and who was not supremely, if not desperately, interested in what he planned to do.

In June, 1890, I received my bachelor's degree from Harvard *cum laude* in philosophy. I was one of the five graduating students selected to speak at commencement. My subject was "Jefferson Davis." I chose it with the deliberate intent of facing Harvard and the nation with a discussion of slavery as illustrated in the person of the president of the Confederate States of America. Naturally, my effort made a sensation. I said, among other things: "I wish to consider not the man, but the type of civilization which his life represented: its foundation is the idea of the strong man—individualism coupled with the rule of might—and it is this idea that has made the logic of even modern history, the cool logic of the Club. I made of a naturally brave and generous man, Jefferson Davis, one who advanced civilization by murdering Indians; then a hero of a national disgrace, called by courtesy the Mexican War; and finally, as the crowning absurdity, the peculiar champion of people fighting to be free in order that another people should not be free. Whenever this idea has for a moment escaped from the individual realm, it has found an even more secure foothold in the policy and philosophy of the State. The strong man and his mighty right arm has become the strong nation with its armies. However, under whatever guise a Jefferson Davis may appear as man, as race, or as a nation, his life can only logically mean this: the advance of a part of the world at the expense of the whole; the overwhelming sense of the I, and the consequent forgetting of the Thou. It has thus happened that advance in civilization has always been handicapped by shortsighted national selfishness. The vital principle of division of labor has been stifled not only in industry, but also in civilization; so as to render it well-nigh impossible for a new race to introduce a new idea into the world except by means of the cudgel. To say that a nation is in the way of civilization is a contradiction in terms, and a system of human culture whose principle is the rise of one race on the ruins of another is a farce and a lie. Yet this is the type of civilization which Jefferson Davis represented: it represents a field for stalwart manhood and heroic character, and at the same time for moral obtuseness and refined brutality. These striking contradictions of character always arise when a people seemingly become convinced that the object of the world is not civilization, but Teutonic civilization."

A Harvard professor wrote to *Kate Field's Washington*, then a leading periodical: "Du Bois, the colored orator of the commencement stage, made a ten-strike. It is agreed upon by all the people I have seen that he was the star of the occasion. His paper was on 'Jefferson Davis,' and you would have been surprised to hear a colored man deal with him so generously. Such phrases as a 'great man,' a 'keen thinker,' a 'strong leader,' and others akin occurred in the address. One of the trustees of the University told me yesterday that the paper was considered masterly in every way. Du Bois is from Great Barrington, Massachusetts, and doubtless has some white blood in his veins. He, too, has been in my classes the past year. If he did not head the class, he came pretty near the head, for he is an excellent scholar in every way, and altogether the best black man that has come to Cambridge."

Bishop Potter of New York wrote in the *Boston Herald*: "When at the last commencement of Harvard University, I saw a young colored man appear . . . and heard his brilliant and eloquent address, I said to myself: 'Here is what an historic race can do if they have a clear field, a high purpose, and a resolute will.'"

Already I had now received more education than most young white men, having been almost continuously in school from the age of six to twenty-two. But I did not yet feel prepared. I felt that to cope with the new and extraordinary situations then developing in the United States and the world I needed to go further and that as a matter of fact I had just well begun my training in knowledge of social conditions.

I revelled in the keen analysis of William James, Josiah Royce, and young George Santayana. But it was James with his pragmatism and Albert Bushnell Hart with his research method who turned me back from the lovely but sterile land of philosophic speculation to the social sciences as the field for gathering and interpreting that body of fact which would apply to my program for the Negro. As an undergraduate, I had talked frankly with William James about teaching philosophy, my major subject. He discouraged me, but not by any means because of my record in his classes. He used to give me "A's" and even "A-plus," but as he said candidly, there is "not much chance of anyone earning a living as a philosopher." He was repeating just what Chase of Fisk had said a few years previously.

I knew by this time that practically my sole chance of earning a living combined with study was to teach, and after my work with Hart in United States history I conceived the idea of applying philosophy to an historical interpretation of race relations. In other words, I was trying to take my first steps toward sociology as the science of human action. It goes without saying that no such field of study was then recognized at Harvard or came to be recognized for twenty years after. But I began with some research in Negro history and finally, at the suggestion of Hart, I chose the suppression of the African slave trade to America as my doctor's thesis. Then came the question as to whether I could continue study in the graduate school. I had no resources in wealth or friends. I applied for a fellowship in the graduate school of Harvard, was appointed Henry Bromfield Rogers Fellow for a year, and later the appointment was renewed; so that from 1890 to 1892, I was a fellow in Harvard University, studying history and political science and what would have been sociology if Harvard had yet recognized such a field.

I finished the first draft of my thesis and delivered an outline of it at the seminars of American history and political economy December 7, 1891. I [had] received my master's degree in the spring. I was thereupon elected to the American Historical [Association] and asked to speak in Washington at their meeting in December, [1891]. The *New York Independent* noted this among the "three best papers presented," and continued:

The article upon the "enforcement of the Slave Laws" was written and read by a black man. It was thrilling when one could, for a moment, turn his thoughts from listening to think that scarcely thirty years have elapsed since the war that freed his race, and here was an audience of white men listening to a black man—listening, moreover, to a careful, cool, philosophical history of the laws which had not prevented the enslavement of his race. The voice, the diction, the manner of the speaker were faultless. As one looked at him, one could not help saying, "Let us not worry about the future of our country in the matter of race distinctions."

I had begun with a bibliography of Nat Turner and ended with a history of the suppression of the African slave trade to America; neither would need be done again, at least in my day. Thus in my quest for basic knowledge with which to help guide the American Negro, I came to the study of sociology, by way of philosophy and history rather than by physics and biology. After hesitating between history and economics, I chose history. On the other hand, psychology, hovering then on the threshold of experiment under Münsterberg, soon took a new orientation which I could understand from the beginning.

Already I had made up my mind that what I needed was further training in Europe. The German universities were at the top of their reputation. Any American scholar who wanted preferment went to Germany for study. The faculties of Johns Hopkins and the new University of Chicago were beginning to be filled with German Ph.D.'s, and even Harvard, where Kuno Francke had long taught, had imported Münsterberg. British universities did not recognize American degrees and French universities made no special effort to encourage American graduates. I wanted then to study in Germany. I was determined that any failure on my part to become a recognized American scholar must not be based on lack of modern training.

I was confident. So far I had met no failure. I willed and lo! I was walking beneath the elms of Harvard—the name of allurement, the college of my youngest, wildest visions! I needed money; scholarships and prizes fell into my lap—not all I wanted or strove for, but all I needed to keep me in school. Commencement came, and standing before governor, president, and grave, gowned men, I told them certain truths, waving my arms and breathing fast! They applauded with what may have seemed to many as uncalled-for fervor, but I walked home on pink clouds of glory! I asked for a fellowship and got it. I announced my plan of studying in Germany, but Harvard had no more fellowships for me. A friend, however, told me of the Slater Fund and that the Board was looking for colored men worth educating.

No thought of modest hesitation occurred to me. I rushed at the chance. It was one of those tricks of fortune which always seem partly due to chance. In 1882, the Slater Fund for the education of Negroes had been established and the board in 1890 was headed by ex-President R. B. Hayes. Ex-President Hayes went down to Johns Hopkins University, which admitted no Negro students, and told a "darkey" joke in a frank talk about the plans of the fund. The *Boston Herald* of November 2, 1890, quoted him as saying: "If there is any young colored man in the South whom we find to have a talent for art or literature or any special aptitude for study, we are willing to give him money from the education funds to send him to Europe or give him advanced education." He added that so far they had been able to find only "orators." This seemed to me a nasty fling at my black classmate, Morgan, who had been Harvard class orator a few months earlier.

The Hayes statement was brought to my attention at a card party one evening; it not only made me good and angry but inspired me to write ex-President Hayes and ask for a scholarship. I received a pleasant reply saying that the newspaper quotation was incorrect; that his board had some such program in the past but had no present plans for such scholarships. I responded referring him to my teachers and to others who knew me, and intimating that his change of plan did not seem to me fair nor honest. He wrote again in apologetic mood and said that he was sorry the plan had been given up, that he recognized that I was a candidate who might otherwise have been given attention. I then sat down and wrote Mr. Hayes this letter:

May 25, 1891

Your favor of the 2nd. is at hand. I thank you for your kind wishes. You will pardon me if I add a few words of explanation as to my application. The outcome of the matter is as I expected it would be. The announcement that any agency of the American people was willing to give a Negro a thoroughly liberal education and that it had been looking in vain for men to educate was to say the least rather startling. When the newspaper clipping was handed me in a company of friends, my first impulse was to make in some public way a categorical statement denying that such an offer had ever been made known to colored students. I saw this would be injudicious and fruitless, and I therefore determined on the plan of applying myself. I did so and have been refused along with a "number of cases" beside mine.

As to my case, I personally care little. I am perfectly capable of fighting alone for an education if the trustees do not see fit to help me. On the other hand the injury you have—unwittingly I trust—done the race I represent, and [am] not ashamed of, is almost irreparable. You went before a number of keenly observant men who looked upon you as an authority on the matter, and told them in substance that the Negroes of the United States either couldn't or wouldn't embrace a most liberal opportunity for advancement. That statement went all over the country. When now finally you receive three or four applications for the fulfillment of that offer, the offer is suddenly withdrawn, while the impression still remains.

If the offer was an experiment, you ought to have had at least one case before withdrawing it; if you have given aid before (and I mean here toward liberal education—not toward training plowmen) then your statement at Johns Hopkins was partial. From the above facts I think you owe an apology to the Negro people. We are ready to furnish competent men for every European scholarship furnished us off paper. But we can't educate ourselves on nothing and we can't have the moral courage to try, if in the midst of our work our friends turn public sentiment against us by making statements which injure us and which they cannot stand by.

That you have been looking for men to liberally educate in the past may be so, but it is certainly strange so few have heard [of] it. It was never mentioned during my three years stay at Fisk University. President [J.C.] Price of Livingstone [then a leading Negro spokesman] has told me that he never heard of it, and students from various other Southern schools have expressed great surprise at the offer. The fact is that when I was wanting to come to Harvard, while yet in the South, I wrote to Dr. Haygood [Atticus G. Haygood, a leader of Southern white liberals], for a loan merely, and he never even answered my letter. I find men willing to help me thro' cheap theological schools, I find men willing to help me use my hands before I have got my brains in working order, I have an abundance of good wishes on hand, but I never found a man willing to help me get a Harvard Ph.D.

Hayes was stirred. He promised to take up the matter the next year with the board. Thereupon, the next year I proceeded to write the board: "At the close of the last academic year at Harvard, I received the degree of Master of Arts, and was reappointed to my fellowship for the year 1891-92. I have spent most of the year in the preparation of my doctor's thesis on the suppression of the Slave Trade in America. I prepared a preliminary paper on this subject and read it before the American Historical Association at its annual meeting at Washington during the Christmas holidays. . . . Properly to finish my education, careful training in a European university for at least a year is in my mind and the minds of my professors, absolutely indispensable." I thereupon asked respectfully "aid to study at least a year abroad under the direction of the graduate department of Harvard or other reputable auspices" and if this was not practicable, "that the board loan me a sufficient sum for this purpose." I did not of course believe that this would get me an appointment, but I did think that possibly through the influence of people who thus came to know about my work, I might somehow borrow or beg enough to get to Europe.

I rained recommendations upon Mr. Hayes. The Slater Fund Board surrendered, and I was given a fellowship of seven hundred and fifty dollars to study a year abroad, with the promise that it might possibly be renewed for a second year. To salve their souls, however, this grant was made half as gift and half as repayable loan with five percent interest. I remember rushing down to New York and talking with ex-President Hayes in the old Astor House, and emerging walking on air. I saw an especially delectable shirt in a shop window. I went in and asked about it. It cost three dollars, which was about four times as much as I had ever paid for a shirt in my life; but I bought it.

Massachusetts Review (1960)

W. Monroe Trotter on entering Harvard in 1891
(previously unpublished)

W. Monroe Trotter in midcareer

W. MONROE TROTTER

William Monroe Trotter was born on 7 April 1872 in Ohio, but grew up in a Boston suburb. At Harvard not only was he the first black student ever elected to Phi Beta Kappa, but he also received this honor as one of the First Eight chosen in the spring of his junior year. After being graduated *magna cum laude* in 1895 he took more courses and earned an A.M. degree in 1896.

After a few years of negotiating real-estate mortgages, Monroe Trotter found his true calling by establishing a weekly black newspaper, the *Guardian*, which made its debut on 9 November 1901, bearing the motto, "For every right, with all thy might." Trotter took pride in the fact that his paper issued from the same floor of the same building whence William Lloyd Garrison had published his celebrated abolitionist paper, the *Liberator* (1831-65).

Trotter vehemently attacked Booker T. Washington, but also eventually broke with his one-time ally W.E.B. Du Bois. An inveterate agitator and activist, he spent a month in jail for disrupting a speech by Washington; got into a shouting match with President Woodrow Wilson in the White House; and was arrested, tried, and acquitted of leading a demonstration against the Boston screening of D. W. Griffith's movie *Birth of a Nation* (1915).

He continued to publish the *Guardian* until his death on his 62nd birthday, an apparent suicide. His sister Maude and brother-in-law Charles G. Steward (A.B. 1896) kept the paper going until 1957.

W. Monroe Trotter at Harvard

STEPHEN R. FOX

Given his father's expectations and his own talent, young Monroe was perforce a good student, leading both his grammar and high school classes. His twenty-one white high school classmates elected him president of the senior class. He gave some thought to becoming a minister, and was urged toward such a course by the pastor and deacons of the white First Baptist Church of Hyde Park, where he spent most of every Sunday. "His father disliked so strong a religious tendency," one of his sisters later recalled, "fearing he might not like to go out in the world and fight the world's problems." Further, the father argued, a black minister would end up serving a segregated congregation. So the son left the ministry notion behind. After graduating from high school he worked as a shipping clerk in Boston for a year and then entered Harvard College in the fall of 1891. . . .

Monroe Trotter had no trouble making the transition from shipping clerk to Harvard undergraduate. His lowest mark as a freshman was a B in English. That year had an interlude of sorrow, however, as his father died in February, at the age of fifty. A severe case of pneumonia during his recordership in Washington had destroyed James Trotter's health, leading to tuberculosis and a slow decline. His son was now the head of the family for his mother and two younger sisters. Money was no particular problem—the family owned considerable property in Boston, thanks mostly to the income from the recordership. Over the next three years Trotter won a total of $800 in Harvard scholarships. He supplemented that with jobs during his vacations. In the summer of 1892, for example, he sold desks from door to door in towns near his home (and remarked of this experience, with a touch of condescension, that "I sell more among the laboring people than among the better class . . . No house is too poor for me to call"). At Harvard he lived in a single room in College House, the cheapest student dormitory, and, with tuition only $150 a year, he paid for most of his education himself.

He worked hard at his studies, taking extra courses, and continued to be active in church work. Not that he was *always* so serious: he enjoyed playing tennis and wheeling around Cambridge and Boston on his bicycle. He also cheered on Harvard's athletic teams, and once jestingly considered going out for crew "in order to break Yale's long chain (two or three links) of victories." But in general he indulged in few of the frivolities of college life, at least on an organized basis. His formal extracurricular activities reflected a no-nonsense earnestness: the Wendell Phillips Club, the Young Men's Christian Association, and the Prohibition Club. In addition, he helped organize and was president of the Total Abstinence League, a group of about thirty ascetic undergraduates. He was a teetotaler all his life and, his brother-in-law once remarked, "believed that beer-drinking students were headed straight for Hell."

Like most Harvard students of the day, he took a great variety of courses without going deeply into anything and had no major subject. His first two years he concentrated in English, foreign languages, and mathematics, and then moved into history, philosophy, government, and political economy. In his introductory philosophy course he heard lectures by George Herbert Palmer, Josiah Royce, George Santayana, and William James. Senior year was probably the most rewarding, highlighted by Francis Peabody's social ethics course, Edward Cummings' sociology course and American constitutional and political history under Albert Bushnell Hart and his young assistant, Oswald Garrison Villard.

Trotter's academic performance was a confirmation, if he needed it, of his father's claims for the black man's intellect. Competing with some of the best white students in the country, he stood third in his class of 376 as a freshman and never ranked lower than eighth. He was especially good at foreign languages. His worst marks were a C and a C+ in English composition courses. (Though he would spend a career in journalism, his lifelong quarrel with the English language remained at best a stalemate. "It's" was his characteristic spelling of the neuter possessive pronoun.). . . .

Being a Harvard student was no protection from white America's peculiar mores. In the spring of 1893 a Negro at Harvard Law School named William H. Lewis—a brilliant scholar and later an All-American football player as well—was twice denied service at a Harvard Square barbershop. Within the Yard, though, there seemed to be remarkably little prejudice. Trotter of course could not have joined the exclusive clubs, but probably he had no interest in them anyway. His friendships were cosmopolitan, including white students from Europe and the United States. Later in life he would cherish the memory of his college years, for a greater reason than the usual nostalgia of the old alumnus.

From *The Guardian of Boston: William Monroe Trotter* (1970)

[Editors' note: See "Negro Graduate Protests" in section on Harvard Dormitory Crisis, below.]

Negro Delegate Tells of His Work

Only One of the Eleven Chosen
In the United States Who
Actually Reached France
Describes How He Got to Paris

Specially for the *Christian Science Monitor*

BOSTON, Massachusetts—William Monroe Trotter, of this city, the only one of eleven delegates chosen by American Negroes to represent them at the Paris Peace Conference who actually reached France, last night, at a public meeting in Tremont Temple, told of his difficulties in getting abroad, and gave an account of his work in the French capital.

The eleven delegates were chosen at a national assembly of the Negroes of this country, held under the auspices of the National Equal Rights League in Washington last December. They were instructed to place before the Peace Conference the claims of the estimated 14,000,000 Negroes in the United States for equal rights and no discrimination. All the elected delegates but Mr. Trotter applied for passports and failed to receive them.

The Negroes felt that the State Department had wronged them, Mr. Trotter said, in refusing to grant passports, because, when soldiers and civilians were needed to win the war, the promise of world democracy was held out and was accepted as genuine by the Negroes. The Negroes, Mr. Trotter said, are practically the only element in this country who are denied complete democracy, and therefore they need it. "To deny even the right of petition we felt was extraordinary tyranny," he said, "flagrant enough to justify us in seeking to overcome it."

Got a Job as Second Cook

Mr. Trotter took the money raised for his trip to Paris, after having arranged his own affairs, and went to a seaport city, disguised, where he tried to obtain passage without a passport. This means failed, but to avoid violating any laws, he obtained a seaman's passport. He had considerable difficulty in getting a job on a ship, but after a course in cooking in a lodging house he gained, through his persistence, the sympathy of a Negro cook on a small steamship and was signed as second cook. The job hunt took six weeks.

On reaching Havre, the ship did not dock for several days, but at last the opportunity came to go ashore. Mr. Trotter found that all members of the crew were prohibited from landing, but got a chance to go on the wharf to mail a letter written by the cook. Then, although he was in his working clothes, he continued into Havre, and found that no train was available till morning. He had been obliged to leave all his belongings on shipboard, but had a small sum of money with him. He boarded an early morning train to Paris, where he learned that the peace terms had just been handed Germany. He also found at about this time that the State Department had ruled against granting any passports to American Negroes, and considered his course thereby justified.

Mr. Trotter promptly sent protests to the Council of Five, and to General Foch, against the denial of passports to American Negroes and against the failure to insert in the peace treaty a clause guaranteeing them life and liberty. The protest charged that war pledges had been violated. He then presented copies of the protest to the Paris newspapers and to the American newspaper offices in that city.

"The next day," said Mr. Trotter, "I began my work of letting the world know that the Negro race wants full liberty and equality of rights, as the fruit of the world war. The *Journal des Débats, L'Intransigeant* and *Le Petit Journal* used the communications I sent them. I sent copies of the protest to every peace delegate and received sympathetic acknowledgments from many of them.

Jews Received Everything

"The Jews have received everything they asked from the Peace Conference. But here, in the United States, is an ethnical minority denied equal rights and we are asking that we be accorded only what every one else has. After the Memorial Day speech of President Wilson, I prepared a statement recalling that many of the American troops were Negroes, and, in view of a lynching which had just occurred in Missouri, demanding that in justice to them he ask Congress for a federal law against lynching. This statement was widely published in the French press and was cabled to this country by The Associated Press.

"The colored soldiers in France charged that they had been discriminated against in France. Leave was regulated by the color line, and Negro troops were restricted from visiting large cities, certain streets, and certain cafés. The white soldiers spread damaging stories about the colored men, in order to make the French people fear them. All menial tasks were shouldered upon colored soldiers. I prepared a protest to President Wilson in behalf of the colored soldiers, which was also widely printed in France. I also gave to the French press the facts about a particularly atrocious lynching in the south.

"I was unable to obtain an audience with President Wilson or Premier Clemenceau. On the day that the Germans signed the peace treaty, I felt that my work had been completed, and on July 4 I sent to Sir Eric Drummond, of the secretariat of the League of Nations, suggestions for amendment of the covenant in the interest of American Negroes. I then returned to America as a passenger."

Christian Science Monitor (1919)

William Monroe Trotter

W.E.B. DU BOIS

Monroe Trotter was a man of heroic proportions, and probably one of the most selfless of Negro leaders during all our American history. His father was Recorder of Deeds for the District of Columbia, at the time when Recorders were paid by fees; and as a result, he retired from office with a small fortune, which he husbanded carefully. Thus, his son was born in comfortable circumstances, and with his talent for business, and his wide acquaintanceship with the best class of young Massachusetts men in his day, might easily have accumulated wealth.

But he turned aside. He had in his soul all that went to make a fanatic, a knight errant. Ready to sacrifice himself, fearing nobody and nothing, strong in body, sturdy in conviction, full of unbending belief.

I remember when I first saw him as a student at Harvard. He was several classes below me. I should like to have known him and spoken to him, but he was curiously aloof. He was even then forming his philosophy of life. Colored students must not herd together, just because they were colored. He had his white friends and companions, and they liked him. He was no hanger-on, but a leader among them. But he did not seek other colored students as companions. I was a bit lonesome in those days, but I saw his point, and I did not seek him.

Out of this rose his life-long philosophy: Intense hatred of all racial discrimination and segregation. He was particularly incensed at the compromising philosophy of Booker T. Washington; at his industrialism, and his condoning of the deeds of the South.

In the first years of the 20th Century, with George Forbes, Monroe Trotter began the publication of the *Guardian*. Several times young men have started radical sheets among us, like *The Messenger*, and others. But nothing, I think, that for sheer biting invective and unswerving courage, ever quite equaled the *Boston Guardian* in its earlier days. Mr. Washington and his followers literally shrivelled before it, and it was, of course, often as unfair as it was inspired.

I had come to know Trotter, then, especially because I knew Deenie Pindell as a girl before they were married. We were to stop with them one summer. Mrs. Du Bois was already there when I arrived in Boston, and on the elevated platform, I learned of the Zion Church riot. It was called a riot in the newspapers, and they were full of it. As a matter of fact, Trotter and Forbes had tried to ask Booker T. Washington certain pointed questions, after a speech which he made in the colored church; and immediately he was arrested according to the careful plans which William H. Lewis, Washington's attorney, had laid. I was incensed at Trotter. I thought that he had been needlessly violent, and had compromised me as his guest; but when I learned the exact facts, and how little cause for riot there was, and when they clapped Trotter in the Charles Street Jail, all of us more conservative, younger men rose in revolt.

Out of this incident, within a year or two, arose the Niagara movement, and Trotter was present.

But Trotter was not an organization man. He was a free lance; too intense and sturdy to loan himself to that compromise which is the basis of all real organization. Trouble arose in the Niagara movement, and afterward when the Niagara movement joined the new N.A.A.C.P., Trotter stood out in revolt, and curiously enough, did not join the new organization because of his suspicion of the white elements who were co-operating with us.

He devoted himself to the *Guardian*, and it became one of the first of the nation-wide colored weeklies. His wife worked with him in utter devotion; giving up all thought of children, giving up her pretty home in Roxbury; living and lunching with him in the *Guardian Office*, and knowing hunger and cold. It was a magnificent partnership, and she died to pay for it.

The Trotter philosophy was carried out remorselessly in his paper, and his philosophy. He stood unflinchingly for fighting separation and discrimination in church and school, and in professional and business life. He would not allow a colored Y. M. C. A. in Boston, and he hated to recognize colored churches, or colored colleges. On this battle line he fought a long, exhausting fight for over a quarter of a century. What has been the result? There are fewer Negroes in Boston churches today than when Trotter began a crusade, and colored people sat in the pews under Phillips Brooks' preaching. There may be more colored teachers in the schools, but certainly they are playing no such part as Maria Baldwin did, as principal of the best Cambridge Grammar School.

When Trotter began, not a single hotel in Boston dared to refuse colored guests. Today, there are few Boston hotels where colored people are received. There is still no colored Y. M. C. A., but on the other hand, there are practically no colored members of the white "Y," and young colored men are deprived of club house and recreational facilities which they sorely need. In the professions, in general employment, and in business, there is certainly not less, and probably more discrimination than there used to be.

Does this mean that Monroe Trotter's life was a failure? Never. He lived up to his belief to the best of his ability. He fought like a man. The ultimate object of his fighting was absolutely right, but he miscalculated the opposition. He thought that Boston and America would yield to clear reason and determined agitation. They did not. On the contrary, to some extent, the very agitation carried on in these years has solidified opposition. This does not mean that agitation does not pay; but it means that you cannot necessarily cash in quickly upon it. It means that sacrifice, even to blood and tears, must be given to this great fight; and not one but a thousand lives, like that of

Monroe Trotter, is necessary to victory.

More than that, inner organization is demanded. The free lance like Trotter is not strong enough. The mailed fist has got to be clenched. The united effort of twelve millions has got to be made to mean more than the individual effort of those who think aright. Yet this very inner organization involves segregation. It involves voluntary racial organization, and this racial grouping invites further effort at enforced segregation by law and custom from without. Nevertheless, there is no alternative. We have got to unite to save ourselves, and while the unbending devotion to principle, such as Monroe Trotter shows, has and must ever have, its value, with sorrow, and yet with conviction, we know that this is not enough.

. . .

I can understand his death. I can see a man of sixty, tired and disappointed, facing poverty and defeat. Standing amid indifferent friends and triumphant enemies. So he went to the window of his Dark Tower, and beckoned to Death; up from where She lay among the lilies. And Death, like a whirlwind, swept up to him. I shall think of him as lying silent, cold and still; at last at peace, dreamless and serene. Let no trump of doom disturb him from his perfect and eternal rest.

The Crisis (1934)

BOOKER T. WASHINGTON

Booker Taliaferro Washington was born a plantation slave near Hale's Ford, Virginia, on 5 April 1856. He acquired a rudimentary education and eventually worked his way through Hampton Institute, graduating in 1875. In 1881 he was chosen to be the founding principal of Tuskegee Institute in Alabama, a post he kept until his death from arteriosclerosis and overwork on 14 November 1915, by which time he had built the school into an internationally renowned institution with more than a hundred buildings for its 1500 black students.

Washington's first contact with Harvard came in 1887, when his wife Olivia felt his physical condition needed improvement. She arranged for her husband to enroll in Harvard's first annual intensive five-week summer course in physical training, given by Professor Dudley A. Sargent, Director of the Hemenway Gymnasium. Sargent's course, which was designed especially for teachers and physicians—"for those who can arouse enthusiasm for health and bodily development rather than for gymnastic feats"—was both theoretical (with lectures and assigned reading in such topics as applied anatomy, hygiene, and anthropometry) and practical (calisthenics, gymnastics, Delsarte movements, and outdoor athletics). On July 6 Washington was one of 18 men and 39 women to begin the course, and a fortnight later he wrote a friend, "I am enjoying my work at Harvard though it is somewhat difficult."

A milestone in Washington's life was the invitation to give an address at the Atlanta International Exposition on 18 September 1895. His accommodationist speech, known as "the Atlanta Compromise," was hailed by white society in both the North and the South. And now that the great Frederick Douglass had died a few months before, Washington was catapulted into the role of foremost spokesman for his race and for twenty years gladly wielded unprecedented power and influence. It was at the next Harvard commencement (24 June 1896) that Washington received an honorary Master of Arts degree, the second such honor bestowed on a Negro by a New England institution (Middlebury College had made the famous

Vermont preacher Lemuel Haynes an M.A. in 1804). After Harvard's graduation ceremonies ended, Washington and his fellow honorees offered remarks at an alumni dinner that evening.

Over the years thereafter, Washington returned to Harvard several times to speak in Sanders Theatre, Agassiz, and the Freshman Union on the subject of Negro education, partly with an eye to stimulating financial contributions to Tuskegee. In 1904, Harvard's chapter of Phi Beta Kappa elected him to honorary membership, the only time a Negro was so chosen until 1960.

Washington's second autobiography, *Up From Slavery* (to a considerable extent ghostwritten by a Bostonian, Max Bennett Thrasher), began serialization in the *Outlook* in 1900 and appeared in book form the next year. It was widely read, soon translated into at least fifteen foreign languages, and has been frequently reprinted. The book elicited a letter (12 April 1901) to Washington from Harvard professor Barrett Wendell, in which the celebrated authority on English composition stated: "I have grown less and less patient of all writing which is not simple and efficient; and more and more of a style which does its work with simple, manly distinctness. It is hard to remember when a book, casually taken up, has proved, in this respect, so satisfactory as yours. No style could be more simple, more unobtrusive; yet few styles which I know seem to be more laden—as distinguished from overburdened—with meaning." An excerpt from the chapter "Last Words" is reprinted here.

Last Words

More than once I have been asked what was the greatest surprise that ever came to me. I have little hesitation in answering that question. It was the following letter, which came to me one Sunday morning when I was sitting on the veranda of my home at Tuskegee, surrounded by my wife and three children:—

HARVARD UNIVERSITY, CAMBRIDGE, MAY 28, 1896.

PRESIDENT BOOKER T. WASHINGTON,

MY DEAR SIR: Harvard University desires to confer on you at the approaching Commencement an honorary degree; but it is our custom to

Booker T. Washington as a Hampton Institute student ca. 1873

Booker T. Washington at his Tuskegee desk in 1902

confer degrees only on gentlemen who are present. Our Commencement occurs this year on June 24, and your presence would be desirable from about noon till about five o'clock in the afternoon. Would it be possible for you to be in Cambridge on that day?

Believe me, with great regard,

Very truly yours,

CHARLES W. ELIOT.

This was a recognition that had never in the slightest manner entered into my mind, and it was hard for me to realize that I was to be honoured by a degree from the oldest and most renowned university in America. As I sat upon my veranda, with this letter in my hand, tears came into my eyes. My whole former life—my life as a slave on the plantation, my work in the coal-mine, the times when I was without food and clothing, when I made my bed under a sidewalk, my struggles for an education, the trying days I had had at Tuskegee, days when I did not know where to turn for a dollar to continue the work there, the ostracism and sometimes oppression of my race,—all this passed before me and nearly overcame me.

I had never sought or cared for what the world calls fame. I have always looked upon fame as something to be used in accomplishing good. I have often said to my friends that if I can use whatever prominence may have come to me as an instrument with which to do good, I am content to have it. I care for it only as a means to be used for doing good, just as wealth may be used. The more I come into contact with wealthy people, the more I believe that they are growing in the direction of looking upon their money simply as an instrument which God has placed in their hand for doing good with. I never go to the office of Mr. John D. Rockefeller, who more than once has been generous to Tuskegee, without being reminded of this. The close, careful, and minute investigation that he always makes in order to be sure that every dollar that he gives will do the most good—an investigation that is just as searching as if he were investing money in a business enterprise—convinces me that the growth in this direction is most encouraging.

At nine o'clock, on the morning of June 24, I met President Eliot, the Board of Overseers of Harvard University, and the other guests, at the designated place on the university grounds, for the purpose of being escorted to Sanders Theatre, where the Commencement exercises were to be held and degrees conferred. Among others invited to be present for the purpose of receiving a degree at this time were General Nelson A. Miles, Dr. [Alexander Graham] Bell, the inventor of the Bell telephone, Bishop [John Heyl] Vincent, and the Rev. Minot J. Savage. We were placed in line immediately behind the President and the Board of Overseers, and directly afterward the Governor of Massachusetts, escorted by the Lancers, arrived and took his place in the line of march by the side of President Eliot. In the line there were also various other officers and professors, clad in cap and gown. In this order we marched to Sanders Theatre, where, after the usual Commencement exercises, came the conferring of the honorary degrees. This, it seems, is always considered the most interesting feature at Harvard. It is not known, until the individuals appear, upon whom the honorary degrees are to be conferred, and those receiving these honours are cheered by the students and others in proportion to their popularity. During the conferring of the degrees excitement and enthusiasm are at the highest pitch.

When my name was called, I rose, and President Eliot, in beautiful and strong English, conferred upon me the degree of Master of Arts. After these exercises were over, those who had received honorary degrees were invited to lunch with the President. After the lunch we were formed in line again, and were escorted by the Marshal of the day, who that year happened to be Bishop William Lawrence, through the grounds, where, at different points, those who had been honoured were called by name and received the Harvard yell. This march ended at Memorial Hall, where the alumni dinner was served. To see over a thousand strong men, representing all that is best in State, Church, business, and education, with the glow and enthusiasm of college loyalty and college pride—which has, I think, a peculiar Harvard flavour—is a sight that does not easily fade from memory.

Among the speakers after dinner were President Eliot, Governor Roger Wolcott, General Miles, Dr. Minot J. Savage, the Hon. Henry Cabot Lodge, and myself. When I was called upon, I said, among other things:[*]

---

[*]Here we have substituted the full and annotated version of "An Address at the Harvard University Alumni Dinner," reprinted in Louis R. Harlan,

Mr. President and Gentlemen: It would in some measure relieve my embarrassment if I could, even in a slight degree, feel myself worthy of the great honor which you do me to-day. Why you have called me from the Black Belt of the South, from among my humble people, to share in the honors of this occasion, is not for me to explain; and yet it may not be inappropriate for me to suggest that it seems to me that one of the most vital questions that touch our American life, is how to bring the strong, wealthy and learned into helpful touch with the poorest, most ignorant, and humble and at the same time, make the one appreciate the vitalizing, strengthening influence of the other. How shall we make the mansions on yon Beacon Street feel and see the need of the spirits in the lowliest cabin in Alabama cotton fields or Louisiana sugar bottoms? This problem Harvard University is solving, not by bringing itself down, but by bringing the masses up.

If through me, an humble representative, seven millions of my people in the South might be permitted to send a message to Harvard—Harvard that offered up on death's altar, young Shaw, and Russell, and Lowell and scores of others, that we might have a free and united country—that message would be, "Tell them that the sacrifice was not in vain. Tell them that by the way of the shop, the field, the skilled hand, habits of thrift and economy, by way of industrial school and college, we are coming. We are crawling up, working up, yea, bursting up. Often through oppression, unjust discrimination and prejudice, but through them all we are coming up, and with proper habits, intelligence and property, there is no power on earth that can permanently stay our progress."

If my life in the past has meant anything in the lifting up of my people and the bringing about of better relations between your race and mine, I assure you from this day it will mean doubly more. In the economy of God there is but one standard by which an individual can succeed—there is but one for a race. This country demands that every race measure itself by the American standard. By it a race must rise or fall, succeed or fail, and in the last analysis mere sentiment counts for little. During the next half century and more, my race must continue passing through the severe American crucible. We are to be tested in our patience, our forbearance, our perseverance, our power to endure wrong, to withstand temptations, to economize, to acquire and use skill; our ability to compete, to succeed in commerce, to disregard the superficial for the real, the appearance for the substance, to be great and yet small, learned and yet simple, high and yet the servant of all. This, this is the passport to all that is best in the life of our

Stuart B. Kaufman, Barbara S. Kraft, and Raymond W. Smock, eds., *The Booker T. Washington Papers*, Vol. 4, 1895-98 (Urbana: University of Illinois Press, 1975), pp. 183-185.—Eds.

republic, and the Negro must possess it, or be debarred.

While we are thus being tested, I beg of you to remember that wherever our life touches yours, we help or hinder. Wherever your life touches ours, you make us stronger or weaker. No member of your race in any part of our country can harm the meanest member of mine, without the proudest and bluest blood in Massachusetts being degraded. When Mississippi commits crime, New England commits crime, and in so much, lowers the standard of your civilization. There is no escape—man drags man down, or man lifts man up.

In working out our destiny, while the main burden and center of activity must be with us, we shall need, in a large measure in the years that are to come, as we have in the past, the help, the encouragement, the guidance that the strong can give the weak. Thus helped, we of both races in the South, soon shall throw off the shackles of racial and sectional prejudice and rise, as Harvard University has risen and as we all should rise, above the clouds of ignorance, narrowness and selfishness, into that atmosphere, that pure sunshine, where it will be our highest ambition to serve MAN, our brother, regardless of race or previous condition.[1]

As this was the first time* that a New England university had conferred an honorary degree upon a Negro, it was the occasion of much newspaper comment throughout the country. A correspondent of a New York paper said:

When the name of Booker T. Washington was called, and he arose to acknowledge and accept, there was such an outburst of applause as greeted no other name except that of the popular soldier patriot, General Miles. The applause was not studied and stiff, sympathetic and condoling; it was

---

[1]BTW was one of thirteen persons receiving honorary degrees at Harvard that day. By custom, the names of recipients were kept confidential until the moment of their announcement, and the students' applause was a measure of their popularity. Washington received applause equaled only by that for General Nelson A. Miles. It was at the alumni dinner that evening, when each recipient made a short speech, however, that Washington shone. According to the later recollection of Roger Baldwin, BTW won his audience by his first sentence: "I feel like a huckleberry in a bowl of milk." (Reminiscences of Roger Nash Baldwin, Oral History Research Office, Columbia University, 1954.)

*BTW apparently did not know of Lemuel Haynes's 1804 M.A. from Middlebury College.—Eds.

enthusiasm and admiration. Every part of the audience from pit to gallery joined in, and a glow covered the cheeks of those around me, proving sincere appreciation of the rising struggle of an ex-slave and the work he has accomplished for his race.

A Boston paper said, editorially:

In conferring the honorary degree of Master of Arts upon the Principal of Tuskegee Institute, Harvard University has honoured itself as well as the object of this distinction. The work which Professor Booker T. Washington has accomplished for the education, good citizenship, and popular enlightenment in his chosen field of labour in the South entitles him to rank with our national benefactors. The university which can claim him on its list of sons, whether in regular course or *honoris causa*, may be proud.

It has been mentioned that Mr. Washington is the first of his race to receive an honorary degree from a New England university. This, in itself, is a distinction, but the degree was not conferred because Mr. Washington is a coloured man, or because he was born in slavery, but because he has shown, by his work for the elevation of the people of the Black Belt of the South, a genius and a broad humanity which count for greatness in any man, whether his skin be white or black.

Another Boston paper said:

It is Harvard which, first among New England colleges, confers an honorary degree upon a black man. No one who has followed the history of Tuskegee and its work can fail to admire the courage, persistence, and splendid common sense of Booker T. Washington. Well may Harvard honour the ex-slave, the value of whose services, alike to his race and country, only the future can estimate.

The correspondent of the New York *Times* wrote:

All the speeches were enthusiastically received, but the coloured man carried off the oratorical honours, and the applause which broke out when he had finished was vociferous and long-continued.

From *Up from Slavery* (1901), chapter 17.

Principal Washington at Harvard University

MARCH 12, 1907

Dr. Booker T. Washington of the Tuskegee Institute, spoke to Harvard students in the Harvard Union Building last night. The room was crowded and even the windows and gallery were filled. The speaker was introduced by President Eliot who emphasized the importance of young men getting a clear conception of Dr. Washington's life and work. The address was full of enthusiasm and candor and wisdom; it was oratorical and witty and forceful from beginning to end, and time and time again the speaker was cheered to the echo.

The applause went wild when the speaker, raising himself to his full height, and taking on a most serious and earnest look, remarked with a slightly nervous tremor of the hand and lips:

"If I could be born again and the Great Spirit should say to me: 'In what skin do you wish to be clothed,' I should answer, 'make me an American Negro!'"

These words lent inspiration to every Negro present, and won for the speaker and the race immeasurable respect from the whites.

After the address, Messrs. Edwin French Tyson[1] and Walter S. Buchanan,[2] both of the class of 1907 at Harvard University, escorted Dr. Washington to their room, 22 Hastings Hall, where he met and addressed informally all of the young colored men in the University. Mr. Buchanan graduated from Tuskegee Institute with the class 1899.

Booker T. Washington, Jr. and Mr. Charles Alexander, Editor of Alexander's Magazine, were in the party.

[1]Edwin French Tyson (1885-1962) received an M.D. degree from Howard University Medical School in 1911.

[2]Walter Solomon Buchanan (1882-1954) later became a president of Alabama State A & M College for Negroes in Normal, and a director of the Standard Life Insurance Co.

Extracts from an Address at Harvard University

FEBRUARY 4, 1914

Every man going out from this great University has a duty to perform not only in relation to his personal success, but in helping to solve the various problems relating to state and nation. Because of the superior advantages which you are enjoying, in a peculiar manner the solution of these problems will rest upon you. Just in the same degree in which you have received broad liberal culture, you should be willing and anxious to give your service in lightening the burdens of others; in seeing that every man, no matter what his race or color is, has a fair chance, is permitted to have all the opportunities for growth and usefulness that is accorded to every other human being.

I hope that when you go away from here and enter upon your life career, whether it is in private business or in some public service, that you will seek an opportunity to let the members of my race know that you are interested in it; not only interested in the race as a whole, but interested in the individual members of the race. It is not always an easy task for one to manifest interest in persons who are members of what is commonly considered an unpopular race, but just in the degree that you manifest the courage and the deep interest to break through prejudice and custom and show that you are interested in the members of all the human family and desire to benefit humanity regardless of race or color, just in the same degree you will yourselves be strengthened and broadened and your life sweetened.

* * *

My race owes much to Harvard University; much for its spirit of fairness and justice. Here above all places a man is measured by his ability, and I hope that this spirit and this disposition will always be manifest at Harvard.

* * *

My race is often classed as an unfortunate race. I do not sympathize with such classification. On the other hand, I am proud that I am identified with the colored race in America. I would rather be classed as a black man in this country than as a white man. I belong to a race that has problems to solve, difficulties to overcome every day in the year, and one of the means by which the young colored men and women throughout this country are developing themselves in mind and in spirit is through the service which they are rendering to their less fortunate brothers and sisters, and in proportion as educated colored men and women render this service they receive a breadth of mind and sympathy and have brought into their lives a sweetness and satisfaction which rarely comes to the educated men and women of any race.

I would not care to live in any age or in any country where there were not problems to be solved and difficulties to overcome, and the educated men and women of my race are striving to do their share in solving America's problems, and just in proportion as they strive to do this they should have the sympathy, the encouragement and the cooperation of every American citizen and especially of those who are placed as you are with the opportunities of receiving the highest and best university training.

WILLIAM H. FERRIS

William Henry Ferris was born on 20 July 1874 in New Haven, Connecticut, where he was graduated from Hillhouse High School in 1891. In 1895, he received an A.B. from Yale University, which also awarded him an M.A. in 1899. He accepted an invitation to become a charter member of the American Negro Academy in 1897, at which time he entered Harvard Divinity School for two years, switching to the Graduate School of Arts and Sciences for a year and taking a second M.A. in 1900. He did a little teaching in the South, and then was pastor of churches briefly in North Carolina and Massachusetts, during which time he began research for his magnum opus, the two-volume *The African Abroad; or, His Evolution in Western Civilization* (1913). He then worked for several periodicals, notably as associate editor of the *Champion* (1916-17), and as literary editor of Marcus Garvey's *Negro World* (1919-23) and of the short-lived *Spokesman* (1924-27). From 1930 to 1935, he served as dean of the Normal and Theological Institute in Glasgow, Kentucky, also doing some editorial work for the fledgling *Louisville Defender* and later for the moribund *Christian Review*. He died in penniless obscurity on 23 August 1941 in his Harlem room, and was saved from a pauper's burial by a college classmate who was treasurer of Yale.

Douglass as an Orator

While a student at Yale and Harvard, it was my privilege to hear some of the world's greatest preachers and orators. Of the English preachers, I heard Fairbarn, Robert Forman Horton, Ian Maclaren Berry and George Adam Smith. Of the American preachers, I heard McKenzie, Gordon, Bradford, Storrs, Hall, Babcock, Purvis, Smythe,

Munger, Talmadge, Cuyler, Edward Everett Hale, Dewey, Hillis, Barrows, Behrends, Dwight, Tucker, Bishop S. Greer and Foss. Then I have been privileged to hear Thomas B. Reed, Joseph Benson Foraker, Senator Spooner, C. Emery Smith, McKinley, Bob Ingersoll, Wallace Bruce, Judge Howland, Wayne McVeagh, Edward Howard Griggs, James Coolidge Carter, Dr. Nicholas Murray Butler, Lodge, Depew, Roosevelt, Bryan, Bourke Cochran and Dr. C. Eliot of Harvard. Furthermore, I have heard Dr. Otto Pfleiderer, the German theologian, Prof. William Knight, the Scotch philosopher, and Swami Abhedananda, Mozoombar and Bita Chandra Pal, the Hindoo philosophers, speak.

Out of this group, I have heard men who surpassed Frederick Douglass for breadth of knowledge and profundity of thought, but have never heard a speaker who was endowed with the natural gifts of the orator to the same degree that he was.

Then, too, I have been privileged to hear some of the addresses which have entered into the history of oratory. I heard Bourke Cochran's famous speech upon Anti-Imperialism in Faneuil Hall in the spring of 1900, when, with Harvard professors and the blue bloods of Boston behind him on the platform and a mixed audience in front of him, he closed his two-hour address with a peroration which lasted fully fifteen minutes, rising from one climax to another, as he threw back his head and hurled climaxes, or paced restlessly back and forth like a caged lion or pounded on the desk in front of him to emphasize a point.

In June of the same year I heard James Coolidge Carter, the leader of the New York bar, whom President Hadley, of Yale University, called the "Nestor and the Chesterfield of the legal profession in America," deliver his famous address at the Harvard Alumni dinner. That address has now been published in one of the specimens of eloquence. I saw a rather large man with broad, high brow, surmounting a face that was adorned with gray side-whiskers, and a mustache, rise to his feet and begin to speak calmly and deliberately, with a heavy brass voice and with dignity and grace of manner and gesture. Soon the orator launched forth with uplifted hand into that peroration which has entered into the annals of eloquence. He contrasted the heroic days of his youth, when the Concord School of Philosophy, the famous group of American poets and writers and the anti-slavery movement held the center of the stage, with the present commercial age. His voice rang out, when he

William H. Ferris in 1927

Frederick Douglass in his thirties

expressed the hope that, if truth should ever be banished from the forum, driven from the market place and exiled from our legislative halls, she would still have a sacred shrine in Harvard University, an ancient seat and center of learning, which had ever been consecrated to the highest ideals. I didn't know, until I saw Col. Higginson that evening, who James Coolidge Carter was, but I realized that Wednesday afternoon that I was listening to a wonderful oratorical effort.

And yet neither of these two famous addresses electrified and thrilled their audiences as did Frederick Douglass when he spoke in the Hyperion of New Haven in a presidential campaign. I heard the noted orator three times, on the occasion just mentioned, in the same opera house, after his return from Hayti, and in the Grand Avenue Congregational Church of New Haven, a few weeks before his death. On the last two occasions, he was interesting and impressive, but on the first occasion, he was overwhelming and irresistible.

Of all the impressions stamped upon my mind, when a school boy in New Haven and a student at Yale, the most striking and vivid are those of the times when I heard Frederick Douglass. The first Yale-Harvard baseball game and the first Yale-Harvard football game I saw are the only other occasions that stand out so vividly in my mind.

This may seem a rather extravagant estimate, but it coincided somewhat with Col. Higginson's estimate. Col. T. W. Higginson, of Boston, in his eighties, with the exception of Julia Ward Howe, Edward Everett Hale and Frank Sanborn, was the last survivor of the old literary set of Boston, and of the old-time abolitionists. He was an associate of Emerson, Whittier, Longfellow, Lowell, Holmes and Bryant. He led the abolitionists who attempted to rescue Anthony Burns, a fugitive slave, in broad daylight, from the Boston court house. He fought under John Brown's banner in Kansas and was with Hallowell and Shaw among the first white men to risk their lives, commanding Negro troops in the late Civil War. Standing six feet in height, symmetrical in form, graceful in movement and commanding in his personality, he looked the born soldier and leader of men. And yet, he told me that he hated to walk down the street with Frederick Douglass, because Fred Douglass towered two inches above him in stature and was more colossal in figure and picturesque in face. When one looked upon Frederick Douglass he felt like saying, "And the elements were so mixed in him that Nature might cry out—'This was a man.'"

Furthermore, Col. Higginson said that even when Frederick

Douglass spoke extemporaneously, his English was well nigh perfect and his words flowed forth in a clear, limpid stream of eloquence. Very rarely was Frederick Douglass compelled to revise and correct his extemporaneous speeches.

Frank Sanborn, the Concord sage, who had heard Gladstone, rated Douglass highly as an orator. The companion of the leading statesmen and scholars of America and Europe, Frederick Douglass impressed everyone by his intelligence and nobility of soul.

Standing over six feet in height, blessed with a magnificent physique, a kingly brow and face and a royal bearing, he attracted attention wherever he went. There was something elemental, magnetic and majestic about the man. The repose of the lion was seen in that face. On the platform, the grace and dignity of his movements and gestures, the organ swell and roll of his sonorous voice, the flash of his eagle eye, the tremendous reserve powers of the man, the volcanic outburst of pent up indignation and wrath, when he was thoroughly aroused, rank Frederick Douglass with Mirabeau, Daniel O'Connell, the Elder Pitt, and Daniel Webster, as one who was born a leader of men, as one who possessed from birth those native gifts which enabled him to sway audiences or move men.

Now for the three occasions in which I heard Frederick Douglass. The Hyperion in days of yore was the largest and finest opera house in New Haven, Conn. Situated in Chapel Street, opposite Yale University, with a seating capacity of 2,200, it catered to the university and society crowd. Consequently when the news spread over the city that Frederick Douglass, the colored orator, was scheduled to speak there in the Harrison presidential campaign, enthusiasm knew no bounds. The meeting was preceded by a brass band and torch light procession and the Hyperion was packed and crowded to its utmost seating and standing capacity. The preliminaries were soon disposed of. Mr. Willis Bonner, the president of the colored Republican club, introduced Rev. A. P. Miller, the chairman of the meeting, who introduced the distinguished white and colored speakers.

That night Frederick Douglass had a difficult task set out for him. He was sandwiched in between one of the most brilliant scholars and one of the most magnetic orators in the colored race. He was preceded as a speaker by Hon. E. D. Bassett, formerly principal of the Institute for Colored Youth in Philadelphia, and former U. S. Minister to Hayti. He was followed by Charles Satchell Morris, who later rose in the ministry, pastored the Abyssinia Baptist Church in New York

City, and is now pastor in Norfolk, Va. But even on such a trying occasion, the "Grand Old Man" loomed up as an oratorical colossus. Every eye was riveted upon the stage when Frederick Douglass was announced. The audience saw an unusually tall and well proportioned man rise slowly from his seat on the platform, step forward and face it. With his lion-like face, crowned with waving gray hair, adorned with an iron-gray beard of medium growth, illumined by flashing eyes and set upon a magnificent physique, he was both a distinguished and picturesque-looking man. He impressed the audience by his personality before he uttered a single word.

His voice was low, deep, and heavy. He spoke slowly, calmly and deliberately. His movements on the platform were dignified and graceful. In a word, his attitude, bearing, gestures and manner of speaking indicated a gentleman who was perfectly calm and self-possessed, upon a platform upon which some of the world's greatest actors and singers had appeared and before a vast audience, four-fifths of which was white.

In his style and manner of speaking he was a gentleman conversing with a perfectly well modulated and controlled voice, who now and then rose to an impassioned outburst of eloquence. He calmly and dispassionately discussed the race question in all of its phases and aspects. He was lucid and clear in his presenting his facts and data, and logical and cogent in his reasoning. But he by no means gave a dry discussion of a hackneyed theme. That discussion was enlivened by anecdote, illustration, wit and humor. Douglass' observations upon men and affairs were keen and penetrating. His reflections showed that he was thoughtful and prudent. In a word, he seemed to have some of that worldly wisdom which made Solomon and Lord Bacon famous. His fundamental thought was that the colored brother was made out of the same clay as the rest of mankind.

But what impressed the audience most was the fact that Douglass had some tremendous force or power which he was holding in reserve and which he had not yet let out. And it was not disappointed. The outburst of eloquence, which lifted the audience off its feet and threw it into pandemonium, finally came. Douglass began that outburst by telling the audience that it was the brawn and muscle of black men, who toiled in the sun, and bled under the lash, which for two centuries and a half had built up the wealth and prosperity of the Southland. His eye flashed, his face lighted up, his voice rose and swelled like the notes of an organ and rang out in stentorian tones over the audience, he moved more rapidly about the platform and his gestures grew more animated, as he rose to his grand climax. He said: "During the trying days of the Civil War, we gave your sons food to eat when they were hungry and water to drink when they were thirsty, we led them through the forests when they had lost their way and we binded up their wounds when they were wounded." Then, stepping to the front of the platform with head thrown back, outstretched arms and voice that rang out like a clarion, Douglass said: "And when Abraham Lincoln sent forth his call for volunteers, we came, we came two hundred thousand strong."

Then the pent up and long suppressed enthusiasm of the audience released itself. Men and women rose to their feet and cheered and applauded the "Old Man Eloquent" again and again. It were as though he had calmly and deliberately warmed the hearts of his hearers and then uncorked the bottle, when the contents were about to effervesce.

In that address Frederick Douglass told of the conversation that he had with Abraham Lincoln, when Lincoln expressed great interest in and sympathy for the colored people. He said that he knew what to do with regard to every nationality except the Negro.

Douglass replied, "Give us our freedom and the same protection of the law as you give the other nationalities and we will do for ourselves."

The audience did not rush out of the Hyperion, as it usually did after a three-hour sitting, but many lingered long to catch one last fleeting glimpse or grasp the hand of the noted orator. By some unknown and mysterious channel of communication the news had been whispered around that a reception would be held in honor of Fred Douglass at one of the aristocratic white clubs. And when Douglass and his escorts left the Hyperion and walked a block or so down Chapel Street, a large crowd assembled on the sidewalk to again cheer the "Grand Old Man" as he passed by. And he towered head and shoulders above his companions like King Saul.

I heard Frederick Douglass again in the Hyperion after his return from Hayti, when he ably defended his course in refusing to persuade the Haytians to sell the Mole St. Nicholas to the United States government. His great climax came in that address when he said, "Measure us not by the heights to which we have attained, but by the depths from which we have come."

The last time that I heard Fred Douglass speak in New Haven was in the Grand Avenue Congregational Church in the fall of 1894, a few weeks before his death. He was then speaking in the interest of the Industrial Institute in Virginia, in which a grand-daughter, Miss Rosette Sprague, was a teacher. I believe that Mr. Wheaton was principal. It is a significant fact that, ten months before Booker Washington delivered his Atlanta speech, Frederick Douglass had recognized the value of industrial education and perceived that the colored race needed both the ballot and the bank book. Mr. Douglass was not as vigorous physically as when I last heard him, but there was still the same dignity and grace and self-possession and at times flashes of his former eloquence.

A group of colored students went forward to meet Mr. Douglass. One of us, William Fletcher Penn, knew him personally, so we had the honor of walking with the noted orator to the trolley car and riding in the car with Mr. Douglass from Fairhaven to the street, where he left the car to go to his hotel. He was easily the most attractive person in the whole car, and when he arose to leave the car with his towering form, patrician bearing and distinguished countenance, people asked "Who was that?" and the answer was whispered around in hushed awed tones, "That is Fred Douglass." That was the last I saw of the noted orator.

Mankind has ever honored and deified those men who embodied and incarnated its ideals in their personalities and realized its dreams in their achievements; and that is why Fred Douglass electrified and thrilled me the first time that I heard him when a school boy. He was not only a man who fought his way from slavery to the pinnacle of fame, but his personality and his manliness liberated the heroic in his hearers. There was that indefinable and indescribable something, in the man and his eloquence, which appealed to the sublime in one. There is something uplifting and inspiring in a church spire, in a Gothic cathedral, in the Colossus of Rhodes and in a towering Alpine peak. There is also something uplifting and inspiring in the career of a Hercules or Julius Caesar and in the eloquence of a Pitt, a Webster and a Douglass. Frederick Douglass was thus both a call and an inspiration to higher effort.

Champion Magazine (1917)

[Editors' note: A passage in Frederick Douglass's 1881 autobiography tells the story of a relationship that might have developed, but never did. Douglass recalled, "The 2nd of June, 1872, brought me a very grievous loss. My house in Rochester was burnt to the ground, and among other things of value, twelve volumes of my paper, covering the period from 1848 to 1860, were devoured by the flames. I have never been able to replace them, and the loss is immeasurable. Only a few weeks before, I had been invited to send these bound volumes to the library of Harvard University where they would have been preserved in a fire-proof building, and the result of my procrastination attests the wisdom of more than one proverb." See *Life and Times of Frederick Douglass, Written by Himself* (Hartford, Conn.: Park Publishing Co., 1882), p. 270.]

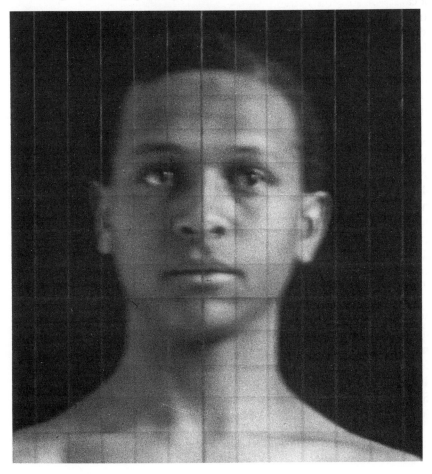

Leslie P. Hill on entering Harvard in 1899 (previously unpublished)

LESLIE PINCKNEY HILL

Leslie Pinckney Hill was born in Lynchburg, Virginia on 14 May 1880, the son of a former slave. As a youth he mastered the trumpet and envisioned a career in music. When his family moved to East Orange, New Jersey, he transferred to the local high school and, by accelerated study, was able to skip the junior year, winding up near the top of his graduating class in 1898. In the fall of 1899 he entered Harvard, supplementing scholarship aid by working as a waiter. He studied Classics, history, English composition and literature, and fine arts. Active in debating from the start, he took an official elocution course as a sophomore, and as a junior won second place in the Boylston Prize oratory competition.

An introductory philosophy course inspired him to include a philosophy course every term thereafter. He formed a particularly close tie with William James (M.D. 1869), who started out teaching physiology but in 1880 switched to philosophy and psychology until his retirement in 1907. A decade after James' death, Hill would write a sonnet in tribute to his former mentor. In his senior year Hill was elected to Phi Beta Kappa and awarded his degree *cum laude*. He also had the honor of being one of the three candidates invited to give a commencement address, a well-received disquisition entitled "The Place of Religion in the Education of the Negro." Hill stayed on another year to take courses in education, receiving an A.M. degree in 1904.

In 1904 Hill began teaching education and English at Booker T. Washington's Tuskegee Institute, where the academic department was headed by his black Harvard schoolmate Roscoe Conkling Bruce '02. Both men found Washington's policies uncongenial; Bruce left in 1906, and Hill followed a year later to head the Manassas Industrial School in Virginia. In 1913 Hill was persuaded to assume the presidency of what is today Cheyney State College in Pennsylvania, which grew out of an Institute for Colored Youth chartered in 1837. He resumed his musical activity by conducting the College chorus, and retired from the presidency in 1951. Author of essays, poems, and plays, and the recipient of four honorary degrees, he died on 15 February 1960.

The Place of Religion
in the Education of the Negro

The problem of the Negro in this country, pressing upon us as it is, we cannot lightly put aside. For thirty years it has found a widening sphere of influence in politics. It has been interwoven with the whole industrial growth of the South. It lay at the bottom of the most frightful war of modern times. And now of more urgent importance than the reform of our civil service, or the question of the rights of labor and capital, or the government of our new dependencies, it is the first matter of concern for the thinking men of this nation. And yet for all its prominence and urgency how little attention has been given to one side of the problem from which it seems a real approach to its solution might ultimately be made!

We have spoken and acted with regard to the Negro hitherto almost wholly from the point of view of his economic value, his material status, without taking into due account the opposite balance of his inner nature. Chiefly he has been an *object* of pity, or contempt, or philanthropy, or legislation, seldom a living human soul. Always we are told that he must seek hopefully and earnestly to find his place and power in the world of competition about him, that he must live a clean, thrifty life, must acquire property and increase his intelligence: but hardly at all is there heard now any word as to the use of that force so peculiarly the endowment of the black man by which he might be impelled forward to these same ends.

Certainly the economic aspect of the Negro in this country to-day, his actual worth in the world of industry or of politics, is a question of momentous import well worthy of the great expenditure of energy and the earnest application of brain now so happily devoted to it. But it must be remembered that beneath the material progress and the outer strivings of the race there has always run the deep vein of its religion.

"If the genus man is a religious being," says a recent writer, "the species Negro is pre-eminently so." And it is not enough, nor is it true, to say that this religion has been a mere unreasoning emotion.

What has been its value, its effect? Even in its first appearances in primitive society there was in it something better. The black man there indeed "paid foolish honors to this ugly fetich," but he had also noble conceptions of a "Nyangmo who sends the sunshine and the rain, who veils his face with the clouds and makes the stars his jewels." In civilization the religious instinct of the race has been clear and productive of solid results. It has had to grow slowly and painfully through the camp meeting with its professional shouters and prayer-makers, through the revival with its superstitions of the mourner's bench, its picturesque exhorters and emotional audiences, through the leadership of a misguided or ill instructed clergy, through that enthusiasm of faith which could not stand the test of moral practice. All this should have been expected of a race thrust so suddenly and without preparation into the life of a people indefinitely advanced beyond its primitive ideas. Still, when all has been said, it remains indisputable that this people has given to mankind an example of the power of the Christian religion surprising and unique.

Men of science have wondered that the greater part of the Negroes did not die of nostalgia. From a life of freedom and ignorance they were brought from their home in the tropics to a climate wholly unlike their own, and to a civilization of which they could not then have had the poorest conception. They had no books or instruction. The schools, even the churches, were closed upon them. For the meanest menial labor there was no reward but the most necessary physical sustenance. Generations passed with no prospect but continuance in that state. But there was no despair. These people heard from their masters the name of Christ. The story of the cross, but little understood, came to them, nevertheless, as the story of their own hard life, and there in all their ignorance and destitution they thought it a noble thing to suffer for the reward of the faithful. In the cornfield and the cottonfield it was not complaining, but the expression of their faith through those sad melodies which are now considered the one original contribution of America to music. On the block it was not imprecation and abuse but often prayer for the slave dealer. And when the crisis had come and the masters of the Southland marched to the front and offered their lives for a cause whose success meant the perpetuation of the Negro's bondage, they left behind them as protector of their families and guardian of their estates this same black man who did not prove false to what he thought even then a trust. Whether faith and prayer were all they were held to be or not, these were the comfort and the strength of the race throughout its darkest hours.

Those bitter times are gone, and the Negroes are citizens of the republic. Their presence here for a generation in that capacity has given rise to the gravest, most practical problem this nation has yet been called upon to face. How are these people, now rapidly increasing in numbers, exerting for good or ill a greater and greater influence, to be adjusted to the new conditions of their national life? How can this mass of black folk be made to contribute most to the realization of the ideals of democracy? Many an answer one hears of all degrees of sanity and thoughtlessness. The wisest, however, can recognize but one: by an education that shall not stop short of what is highest in the black man's nature, by an education, it seems to me, that should carefully cultivate his deep innate sense of religion. For the Negro is still, in spite of his material advancement, primarily of a religious temperament. About every third Negro is a communicant. Rightly or wrongly he devotes just ten times as much money to the building of churches as he devotes to the erection of schools. It is still through the church and not through the school that the great masses of the people are most effectively reached.

Emanuel Swedenborg, that prodigious student of religious phenomena whom Emerson entitles to "a place vacant for some ages among the law-givers of mankind," affirms that the African has a greater "genius and faculty of receiving light through the heavens from the Lord" than any of the rest of the Gentiles. And Emerson himself has said:

> He has avenues to God
> Hid from men of Northern brain,
> Far beholding, without cloud,
> What these with slowest steps attain.

Why should not this high faculty, already so effective in the past, be made to exercise a still larger function as the education of the Negro advances? If only the efforts and attainments of the race might be made the expression of its deepest religious feeling many a perplexing material problem now before us would soon enough be gone. Surely, at all events, nothing less should be a primary aim of instruction for the race henceforth—an aim to justify more fully, indeed to set in a clearer light, the remark of the man who stands first among the leaders of education in America to-day, that "the Negro needs absolutely" the "higher facilities of education."

These higher facilities it is the duty and opportunity of the nation in larger measure to provide. It has been said that if democracy has any loftier ideal than another form of government, or any diviner mission it is "to help all the weak, to lift up all the fallen, to raise to the highest culture of which he is capable every son of Adam." That highest culture for any man in this country to-day, the Negro preëminently, is the culture proceeding from a true conception of the ideals of Christianity. In slavery Christianity, rudely understood, was the Negro's pillar of cloud by day and pillar of fire by night. In freedom and citizenship a truer Christianity should serve the same high purpose. The common ranks of the race must now be lifted to a higher plane of Christian thought and conduct. A broader, more adequate education must lead "the raw unkindled masses" to see the beauty and the value of the higher Christian life. This nation must know that ten millions of black people, inseparable part of its very life, will either help it forward or hold it back. It must be clear that any system of education, or any method of approaching the race problem which makes of the Negro a mere object of economic consideration, without emphasizing the paramount importance of getting out of my people the highest qualities of which they are capable, is a system or a method which must forever defeat its own end, and keep within the borders of this country a problem that will ever tend to drag our nation down.

Harvard Advocate (1903)

To William James

Devotedly he watched the silent stream
Of consciousness, and from the shifting brink,
In lucid phrase, taught thousands how to think.
No straightened logic's thrall, he prized the gleam
Of truth in all experience: the dream
To him was precious too. He dared to link
Reality with wonder, and to sink
The plumb of thought down where all mysteries teem.
Where is the light we knew upon his face—
The zest for knowledge, searching and intense?
Gone out for aye in darkness deep and strange?
Or do they now at last find scope and place
Where Thales still propounds the elements,
And Heraclitus broods, "'Tis only Change"?

From *The Wings of Oppression* (1921)

ALAIN LOCKE

Alain LeRoy Locke was born to schoolteacher parents on 13 September 1886 in Philadelphia, where he attended Central High School and the Philadelphia School of Pedagogy. A member of the Harvard class of 1908, he completed his requirements in three years, and received his A.B. *magna cum laude* in 1907, also winning the top Bowdoin Prize for an essay on Tennyson as well as election to Phi Beta Kappa. He became the first and, until 1963, only black American to win a Rhodes scholarship to Oxford, from which he took a Litt.B. degree in 1912.

In 1918 he became—after W.E.B. Du Bois and historian Carter G. Woodson—the third black recipient of a Harvard Ph.D. degree, with a dissertation in philosophy on the theory of value. He had in 1912, after a year's study at the University of Berlin, already begun teaching English, education, and then philosophy at Howard University, where he was also instrumental in establishing a drama program, art gallery, and literary magazine. Best known for his writing on literature, he was the godfather of the so-called Harlem Renaissance of the 1920s. He also wrote extensively on the fine arts (including those of Africa) and on music (he was a trained classical pianist). At the time Du Bois termed him "by long odds the best trained man among the younger American Negroes."

In mid-career Locke acknowledged his debt to Harvard, where "I was exposed to the Golden Age of liberalism and deeply influenced by Barrett Wendell, Copeland, Briggs and Baker, shed the Tory restraints for urbanity and humanism, and under the spell of Royce, James, Palmer, and Santayana, gave up Puritan provincialism for critical-mindedness and cosmopolitanism." Locke spoke of his "not regretted vocation—a decent livelihood teaching philosophy; and . . . an avocation of mid-wifery to younger Negro poets, writers and artists. . . . I am sure it has all been due to Harvard, at least what there has been creditable and productive."

In February of 1942, the Harvard chapter of Phi Delta Kappa (the national fraternity in professional education), whose constitution forbade non-white members, demonstrated its disgust with this exclusionary policy by inviting Locke to give an address, "Democracy Faces a New World Order." Later that year Locke was one of twelve blacks named in the Honor

Roll of Race Relations. He continued teaching at Howard until heart trouble forced his retirement in 1953. He died in New York City on 9 June 1954, leaving his partly written *magnum opus* to be completed and published by a colleague's devoted daughter, Margaret Just Butcher—*The Negro in American Culture* (1956; 2nd ed. 1972).

Two Letters from Harvard

[7 December 1905]

My dear Mamma:

Don't blame the postman and the postal service for this delay—for God knows their souls are black with enough guilt—but this delay is mine, partly carelessness and partly work. As usual I shall try to make it up. Well, one piece of good news—I have paid the entire $90 tuition so that's off our hands. $50 I had on hand as I told you. I went to Dean Hurlbut [Byron S. Hurlbut, Dean of Harvard College, 1902-16] and got $40 of my scholarship money so that's paid, and we have nothing more to pay the university until the term bill on February 10th. I am very glad as it tides us over the critical Xmas period very nicely. Besides, I got my invitation to the Award of Academic Distinctions. Quite an elaborately engraved invitation—we who have won scholarships and those who have won prizes go to Sanders Theatre and sit on the floor of the theatre—what would be the parquet, I mean, of course—and hear the awards and then have a collation afterwards—this happens a week from tomorrow and makes a very pleasant celebration as a double reward of last year's work.

Now for other news. Tuesday we had a simply delightful meeting of the Ethical Society—a closed meeting, only about 25 or 30 of us in the parlor of Phillips Brooks House, with [President Charles W.] Eliot to address us. His talk was very interesting, and he himself more so— we all had an excellent chance to meet him, of course. After the meeting we went to Beckhard's room [Bruno Beckhard '07] and had a little supper, then went to Pfromm's room [David A. Pfromm '08] and played (piannie) till 11:30, then Dickerman [Charles H. Dickerman '07] suggested a walk—we all took it and finally winded up in Pottinger's room [David T. Pottinger '06], where after some tea and

Alain Locke in 1908

Alain Locke in 1933

crackers we reluctantly departed at 3 A.M.

You see that meant no letter. Well, Wednesday—yesterday (this is Thursday) I got up so late as to have a great hurry to get to my classes—Wednesday is a busy day for me anyway, and no sooner had I settled down to write—I started by finishing a letter overdue to Rowland—than I remembered a meeting of the debating society at which our shingles were to be given out. Shingles for your edification, I may explain, are certificates of membership that almost every Harvard club gives—they are not as you would suppose of wood—but paper—another example of the contradictions of college life. Well, we went for our shingles and had the usual jubilation meeting that generally results—beer, ginger ale, crackers, cheese, pretzels and the like. Well, I left that early and had barely time to finish a report on English literature due today. I finished the report at 2 A.M. and promptly went to bed. This morning—or rather this afternoon I had my English conference and a more delightful conference I have never had. Our professor is Barrett Wendell [faculty, 1880-1917]—whom you have heard of as the Harvard professor who went to Paris last year to lecture at the Sorbonne. He is decidedly French—wears garters, smokes cigarettes and twirled his cane all during the conference but talked most entertainingly. The others left and I found myself with his highness and a Jewish rabbi—what a combination!—and we talked for an hour or so on literary topics, which chiefly consisted in Barrett Wendell's reminiscences and jokes, issue[d] forth from such erudition and over-frenchified culture to the Union, where I am now writing you this letter. . . . I have received a copy of the Central High School March and am raving mad to have to acknowl-edge it and say what is expected to say. It's good training in the suppression of feeling and in the art of deceit—but perhaps I do not need it. Glad of Harry's success—it's about time I wrote them anyway. I beg to disagree with the universal sanction that seems to be given Mr. Robinson's ideas of how a gentleman should dress. The benefit of Harvard is that you learn what is proper, with perfect permission to be a non-conformist and be and dress and act as inde-pendently as you please. . . . Well, there's but one thing I request of you by all that's holy: do not reserve Cousin Hortense for my first Sunday home, or by thunder you'll get your teapot for I['ll] do away with her.

I may soon have to take to glasses so I shall be silent lest retribution go down another generation—you remember Dr. Brandt's figure of Elijah's mantle. By the way, that reminds me to tell you that

I went to chapel Sunday and heard a sermon worth hearing. Lyman Abbott [Preacher to the University, 1903-09] is simply great; he is worth the whole bunch of the others put together—in the first place he is very broad and very liberal.

The room looks very nice now and will look still better when I come back from the Xmas recess. By the way, don't worry about worthless tickets—ticket brokering is a regular legal business in Massachusetts. I must close now, as the rustics say, for I have still work on hand and am anxious to rest up a bit from the week's dissipations and excitement. I am very well and work is going on nicely. With the usual cautions to take care of yourself and to try to live comfortably, with strict injunctions to sidetrack, or do anything legitimate to Hortense, that she and I may not conflict at the beginning of my holiday, and of course with lots of love,

Your loving boy

Roy

[15 December 1905]

My dear Mamma:

Tonight was the Award of Distinctions and I want to write you to tell you what your spirit saw. I send you the program along with this letter. 'Twas as usual a very brilliant and a very boresome affair. You may think the two things a little contradictory but they are not for an academic function. The majority of the faculty attend and you cannot imagine a more brilliant scene than they make with their gowns and hoods, since the Oxford doctors' are crimson silk with long flowing sleeves. I noticed a Paris degree—purple and buff silk etc. They only wear them on this occasion and at commencement, so it was one of our two annual opportunities to see a professor dressed respectably. Some of the professors—the younger men—usher, and you feel quite important having a teacher in a gorgeous Mother Hubbard showing you to your seat on the floor of the theatre. The programme you can see for yourself. The usual singing of the Harvard Hymn etc. was quite impressive. The orator of the evening was as usual not interesting so we spent [the] best part of the time, or at least I did, hunting up each other's names and seeing who all got scholarships—as you see I am in second group—sorry I did not make first group—but still only 8 of our class did—that's some consolation—I hoped to have 1st group cinched this year. Harley [Harley H. Bartlett '08] is the only other brother who got a scholarship—he is in second group too. You will notice his name. . . .

Your loving boy

Roy

Youth Speaks

We might know the future but for our chronic tendency to turn to age rather than to youth for the forecast. And when youth speaks, the future listens, however the present may shut its ears. Here we have Negro youth, foretelling in the mirror of art what we must see and recognize in the streets of reality tomorrow.

Primarily, of course, it is youth that speaks in the voice of Negro youth, but the overtones are distinctive; Negro youth speaks out of an unique experience and with a particular representativeness. All classes of a people under social pressure are permeated with a common experience; they are emotionally welded as others cannot be. With them, even ordinary living has epic depth and lyric intensity, and this, their material handicap, is their spiritual advantage. So, in a day when art has run to classes, cliques and coteries, and life lacks more and more a vital common background, the Negro artist, out of the depths of his group and personal experience, has to his hand almost the conditions of a classical art.

Negro genius today relies upon the race-gift as a vast spiritual endowment from which our best developments have come and must come. Racial expression as a conscious motive, it is true, is fading out of our latest art, but just as surely the age of truer, finer group expression is coming in—for race expression does not need to be deliberate to be vital. Indeed at its best it never is. This was the case with our instinctive and quite matchless folk-art, and begins to be the same again as we approach cultural maturity in a phase of art that promises now to be fully representative. The interval between has been an awkward age, where from the anxious desire and attempt to be representative much that was really unrepresentative has come; we have lately had an art that was stiltedly self-conscious, and racially rhetorical rather than racially expressive. Our poets have now stopped speaking for the Negro—they speak as Negroes. Where formerly they spoke to others and tried to interpret, they now speak to their own and try to express. They have stopped posing, being nearer to the attainment of poise.

The younger generation has thus achieved an objective attitude toward life. Race for them is but an idiom of experience, a sort of added enriching adventure and discipline, giving subtler overtones to life, making it more beautiful and interesting, even if more poignantly so. So experienced, it affords a deepening rather than a narrowing of social vision. The artistic problem of the Young Negro has not been so much that of acquiring the outer mastery of form and technique as that of achieving an inner mastery of mood and spirit. That accomplished, there has come the happy release from self-consciousness, rhetoric, bombast, and the hampering habit of setting artistic values with primary regard for moral effect—all those pathetic over-compensations of a group inferiority complex which our social dilemmas inflicted upon several unhappy generations. Our poets no longer have the hard choice between an over-assertive and appealing attitude. By the same effort, they have shaken themselves free from the minstrel tradition and the fowling-nets of dialect, and through acquiring ease and simplicity in serious expression, have carried the folk-gift to the altitudes of art. There they seek and find art's intrinsic values and satisfactions—and if America were deaf, they would still sing.

But America listens—perhaps in curiosity at first; later, we may be sure, in understanding. But—a moment of patience. The generation now in the artistic vanguard inherits the fine and dearly bought achievement of another generation of creative workmen who have been pioneers and path-breakers in the cultural development and recognition of the Negro in the arts. Though still in their prime, as veterans of a hard struggle, they must have the praise and gratitude that is due them. We have had, in fiction, Chesnutt and Burghardt Du Bois; in drama, Du Bois again and Angelina Grimke; in poetry Dunbar, James Weldon Johnson, Fenton and Charles Bertram Johnson, Everett Hawkins, Lucien Watkins, Cotter, Jamison; and in another file of poets, Miss Grimke, Anne Spencer, and Georgia Douglas Johnson; in criticism and *belles lettres*, Braithwaite and Dr. Du Bois; in painting, Tanner and Scott; in sculpture, Meta Warrick and May Jackson; in acting Gilpin and Robeson; in music, Burleigh. Nor must the fine collaboration of white American artists be omitted; the work of Ridgeley Torrence and Eugene O'Neill in drama, of Stribling, and Shands and Clement Wood in fiction, all of which has helped in the bringing of the materials of Negro life out of the shambles of conventional polemics, cheap romance and journalism into the domain of pure and unbiassed art. Then, rich in this legacy, but richer still, I think, in their own endowment of talent, comes the youngest generation of our Afro-American culture: in music, Diton, Dett, Grant Still, and Roland Hayes; in fiction, Jessie Fauset, Walter White, Claude McKay (a forthcoming book); in drama, Willis Richardson; in the field of the short story, Jean Toomer, Eric Walrond, Rudolf Fisher; and finally a vivid galaxy of young Negro poets, McKay, Jean Toomer, Langston Hughes and Countée Cullen.*

These constitute a new generation not because of years only, but because of a new aesthetic and a new philosophy of life. They have all swung above the horizon in the last three years, and we can say without disparagement of the past that in that short space of time they have gained collectively from publishers, editors, critics and the general public more recognition than has ever before come to Negro creative artists in an entire working lifetime. First novels of unquestioned distinction, first acceptances by premier journals whose pages are the ambition of veteran craftsmen, international acclaim, the conquest for us of new provinces of art, the development for the first time among us of literary coteries and channels for the contact of creative minds, and most important of all, a spiritual quickening and racial leavening such as no generation has yet felt and known. It has been their achievement also to bring the artistic advance of the Negro sharply into stepping alignment with contemporary artistic thought, mood and style. They are thoroughly modern, some of them ultra-modern, and Negro thoughts now wear the uniform of the age.

But for all that, the heart beats a little differently. Toomer gives a folk-lilt and ecstasy to the prose of the American modernists. McKay adds Aesop and irony to the social novel and a peasant clarity and naïveté to lyric thought, Fisher adds Uncle Remus to the art of Maupassant and O. Henry. Hughes puts Biblical fervor into free verse, Hayes carries the gush and depth of folk-song to the old masters,

---

*The full names are: [Charles W.] Chesnutt, [W.E.] Burghardt Du Bois, [Paul Laurence] Dunbar, [Joseph S.] Cotter [Jr.], [Roscoe Conkling] Jamison, [William S.] Braithwaite, [Henry O.] Tanner, [William Edouard] Scott, [Charles] Gilpin, [Paul] Robeson, [Harry T.] Burleigh, [Thomas S.] Stribling, [Hubert A.] Shands, [Carl R.] Diton, [R. Nathaniel] Dett (Harv. spec. student 1919-20), and [William] Grant Still.—Eds.

Cullen blends the simple with the sophisticated and puts the vineyards themselves into his crystal goblets. There is in all the marriage of a fresh emotional endowment with the finest niceties of art. Here for the enrichment of American and modern art, among our contemporaries, in a people who still have the ancient key, are some of the things we thought culture had forever lost. Art cannot disdain the gift of a natural irony, of a transfiguring imagination, of rhapsodic Biblical speech, of dynamic musical swing, of cosmic emotion such as only the gifted pagans knew, of a return to nature, not by way of the forced and worn formula of Romanticism, but through the closeness of an imagination that has never broken kinship with nature. Art must accept such gifts, and revaluate the giver.

Not all the new art is in the field of pure art values. There is poetry of sturdy social protest, and fiction of calm, dispassionate social analysis. But reason and realism have cured us of sentimentality: instead of the wail and appeal, there is challenge and indictment. Satire is just beneath the surface of our latest prose, and tonic irony has come into our poetic wells. These are good medicines for the common mind, for us they are necessary antidotes against social poison. Their influence means that at least for us the worst symptoms of the social distemper are passing. And so the social promise of our recent art is as great as the artistic. It has brought with it, first of all, that wholesome, welcome virtue of finding beauty in oneself; the younger generation can no longer be twitted as "cultural nondescripts" or accused of "being out of love with their own nativity." They have instinctive love and pride of race, and, spiritually compensating for the present lacks of America, ardent respect and love for Africa, the motherland. Gradually too under some spiritualizing reaction, the brands and wounds of social persecution are becoming the proud stigmata of spiritual immunity and moral victory. Already enough progress has been made in this direction so that it is no longer true that the Negro mind is too engulfed in its own social dilemmas for control of the necessary perspective of art, or too depressed to attain the full horizons of self and social criticism. Indeed, by the evidence and promise of the cultured few, we are at last spiritually free, and offer through art an emancipating vision to America. But it is a presumption to speak further for those who have spoken and can speak so adequately for themselves.

Survey Graphic (1925)

Sterling Brown: The New Negro Folk-Poet

Many critics, writing in praise of Sterling Brown's first volume of verse, have seen fit to hail him as a significant new Negro poet. The discriminating few go further; they hail a new era in Negro poetry, for such is the deeper significance of this volume (*The Southern Road*, Sterling A. Brown, Harcourt Brace, New York, 1932). Gauging the main objective of Negro poetry as the poetic portrayal of Negro folk-life true in both letter and spirit to the idiom of the folk's own way of feeling and thinking, we may say that here for the first time is that much-desired and long-awaited acme attained or brought within actual reach.

Almost since the advent of the Negro poet public opinion has expected and demanded folk-poetry of him. And Negro poets have tried hard and voluminously to cater to this popular demand. But on the whole, for very understandable reasons, folk-poetry by Negroes, with notable flash exceptions, has been very unsatisfactory and weak, and despite the intimacy of the race poet's attachments, has been representative in only a limited, superficial sense. First of all, the demand has been too insistent. "They required of us a song in a strange land." "How could we sing of thee, O Zion?" There was the canker of theatricality and exhibitionism planted at the very heart of Negro poetry, unwittingly no doubt, but just as fatally. Other captive nations have suffered the same ordeal. But with the Negro another spiritual handicap was imposed. Robbed of his own tradition, there was no internal compensation to counter the external pressure. Consequently the Negro spirit had a triple plague on its heart and mind—morbid self-consciousness, self-pity and forced exhibitionism. Small wonder that so much poetry by Negroes exhibits in one degree or another the blights of bombast, bathos and artificiality. Much genuine poetic talent has thus been blighted either by these spiritual faults or their equally vicious over-compensations. And so it is epoch-making to have developed a poet whose work, to quote a recent criticism, "has no taint of music-hall convention, is neither arrogant nor servile"—and plays up to neither side of the racial dilemma. For it is as fatal to true poetry to cater to the self-pity or racial vanity of a persecuted group as to pander to the amusement complex of the overlords and masters.

I do not mean to imply that Sterling Brown's art is perfect, or even completely mature. It is all the more promising that this volume represents the work of a young man just in his early thirties. But a Negro poet with almost complete detachment, yet with a tone of persuasive sincerity, whose muse neither clowns nor shouts, is indeed a promising and grateful phenomenon.

By some deft touch, independent of dialect, Mr. Brown is able to compose with the freshness and naturalness of folk balladry—*Maumee Ruth, Dark O' the Moon, Sam Smiley, Slim Green, Johnny Thomas,* and *Memphis Blues* will convince the most sceptical that modern Negro life can yield real balladry and a Negro poet achieve an authentic folk-touch.

Or this from *Sam Smiley*:

> The mob was in fine fettle, yet
> The dogs were stupid-nosed, and day
> Was far spent when the men drew round
> The scrawny woods where Smiley lay.
>
> The oaken leaves drowsed prettily,
> The moon shone down benignly there;
> And big Sam Smiley, King Buckdancer,
> Buckdanced on the midnight air.

This is even more dramatic and graphic than the fine but more melo-dramatic lyric of Langston Hughes:

> Way down South in Dixie
> (Break the heart of me!)
> They hung my black young lover
> To a cross-road's tree.

With Mr. Brown the racial touch is quite independent of dialect; it is because in his ballads and lyrics he has caught the deeper idiom of feeling or the peculiar paradox of the racial situation. That gives the genuine earthy folk-touch, and justifies a statement I ventured some years back: "the soul of the Negro will be discovered in a characteristic way of thinking and in a homely philosophy rather than in a jingling and juggling of broken English." As a matter of fact, Negro dialect is extremely local—it changes from place to place, as do white dialects. And what is more, the dialect of Dunbar and the other early Negro poets never was on land or sea as a living peasant speech; but it has had such wide currency, especially on the stage, as to have successfully deceived half the world, including the many Negroes who for one reason or another imitate it.

Sterling Brown's dialect is also local, and frankly an adaptation, but he has localized it carefully, after close observation and study, and varies it according to the brogue of the locality or the characteristic jargon of the *milieu* of which he is writing. But his racial effects, as I have said, are not dependent on dialect. Consider *Maumee Ruth*:

> Might as well bury her
> And bury her deep,
> Might as well put her
> Where she can sleep.
>
>   . . .
> Boy that she suckled—
> How should he know,
> Hiding in city holes
> Sniffing the "snow"?[1]
>
> And how should the news
> Pierce Harlem's din,
> To reach her baby gal
> Sodden with gin?
>
> Might as well drop her
> Deep in the ground,
> Might as well pray for her,
> That she sleep sound.

That is as uniquely racial as the straight dialect of *Southern Road*:

---

[1]Cocaine.

White man tells me—hunh—
Damn yo' soul;
White man tells me—hunh—
Damn yo' soul;
Got no need, bebby,
To be tole.

If we stop to inquire—as unfortunately the critic must—into the magic of these effects, we find the secret, I think, in this fact more than in any other: Sterling Brown has listened long and carefully to the folk in their intimate hours, when they were talking to themselves, not, so to speak, as in Dunbar, but actually as they do when the masks of protective mimicry fall. Not only has he dared to give quiet but bold expression to this private thought and speech, but he has dared to give the Negro peasant credit for thinking. In this way he has recaptured the shrewd Aesopian quality of the Negro folk-thought, which is more profoundly characteristic than their types of metaphors or their mannerisms of speech. They are, as he himself says,

Illiterate, and somehow very wise,

and it is this wisdom, bitter fruit of their suffering, combined with their characteristic fatalism and irony, which in this book gives a truer soul picture of the Negro than has ever yet been given poetically. The traditional Negro is a clown, a buffoon, an easy laugher, a shallow sobber and a credulous christian; the real Negro underneath is more often an all but cynical fatalist, a shrewd pretender, and a boldly whimsical pagan; or when not, a lusty, realistic religionist who tastes its nectars here and now.

Mammy
With deep religion defeating the grief
Life piled so closely about her

is the key picture to the Negro as christian; Mr. Brown's *When the Saints Come Marching Home* [Brown's title is "When de Saints Go Ma'ching Home"] is worth half a dozen essays on the Negro's religion. But to return to the question of bold exposure of the intimacies of Negro thinking—read that priceless apologia of kitchen stealing in the *Ruminations of Luke Johnson*, reflective husband of Mandy Jane, tromping early to work with a great big basket, and tromping wearily back with it at night laden with the petty spoils of the day's picking:

> Well, tain't my business noway,
> An' I ain' near fo'gotten
> De lady what she wuks fo',
> An' how she got huh jack;
> De money dat *she* live on
> Come from niggers pickin' cotton,
> Ebbery dollar dat she squander
> Nearly bust a nigger's back.
>
> So I'm glad dat in de evenin's
> Mandy Jane seems extra happy,
> An' de lady at de big house
> Got no kick at all, I say;—
> Cause what huh "dear grandfawthaw"
> Took from Mandy Jane's grandpappy—
> Ain' no basket in de worl'
> What kin tote all dat away.

Or again in that delicious epic of *Sporting Beasley* entering heaven:

> Lord help us, give a *look* at him,
> Don't make him dress up in no night gown, Lord.
> Don't put no fuss and feathers on his shoulders, Lord.
>   Let him know it's heaven,
> Let him keep his hat, his vest, his elkstooth,
>   and everything.
> Let him have his spats and cane.

It is not enough to sprinkle "dis's and dat's" to be a Negro folk-poet, or to jingle rhymes and juggle popularized clichés traditional to sentimental minor poetry for generations. One must study the intimate thought of the people who can only state it in an ejaculation, or a metaphor, or at best a proverb, and translate that into an articulate attitude, or a folk philosophy or a daring fable, with Aesopian clarity and simplicity—and above all, with Aesopian candor.

The last is most important; other Negro poets in many ways have been too tender with their own, even though they have learned with the increasing boldness of new Negro thought not to be too gingerly and conciliatory to and about the white man. The Negro muse weaned itself of that in McKay, Fenton Johnson, Toomer, Countée

Cullen and Langston Hughes. But in Sterling Brown it has learned to laugh at itself and to chide itself with the same broomstick. I have space for only two examples: *Children's Children*:

> When they hear
> These songs, born of the travail of their sires,
> Diamonds of song, deep buried beneath the weight
> Of dark and heavy years;
> They laugh.
>
> They have forgotten, they have never known
> Long days beneath the torrid Dixie sun,
> In miasma'd riceswamps;
> The chopping of dried grass, on the third go round
> In strangling cotton;
> Wintry nights in mud-daubed makeshift huts,
> With these songs, sole comfort.
>
> They have forgotten
> What had to be endured—
>
> That they, babbling young ones,
> With their paled faces, coppered lips,
> And sleek hair cajoled to Caucasian straightness,
> Might drown the quiet voice of beauty
> With sensuous stridency;
>
> And might, on hearing these memoirs of their sires,
> Giggle,
> And nudge each other's satin-clad
> Sleek sides.

Anent the same broomstick, it is refreshing to read *Mr. Samuel and Sam*, from which we can only quote in part:

> Mister Samuel, he belong to Rotary,
> Sam to de Sons of Rest;
> Both wear red hats lak monkey men,
> An' you cain't say which is de best.
>   . . .
>
> Mister Samuel die, an' de folks all know,

Sam die widout no noise;
De worl' go by in de same ol' way,
And dey's both of 'em po' los' boys.

There is a world of psychological distance between this and the
rhetorical defiance and the plaintive, furtive sarcasms of even some of
our other contemporary poets—even as theirs, it must be said in all
justice, was miles better and more representative than the sycophan-
cies and platitudes of the older writers.

In closing it might be well to trace briefly the steps by which
Negro poetry has scrambled up the sides of Parnassus from the ditches
of minstrelsy and the trenches of race propaganda. In complaining
against the narrow compass of dialect poetry (dialect is an organ with
only two stops—pathos and humor), Weldon Johnson tried to break
the Dunbar mould and shake free of the traditional stereotypes. But
significant as it was, this was more a threat than an accomplishment;
his own dialect poetry has all of the clichés of Dunbar without
Dunbar's lilting lyric charm. Later in the *Negro Sermons* Weldon
Johnson discovered a way out—in a rhapsodic form free from the verse
shackles of classical minor poetry, and in the attempt to substitute an
idiom of racial thought and imagery for a mere dialect of peasant
speech. Claude McKay then broke with all the moods conventional
in his day in Negro poetry, and presented a Negro who could
challenge and hate, who knew resentment, brooded intellectual
sarcasm, and felt contemplative irony. In this, so to speak, he pulled
the psychological cloak off the Negro and revealed, even to the Negro
himself, those facts disguised till then by his shrewd protective mimicry
or pressed down under the dramatic mask of living up to what was
expected of him. But though McKay sensed a truer Negro, he was at
times too indignant at the older sham, and, too, lacked the requisite
native touch—as of West Indian birth and training—with the local color
of the American Negro. Jean Toomer went deeper still—I should say
higher—and saw for the first time the glaring paradoxes and the deeper
ironies of the situation, as they affected not only the Negro but the
white man. He realized, too, that Negro idiom was anything but trite
and derivative, and also that it was in emotional substance pagan—all
of which he convincingly demonstrated, alas, all too fugitively, in *Cane*.
But Toomer was not enough of a realist, or patient enough as an
observer, to reproduce extensively a folk idiom.

Then Langston Hughes came with his revelation of the emotional color of Negro life, and his brilliant discovery of the flow and rhythm of the modern and especially the city Negro, substituting this jazz figure and personality for the older plantation stereotype. But it was essentially a jazz version of Negro life, and that is to say as much American, or more, as Negro; and though fascinating and true to an epoch this version was surface quality after all.

Sterling Brown, more reflective, a closer student of the folk-life, and above all a bolder and more detached observer, has gone deeper still, and has found certain basic, more sober and more persistent qualities of Negro thought and feeling; and so has reached a sort of common denominator between the old and the new Negro. Underneath the particularities of one generation are hidden universalities which only deeply penetrating genius can fathom and bring to the surface. Too many of the articulate intellects of the Negro group—including sadly enough the younger poets—themselves children of opportunity, have been unaware of these deep resources of the past. But here, if anywhere, in the ancient common wisdom of the folk, is the real treasure trove of the Negro poet; and Sterling Brown's poetic divining-rod has dipped significantly over this position. It is in this sense that I believe *Southern Road* ushers in a new era in Negro folk-expression and brings a new dimension in Negro folk-portraiture.

From *Negro: An Anthology* (1934)

The Myth of the New Negro

WILLIAM H. FERRIS

A review of *The New Negro: An Interpretation*, edited by Alain Locke, published by Albert & Charles Boni, New York, 1925.

In a 446-page book, with attractive book decorations and portraits by Winold Reiss, Mr. Alain Locke, a former Rhodes Scholar, has gathered together interesting stories, poems and essays by well-known and promising Colored writers. Nearly forty colored writers swell the list of contributors.

Alain Locke, Albert C. Barnes, William Stanley Braithwaite, Arthur A. Schomburg, Charles S. Johnson, James Weldon Johnson, Kelly Miller and W.A. Domingo, Dr. W.E.B. Du Bois and others contribute essays. Jean Toomer, Zora Neale Hurston, Rudolph Fisher, John Matheus, Bruce Nugent and Eric Walrond give us a series of stories. Countée Cullen, Claude McKay, Jean Toomer, James Weldon Johnson, Langston Hughes, Georgia Douglas Johnson, Anne Spencer, Angelina Grimke and Lewis Alexander regale the readers with poetic gems that would show up well in the leading white magazines.

The essayists treat of "The Negro Renaissance," "Drama," "Music," "The Negro Digs Up His Past," "The New Negro in a New World," "The Negro and the American Tradition." Alain Locke, Paul U. Kellogg, Charles S. Johnson, James Weldon Johnson, Kelly Miller and W.E.B. Du Bois give the reader food for thought. Albert C. Barnes, William Stanley Braithwaite, and Arthur A. Schomburg and Arthur Huff Fauset dig up plenty of facts. Dr. Du Bois' "The Negro Mind Reaches Out," reprinted with revisions by the author from *Foreign Affairs*, an American Quarterly Review, presents a masterly study of the Negro's status in foreign lands.

Jean Toomer in two short stories, "Carma" and "Fern" from *Cane*, indicates that he has a sense for plot and a racy style that make him a short story teller of which any race could justly be proud. *The New Negro* has spice and variety. It is an entertaining volume. It would be a splendid companion on a rainy day, on a summer's vacation or an ocean voyage. But I am not sure whether the reader will get a broader perspective in philosophy or a more comprehensive grasp on sociological problems or new vistas in psychology, after perusing the volume.

The Reviews

Never did the works of Paul Laurence Dunbar, Charles W. Chesnutt and Dr. W.E.B. Du Bois receive the fulsome praise that *The New Negro* has received. Carl Van Doren in the *Century* and other reviews in the *American Mercury*, the *New York Times*, the *New York Tribune* and other journals were more than appreciative and sympathetic. They indulged in superlatives. They had the enthusiasm of a discoverer of a new continent, of a discoverer of a new world of thought and feeling. For the first time since the fall of 1895, when Industrial Education was regarded as the panacea for all of the Negro's ills, his higher aspirations in literature, art, music and poetry are taken seriously. And this is a very hopeful sign of the change in the attitude of the American mind towards the Negro intellect.

The Myth of the New Negro

There has been so much talk and writing about *The New Negro* that it is well to ask, "Is the Negro of 1926 different from the Negro of 1895, 1900 and 1905?" If in the summer of 1906, when the Atlanta Riot had occurred and when [Jesse] Max Barber, the editor of *Voice of the Negro*, was forced to leave Atlanta, Ga., and to give up his paper, all of the issues of his brilliant magazine had been bound together and published in a single volume, I am inclined to believe that the book would have been similar in plan and scope and equally as instructive and entertaining as *The New Negro*.

And if the papers read before the American Negro Academy in March, 1897, when Dr. Alexander Crummell spoke on "Civilization, the Primal Need of the Negro Race," and "The Attitude of the American Mind Toward the Negro Intellect," Dr. Du Bois on "The Conservation of Races" and Prof. Kelly Miller on "Hoffman's 'Race Traits and Tendencies of the American Negro,'" the papers read before the same organization in December, 1897, on "The Race Problem in the Light of the Evolution Hypothesis" and "The Race Problem in the Light of Sociology," if the papers read around 1900 on "Disfranchisement," the papers read in December, 1902, on "The Negro's Religion" and the papers read in December, 1906, on "Negro Labor and Foreign Emigrant Labor" could be published in a single volume, the scholarship, philosophical analysis, sociological insight displayed would have startled the world and made as strong an impression as the essays on the New Negro.

Some may claim that the New Negro is more poetic than the Negro of 1896 and 1906, but in those days Paul Laurence Dunbar, Rev. James D. Corrothers, D. Webster Davis, Silas Floyd, [Richard E.S.] Toomey and others produced excellent poetry and Lillian Lewis, Victoria Earle Matthews and Alice Ruth Moore wrote interesting sketches.

Some may claim that the New Negro is more assertive regarding his civil and political rights than the old Negro, but at the Faneuil Hall, Mass. Meeting of the Colored National League in February, 1898, the state Sumner League Convention in Savin Rock, Conn. in August, 1898, when James W. Peaker, Counsellor D. Macon Webster of New York and T. Thomas Fortune, editor of the *New York Age*, spoke, and at the Afro-American Council, called by Bishop Alexander Walters and T. Thomas Fortune in Washington, D.C., in December, 1898, speeches were delivered as bold and fearless as any heard today.

The Faneuil Hall Mass Meeting of the Colored National League caused Henry Cabot Lodge to introduce in Congress, a discussion on the floor of Congress the heralding the same through the Associated Press, [sic] the printing of the same in the Congressional Record and the appointment of a Senatorial Committee to investigate the [22 Feb. 1898] murder of [black] Postmaster [Frazier B.] Baker of Lake City, S.C. The State Sumner League was so potent in the closing days of the nineteenth century that President McKinley appointed Dr. [George H.] Jackson of New Haven, Conn., consul to Cognac and LaRochelle, France [1897ff.]. One of the statements in the resolution of the Afro-American Council in December, 1898, read, "We regret that the President saw fit to pass over in silence in his recent message to Congress the Wilmington race riot, etc." And these things occurred before Dr. Du Bois published his *Souls of Black Folk* [1903] and organized the Niagara Movement [1905], before even Wm. Monroe Trotter published the *Boston Guardian* [1901] and organized the New

England Suffrage League [1904].

Some may claim that the New Negro has more interest in Literature per se than the Old Negro. But in the fall of 1898 an Omar Khayyam Club was organized by Mr. George W. Forbes in Miss Maria Baldwin's home in Cambridge, Mass., to study the *Rubaiyat* of Omar Khayyam and Dante's *Divine Comedy.* Soon after, a Book Lover's Club was organized in Washington, and a Shakespeare's Club in New Haven, Conn. In the spring of 1896, Rev. Butler, a Methodist preacher, read a paper on "The Neo-Platonic Philosophy" before the St. Mark's Lyceum. In the summer of 1909, Hon. James D. Carr, Assistant Corporation Counsel, read a paper on "Evolution" before the Philosophical Club, which met in the home of Mrs. A.C. Cowan of Brooklyn, N.Y.

Yes, the Black Man has been revealing his mind for the past thirty years; but the country did not take the revelation seriously. It is a very hopeful sign that the colored man's higher aspirations are now taken seriously.

Spokesman (1925)

Edward Smyth Jones in 1915

EDWARD SMYTH JONES

Edward Smyth Jones was born in Natchez, Mississippi, sometime in March of 1881. His slave parents, Hawk and Rebecca, lacked formal education, but he attended local schools and developed a taste for reading and writing. For fourteen months during 1902-03 he studied at nearby Alcorn Agricultural and Mechanical College in exchange for labor. Continuing his reading and writing in Louisville, Kentucky, he brought out, under the nickname "Invincible Ned," a book of poems entitled *The Rose That Bloometh in My Heart* (1908). Among its thirty poems was "A Psalm of Love," a parody of the well-known "A Psalm of Love" written by Longfellow while a professor at Harvard.

After moving to Indianapolis, Jones won praise for his poetry. But his greatest desire was to attend Harvard. With almost no money in his pocket, he set out in July 1910—hiking, stealing freight-train rides, and sleeping outdoors. He covered the 1200 miles and arrived after dark in Harvard Yard, where he found a printer working overtime in the basement of University Hall and asked to see the president. Looking at the dirty and shabby traveler, the printer took him for a crazy tramp and summoned a policeman, who jailed Jones for vagrancy. Arraigned before Judge Arthur P. Stone '93, LL.B. '95, Jones was able to produce letters of congratulation from numerous people including the mayor of Indianapolis, the governor of Indiana and former Vice-President Charles Fairbanks, along with two of his poems. The judge was impressed by the long "Ode to Ethiopia," which hailed a parade of Negro achievers, including several Harvard alumni.

Jones was offered assistance by black lawyer Clement Morgan '90, LL.B. '93, and by William H. Holtzclaw, founding principal of all-black Utica Normal and Industrial Institute in Mississippi, who happened to be studying then at the Harvard Summer School. Jones was released, but not before writing a new poem, "Harvard Square," during his three-day incarceration. Harvard's janitorial supervisor put Jones to work, enabling the would-be student to attend Boston Latin School for a year. During this period, Jones published his second book, *The Sylvan Cabin and Other Verse*, which contained the Harvard poem and bore a dedication to Judge Stone. (The Harvard Library has a copy presented to it by former president Charles W.

Eliot.)

Lack of funds prevented Jones from finishing at Boston Latin School and entering Harvard, and he moved from place to place until he secured a job as a waiter in the Faculty Club at Columbia University. The *New York Times* published an article about him and lauded his long new poem about the sinking of the Titanic. By the 1920s Jones was living in Chicago, where he worked as a general laborer until he succumbed to a cerebral thrombosis on 28 September 1968.

Harvard Square

'Tis once in life our dreams come true,
          The myths of long ago,
Quite real though fairy-like their view,
          They surge with ebb and flow;
Thus thou, O haunt of childhood dreams,
          More beauteous and fair
Than Nature's landscape and her streams,
          Historic Harvard Square.

My soul hath panted long for thee,
          Like as the wounded hart
That vainly strives himself to free
          Full from the archer's dart;
And struggled oft all, all alone
          With burdens hard to bear
But now I stand at Wisdom's throne
          To-night in Harvard Square.

A night most tranquil,—I was proud
          My thoughts soared up afar,
To moonbeams pouring through the cloud,
          Or some lone twinkling star;
And musing thus, my quickened pace
          Beat to the printery's glare,
Where first I saw a friendly face
          In classic Harvard Square.

"Ho! stranger, thou art wan and worn
      Of journey's wear and tear;
Thy face all haggard and forlorn,
      Pray tell me whence and where?"
"I came—from out—the Sunny South—
      The spot—on earth—most fair,"
Fell lisping from my trembling mouth—
      "In search—of—Harvard Square."

"Here rest, my friend, upon this seat,
      And feel thyself at home;
I'll bring thee forth some drink and meat,
      'Twill give thee back thy form."
And then I prayed the Lord to bless
      Us, and that little lair—
Quite sure, I thought, I had found rest
      Most sweet in Harvard Square.

"I came," I said, "o'er stony ways,
      Through mountain, hill and dale,
I've felt old Sol's most scorching rays,
      And braved the stormy gale;
I've done this, Printer, not for gold,
      Nor diamonds rich and rare—
But for a burning in my soul
      To learn in Harvard Square.

"I've journeyed long without a drink
      Nor yet a bite of bread,
While in this state, O Printer, think—
      No shelter for my head.
I mused, 'Hope's yet this side the grave'—
      My pluck and courage there
Then made my languid heart bear brave—
      Each throb for Harvard Square."

A sound soon hushed my heart's rejoice—
      "The watchman on his search?"
"No!" rang the printer's gentle voice,
      "'Deak' Wilson in from church.

O'er there, good 'Deak'," the printer said,
        "The wanderer in that chair,
Hath come to seek the lore deep laid
        Up here in Harvard Square."

"It matters not how you implore,
        He can no longer stay;
But on the night's 'Plutonian shore,'
        Await the coming day.
I'm sorry, sir," he calmly said,
        "Though hard, I guess 'tis fair,
Thou hast no place to lay thy head—
        Not yet in Harvard Square!"

"Good night!" he said, and we the same—
        I sighed, "Where shall I go?"
He soon returned and with him came
        An officer and—Oh!
"Now sir, you take this forlorn tramp
        With all his shabby ware,
And guide him safely off the 'Camp'
        Of dear old Harvard Square."

As soon as locked within the jail,
        Deep in a ghastly cell,
Methought I heard the bitter wail
        Of all the fiends of hell!
"O God, to Thee I humbly pray
        No treacherous prison snare
Shall close my soul within for aye
        From dear old Harvard Square."

Just then I saw an holy Sprite
        Shed all her radiant beams,
And round her shone the source of light
        Of all the poets' dreams!
I plied my pen in sober use,
        And spent each moment spare
In sweet communion with the Muse
        I met in Harvard Square!

I cried: "Fair Goddess, hear my tale
      Of sorrow, grief and pain."
That made her face an ashen pale,
      But soon it glowed again!
"They placed me here; and this my crime,
      Writ on their pages fair:—
'He left his sunny native clime,
      And came to Harvard Square!'"

"Weep not, my son, thy way is hard,
      Thy weary journey long—
But thus I choose my favorite bard
      To sing my sweetest song.
I'll strike the key-note of my art
      And guide with tend'rest care,
And breathe a song into thy heart
      To honor Harvard Square.

"I called old Homer long ago,
      And made him beg his bread
Through seven cities, ye all know,
      His body fought for, dead.
Spurn not oppression's blighting sting,
      Nor scorn thy lowly fare;
By them I'll teach thy soul to sing
      The songs of Harvard Square.

"I placed great Dante in exile,
      And Byron had his turns;
Then Keats and Shelley smote the while,
      And my immortal Burns!
But thee I'll build a sacred shrine,
      A store of all my ware;
By them I'll teach thy soul to sing
      'A place in Harvard Square.'

"To some a store of mystic lore,
      To some to shine a star:
The first I gave to Allan Poe,
      The last to Paul Dunbar.

Since thou hast waited patient, long,
    Now by my throne I swear
To give to thee my sweetest song
    To sing in Harvard Square."

And when she gave her parting kiss
    And bade a long farewell,
I sat serene in perfect bliss
    As she forsook my cell.
Upon the altar-fire she poured
    Some incense very rare;
Its fragrance sweet my soul assured
    I'd enter Harvard Square.

Reclining on my couch, I slept
    A sleep sweet and profound;
O'er me the blessed angels kept
    Their vigil close around.
With dawning's smile, my fondest hope
    Shone radiant and fair:
The Justice cut each chain and rope
    'Tween me and Harvard Square!

Cell No. 40, East Cambridge Jail,
Cambridge, Mass., July 26, 1910

EVA B. DYKES

Eva Beatrice Dykes was born on 13 August 1893 in Washington, D.C., where she attended the famous M Street (later Dunbar) High School and went on to get an A.B. from Howard University in 1914. With financial assistance from her uncle and from scholarship funds, she entered Radcliffe, majored in English, and in 1917 received a second A.B. *magna cum laude*, followed by an A.M. the next year. With a dissertation on Alexander Pope and his influence, she took a Radcliffe Ph.D. in 1921—one of the first three black women to earn this degree (with Sadie T.M. Alexander in economics at the University of Pennsylvania, and Georgiana R. Simpson in German at the University of Chicago, both in 1921).

After teaching stints at Walden College in Nashville, Tennessee, and at her own Dunbar High School, she returned to Howard in 1929 to teach English for fifteen years, and was voted "best all-around teacher" by her faculty colleagues. In 1944 she moved to Oakwood College in Alabama, where she continued working with students after her formal retirement in 1968 at the age of 75. The College named a library for her in 1973. Active as a musician and writer on literature (we here reprint the conclusion of her 1942 book *The Negro in English Romantic Thought*), she was elected to Phi Beta Kappa by Radcliffe as an alumna in 1940. In 1977, as part of the Black Women Oral History Project at Radcliffe, Dykes was interviewed by Merze Tate, herself a holder of a Radcliffe Ph.D. (1941) and a long-time professor of history at Howard University. Dykes died in Huntsville, Alabama, on 29 October 1986.

Eva Dykes in 1917

Conclusion to
The Negro in English Romantic Thought
or
A Study of Sympathy for the Oppressed

There is no doubt that English romantic thought included the Negro and the amelioration of his condition as vital factors in the program of romanticism. Literary men and women of all types were more or less active in voicing their protest against the evils of slavery. From the heterogeneous array of literature we have seen various arguments advanced against this institution: first, from a moral and sentimental aspect, slavery is a transgression of the law of God and of the principles of right and justice; secondly, from an economic standpoint slave labor is in the long run more costly than free labor and the maintenance of slave colonies is a great expense to the mother country; and thirdly, from the physical aspect, slavery involves separation from families, the horrors of the Middle Passage, the scourge of pestilence and disease, the brutality of the lash, and the loss of human life. Many of those who advanced these arguments could not be contented while the Negro was reduced to a status a little above that of an animal. They were farsighted enough to see that any institution which deprived their fellowmen of intellectual, economic, and spiritual development was a hindrance to the progress of the human race as a whole.

From this study three interesting facts are worthy of notice. One is that many of these writers were not prompted by any consideration of social equality for the Negro as the following account from Benjamin Haydon reveals: "When I was painting the 'Anti-Slavery Convention' in 1840, I said to Scobell, one of the leading emancipation men, 'I shall place you, Thompson, and the Negro, together.' This was the touchstone. He sophisticated immediately on the propriety of placing the Negro in the distance. Now, a man who wishes to place the Negro on our level must no longer regard him having been a slave and feel annoyed at sitting by his side."[1] Another interesting fact is the variety of forms assumed by the material devoted to the Negro. There appear poems ranging from the short sonnet and poem of two stanzas to the longer poem,—poems in heroic couplets, Miltonic octosyllabic couplets, in elegiac quatrains, and in other varied stanzaic forms. Some writers like Burns, Blake, Wordsworth, Coleridge, Hunt, Harriet Martineau, Maria Edgeworth and Landor devoted complete poems, tales, or essays to the Negro while others like Shelley and Byron were satisfied with incidental passages. Furthermore, almost all the well-known writers of the eighteenth and early nineteenth centuries wrote against slavery; yet they are remembered by the general student of English literature not for their anti-slavery utterances but for their conforming more or less to those principles of writing which make their works take place among the classics of English literature.

Just as a musical composition has ever-recurring motifs and characteristic stock features, so anti-slavery literature contains ever-recurring patterns of ideas and imagery. Some of these stock features are the beauty of Africa, an ideal land, as it were, the happiness of the natives in their primitive home-lands, the approach of the slave-ship, the hospitality of the unsuspecting natives, the treachery of the whites, the brave resistance of the natives, the misery caused by the separation of kindred and friends, the cruelties on the slave-ship, the arrival in a strange land, the brutality of the slave-masters, the frequent occurrence of storms and tornadoes sent to avenge the slave, the pathetic dejection of the captives, and the hope of happiness and reconciliation after death.   Unlike the Negro spiritual, which is exceptional in that it is almost free from the element of revenge, much of this anti-slavery literature (no doubt because much of it is the product of the white man's brain) calls upon Heaven to avenge the suffering of the slave. Again and again ironical attacks on the bigotry, the inconsistency, and the hypocrisy of Christians appear.

The characters in this literature are as varied as the motifs. There is, of course, the typical cruel slave-dealer and master, who may or may not repent of his inhumanity to man; there is also the humane slave-master who realizes that kindly treatment of the slaves produces the best results. The Negro woman appears usually as a beautiful

[1]Benjamin Robert Haydon, *Life, Letters, and Table Talk*, pp. 292, 293.

maiden, left behind in Africa, prostrate with grief over the loss of her lover, or as a mother stricken with sorrow over the loss of her children. Since most of the anti-slavery literature was written with a view to gaining sympathy for the slave and effective action in his behalf, the Negro male appears most frequently as slave and toiler. There is also the "dying" Negro, who, rather than submit to an ignominious life of slaver, prefers the peace afforded by death.

The Negro appears also as a prince, rescuer, and soldier. A figure of popular appeal was Toussaint Louverture. Edward Seeber says that in France Toussaint "was regarded as a sort of glamorous hero, the incarnation of the numerous literary progeny of Oroonoko and the fulfillment of frequent petitions for a 'nouveau Spartacus' to lead the wretched slaves to freedom."[2] In England his tragic fate appealed . . . to such writers as Rushton, Harriet Martineau, Rogers, Wordsworth, and Landor. Attention may be called to the Negro who speaks in his own behalf as in Samuel Bowden's "An Epitaph on a Negro Servant," Blake's "The Little Black Boy," Burns' "The Slave's Lament," Hunt's "The Negro Boy," and Amelia Opie's "The Negro Boy's Tale." Attempts to represent Negro dialect are few and rather unsuccessful as in Robert Anderson's "Negro Affection" and Amelia Opie's "The Negro Boy's Tale."

The numerous tributes to such abolitionists as Cowper, Wilberforce, Clarkson and Sharp* indicate the gratitude of both whites and Negroes for the efforts of the anti-slavery crusaders. Similarly today those who believe that "a man's a man for a' that" cannot help appreciating these varied manifestations of sympathy for the oppressed in English romantic thought. The growing consciousness of the inhumanity of slavery which finds its reflection in literature of the eighteenth century, the rising tide of popular opposition and indignation which reached its crest during the romantic period and was responsible for the abolition of slavery in the British colonies, and the concern for the slave in America,—all of these facts bespeak a sincere

---

[2]Edward Derbyshire Seeber, *Anti-slavery Opinion in France During the Second Half of the Eighteenth Century* (Baltimore: The Johns Hopkins Press, 1937), p. 194.

*William Cooper (1731-1800); William Wilberforce (1759-1833); Thomas Clarkson (1760-1846); Granville Sharp (1735-1813).—Eds.

desire to keep the torch of liberty burning and pass it on undimmed to those who follow.

Carlyle once said to an American visitor in England, "All the worth you have put into your cause will be returned to you personally; but the America for which you are hoping you will never see: and you will never see the whites and the blacks in the South dwelling together as equals in peace."[3] The torch of liberty has been handed down to the twentieth century with the prophecy of Carlyle yet unfulfilled.

(1942)

[3]Moncure Daniel Conway, *Autobiography, Memory and Experiences*, Vol. 1, p. 400.

Preface to *Readings from Negro Authors*

OTELIA CROMWELL, LORENZO DOW TURNER [A.M. '17]
& EVA B. DYKES

The purpose of this volume is not to present another anthology of Negro literature, but to offer for classroom study or supplementary reading a selection of types of writings by Negro authors. Although many young people develop their reading habits independently of formal direction, teachers of English have a clear duty toward their students; namely, "To teach them to read thoughtfully and with appreciation, to form in them a taste for good reading, and to teach them how to find books that are worth while." This dogma, recognized as one of the fundamental aims of the English course as stated by the National Joint Committee on English, suggests a method of selecting and reading books that admits of extensive possibilities in the choice of reading while it imposes literary criteria more or less elastic. For the program of readings, therefore, the teacher of English has a wide range of choice; and for the specific program of American literature,—the opportunity to embrace in true catholicity of spirit writings that constitute a significant part of the total American output. Of some significance are the worth-while productions of Negro authors. Negro literature demands no unique method of approach, no special interpretation of the rules of craftsmanship, because the standards of literary form are based upon universal principles. A short story written by a Negro is good, bad, or indifferent in so far as it is a good, a bad, or an indifferent short story.

In emphasizing what, for a more comprehensive term, is called technique, the editors are not unmindful of the fact that, form being always subordinate to content, the presentation of cross-sections of Negro life is, perhaps, the essential appeal of Negro literature. What has been guarded against is, as Amy Lowell puts it, "a tendency to think that a fine idea excuses slovenly workmanship." Moreover, it is believed that an intelligent appreciation of these writings will be stimulated, a sane balance will be preserved, if the writings are introduced to students by the methods used in the study of types of general literature. Toward the accomplishment of these ends, students should be encouraged to make parallel readings, or at least to compare types of Negro writings with similar types of writings by authors of other races. Such a method does not imply a desire to underestimate Negro talent, but rather one to widen the reading interests of students and to develop the habit of looking for relative and absolute values.

In selecting material for this volume, the editors have been constrained to keep in mind their purpose, namely, the presentation of certain readings for definite study. No apology, therefore, is made for the offering of much that has appeared in print many times already or for the exclusion of writings that are of intrinsic worth yet not wholly suitable for textbook adoption. The particular slant of the realism of a few representative Negro writers and the marked predilection on the part of some others for a bafflingly incoherent style explain the absence from this volume of productions by one or two well-known writers. In the field of poetry, much that was desirable had to be omitted because of the necessity of preserving a semblance of proportion. In some other fields, the output was disappointingly meager. Prose fiction has been limited to the short story and the sketch because of the debatable value of the study of excerpts from novels. First and last, it was the question of what would serve best the needs of the text.

The method of using the text will be determined by the attitude of the teacher, the object of the course, and the ability and progress of the class. Experience has shown that the plan of starting pupils with the writings of authors—*not* with what some one has said about the authors—is not only a logical procedure in the teaching of literature, but one calculated to challenge the imagination of the student. The introductory essays, placed at the beginnings of each group of readings, may, if the teacher so wishes, be postponed for study until after the readings are concluded. In like manner, the Suggestions for Study are to be treated as suggestions merely. The alert teacher will, of course, use the plan that his initiative and sense of values will choose. What is of vast importance is the need of stimulating the student to read, to read, and to read again; to get joy out of the printed page; and to cherish his own responses to what is read. When a student's interest and reactions have been awakened, it is but another step for him to make an intelligent criticism of his reading. The tragic mistake made by inexperienced teachers of literature is to attempt criticism—usually by having the student read the opinions of literary historians—before the student has been spurred to read and to think for himself. This error may be avoided if responses to reading, especially first readings, are awakened through a few stimulating questions or topics given with reading assignments. Typical questions and topics are contained in the Suggestions for Study, but the teacher and the students themselves will supply others.

(1931)

Caroline Bond Day in 1919

CAROLINE BOND DAY

Caroline Stewart Bond Day was born in Montgomery, Alabama, on 18 November 1889, the daughter of Moses and Georgia Stewart. Upon her mother's second marriage, to John Bond, Caroline Stewart took her stepfather's surname. She attended Atlanta University, from which she received an A.B. in 1912. For a year she taught at Alabama Agricultural and Mechanical College, and then spent time working for the YWCA in Montclair, N.J. In 1916 she entered Radcliffe and received a second A.B. in 1919. Following her marriage to Aaron Day in 1920, she spent a year as dean of women at Paul Quinn College in Waco, Texas, and another as head of the English department at Prairie View State College in Texas. In 1922 she moved to Atlanta University, where she supervised dramatics in addition to teaching English. During 1927-28 and 1929-30 she was on leave to do research and take courses at Radcliffe—this time in anthropology, mainly under Professor Earnest A. Hooton. In 1930 she received her A.M., primarily for amassing and analyzing data on race-mixing in 346 families, including her own. The result was published by Harvard's Peabody Museum under the title *A Study of Some Negro-White Families in the United States* (1932). A brief sampling from this study, which drew praise from W.E.B. Du Bois in a 1935 essay, is reprinted here.

Between 1919 and 1933 Day published some essays and short stories, of which the best is the clearly autobiographical tale "The Pink Hat" (*Opportunity*, December 1926). In the 1930s she taught at Howard University for two years, and then went into social work—first as a settlement-house supervisor in Washington, D.C., then as general secretary of the nearby Phillis Wheatley YWCA. Never in robust health, she retired to Durham, North Carolina, in 1939. She tried a bit of teaching at the North Carolina College for Negroes, but had to give it up. After some years of hypertension and myocarditis, she succumbed to cerebral apoplexy in a Durham hospital on 5 May 1948.

Selections from *A Study of Some Negro-White Families in
the United States*

F13 FAGAIN (PLATE 34)

James Fagain was the son of Nancy Knight, mulatto, and Harold
Fagain, white, of Scotch and Irish ancestry. Nancy Knight was an F1
generation, the offspring of a white mother and Negro father. James
Fagain was stockily built, with a ruddy complexion and light brown,
very crinkly hair. His nose was straight with a moderately high bridge
and medium wide alae. His lips were fairly thin.

He married about 1860 Caroline Reese, 1/4N 3/4W, born in 1846.
She was the daughter of Anna Tucker, an F1 mulatto, the offspring
of a white father of English ancestry and a Negro mother. Caroline
Reese looked like a light Italian with long, straight, dark brown hair
with the suggestion of a low wave. Her nose was medium as to bridge
height and width and her lips were thin.

From the marriage of these two quadroons there resulted seven
children: John, Lilla, Edward, James, Georgia, Charles, and Florence,
the last-named two having died in infancy. Of the five older children,
except Edward, all were married and had children in the following
numbers: John, five; Lilla, five; James (who married late), one; and
Georgia, three children by two husbands, she having been a widow for
an interim of eight years.

John, Lilla, James, and Florence inherited the dark hair, dark eyes,
and creamy complexion of the mother, while Edward, Georgia, and
Charles inherited the light, reddish brown hair, and mixed eyes of the
father as well as the ruddy complexion. Although neither father nor
mother had blue eyes, one of the children had greenish gray eyes and
one hazel.

While hair color was almost equally divided in the children between light and very dark, hair form varied only slightly. Curly hair,
inherited by James Fagain, 1/4N, from Nancy Knight, 1/2 N, seems to
have been lost to a great extent in the children of James Fagain and

Caroline Reese, 1/4N, whose hair was of the low waved variety. Hair curve diminishes in this family through the three generations. The hair of all the children might easily be classed as having low waves, but those with lighter hair have a slight fuzziness at the front.

No prognathism is noticeable in any of the quadroons and none show more than moderate lip thickness. Nasal tips are in all cases of medium thickness and alae of moderate breadth. Nasal bridges are high or of medium height and narrow to medium in breadth.

The two most widely distinct types of the living children, Georgia and Lilla, illustrate the range of variations. Lilla, having the most negroid features, has the straightest hair. Georgia, the least negroid, has the lightest and most frizzly hair. This frizzliness, however, seems to be confined to the front of the hair and tendrils at the base of the neck.

C29 STEWART-BOND (PLATES 34,35)

Georgia Fagain married Moses Stewart, 5/8N 1/8I 2/8W, in 1888. Of this union was born one daughter, Caroline, who is married but has no children. In 1905 Georgia Fagain was again married, to John Bond, 3/4N 1/4W, from which union there came two children, Wenonah and John.

John Bond was the son of John Bond, a mulatto sailor who was born in Liverpool, and an approximately full-blooded Negro woman. He inherited a slight degree of alveolar prognathism from her, also a slightly pendulous, everted lower lip. His hair was frizzly, but coarse and wiry rather than soft.

The two children in this family represent a type of variation similar to that shown in the Fagain family between the sisters Lilla and Georgia, i.e. Wenonah, the darker, of a dark olive complexion, has the darker, straighter hair, while John 3rd has light brown, frizzly hair and is a yellowish color. Before second dentition, however, the hair of the boy was of a blond color, and while somewhat curly was fine and silky. With the new teeth a new growth of coarser and darker hair took its place.

C21 DU BOIS (PLATE 50)

W.E.B. Du Bois, 5/8N 3/8W, apparently a third generation cross, has a light brown skin color with frizzly black hair, Grade A9. His nose is narrow-bridged, long, convex with moderate alae and a narrow tip. His lips are medium thickness, the lower being slightly heavier

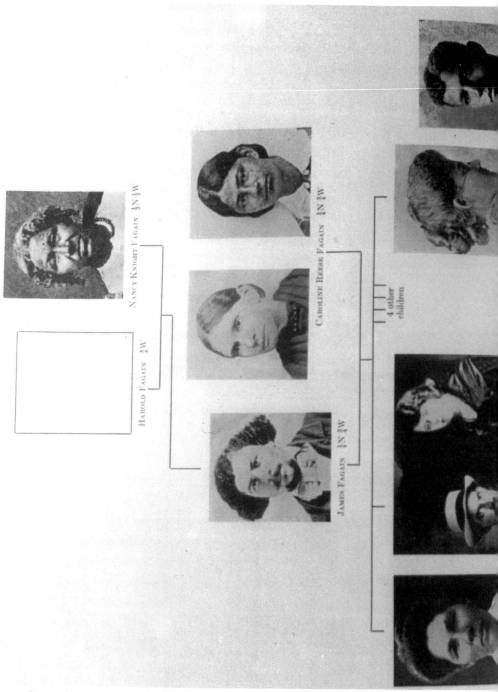

Day: three genealogical plates

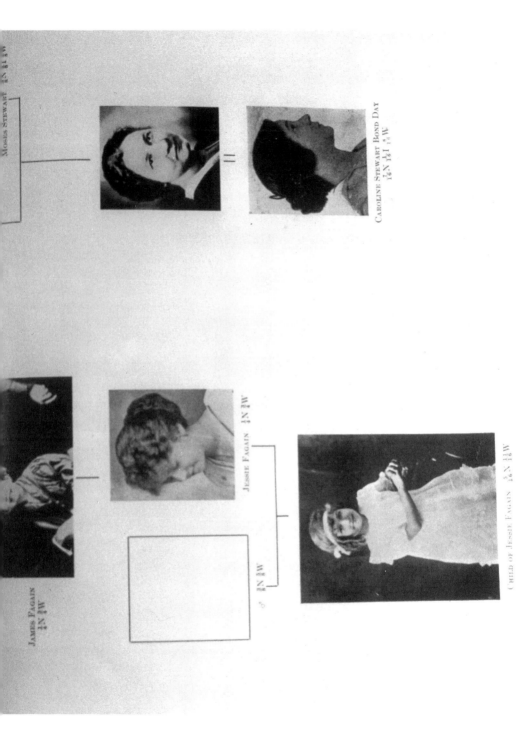

Moses Stewart ½N ¼I¼W

Caroline Stewart Bond Day
1⁄8 N 1 6/16 I 1⁄8 W

James Fagain ½N ½W

Jessie Fagain ½N ¾W

♂ ½N ¾W

Child of Jessie Fagain ⅜N ⅜W

PLATE 35

JOHN BOND ¼N ¼W (?)

MRS. J. P. BOND, SR., AND DAUGHTERS LENA AND MARY
¼N ⅜N ¼W

LENA MARY

JOHN BOND ⅜N ¼W

GEORGIA F. BOND ¼N ¾W
Second marriage

JOHN BOND III ¼N ½W

WENONAH BOND ½N ½W

Day: three genealogical plates

PLATE 50

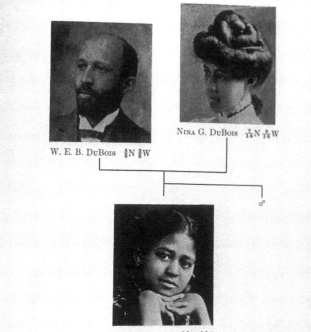

W. E. B. DuBois $\frac{5}{8}$N $\frac{3}{8}$W

NINA G. DuBois $\frac{7}{16}$N $\frac{9}{16}$W

YOLANDE DuBois $\frac{17}{32}$N $\frac{15}{32}$W

than the upper.   He married Nina Gomer, 7/16N 9/16W, also a probable third generation cross on the paternal side.   Her mother was a French woman.

She has skin color #12, straight, rather coarse hair of exceedingly great length and abundance.   It has a high natural gloss.   Her features are medium, the nose being slightly thick at the tip.

They had two children, the eldest, a son, being the dominant, with a yellow skin color, light brown, curly hair, and gray-brown eyes.   The daughter is the recessive, being light brown in color with frizzly hair and a nose unlike either father or mother.   Her lips are medium.

The family is notable for the appearance in the daughter of distinctly more negroid features than occur in either parent.

(1932)

The Pink Hat

This hat has become to me a symbol. It represents the respective advantages and disadvantages of my life here. It is at once my magic-carpet, my enchanted cloak, my Aladdin's lamp. Yet it is a plain, rough, straw hat, "pour le sport," as was the recently famous green one.

Before its purchase, life was wont to become periodically flat for me. Teaching is an exhausting profession unless there are wells to draw from, and the soil of my world seems hard and dry. One needs adventure and touch with the main current of human life, and contact with many of one's kind to keep from "going stale on the job." I had not had these things and heretofore had passed back and forth from the town a more or less drab figure eliciting no attention.

Then suddenly one day with the self-confidence bred of a becoming hat, careful grooming, and satisfactory clothes I stepped on to a street car, and lo! the world was reversed. A portly gentleman of obvious rank arose and offered me a seat. Shortly afterwards as I alighted a comely young lad jumped to rescue my gloves. Walking on into the store where I always shopped, I was startled to hear the sales-girl sweetly drawl, "Miss or Mrs.?" as I gave the customary initials. I heard myself answering reassuringly "Mrs." Was this myself? I, who was frequently addressed as "Sarah." For you see this is south of the Mason and Dixon line, and I am a Negro woman of mixed blood unaccustomed to these respectable prefixes.

I had been mistaken for other than a Negro, yet I look like hundreds of other colored women—yellow-skinned and slightly heavy featured, with frizzy brown hair. My maternal grand-parents were Scotch-Irish and English quadroons; paternal grand-parents Cherokee Indian and full blooded Negro; but the ruddy pigment of the Scotch-Irish ancestry is my inheritance, and it is this which shows through my yellow skin, and in the reflection of my pink hat glows pink. Loosely speaking, I should be called a mulatto—anthropologically speaking, I am a dominant of the white type of the F^3 generation of secondary crossings. There is a tendency known to the initiated persons of mixed Negro blood in this climate to "breed white" as we say, propagandists to the contrary notwithstanding. In this sense the Proud Race is, as it were, really dominant. The cause? I'll save that for another time.

Coming back to the hat—when I realized what had made me the recipient of those unlooked for, yet common courtesies, I decided to experiment further.

So I wore it to town again one day when visiting an art store looking for prints for my school room. Here, where formerly I had met with indifference and poor service, I encountered a new girl today who was the essence of courtesy. She pulled out drawer after drawer of prints as we talked and compared from Giotto to Sargent. Yet she agreed that Giorgione had a sweet, worldly taste, that he was not sufficiently appreciated, that Titian did over-shadow him. We went back to Velasquez as the master technician and had about decided on "The Forge of Vulcan" as appropriate for my needs when suddenly she asked, "but where do you teach?" I answered, and she recognized the name of a Negro university. Well—I felt sorry for her. She had blundered. She had been chatting familiarly, almost intimately with a Negro woman. I spared her by leaving quickly, and murmured that I would send for the package.

My mood forced me to walk—and I walked on and on until I stood at the "curb-market." I do love markets, and at this one they sell flowers as well as vegetables. A feeble old man came up beside me. I noticed that he was near-sighted. "Lady," he began, "would you tell me—is them dahlias or peernies up there?" Then, "market smells so good—don't it?"

I recognized a kindred spirit. He sniffed about among the flowers, and was about to say more—a nice old man—I should have liked to stop and talk with him after the leisurely southern fashion, but he was a white old man—and I moved on hastily.

I walked home the long way and in doing so passed the city library. I thought of my far away Boston—no Abbey nor Puvis de Chauvannes here, no marble stairs, no spirit of studiousness of which I might become a part. Then I saw a notice of a lecture by Drinkwater at the women's club—I was starved for something good—and starvation of body or soul sometimes breeds criminals.

So then I deliberately set out to deceive. Now, I decided, I would enjoy all that had previously been impossible. When necessary I would add a bit of rouge and the frizzy hair (thanks to the marcel) could be crimped into smoothness. I supposed also that a well-modulated voice and assurance of manner would be assets.

So thus disguised, for a brief space of time, I enjoyed everything from the attentions of an expert Chiropodist, to grand opera, avoiding only the restaurants—I could not have borne the questioning eyes of colored waiters.

I would press on my Aladdin's lamp and presto, I could be comforted with a hot drink at the same soda-fountain where ordinarily I should have been hissed at. I could pull my hat down a bit and buy a ticket to see my favorite movie star while the play was still new.

I could wrap my enchanted cloak about me and have the decent comfort of ladies' rest-rooms. I could have my shoes fitted in the best shops, and be shown the best values in all of the stores—not the common styles "which all the darkies buy, you know." At one of these times a policeman helped me across the street. A sales-girl in the most human way once said, "I wouldn't get that, Sweetie, you and me is the same style and I know." How warming to be like the rest of the world, albeit a slangy and gum-chewing world!

But it was best of all of an afternoon when it was impossible to correct any more papers or to look longer at my own Lares and Penates, to sit upon my magic-carpet and be transported into the midst of a local art exhibit, to enjoy the freshness of George Inness and the vague charm of Brangwyn, and to see white-folk enjoying Tanner—really nice, likable, folk too, when they don't know one. Again it was good to be transported into the midst of a great expectant throng, awaiting the pealing of the Christmas carols at the Municipal Pageant. One could not enjoy this without compunction, however, for there was not a dark face to be seen among all of those thousands of people, and my two hundred bright-eyed youngsters should have been there.

Finally—and the last time that I dared upon my carpet, was to answer the call of a Greek play to be given on the lawn of a State University. I drank it all in. Marvellous beauty! Perfection of speech and gesture on a velvet greensward, music, color, life!

Then a crash came. I suppose I was nervous—one does have "horrible imaginings and present fears" down here, sub-conscious pictures of hooded figures and burning crosses. Anyway in hurrying out to avoid the crowd, I fell and broke an anklebone.

Someone took me home. My doctor talked plaster-casts. "No," I said, "I'll try osteopathy," but there was no chance for magic now. I was home in bed with my family—a colored family—and in a colored section of the town. A friend interceded with the doctor whom I had named. "No," he said, "it is against the rules of the osteopathic association to serve Negroes."

I waited a day—perhaps my foot would be better—then they talked bone-surgery. I am afraid of doctors. Three operations have been enough for me. Then a friend said, "try Christian Science." Perhaps I had been taking matters too much in my own hands, I thought. Yes, that would be the thing. Would she find a practitioner for me?

Dear, loyal daughter of New England—as loyal to the Freedmen's children as she had been to them. She tried to spare me. "They will give you absent treatments and when you are better we will go down." I regret now having said, "Where, to the back door?" What was the need of wounding my friend?

Besides, I have recovered somehow—I am only a wee bit lame now. And mirabile dictu! My spirit has knit together as well as my bones. My hat has grown useless. I am so glad to be well again, and back at my desk. My brown boys and girls have become reservoirs of interest. One is attending Radcliffe this year. My neighborly friend needs me now to while away the hours for her. We've gone back to Chaucer and dug out forgotten romances to be read aloud. The little boy next door has a new family of Belgian hares with which we play wonderful games. And the man and I have ordered seed catalogues for spring.

Health, a job, young minds and souls to touch, a friend, some books, a child, a garden, Spring! Who'd want a hat?

Opportunity: A Journal of Negro Life (1926)

Race Crossings in the United States

Here is an account of the results of three scientific studies of race intermixture in the United States done by graduate students at Harvard and Chicago universities.

One of the phases of the race problem which is of vital interest to the public yet least written about, is the question of intermarriage and race mixture. Few popular writers have dared attempt the subject and few scientists have had sufficient material at their disposal to warrant venturing conclusions.

At the present time, however, there are three unpublished studies on this subject which might prove interesting if reviewed in a cursory manner. One of them is an article entitled "The Social Significance of the Intermixture of Races in the Colonial and National Period," by James H. Johnston, Jr.; another is entitled "Race Crosses," by George T. Dixon, and both are careful analyses of the subject from the historical and literary standpoints, respectively. The first, a scholarly study which served as a thesis for the M.A. degree of the author at Chicago University, is a careful compilation of data taken from innumerable old records and arranged into a most coherent and illuminative treatise. The latter is a thorough and comprehensive survey of more recent literature, covering the ground from approximately the period between 1864 to 1926. This work was also done under the supervision of the Department of Anthropology of Chicago University. The third is the report of an original investigation made by myself under the auspices of the Bureau of International Research of Harvard University and Radcliffe College,[1] and has as its subject "The Sociological, Genealogical and Physiological Aspects of Negro-

[1]This research was done under the direction of Dr. E.A. Hooton of the Department of Anthropology, Harvard University.

White Crosses in the United States." The emphasis here is placed on such data as was obtained from living subjects in 1927-8, in contrast to that of the other two papers which consist largely of evidence from documents and other treatises.

As it happens, these three articles form a chronological trio in that they cover, through their bibliographies (which, in the first two instances, are very extensive) what has been said and done in this field in the United States from colonial times to the present. Furthermore, it is significant that although these studies were prepared independently, there is a continuity of thought running through them which, to a slight extent, amounts to overlapping. They might be listed, therefore, in the following chronological order:

1. "The Social Significance of the Intermixture of the Races in the Colonial and National Period" (1630-1864)
2. "Race Crosses" (1864-1926)
3. "The Sociological, Genealogical, and Physiological Significance of Negro-White Crosses in the United States" (1926-1929)

In the first article of the series Mr. Johnston has analyzed the immense mass of data gathered on his subject.

Upon the question of the intermixture between Negroes and Indians, the significant points of interest to me are the facts, first, that during the Colonial Period the same attitude of mind was exercised toward the Indian as toward the Negro on the part of the white man, and second, that there was an extremely sympathetic attitude existing between Negroes and Indians. These points are illustrated by the following quotation from Mr. Johnston: "In the colonial period there was also much mixture of the Indian with the Negro, both the slave and free Negro. Sympathies existed between the two races. It is interesting to note that in the massacre of 1622, not a Negro was slain. Neither law nor social barriers forbade the intermixture of the Indian and the Negro, both shared the antipathies of the white man, while as slaves their treatment differed in no essential degree. Conditions of their life, slave and free, often led to the union of these races, also the final extinction of Indian Slavery was, in part, due to the absorption of the Indian Slave by the more numerous Negro."

Concerning Negro and Indian marriages, one of the interesting quotations which he gives from other sources is the following from E. A. Kendell in "Travels Through the Northern Part of the United

States." "There was much of Negro and Indian intermixture in New Jersey and Massachusetts. The fact that in Massachusetts the children of an Indian mother would be declared free is said to have served as a temptation to the Negro to take Indian wives."

Under the larger topic of intermixture between Negroes and Whites Mr. Johnston begins his treatment by citing specific laws against intermarriage such as those made in Maryland in 1664, and in Virginia [in] 1671. He stresses the significance of those laws. Then he traces the development of the present attitude of the South on this question as it grew through two centuries of a system of concubinage. Many interesting "side-lights" are thrown on this system by quotations from a successive series of letters, memoirs and records of the times. He also cites specific cases of individuals which are supported by ample documentary evidence before advancing any of the generalizations which he makes.

Perhaps however, one of the most pertinent conclusions reached concerning this long era of attempted repression of human passion is not given by Mr. Johnston himself, but is one which he quotes from the Edinburgh Review of March 1827 and which reads as follows:

"Contemporary testimony seems to support the belief that the long established laws prohibiting intermarriage between Negroes and whites tended to increase rather than to hinder the intermixture of races."

Mr. Dixon deals also with the same three groups of crossings as does Mr. Johnston, namely, Negroes and whites, Negroes and Indians, and Indians and whites. However, he considers them purely from the standpoint of the physical anthropologist, whereas Mr. Johnston's material is more that of the sociologist and the historian.

Mr. Dixon says of his own paper: "It is largely a review of the literature upon the subject, with an attempt to present the evidence in a brief and concise form. Unfortunately very little counteractive work has been done upon the subject. There are few records of extended measurements and genealogies, which would allow for compilation and comparison with the work of others. Most of the literature contains merely hypotheses and opinions based upon casual observations. How largely these opinions are colored by the personal views of the authors is impossible to state."

Nevertheless, he gives us a most careful analysis of the works of such writers as Boas, Davenport, Reuter, Rowe, Castle and Herskovits, and then as a result of his own study he advances the following summary and conclusions:

"So little definite work has been done upon the subject and so few cases studied, in which genealogies have been obtained, that we can draw few definite conclusions. In many cases results contradict each other. In some instances students have assumed that they were dealing with mixtures of pure-bloods, when in reality there had been previous intermixture, which fact has materially colored the results obtained. How far environmental and sociological factors have entered in to alter results is not yet known. We are not agreed on all the criteria of race; nor have we any satisfactory method of measuring intelligence. Not being able to definitely analyze the pure-blood race, we are still farther afield and encounter numerous other problems in our study of the hybrid groups."

However, the data presented seem to Mr. Dixon to substantiate the following tentative conclusions:

1. In general hybrids tend to be intermediate to the parents in general body form and all other characteristics which are not usually considered distinctly racial.
2. In skin color the tendency is for the hybrid to more closely approach the darker parent. This is explained by the fact that he has inherited a positive skin pigmentation on one side and a blank on the other.
3. In regard to hair, the exceptions to any rule, which might be formulated, seem too numerous to make the statement interesting.
4. Hybrids are as fertile as the parent races. If there is any difference, it seems to be in favor of the hybrid race.
5. Variability within the group is very much higher than in the full-blood races.
6. In general the hybrid is more intelligent than the more backward of the two full-blooded races. However, this fact seems accounted for by the difference in environmental conditions and social status and not as the result of inheritance.

The third paper of the series furnishes just the material which Mr. Dixon at the time of writing his article, felt was lacking. It represents a genealogical study of a limited number of families of mixed blood. While it proposes to be a study of the mulatto family (to use the term loosely) it also involves, naturally, the records of many Indian-Negro and Indian-White unions, as well as the Negro-White crosses.

We have records of 2,537 adults included in this series, representing 346 families. This material was gathered by the questionnaire method, and records substantiating their evidence are on file at the Peabody Museum at Harvard University.

Naturally the sociological topics of this paper coordinate with certain general theories brought out in Mr. Johnston's work. But a consideration of the physiological characteristics of the group, under such headings as "Personal Appearance", and "Health", brings us into the field of physical anthropology as does Mr. Dixon's article. A discussion of the latter type of scientific investigation involves, however, an explanation of terminology and scientific laws which the length of this article does not permit. Furthermore, my findings from real life in this field are with one exception, so similar to Mr. Dixon's conclusion that with reference only to that exception, I shall pass on to other more general subject matter.

He states as the second item of his conclusions, that there is a tendency for the hybrid to approach the skin color of the darker parent. While this may seem plausible theoretically, I have not observed it to be true. In primary crosses between white and blacks the skin color is usually intermediate. In second and third generation crosses between the mulattoes studied here, there is much variability, but as many of the offspring resemble the fairer parents as the darker. In fact, we have observed a tendency on the part of mixed bloods in this country to "breed white" as we say.

Let us then look at some of the facts brought out by the testimonies of the questionnaires which are substantiated by the documentary evidence from the first article.

First, the large admixture of Indian blood as reported by half of the Negroes questioned, seems most plausible in the light of the laws and customs mentioned above.

Another interesting feature which our summaries disclose is the high percentage of persons of mixed blood who have been absorbed into the white group with or without knowledge of this blood. About 20 per cent of these families in this group have one or more members who are "passing" as it is commonly called. This does not include those who temporarily leave the family ranks for economic or other reasons of convenience, and eventually return. One of the greatest handicaps in collecting this material was caused by the reluctance of the members of such families to place on record any information which might serve later as a means of identifying such relatives.

Contrary to the popular idea, that one must be a quadroon or an

octoroon to "pass," some persons of little more than one-half white
blood (particularly if there be a slight strain of Indian) are frequently
mistaken for Europeans, and are often addressed as Spaniards or
Italians. This is a point on which the American public seems to be
most stupid. One reason no doubt is the fact that many Negroes
themselves have been mistaken in their calculations and when
questioned have misrepresented themselves as having from an eighth
to a fourth more white blood than they really possess.

A large part of this misapprehension has been caused by a lack of
knowledge of the laws of inheritance. The extreme variability
sometimes seen in the third generation crossings of mulattoes, may
produce two brothers of very different types, one of whom might be
easily considered an octoroon and the other a mulatto. These persons
of the fairer type, then, when referred to by distant descendants, have,
sometimes been identified as quadroons or octoroons until evidence
from some other branch of the family, or friends of the family have
counteracted this opinion. Hence, the almost incredible amount of
"passing" done in this country is readily understood when we realize
that if persons of approximately only one-half white blood can be
mistaken for quadroons or octoroons, certainly the quadroons and
octoroons have long ceased to be suspected of identification with this
group at all.

Mr. Johnston tells the ridiculous story of one Monsieur Dukey
from New Orleans, who visited the city of Memphis in the year of
1838, and who, because of his charming personality was received by
the best society, entertained elaborately, and made the recipient of
many favors. He then returned home, laid aside his grand manner,
and his French name, and resumed his real role of quadroon barber.
Many such instances sufficiently far removed by time, might be quoted
to show the gullibility of the white man then as now, when he refuses
to believe that a person of culture, charm and physical attractions can
have any appreciable amount of Negro blood.

Again, our evidence that the volume of white blood inherited by
this group is not all from the poorer class of whites or from white
males, is augmented by Mr. Johnston's records of settlements of
money and grants of land shown on county records by prominent
white citizens in the colonial and national periods. Out of our group
of 346 families, 114 of them bore the names and had some personal
reminiscence of their white progenitors. In 76 cases there were
heirlooms, photographs, and in some cases other unmistakable proof

of these relationships. There were twenty instances of white mothers, 11 of these, however, were foreign born.

Other points of interest which were found by the summarizing of these statistics were: the fact of an undiminishing birth-rate, only a moderate number of deaths from pulmonary troubles, and a favorable amount of property owned in relation to the salaries of the wage earners.

However, the most significant, to the average reading citizen, would probably be those figures which show the cultural and educational achievements of the group. Representatives from 50 of these families have had European travel, 20 have the degree of Master of Arts, 5 have the degree of Ph.D. and 5 are Phi Beta Kappa members out of 40 who have attended colleges where it is granted. There are many others who are without degrees, yet who are teachers and professional persons of great influence and high standing in their respective communities.

Yet, this study was by no means attempted as any proof of the superiority of the mixed blood over the full-blooded Negro. In fact interesting comparisons have occurred all through the compilation of the data, to refute such a theory. The two wealthiest men of the group were, one almost white and one almost black; and again two of the most intellectual, were exact opposites as to color and type.

However, some of the older theories concerning mulattoes do seem to be refuted by the data concerning this group. One is, that in the third generation mulattoes become infertile, another that the mental and physical calibre of mulattoes is inferior to either parent stock. Perhaps, most vicious of all is the popular superstition that two fair colored people or one colored person fair enough to be mistaken for white, and a white person, are apt to produce a black child. We have found no evidence to prove the truth of any of these theories.

The Crisis (1930)

*Marcus Garvey in annual U.N.I.A. convention parade,
New York City, 1922*

MARCUS GARVEY

Marcus Mosiah Garvey was born in St. Ann's Bay, Jamaica, on 17 August 1887, the youngest of eleven children. A period of foreign travel, observation, and reading (1909–14) led him on his return to Jamaica to found the Universal Negro Improvement Association, whose goal was "the general uplift of the Negro peoples of the world," and whose motto was "One God! One Aim! One Destiny!" Making little headway at home, he moved to New York's Harlem in 1916 and found fertile ground for an unprecedented black mass movement. Branches of his U.N.I.A. arose around the country, and he raised more money than any other black person before or since. With his steamship company, the *Black Star Line*, he instilled racial pride.

Garvey was convicted of mail fraud in 1925. President Coolidge commuted his five-year sentence in 1927 and ordered his deportation. Finding too much opposition to his endeavors in Jamaica, he spent the last five years of his life in relative obscurity in London, where he died on 10 June 1940. But his decade in the United States had anticipated the modern Black Power movement by a half century.

A Note on Marcus Garvey at Harvard

JOHN M. FITZGERALD AND OTEY M. SCRUGGS

The standard interpretation of relations between Marcus Garvey's black zionism and the black intelligentsia is that they were antagonistic.[1] Does it follow, however, that because few black intellectuals

---

[1]See, for example, Tony Martin, *Race First: The Ideological and Organizational Struggles of Marcus Garvey and the Universal Negro Improvement Association* (Westport, Conn.: Greenwood Press, 1976), esp. chap. 11. The book is in many ways an excellent study of the Garvey movement.

joined Garvey that most opposed him? Or that because a handful of middle class blacks prominent among socialists or in the N.A.A.C.P. seem to have played an important role in Garvey's downfall that most blacks—middle class included—believed that "Garvey must go"? Larger questions obtrude themselves here. How wide, after all, is the chasm between black nationalism and the struggle for full citizenship rights in America? Did not Garvey and non-Garveyites share the same compelling desire for human dignity, especially in their condemnation of the treatment accorded blacks by whites and in a similar desire to advance the interests of the black group? Perhaps a little-known incident of over a half-century ago might help bring these issues into clearer focus.

On a spring evening in 1922,[*] at the height of his power and influence, Marcus Garvey came to a Harvard University which was racially segregated in nearly all respects save the classroom. He came to address the Nile Club, a group composed of all the several dozen black students in the university. Following dinner in the Harvard Union, the charismatic guest of honor spoke at length to the assembled students of his program for the worldwide emancipation of the Negro through the development of racial unity and black pride. The meeting lasted well into the evening, a good deal of time being devoted by the dynamic black leader in responding to students' questions. Of especial interest both to Garvey and the students was the role blacks trained in business, education, and political and military organization might play in the program of black redemption.

Founded a few months earlier, the Nile Club, suggestive of the Black Student Unions of a later generation, was one of the many institutions formed by assertive, race-conscious blacks in the first quarter of the twentieth century in the face of the virulent, widespread hatred of blacks among whites throughout the country. The Club was organized to bring together Negro students on the racist Harvard campus to stimulate interest in black affairs by entertaining the views of outstanding black thinkers and doers. Besides Garvey, for example, such men as W.E.B. Du Bois and William S. Braithwaite, Negro poet and literary critic, addressed the group. That its cultural and political concerns went beyond the confines of the United States

---

[*]In Genna McNeil's *Groundwork: Charles H. Houston* (1983), pp. 51, 260, the date of this gathering is reported to have been January 1921.—Eds.

to embrace the world as far away as Africa is evinced not only by its name and in its choice of guests but by its emblem, pyramid and palm tree.[2] Paradoxically, like Garvey this group of young blacks, some of whom had served overseas during World War I, was moving in the direction of internationalism at the same time white America was attempting to withdraw from the rest of the world behind "fortress America."

Opinions about Garvey among Club members were mixed when not ambivalent. To some he was a "show-off" and a "fool." Others viewed him as a "West Indian schemer" intent upon promoting his own and his countrymen's interests at the expense of American blacks. Most, however, came to hear the most famous black man of his day, who was at the same time a magnetic speaker, articulate what they had always thought about white treatment of blacks and to ponder the implications of his solution to the race problem by means of black self-help and race pride. Among this group, unquestionably, was Charles Houston, the Club's presiding officer.

Charles Hamilton Houston [LL.B. 1922, S.J.D. 1923] was a many-sided person: brilliant, sensitive, playful, highly organized and disciplined, universalist in outlook, unswervingly devoted to excellence and its application to the cause of black advancement, and imbued with the ideal of service to the group.[3] Graduating Phi Beta Kappa from Amherst in 1915 at the age of 19, he had already demonstrated his interest in Black Studies by writing his honors thesis on the Negro poet, Paul Laurence Dunbar. Afterwards, he taught English in Howard University, served overseas as an officer of field artillery in America's Jim Crow army during World War I,[4] and returned home

[2]Such Africa-consciousness reminds one of some of the writings of the contemporary Negro Renaissance. For example in Langston Hughes' poem, "The Negro Speaks of Rivers," there is the line: "I looked upon the Nile and raised the pyramids above it."

[3]For an excellent brief treatment of Houston, see Genna Rae McNeil, "Charles Hamilton Houston," *The Black Law Journal*, III (Summer-Winter: 1973), 123-131.

[4]Houston seems to have viewed military organization and values with the utmost approbation. Not only did he undergo extensive military training during World War I, but as a schoolboy he was commander of the M Street

to face a white mob intent on the destruction of the black community of Washington, D.C. in 1919. During his Harvard days, Charlie Houston demonstrated those qualities of leadership that he was to display so prominently later when as dean he set out to turn the Howard Law School into "the West Point of Negro leadership," and as special counsel for the N.A.A.C.P. he was the "architect and dominant force in the legal program of that organization." In his third year in the Harvard Law School in 1922, Houston was student editor of the prestigious *Harvard Law Review*. But in him intelligence combined with concern for the welfare of others. Older than most students at Harvard, he manifested an abiding brotherly interest in the progress of his younger fellow blacks on campus.[5] Doubtless already settling in Charlie Houston's mind was the conviction that black advancement would only result from black effort.

As presiding officer, the responsibility was Houston's to introduce the distinguished guest. One of the authors, John M. Fitzgerald, a member of the Nile Club and a close friend to Houston, vividly recalls that when the dinner was completed, Houston excused the three white student waiters, asking them to close the door behind them. When they had departed, according to Mr. Fitzgerald, Houston, intending that there be no misunderstanding among his colleagues where he stood, launched with feeling into the following introduction of Marcus

High School (Washington, D.C.) military unit. This partiality toward the military, which clearly did not include its racist policies, seems to have had an impact on his thought. As mentioned [below], he spoke of turning Howard Law School into the "West Point of Negro leadership." In his eulogy, close friend and associate, William Hastie [LL.B. 1930, S.J.D. 1933], said of him that "he had a soldier's faith that winning the fight is all that matters . . ." Garvey, too, had a strong predilection for things military; a case in point is his paramilitary organization, the African Legion. Can it not be said that the two men shared values not uncommon to the military: brotherhood, unity, discipline, service and the need for effective leadership?

[5]The authors wish to thank Mr. Earl Brown [A.B. 1924] of New York City, former editor for Time-Life, ex-member of the New York City Council, and like Mr. Fitzgerald, a long-time friend to Charles Houston, for sharing with us his knowledge of Mr. Houston. He too attended the Nile Club meeting at which Marcus Garvey spoke.

Garvey:

Honored guest and fellow members of the Nile Club, I'd have to say that this is the most exciting moment of my entire educational experience, both as a student and teacher, here at Harvard and elsewhere.

In my capacity as presiding officer of this club, an organization that was conceived for just such purposes as tonight's, I am pleased and privileged to present to you a man whom I personally regard as being not only the greatest leader of men since Moses,[6] but a bearer of good will to all persons of African descent everywhere.

Gentlemen: The Honorable Marcus Garvey, Provisional President of All Africa.

With due allowance for the hyperbole demanded by the occasion, Houston's statement suggests larger questions. Was there not more admiration for Garvey among Negroes of all classes than is commonly supposed? Not only did his indictment of whites fall on receptive ears; so did his view that blacks were a people with a worthy past and a promising future. How different, after all, was the race consciousness of Charlie Houston from Marcus Garvey's? Did not their devotion to race pride, self-reliance, and service to the group constitute a stronger bond than whatever programmatic differences may have separated them? Does not the existence of the Nile Club, like Garvey's U.N.I.A., reflect the quest for an African identity that has existed among American blacks for centuries? Did not Charlie Houston too place a premium on the world-wide unity of Africans in the struggle for human dignity? "He viewed the oppressed condition of Black Americans, Native Americans, colonized Africans, and others, as intolerable," writes Genna Rae McNeil, "and the struggle as indivisible."[7] Indeed, does not his introduction of Garvey on that spring night back in 1922 suggest the cosmopolitan orientation of

---

[6]Ironically, Hastie in his eulogy of Houston nearly thirty years later, spoke of his departed friend as the Moses of the journey through the legal wilderness of second-class citizenship. Given the analogy that blacks as a people well-grounded in biblical lore have always made between their own and the predicament of the ancient Israelites, the comparison of black leaders with Moses is neither new nor coincidental.

[7]McNeil, 131.

oppressed peoples in identifying with all humanity? Was it not the awareness of their submerged position and the commitment to struggle against it that led those black students away from parochialism while white Americans, insecure in their power, struggled vainly to return to isolation and to retain a nonexistent racial purity?[8] For us, looking back, is not this fearless reaching out to embrace others while paradoxically emphasizing black self-reliance, in the final analysis, what bound Marcus Garvey and Charles Houston together as brothers?

The authors wish to thank Professor Lawrence C. Howard [Ph.D. 1956] of the University of Pittsburgh for his contribution to the initial idea of the project. [Note by John M. Fitzgerald and Otey M. Scruggs.]

Journal of Negro History (1978)

[8]The war, of course, was a major influence on the students' internationalism. While all were affected by it, a number of Club members like Houston had served overseas with the A.E.F. Another fact not to be undervalued in their cosmopolitan outlook was the presence of West Indian students on black campuses. Several years previously, for example, Mr. Fitzgerald had a Jamaican room-mate at Howard University.

THE HARVARD DORMITORY CRISIS (1921-23)

The New Negro on Campus

RAYMOND WOLTERS

Harvard's President A. Lawrence Lowell touched off the most publicized college discrimination controversy of the 1920s when he simultaneously barred Negroes from the freshman dormitories and inaugurated a quota system for Jewish students. Lowell's rationale was doubtless complex, but he appears to have been motivated essentially by a desire not to offend white racists and to maintain Harvard's aristocratic tradition. The exclusion of blacks was relatively easy to explain: Residence in the freshman dormitories had recently been made compulsory, Lowell noted, and "we have not thought it possible to compel men of different races to reside together. . . . We owe to the colored man the same opportunities for education that we do to the white man; but we do not owe it to him to force him and the white into social relations that are not, or may not be, mutually congenial."[1]

It was more difficult to explain the limitation of Jews. Lowell claimed that "anti-Semitic feeling is increasing, and it grows in proportion to the increase in the number of Jews." Behind this heightened ethnocentrism lay the fear that admission of large numbers of Jews somehow threatened the dominance of Harvard's established

[1]A. Lawrence Lowell to Roscoe Conkling Bruce, quoted in *New York Age*, 20 January 1923; Lowell to Lewis Gannett, 19 June 1922, Papers of Moorfield Storey, Library of Congress (hereafter cited as Storey Papers); James Weldon Johnson to Lowell, 11 January 1923, NAACP Files.

Roscoe C. Bruce in 1902   *James Weldon Johnson ca. 1902*

Raymond Pace Alexander ca. 1949   Charles W. Chesnutt ca. 1898

tradition. Many of the Jewish students of the early twentieth century were poor, of east-European extraction, and extraordinarily competitive in the classroom while withdrawing from social and athletic life. They were said to "live at home, eat a pocket lunch on the college campus, and leave the university grounds to earn the money for their tuition by night work. Many retain the gregariousness born of life in the Pale, and remain only half-assimilated." There were some Harvard men who believed that these new immigrants endangered the essential Harvard tradition—the flavor that stamped Harvard men as such, in no way to be confused with Yale men, Princeton men, or any other of the many academic breeds. Old Grads allegedly sent their sons to Harvard to attain this flavor, rather than any mere scholarly training, and there were those who claimed that the masters of the institution owed it "to themselves and to the alumni and to everyone else revering the name of Harvard, to maintain the conditions under which this flavor may be imparted."[2]

Summarizing this argument, the *New Republic* noted,

The Harvard flavor can be imparted successfully to men of any race or religion. . . . But it is not to be denied that the flavor is most easily imparted to men of the old New England stock. Others take it effectively only when they are well immersed in social groupings of the original character. They must therefore be present in relatively small numbers. . . . Five Jews to the hundred will necessarily undergo prompt assimilation. Ten Jews to the hundred might assimilate. But twenty or thirty—no. They would form a state within a state. They would cease to take an active part in the general life of the college. . . . What they got out of Harvard might be worth their time and effort, but it would not be the priceless Harvard flavor. Thus it appears that, in the interest of the Jews as well as in the interest of the Gentiles, the number of Jews ought to be kept below the saturation point. Better one true Jewish Harvard man than ten mere Jewish scholars.[3]

President Lowell's racist policies were ultimately repudiated by Harvard's board of overseers. The overseers did not reach their decision without prompting, however, for thousands of students,

[2]A. Lawrence Lowell, quoted in *Literary Digest* 74 (8 July 1922): 28-29; *Nation* 114 (14 June 1922): 708; *New Republic* 31 (16 August 1922): 322-323.

[3]*New Republic* 31 (16 August 1922); 322-323.

professors, and alumni organized to protest against the intrusion of racism at Fair Harvard. James Weldon Johnson was undoubtedly correct when he noted that "President Lowell never for a moment imagined that he was going to raise such a hornet's nest around his ears." Du Bois was uplifted by the protest. "Deep as is the shame and humiliation of Harvard's recent surrender to the Bourbon South," he declared, "the spirited and whole-souled response that it has evinced is perhaps the most heartening sign of sanity on the race problem that has happened in fifty years. Not a single person of importance has yet dared to defend Lowell. . . . " Black and white liberals were convinced that Lowell had taken "an evil and indefensible position which, like a snake, must be scotched at once . . . or else it will, with its venomous bite, poison our entire educational system." Lowell's racist policy was thought to be "as bad for what it portends as for what it immediately inaugurates."[4]

Although it was generally acknowledged that Lowell's Jewish and Negro policies were fundamentally related, most blacks felt that their problem was more manageable than that of the Jews. Lewis Gannett, an editor of the *Nation* who circulated an alumni petition on behalf of the blacks, explained, "The question of discrimination against one class of students after their admission seems to have a much more certain answer than the question of limitation of enrollment."[5]

Blacks insisted that, as Raymond Pace Alexander put it, "no half-dozen men picked at random among the Harvard freshman class could present any better family history or training" than the six blacks who had been excluded from the dormitories. Bertram C. Bland and William J. Knox, Jr., were from eminently respectable New England families; Cecil Blue was the son of a prominent Washington physician; Pritchett Klugh was the son of a distinguished Boston clergyman; Edward W. Wilson was a second generation Harvard man and the son of a noted Boston attorney; and Roscoe Conkling Bruce, Jr., was the

[4]*New York Times*, 10 April 1923; James Weldon Johnson to Butler R. Wilson, 27 January 1923; NAACP Files; W.E.B. Du Bois, "Harvard," *Crisis* 25 (March 1923): 199; *Messenger* 5 (March 1923): 621.

[5]Lewis Gannett to Moorfield Storey, 2 August 1922, Storey Papers; William B. Hixson, Jr., *Moorfield Storey and the Abolitionist Tradition* (New York: Oxford University Press, 1972), p. 120.

son of a Harvard honors graduate and the grandson of a United States senator. Lowell's discrimination against these thoroughly acculturated blacks struck at the very foundation of the middle-class ethos, and this may explain the fervor with which Harvard's president was condemned by the black and white bourgeoisie.[6]

The *New York Amsterdam News* noted that Lowell's discrimination against young Bruce "should convince all of us that our success is not dependent upon individual attainment. The younger Bruce . . . is the grandson of Blanche K. Bruce, former Register of the United States Treasury and United States Senator from Mississippi from 1875 to 1881. His father is a distinguished educator. But to President Lowell and to thousands like him the younger Bruce's distinguished ancestry and preparation are as nothing when placed alongside of the fact that he is a Negro."[7]

The campaign against Harvard's exclusion of Negroes from the freshman dormitories began on the campus in the spring of 1922 when the black students, led by upperclassman* Edwin B. Jourdain, Jr., at that time the world's champion broad jumper, made a special appeal to President Lowell. This was to no avail, and editor Monroe Trotter of the *Boston Guardian*, a black alumnus who fondly recalled "the democracy that I enjoyed at dear old Harvard," then publicized the matter. During the summer Moorfield Storey, Robert Benchley, Lewis Gannett, and four other white alumni circulated a petition among two hundred Harvard men. Altogether some 145 graduates endorsed a statement expressing dismay that "the long tradition of the College as regards Negroes has been broken." It was not sufficient, the graduates insisted, for President Lowell to say that Southern men did not want to live in the same dormitories with blacks. Southern men who came to Cambridge could not rightfully expect the college to surrender its "Northern ideas of democracy" and its "Harvard ideals of justice." One graduate expressed the prevailing spirit when he

[6]Raymond Pace Alexander, "Voices from Harvard's Own Negroes," *Opportunity* 1 (March 1923): 29.

[7]*New York Amsterdam News*, 17 January 1923.

*Jourdain received his degree in 1921, and was a student at the Business School in 1921-22.—Eds.

added, "If any young man should decline to come because of this prejudice against some possible comrade I should say that the college was well rid of so narrow-minded a youth."[8]

In their private correspondence many Harvard men explained their reasons for opposing Lowell's racist policies. George R. Nutter noted that "the hope that individual merit will eventually receive its proper consideration lies at the very basis of what our institutions are trying to accomplish. . . . If a man is found worthy to enter Harvard College, he is worthy to stand on his merits without any of the artificial distinctions of race or color." Roscoe Conkling Bruce, Sr., admitted that "the wind just now is blowing in the direction of reaction," but he insisted that it did not behoove "a great center of enlightenment to be caught, like some paltry straw, in the gust." Moorfield Storey feared that "if Harvard College caters to this unchristian prejudice of some people against Negroes and other people against Jews . . . , it will be responsible for more mischief in this country and the policy will do more injury to the College than those who favor it can possibly conceive." Congressman Hamilton Fish declared that racial discrimination was not consistent with "the spirit of democracy . . . the spirit of New England . . . the spirit of Harvard."[9]

John Jay Chapman pointed out that Southerners were quite accustomed to living in close proximity to blacks.

If any white parent tells President Lowell that he cannot bear the thought of his son's sleeping in a room which abuts on the same quadrangle with a Negro's room, or eating in the same dining-hall with a Negro, that parent deceives Mr. Lowell. What the Southern parent demands is that some stigma be put upon the Negro. He wishes Harvard to hang out a flag

----

[8]Alexander, "Voices from Harvard's Own Negroes," pp. 28-29; Stephen R. Fox, *The Guardian of Boston* (New York: Atheneum, 1970), pp. 261-263; Open Letter to the President and Fellows of Harvard College, attached to Lewis Gannett to Moorfield Storey, 2 June 1922, Storey Papers; *Nation* 116 (31 January 1923): 112.

[9]George R. Nutter, quoted in Lewis Gannett to Moorfield Storey, 26 July 1922, Storey Papers; Roscoe Conkling Bruce telegram to *Brooklyn Eagle,* 13 January 1923, NAACP Files; Storey to Julian W. Mack, 6 June 1922, quoted in Hixson, *Moorfield Storey,* p. 120; Hamilton Fish to A. Lawrence Lowell, quoted in *New York Age,* 20 January 1923.

discriminating against the black man.[10]

This was exactly the point. The *Nation* noted that "Harvard, so long as it follows President Lowell's lead in this matter, is accepting and preaching the Southern doctrine that every man with Negro blood in his veins is inferior to every all-white man." The *New York Evening Post* claimed that Lowell's policy negated the very reason for creating the freshman dormitories: "If the policy of compulsory residence in the freshman halls is to be justified at all, it is precisely because it applies to all freshmen. To say that all white freshmen or all Protestant freshmen or all native American freshmen shall live together, but that all other freshmen shall be barred from the freshmen dormitories, is to make the policy of compulsory residence ludicrous." The *Harvard Alumni Bulletin* observed that "for Harvard to deny to colored men a privilege it accords to whites appears inevitably as a reversal of policy, if not a positive disloyalty to a principle for which the university has hitherto taken an open and unshaken stand."[11]

With the press and the alumni outspoken in their criticism, President Lowell was placed in an untenable position, especially since he had unwisely neglected to discuss the situation with Harvard's board of overseers. "It seems to be a pity that the matter ever came up in this way," wrote overseer Franklin D. Roosevelt. "There were certainly many colored students in Cambridge when we were there and no question ever arose." In January 1923 the overseers held a special meeting to discuss Lowell's racial policies, and a faculty committee was appointed to study the matter. This committee later reported that the principle of "equal opportunity for all, regardless of race and religion," was an essential part of Harvard's tradition. The professors warned that any "covert device to eliminate those deemed racially or socially undesirable" would be interpreted as "a dangerous surrender of traditional ideals." The overseers thereupon unanimously overruled Lowell and banned discrimination for reasons of race or religion. Affirming the Negro's right to equal opportunity on the

[10]John Jay Chapman, quoted in *Nation* 116 (31 January 1923): 112.

[11]*Nation*, 116: 112; *New York Post*, quoted in *Literary Digest* 76 (3 February 1923): 32-33; *Harvard Alumni Bulletin* 25 (1922-1923): 830.

campus, the overseers declared that no man should be excluded from the dormitories "by reason of his color."[12]

Unfortunately the resolution of the dormitory controversy did not usher in an era of interracial brotherhood at Harvard. Members of the various ethnic groups still tended to congregate together in search of familiar company, and the exclusive private clubs barred blacks, Jews, and low-status Gentiles. There were, in addition, nagging problems that followed from the Harvard Medical School's relations with nearby obstetrical clinics. Harvard required its medical students to handle a certain number of obstetrical cases, but problems inevitably arose because many patients at the clinics refused to accept the services of black students. Consequently, it had been customary for blacks to arrange for referrals from the Negro physicians of Boston and Cambridge. This undoubtedly involved racial discrimination, in that black students were treated differently from whites. Black egalitarians inevitably challenged the propriety of this practice.

A case in point occurred in 1905, when a young black by the name of E. D. Brown refused, in the words of Harvard's medical dean, "to accommodate himself to these circumstances which are beyond the jurisdiction of the School, and which other colored students have heretofore cheerfully accepted." Brown acknowledged that Harvard could not force patients to accept an unwelcome student intern, but he demanded "the chance to get the cases if I could." He asked the dean "to put it up to the patients and leave me to face whatever difficulty might arise. . . ." He thought it was far better that he be snubbed by prejudiced patients than that these insults should be used by Harvard as a justification for racial discrimination.[13]

From *The New Negro on Campus* (1975)

---

[12]Franklin D. Roosevelt to R. S. Wallace, 7 February 1923, quoted in Arthur M. Schlesinger, Jr., *The Age of Roosevelt: The Politics of Upheaval* (Boston: Houghton Mifflin Co., 1960), p. 696; *New York Times*, 10 April 1923.

[13]W.L. Richardson to Moorfield Storey, 8 December 1905, Storey Papers; E.D. Brown to Storey, 31 October 1905, Storey Papers; William Pickens to Roscoe Conkling Bruce, 15 January 1923, NAACP Files.

Colored Students at Harvard

Roscoe Conkling Bruce was born on 21 April 1879 in Washington, D.C., the only child of the first black to serve a full term as U.S. Senator. After preparation at Exeter Academy, he attended Harvard, where he demonstrated special talent in debating and served as president of the Debating Club. He was elected to Phi Beta Kappa, was Class Day orator, and took his degree *magna cum laude* in 1902. For several years he headed the academic department of Tuskegee Institute, then served for 13 years as superintendent of the colored schools in Washington. After short stints as a West Virginia school principal and a hen farmer, he became resident manager of the Paul Laurence Dunbar Apartments in Harlem, edited a biweekly newspaper, and did writing under his own name and under pseudonyms. He died in New York City on 16 August 1950.

President Lowell and Roscoe Conkling Bruce, '02, have recently had some correspondence in regard to the admittance of colored students to the Freshman Dormitories at Harvard. Bruce is principal of the Brown's Creek District High School at Kendall, W. Va. Some time ago he applied by letter for a reservation in one of the Freshman Halls for his son, who is a student at Phillips Exeter Academy and intends to enter Harvard College next fall. President Lowell replied as follows:

Dear Mr. Bruce: Your letter to the Registrar about your son has been given to me. I am sorry to have to tell you that in the Freshman Halls, where residence is compulsory, we have felt from the beginning the necessity of not including colored men. To the other dormitories and dining rooms they are admitted freely, but in the Freshman Halls I am sure you will understand why, from the beginning, we have not thought it possible to compel men of different races to reside together.

Bruce then dispatched the following letter to President Lowell:

Your letter of the 14th December reached me duly. I wrote to the Registrar in good faith and not for controversial purposes.
    My delay in responding to your letter is occasioned by my endeavor to

recover beforehand from the shock of your decision to refuse my son placement in the Freshman Halls specifically because he is an American of African descent, a decision applying a general policy upon which your administration has entered deliberately.

I have lived and labored in the South so long since my graduation from Harvard College over twenty years ago that, despite the newspapers, I had fondly cherished the illusion that, step by step with the unquestionable growth of liberal sentiment in the Southern States as a whole, New England was enriching rather than impoverishing her heritage.

The policy of compulsory residence in the Freshman Halls is costly indeed if it is the thing that constrains Harvard to enter open-eyed and brusque upon a policy of racial discrimination. It ill becomes a great mother of culture avoidably to accentuate the consciousness of racial differences among Americans—that seedbed of so many strifes and griefs. Not race, but culture, I had supposed, is the basis of sound nationality. Have the Germans taught us nothing? If America is the melting pot, education is the sacred fire. And Harvard has rendered herself through centuries of high endeavor the Nation's University.

It is my deliberate opinion that some of those young men who, like my son, are after all Negroes by election, will nullify the policy of exclusion so far as they themselves are concerned, by simply not confessing themselves members of the proscribed group. Neither a mental nor a blood test will expose that helpful duplicity. With respect to these individuals (and they outnumber popular estimates), may not the policy of exclusion have the curious effect of promoting that very amalgamation of races which the white North vies with the white South in affecting to dread? It is a thing, may I add in all candor, which all self-respecting Americans of color do not desire. And, be assured, no son of mine will ever deny his name or his blood or his tradition.

To proscribe a youth because of his race is a procedure as novel at Harvard until your administration as it is unscientific. However unpopular the Jew, the Irishman, and the Negro may be in certain minds and certain sections and at certain times (wartime not being one), the fact remains that the distribution of human excellence in each of these races, as in the case of every other race, begins at zero and ends at infinity.

The differences in racial excellence consist in the comparative numbers of individuals to be found in the higher reaches of the vast curve upward of human quality and serviceability. And to assess the relative values of the several stocks of mankind *en masse* is, one must concede, an exceedingly delicate and difficult, indeed perilous, task.

Who shall proscribe a Straus, a Plunkett or a Douglass because of his race? The particular individual may be a personality of charm and power and prospect absolutely apart from the theoretical frequency of inferiorities in the race. From kindergarten to university, I fain believe, the spirit of education approaches children and youth as individuals, not as racial symbols.

After Charles W. Eliot, Harvard cannot escape the grave responsibilities of leadership in American life. And one leads by ascent to higher levels after the manner of scholar and statesman, of poet and prophet; not by descent.

To me whose personal indebtedness to Harvard is immeasurable, the University is neither a mere mechanism of instruction nor a social club, but a centre of enlightenment and idealism and service rendered holy by aspiring centuries.

Few words in the English language, I submit, are susceptible of more poignant abuse than two you have seen fit to employ. The first is "race"; the second, "necessity." As the one is often nothing more than a term of social convenience, so the other is quite often a means of buttress[ing] prejudice. But, "veritas" is less elusive.

President Lowell subsequently sent the following letter to Bruce:

I am sorry that you do not feel the reasonableness of our position about the Freshman Dormitories. It is not a departure from the past to refuse to compel white and colored men to room in the same building. We owe to the colored man the same opportunities for education that we do to the white man; but we do not owe to him to force him and the white into social relations that are not, or may not be, mutually congenial.

We give him freely opportunities for room and board wherever it is voluntary; but it seems to me that for the colored man to claim that he is entitled to have the white man compelled to live with him is a very unfortunate innovation which, far from doing him good, would increase a prejudice that, as you and I will thoroughly agree, is most unfortunate and probably growing.

On the other hand, to maintain that compulsory residence in the Freshman Dormitories—which has proved a great benefit in breaking up the social cliques that did much injury to the College—should not be established for 99-1/2 per cent of the students because the remaining one-half of one percent could not properly be included, seems to me an untenable position.

Regretting very much that we should not agree upon the wisdom of the policy adopted for the Freshman Dormitories, I am,

Very truly yours,

A. Lawrence Lowell.

Harvard Alumni Bulletin (1923)

Attacks Harvard on Negro Question

J. Weldon Johnson Denounces
The Exclusion of Negroes
From Its Dormitories.

[142] ALUMNI SIGN MEMORIAL

Letter of Protest Declares Jim
Crow Policy Augurs Dark Future
For This Country

James Weldon Johnson was born in Jacksonville, Florida, on 17 June 1871.
He received an A.B. from Atlanta University in 1894. Turning down a
scholarship to Harvard Medical School, he became a school principal, lawyer
(the first black admitted to the Florida bar), literature and drama student at
Columbia, U.S. diplomat in South America, newspaper editor, officer of the
NAACP (1916-30), and then professor of literature at Fisk until his death
in a Maine auto accident on 26 June 1938. In addition to poetry, anthologies, and musical-comedy lyrics, his most enduring projects are the classic
novel *The Autobiography of an Ex-Colored Man* (1912); *God's Trombones*
(1927), seven free-verse Negro sermons (which have been recorded by black
actor Harold R. Scott '57); and the historical *Black Manhattan* (1930).

Harvard University, by its exclusion of negro students from the freshman dormitories, is "putting into effect the program proclaimed by the
infamous Ku Klux Klan and its apologists," says James Weldon
Johnson, Secretary of the National Association for the Advancement
of Colored People, 70 Fifth Avenue, in a letter to President A.
Lawrence Lowell of Harvard, made public yesterday. The letter says
that one of the most liberalizing influences at Harvard was to be
found in the opportunity afforded to Southern students to come into
contact with the negro so that they could tolerate and understand him.

Charles C. Burlingham, Harvard, '79, disclosed yesterday that there were 142 signatories to [an earlier] memorial on the exclusion policy of Harvard forwarded to President Lowell by graduates of that institution. In correcting the report that there were only seven signers of that document, Mr. Burlingham explained that seven graduates had distributed the memorial to a selected list of Harvard men.

"There were 142 signers of the memorial," said Mr. Burlingham. "The document was placed in the hands of a little less than 200 men. Of that number there were only eight who disagreed with the sentiments expressed in the memorial. Some of those who would not sign it were governed by delicate positions which they occupied in relation to the university. But the seven men who have been described as the signers of the memorial merely submitted it to other Harvard graduates."

The letter to President Lowell from the Secretary of the National Association for the Advancement of Colored People follows:

A. Lawrence Lowell, Esq., President
Harvard University
Cambridge, Mass.

Jan. 11, 1923.

Sir: In your letter to Mr. Roscoe Conkling Bruce, stating that his son is excluded from the Harvard freshman dormitories because of his color you make the following statement:

".........I am sure you will understand why, from the beginning, we have not thought it possible to compel men of different races to reside together." May I be permitted to amend your statement so that it will accord with the facts? Your statement should read:
".........I am sure you will understand why, from the beginning, we have thought it expedient to compel men of different races to reside apart."

May I further suggest that Harvard's surrender of its tradition and the tradition of liberal America to the slaveholder's prejudice intensifies the very problem which you as Harvard's spokesman are professing to meet. Such amelioration of race problems as has been brought about in this country has occurred in large measure through Southern students who were met in Northern Universities by an unflinching affirmation of the equality of all men in the realm of the arts and of learning. One of the most liberalizing influences on the Southern racial situation has been that the traditional stand of Harvard has afforded to Southern white students the opportunity of coming to know as human beings their fellow colored students with whom they were associated. Deprive those Southern students of their last opportunity to learn the tolerance that comes of living with and understanding men of all races, men with whom they will have perforce to live and mingle in the United States, and Harvard University helps mightily to darken the future of the United States, for by capitulating to anti-negro prejudice in the freshman dormitories or anywhere else, Harvard University affirms that prejudice and strengthens it, and is but putting into effect the program proclaimed by the infamous Ku Klux Klan and its apologists.

Very truly yours, JAMES WELDON JOHNSON, Secretary.

Moorfield Storey of Boston is President of the National Association for the Advancement of Colored People, whose Board of Directors includes Mary White Ovington of New York, Chairman; and the following members:

Bishop John Hurst, Baltimore; Joseph Prince Loud, Butler R. Wilson, Boston; Mary B. Talbert, Buffalo; Jane Addams, Dr. C. E. Bentley, Chicago; Harry E. Davis, Cleveland; Dr. George E. Cannon, Jersey City; E. Burton Ceruti, Los Angeles; R. C. Church, Memphis; George W. Crawford, New Haven; Rev. Hutchens C. Bishop, Dr. W.E.B. Du Bois, Rev. John Haynes Homes, Dr. V. Morton Jones, Florence Kelley, Paul Kennaday, John E. Milholland, Ella Rush Murray, Harry E. Pace, Arthur B. Spingarn, J. E. Spingarn, Charles H. Studin, William English Walling, New York; Dr. J. Max Barber, Dr. William A. Sinclair, Philadelphia; Charles Nagel, St. Louis; Rev G. R. Waller, Springfield; United States Senator Arthur Capper, Topeka; Nannie H. Burroughs, Prof. George William Cook, Archibald H. Grimke, Charles Edward Russell and Neval H. Thomas, Washington, D.C.

Members of the Harvard Corporation and of the Board of Governors who were asked whether they had acted on the exclusion of negroes from the dormitories before President Lowell made known the decision of the University referred all questioners to the offices of the Harvard Corporation, 53 State Street, Boston.

New York Times (1923)

Negro Graduate Protests

Says University Forsakes Freedom for Race Oppression

Cambridge, Mass., Jan. 12—The exclusion of negroes from the freshman dormitories at Harvard was put squarely up to President Lowell today by William Monroe Trotter, negro graduate of Harvard and Secretary of the National Equal Rights League. Speaking officially for the League Trotter held that President Lowell was inconsistent when he advocated a League of Nations and democracy for all at the end of the World War, yet finally turned his back upon the negro race and initiated against its members at Harvard a policy of discrimination.

"In my day and up to the time of President Lowell," said Trotter, discussing the controversy that has been precipitated over the exclusion of young Bruce, "Harvard was an inspiration to me because it was the exemplar of true Americanism, freedom, equality and real democracy.

"Harvard was a place where all races, proscribed in other sections, could find carried out in a practical way the policies and ideals that all beings want, and which is all the Afro-Americans wish.

"Each individual was taken on individual worth, capability and ambition in life. If President Lowell is responsible for race exclusion in the freshman dormitory he is making Harvard turn from democracy and freedom to race oppression, prejudice and hypocrisy.

"President Lowell was, if I remember correctly, an advocate of the League of Nations and all the objects advocated by the War President of the United States. It is inconsistent for him at the close of such a war waged avowedly for democracy, for every man, of every race, of every clime, to be one to initiate a policy of discrimination against Afro-Americans in and for an institution of learning where none such had ever been before."

Official Harvard is silent on the subject of negro exclusion, and it is left to President Lowell, as spokesman for the university, to make any further explanation of the case of Roscoe Conkling Bruce, Jr. Administrative officers of Harvard decline to discuss the case in any way, indicating that President Lowell in his letter to the elder Bruce and to the signers of the memorial recently in conference with him at the Harvard Club in New York City had plainly stated the case for the university.

It became known today that Harvard freshman dormitories had served as homes for negro freshmen already. Edwin B. Jourdain, Jr. had a room in Standish Hall in 1917 and 1918, while Euclid P. Ghee, member of the present senior class, was in Persis Smith Hall in 1919 and 1920. The admission of these students took place in the case of Jourdain during the war upset and in the case of Ghee during the period of readjustment following the war.

New York Times (1923)

Voices from Harvard's Own Negroes

RAYMOND PACE ALEXANDER

Raymond Pace Alexander was born to poor, uneducated black parents in Philadelphia on 13 October 1898. Graduating from Central High School at the top of his class, he won a scholarship to Harvard College. But he could not afford the room and board, so he enrolled at the University of Pennsylvania, finishing the four-year course in three years with a B.S. in economics and highest honors in 1920. He then worked his way through Harvard Law School, receiving his J.D. in 1923. Despite repeated racial rebuffs, he maintained a private law practice in Philadelphia until the 1950s, when he twice won election to the city council and in 1959 ascended the bench. He was senior judge of the Court of Common Pleas when he succumbed to a heart attack in his chambers on 23 November 1974. He was co-founder and editor of the *National Bar Journal*, served a period as president of the National Bar Association, and received several honorary degrees.

Philip Kerr, until recently private secretary to Lloyd George, who sat with the latter at the many international conferences during the past few years, himself an authority on international affairs, said, at a recent lecture before the Harvard student body, "one can hardly appreciate the difficulties involved in solving international problems. They are in a large measure due to the differences in race of the various representatives and the ancient prejudices and antipathies between the races such as the French, Germans, Belgians, and Austrians. In addition to this we were confronted with another and a greater difficulty in the recent conferences and that was arbitrating questions involving races of different *color*.[1] *On these questions nations become irrational.*"

The audience did not sit amazed, neither did it express any surprise nor was this unfortunate confession challenged or inquired into during the time allotted to questioning the speaker.

Could a more damaging confession fall from the lips of so able a statesman? Could it have been better timed to fall upon the ears of those who but a few days before had announced to the world in unflinching terms their going on record to arbitrarily exclude from certain otherwise compulsory features of college life at Harvard a certain racial group because they were "of different color"?

Was Harvard, speaking thru its learned President A. Lawrence Lowell, in prohibiting Negro students from living in the Freshmen Dormitories more rational than the council of nations dealing with their questions or as irrational? Certainly it was not so confessedly irrational. If it was more rational, which is a violent supposition, by what process of reasoning could it have reached such strange results and what factors and elements were considered as the basis of this reasoning? Finally, why in the world can't men, nations or whatnot be rational when a little bit of color is thrown into an issue? Is it possible that the question becomes so onesided?

For a proper treatment of this question it would perhaps be better to sketch briefly the history of the exclusion policy as recently adopted by Harvard.

In the fall of 1921 five colored youths applied for admission to the freshman class, all of them having taken the examinations successfully, were admitted. Three applied for rooms in the freshmen dormitories, which place was a compulsory living quarters for out-of-town freshmen, being optional with local students. These boys were Bertram C. Bland of Newark, N.J., Cecil Blue, Washington, D.C., Pritchett Klugh, Boston, Wm. J. Knox, Jr., New Bedford, Mass., and Edward W. Wilson, Boston. Those requesting dormitory residence were Bland, Blue and Knox, the latter alone being successful. He made application from, and took his examinations in New Bedford, and he was assigned to a room in Standish B. 32, and sent a porter's card to admit his bags and belongings. It happened that one subject,

[1]The speaker had reference to the English Indian problem, Japan and the Shantung controversy and the French use of Colonial soldiers.

chemistry laboratory, had to be taken in Cambridge for which he appeared in person. This was the beginning of all the trouble. He was "spotted" at once, being brown in complexion (incidentally the darkest of the five), found to have been assigned to a room in the exclusive dormitories and by an artful method was made to give it up, in this way. Immediately he was sent a telegram to the effect that there was some error in assigning him to B. 32 in Standish concluding, "will you please return your porter's card so that this error might be adjusted," signed by Dean [Philip P.] Chase of the college. Knox, a native of New Bedford and having lived there all his life, never having been outside of the state of Massachusetts, innocent and unsuspecting, freely complied with the request. Each day he awaited correspondence of equal dignity advising him of his new assignment, but none came. Finally, the light dawned in the nature of a letter of explanation from the Dean stating that "the ruling of the President is that no Negro students shall hereafter be permitted to live in the Freshmen Dormitories." Can anything more depressing be imagined on the mind of this youth than these events, especially in light of the manner in which he was deprived of his assignment?

Knox and a Negro graduate of Harvard of that year, Edwin B. Jourdain, Jr., immediately journeyed to Boston. Jourdain is also a native of New Bedford, and is a son of a prominent attorney of the same name of that city, and lived in the Freshmen Dormitories in 1917 without the least friction, living in the same room with white boys, and eating at the same table. Later he was a member of the same track team that boasted of the famous [Edward O.] Gourdin ['21]. They interviewed Dean Chase who has always been a very fair man, and who cannot now be impeached, but his position was uncompromising, being bound by the orders of President Lowell. It was then thought best to see the President, which was done, Jourdain alone making the interview. President Lowell was a very pleasant person to talk to, but was immovable in his convictions, giving as his reasons, without deliberating in their forthcoming, the following, which is the gist: The southern element in the school is becoming increasingly large while the Negro element is very small, less than one per cent of the entire matriculation. That the southern students have very pronounced prejudices, cannot be disputed, the most acute being their dislike of anything that approaches, or savors of, social equality. *Ergo*, since living in the Freshmen Dormitories is compulsory upon *all* students which would throw southerners in contact with Negroes to their discomfort, and since it is not our policy to compel artificial social contact between Negroes and whites, it is thought that the best policy is to forbid the Negro students this privilege.

The mere assertion of such a statement would raise in the mind of even the untrained a glaring *non sequitur.* Does it follow that because a University enforces a rule that it thought fit and just for all students at its inception which might incidentally mean that a colored student will have to live in the same dormitory with southerners that the University is forcing a sort of social equality between the two types of students, or forcing the southern students to accept the Negro in his social circle, or forcing him to have any social relations with him other than sleeping under the same roof separated by four strongly partitioned walls, and probably some flights of stairs? Does it follow that there is some artificiality in even this most harmless contact, and at the same time legitimate contact, legitimate because the *rules* make it so? Does it follow that because the southern element is increasingly large, and the Negro body very small, that this great institution, which has never been known to suffer from a shortage of students or a boycott because of a policy, must restrict the operation of this rule, enacted for all races, in order to satisfy any racial or geographical element? Does it follow that the only way to meet such an issue as this is to summarily dispose of the question by putting a bar against all further admission of Negroes to the Freshmen Dormitories? Since this question involves a deep principle of ethics, justice, and fairness, would not the most logical and wholesome policy be unqualifiedly to admit the Negro students, and let those objecting make the next move? Would not the "therefore" clause stand with better logic on this ground? All these questions save the last seem to answer themselves in the negative, and we are faced with our original question: "Whether Harvard was any more rational or as irrational in its pronunciation of policy as was the Council of Nations at Versailles?" We submit to the latter that it was.

The present Negro student body of Harvard is particularly proud of the type and bearing of the young Negroes who are entering this University and those against whom this policy was announced. It would probably be not too much to conclude that a great deal of the public sympathy with the Negro on this issue, and popular support, may be directly traceable to the fact that the students were treated in such manner came from very representative Negro families. A word or two concerning them would not be out of place.

Cecil Blue's father is a graduate of Queen's College, British Guiana, and the medical school of Howard University, Washington, D.C., and is at present a successful physician of that city. The Reverend Doctor David Klugh, the father of Pritchett Klugh, a prominent Boston clergyman, is a graduate of Yale, and Butler R. Wilson, Esq. a member of the Boston bar . . . and a successful attorney. And now we add to these the name of Roscoe Conkling Bruce, Jr., the son of Roscoe Conkling Bruce, '02 Harvard, class orator, and Phi Beta Kappa man, grandson of Blanche K. Bruce, United States Senator from Mississippi in 1875, Register of the Treasury under President Garfield in the early eighties. To use the words of a reflecting white student, "He certainly picked out most unfortunate cases to start with," would not be amiss.

It is probably fair to conclude that no half dozen men picked at random among the Harvard freshmen class could present any better family history or training, in a comparative sense, than these young Negroes. It reflects the advent of a new element of Negroes to our colleges and universities; sons of graduates of these larger institutions, as distinct from "the first generation educated" that formed the pioneers among Negro men of letters and science. Not only are these youths better prepared than their fathers were, but their parents have ample means in most cases with which to support these boys in the proper style and comfort. Irrespective of this social progress of the Negro students, we are faced with this pernicious policy of discrimination which strikes at the very source of entrance into the University.

The natural question to ask is what are the aims and underlying purposes of this sudden departure from the great Harvard tradition of fairness and justice to all, irrespective of race or color. Is there an ulterior purpose with its object an immediate limitation in the Negroes attending Harvard and in the future the total exclusion from all departments? One cannot dismiss this question lightly, and rest too assured that Harvard traditions and principles will not allow such when all of its principles, traditions and everything else were freely tossed to the winds in this present affair. One cannot overlook the great significance of this policy, restricted as it is to the Freshmen Dormitories, and the effect that it will have on Negro matriculation. It has already had its effect! In September, 1921, there were six Negroes in the freshman class (one was too fair to be affected by this policy) all of whom were registered before the enunciation of this rule. Last September only one Negro applied for admission to the

Harvard freshman class, and he is the son of the Hon. William H. Lewis, noted Harvard football star centre of all time, and an ex-assistant United States Attorney General. The latter would not be satisfied under any circumstances with another college for his son because his Harvard training has meant too much to him, not to mention his contribution to Harvard, and in this respect, he is not unlike scores of other Negro graduates of Harvard, and hundreds of other parents who want their sons to study under the Harvard system that they themselves were unable to experience.

Young Lewis made no effort to get into the Freshmen Dormitories because his parents live in Cambridge. But was not the apparent desire of the officials fulfilled, with not one Negro requesting to live in the Freshman Dormitory in 1922, and only one Negro in the entire class? It might be asked why is it that the Freshmen Dormitories are indispensable for the quartering of Negro students or why is it that the colored youths do not live with private families. The answer is plain enough. In Cambridge, the colored population, with very few exceptions, is made up of the middle or working class of people with small, modest homes situated some distance from the campus, not too well adapted to lodging college men because of their small, incommodious quarters, inadequate lighting and heating facilities and the utter impossibility of getting board at one's lodging place, or in the one or two instances where board can be got the striking lack of unwholesomeness of the food and culinary art in its preparation. Those persons of the so-called leading families do not make a practice of taking lodgers of any kind, as is true among the upper class of whites.

All things considered the Negro student body is faced with a more momentous question than one readily appreciates and it is only given its full significance when one begins to wonder what will be the next move? Will Harvard next adopt the Yale policy and announce that "because of the growing southern element (sentiment?) and their displeasure at the possibility of coming in contact with Negroes in the voluntary dormitories, it is thought that the best way to preserve the comity of race relations is to hereafter forbid Negroes from living in any of the dormitories." The next most logical step would be to bar them from the college altogether because of the contact in the classrooms! The bare possibility of this registers a shudder and thrill in the heart and soul of the present Negro students; but this is not at all unlikely if one reflects on the significance of the present policy.

"Dormitories or no dormitories, Negroes will always go to

Harvard" is the cry of some; but this is not meeting the issue squarely. Moreover, it is a bare conjecture based on a false assumption if the current freshmen Negro number is at all a fair criterion. The issue must be met by constructive effort on the part of many groups, by the Negroes themselves, i.e., the Negro alumni and present student body, by pressure brought to bear on the General Alumni Association, support from the influential members of the faculty who are fair and impartial, circularizing the white undergraduates or in some manner presenting them with the truth of the situation as herein attempted to be outlined, for their reflection asking for an expression of opinion on their part, finally, by acquainting the Board of Overseers with the magnitude of the significance of their acts on the race in its strides for higher education of its young men, to develop the proper type of leadership, and the psychic effect it will have on the white student body and the citizens of this section of the country in bringing to their minds the fact that *Harvard* realizes that there is an "eternal, fundamental, and inescapable difference" between the two races. No better time affords itself for approaching these groups and working among them than the present, while the matter is still fresh in the minds of the people, and when the press of the country has in a large majority of cases given our cause such great support. It will be of no little interest to state that at present there are movements under way by two of the above groups that stand in a powerfully strategic position. First, there is an organization of white students which is canvassing the undergraduate body in the effort to get a prevailing sentiment against the policy of the President and to present him with a petition, on his return from Europe, to reconsider his stand and revoke the rule on the ground that, "the very persons who would be affected by the admission of Negroes into the dormitories, do not find such a state of affairs objectionable." Secondly, there are reports, not yet verified, that certain members of the faculty are forming a petition to the President and the Board of Overseers, to reconsider such action stating that "any form of racial discrimination is a serious departure from true Harvard principles, and would violate very precious Harvard traditions," substantially the stand of President Emeritus Charles W. Eliot. It is submitted that these two movements, if carried through in full, will have an incalculably great effect.

Harvard does mean something to the Negro. We cannot but look with pride at the list of America's outstanding Negroes and feel an indescribable love for the institution that has honored such men, that has given them their training, industry and resourcefulness, that stamps them as men of calibre, ability and integrity; men who by their deeds have gained the respect and admiration of an entire race, indeed, of the whole country. The University that has cast such men as Greener, W.E.B. Du Bois, William H. Lewis, Carter G. Woodson, Archibald Grimke, and the host of others including Marshall, Matthews, Bruce, Morton, Jackson, and Pope;* that honored Booker T. Washington with a degree for his great achievements, cannot hold only a passive interest for the Negro.

There is much to be gained at Harvard; there is overwhelmingly much to be lost by Harvard closing its doors to our boys, not alone from the loss of the privilege of studying within its walls; but from the loss of the priceless inspiration from the heritage of able Negroes who passed on before, and the ruthless destruction of the significance of their deeds and accomplishments by their own Alma Mater.

Opportunity: Journal of Negro Life (1923)

---

*Napoleon B. Marshall '97, William C. Matthews '05, Ferdinand Q. Morton '06, Alexander L. Jackson '14, Aiken L. Pope, LL.B. '18.—Eds.

Opinion

W.E.B. Du Bois

Deep as is the shame and humiliation of Harvard's recent surrender
to the Bourbon South, the spirited and whole-souled response that it
has evinced is perhaps the most heartening sign of sanity on the race
problem that has happened in fifty years. Not a single person of
importance has yet dared to defend Lowell, while ex-President Eliot
and a score of distinguished graduates have condemned his despicable
action. This does not mean that Lowell has no support. It means
simply that the case is so flagrant that few dare openly to defend what
they secretly sustain.

Above all the Negro race and American democracy owe a debt of
gratitude to Roscoe Conkling Bruce for as fine a statement of the
fundamentals of democracy in college as has ever been made. In its
logic and its English, its flavor and restraint it is as far above
Lawrence Lowell's labored and obscure defense as can be imagined.
Let the Dance of Death go on, but as long as the Black World can
drive the Superior Race to its hole with ammunition like this there
can be—there will be but one end. Imagine, my masters, six decades
after emancipation, a slave's grandson teaching the ABC of democracy
to the Puritan head of Harvard!

The Crisis (1923)

Charles W. Chesnutt to Roscoe Conkling Bruce

Charles Waddell Chesnutt was born in Cleveland, Ohio on 20 June 1858. To help family finances he had to curtail formal education before finishing high school. But self-education served him well and he even became a normal-school principal at 23, supplementing his earnings by giving music and Latin lessons. He studied law in a judge's office and in 1887 passed the Ohio bar with the highest score in his group. Thereafter he conducted a prosperous legal stenographic service. He published his first piece at 14 and his last in 1931. But the bulk of his output appeared from 1887 to 1905—notably three novels, two volumes of short stories, and a biography of Frederick Douglass. He received the Spingarn Medal in 1928. When he died in Cleveland on 15 November 1932, he left unpublished a half dozen other novels, a play, and much short fiction. He joins the short-lived Paul Laurence Dunbar (1872-1906) as one of the period's two foremost black practitioners of creative writing.

                                                    April 10, 1923.

Prof. Roscoe C. Bruce,

Kimball, West Virginia.

My dear Mr. Bruce:

I see from a news item in the morning paper that the authorities of Harvard University have revoked the order with reference to receiving colored students in the dormitories, and also the proposed method of selecting students by other standards than those of scholarship and character. I have no doubt whatever that this action was brought about largely through your masterly presentation of the case through the New York World, and elsewhere, and I think that not only all colored folks but all Harvard men and good Americans owe you a debt of gratitude. I shall await with interest to learn how many southern students leave the university because of this action of the Governing Board.

I hope this may find you and your family well, and Mrs. Chesnutt and my daughters join me in regards to you and Mrs. Bruce.

Sincerely yours,

[Charles W. Chesnutt]

Charles W. Chesnutt and Harvard

J. NOEL HEERMANCE

Perhaps the most dramatic example of [Charles Chesnutt's] continuing concern about the race problem in America and about his role as spokesman is to be found in 1923, when Chesnutt was sixty-five and far less active than before. He was deeply upset at Harvard University's attempt at that time to exclude Black students from its dormitories and dining halls. When a flippant discussion of the controversy appeared in a Cleveland paper, Chesnutt's letter to Charles T. Henderson, editor of the *Cleveland Topics*, was almost massive in its power, showing the same emotional fervor which marked Chesnutt's most dramatic passages in *The Marrow of Tradition*. It was restrained and gentlemanly, to be sure, as his personal writing always was, but within that restraint it was strong and almost savagely direct: the voice of a spokesman still passionately at war with racial injustice and insensitivity even at age sixty-five. After citing some of the more offensive passages in the article, Chesnutt proceeded:

If this utterance had emanated from a Florida "cracker" or a Georgia "red neck," or even an Alabama senator, I should not have been surprised; but from a man brought up in Cleveland, educated in the public schools where he went to school with colored children, and with a mother such as yours, who was widely known as a generous and broad-minded woman, who to my personal knowledge has eaten in public with colored people, it came as a surprise, to say the least.

I really cannot understand the basis of your emotional turmoil, which is apparently so great that you cannot find decent language to express it. I suspected that you did not know what you were writing about, which I have verified by ascertaining that you are not a Harvard man. Colored students have always lived in the dormitories and eaten in the dining halls at Harvard; I have paid the bills of one of them [Edwin J. Chesnutt '05] and ought to know. The "living together" and "eating with white folks" involves no more intimacy than life in a hotel, and you know or ought to know that colored men are received as guests at some of the best hotels in Cleveland, that eight or ten of them are members of the City Club and eat in its dining room, and I have seen brown men eating in the sacred precincts of the Union Club, and at the University Club.

I am quite sure that had you had any such feeling against Jews, you would not have expressed it publicly in any such manner, nor, had you had a hundred subscribers whom you knew to be colored, would you have gone out of your way to insult them, if only as a matter of policy, to say nothing of good taste.

I shall not indulge in the childish gesture of saying "Stop my paper," since I have paid for it in advance, but I shall hereafter take it up with suspicion and qualify my admiration with reflection. (April 20, 1923)

It must have provided Chesnutt with some satisfaction to have the return letter from Henderson express his personal apology to Chesnutt for the "unpardonable stupidity of the 'smart' item"; and Chesnutt was assured that the particular columnist who had written the piece would be supervised thereafter.

From *Charles W. Chesnutt* (1974)

No Racial Discrimination

at Harvard

The committee appointed at Harvard "to consider and report to the Governing Boards principles and methods for more effective sifting of candidates for admission to the University" presented its report to the Board of Overseers on Monday, April 9, through the President, who stated that the report embodied the unanimous conclusions of the committee.

The report was accepted and the Board unanimously adopted the following vote thereon:

"That in the administration of rules for admission Harvard College maintain its traditional policy of freedom from discrimination on grounds of race or religion."

It was further voted that the Board commend the other recom-- mendations of the report to the careful consideration of the Faculty of Arts and Sciences, with the request that any changes in the methods of admission to Harvard College adopted by the Faculty be presented to the Governing Boards for approval.

The committee which prepared the report was appointed by President Lowell last June, in acccordance with a vote of the Board of Overseers which followed a similar vote of the Faculty of Arts and Sciences. The committee included seven representatives of the Faculty of Arts and Sciences: Professor Charles H. Grandgent, '83, chairman; Henry Pennypacker, '88; Professor Theodore Lyman, '97; Dean Chester N. Greenough, '98; Professor Paul J. Sachs, '00; Dr. Roger I. Lee, '02; and Assistant Professor Harry A. Wolfson, '12. On the committee were also Professor Samuel Williston, '82, representing the Faculty of Law; Professors Lawrence J. Henderson, '98, and Milton J. Rosenau, A.M. (hon.) '14, representing the Faculty of Medicine; Professor Harry E. Clifford, representing the Faculty of Engineering; Dean Wallace B. Donham, '98, representing the Faculty of Business Administration; and Dean Henry W. Holmes, '03, representing the Faculty of Education.

The report in full follows:

"1. In accordance with a vote passed by the Board of Overseers on June 5, 1922, the President appointed a committee of thirteen, representing the principal Faculties of the University. This Committee, bearing in mind the functions of an American college and the relations between secondary and higher education, has made a survey of the composition of the student body, and has considered modes, old and new, of determining fitness for entrance. It has collected a comprehensive mass of statistics dealing with admission, college studies, and college life. The compilation has been carefully made by experts, and the results are believed to be as accurate as any figures can be which have to do with necessarily incomplete data and with factors not precisely definable. The attention of the Committee has been concentrated on the College, because it was evident that each of the Graduate Schools has its own entrance requirements based on its special needs. The Committee recognizes that this task has been assigned to it in conformity with the general policy of the University not to adopt new methods or procedures with respect to admission to Harvard College except after careful deliberation and proper authorization.

"2. Foremost, by reason of publicity and apparent urgency, among the matters to be examined by your Committee was the question of racial proportion in the student body. This, however, was only one phase of the problem studied, and as the investigation progressed, the entire Committee became convinced that the whole question should be approached not from the standpoint of race, but in an effort to accomplish a proper selection of individuals among the available candidates for admission to Harvard College. The Committee believes that if the intellectually unfit can be eliminated and if our entrance requirements can be adjusted to the work of good schools not now sending men to Harvard College, our whole problem can be met; and that the student body will be properly representative of all groups in our national life.

"3. Concerning proportional representation, your Committee is unanimous in recommending that no departure be made from the policy that has so long approved itself—the policy of equal opportunity for all, regardless of race and religion. Any action liable to interpretation as an acceptance of the principle of racial discrimination would to many seem like a dangerous surrender of traditional ideals.

"4. Under the circumstances the introduction of any novel process of scrutiny appears inexpedient. Even so rational a method as a personal conference or an intelligence test, if now adopted here as a means of selection, would inevitably be regarded as a covert device to eliminate those deemed racially or socially undesirable, and, however fairly conceived and conducted, could not fail to arouse damaging suspicion."

Harvard Alumni Bulletin (1923)

Negroes in the Freshman Halls

The following vote, passed on March 26 by the president and fellows of Harvard College, was presented by the President to the Board of Overseers on April 9, and was unanimously concurred in by the Board:

"Voted, that up to the capacity of the Freshman Halls all members of the freshman class shall reside and board in the Freshman Halls, except those who are permitted by the Dean of Harvard College to live elsewhere. In the application of this rule, men of the white and colored races shall not be compelled to live and eat together, nor shall any man be excluded by reason of his color."

Harvard Alumni Bulletin (1923)

Marita Bonner in 1922

MARITA O. BONNER

Marieta (later Marita) Odette Bonner was born in Boston on 16 June 1898 and grew up in neighboring Brookline. She attended Brookline High School, where she wrote for the student magazine, *The Sagamore*, and was graduated in 1917. After a year at the Cabot School, she entered Radcliffe in the fall of 1918, and majored in English and Comparative Literature (becoming fluent in German). She was admitted to Charles T. Copeland's famous writing seminar; and one of her sketches, "Dandelion Season," was selected to be read annually to Radcliffe classes. An accomplished pianist (like her sister), she also composed the winning music for the 1919 and 1922 Radcliffe song competitions. During college she did part-time teaching at a Cambridge high school. After her graduation in 1922, she taught for two years at the Bluefield Colored Institute in Virginia.

Moving to Washington, D.C., she taught English at the Armstrong High School from 1924 to 1930, and began publishing essays, plays, and short stories in *The Crisis* and *Opportunity*. (On a few occasions she used the pseudonym Joseph Maree Andrew.) Among her notable literary experiments are the modernist one-act play *The Purple Flower* (1928), the early prize-winning essay "On Being Young—A Woman—and Colored" (1925), which is reproduced here, and "Drab Rambles," the short story that won first prize from W.E.B. Du Bois's *Crisis* in 1927. In the same year her "Scherzo for Orchestra" received the Wanamaker Prize in music.

After her marriage to William Occomy in 1930, she moved to Chicago, and kept writing and publishing short fiction until 1941. She taught there at Phillips High School (1944-49) and the Dolittle School for retarded children (1950-63). She did not, in her lifetime, achieve the recognition that her musical and literary output deserved. It was not until May of 1988 that students mounted in Radcliffe's Agassiz Theatre the apparent premieres of two of her plays, *The Pot Maker* (1927) and *Exit, an Illusion* (1929). On 6 December 1971 Marita Bonner Occomy died from complications after a fire in her Chicago apartment. Some of her manuscripts are now in Radcliffe's Schlesinger Library.

On Being Young—A Woman—And Colored

You start out after you have gone from kindergarten to sheepskin covered with sundry Latin phrases.

At least you know what you want life to give you. A career as fixed and as calmly brilliant as the North Star. The one real thing that money buys. Time. Time to do things. A house that can be as delectably out of order and as easily put in order as the doll-house of "playing-house" days. And of course, a husband you can look up to without looking down on yourself.

Somehow you feel like a kitten in a sunny catnip field that sees sleek, plump brown field mice and yellow baby chicks sitting coyly, side by side, under each leaf. A desire to dash three or four ways seizes you.

That's Youth.

But you know that things learned need testing—acid testing—to see if they are really, after all, an interwoven part of you. All your life you have heard of the debt you owe "Your People" because you have managed to have the things they have not largely had.

So you find a spot where there are hordes of them—of course below the Line—to be your catnip field while you close your eyes to mice and chickens alike.

If you have never lived among your own, you feel prodigal. Some warm untouched current flows through them—through you—and drags you out into the deep waters of a new sea of human foibles and mannerisms; of a peculiar psychology and prejudices. And one day you find yourself entangled—enmeshed—pinioned in the seaweed of a Black Ghetto.

Not a Ghetto, placid like the Strasse that flows, outwardly unperturbed and calm in a stream of religious belief, but a peculiar group. Cut off, flung together, shoved aside in a bundle because of color and with no more in common.

Unless color is, after all, the real bond.

Milling around like live fish in a basket. Those at the bottom crushed into a sort of stupid apathy by the weight of those on top. Those on top leaping, leaping; leaping to scale the sides; to get out.

There are two "colored" movies, innumerable parties—and cards. Cards played so intensely that it fascinates and repulses at once.

Movies.

Movies worthy and worthless—but not even a low-caste spoken stage.

Parties, plentiful. Music and dancing and much that is wit and color and gaiety. But they are like the richest chocolate; stuffed costly chocolates that make the taste go stale if you have too many of them. That make plain whole bread taste like ashes.

There are all the earmarks of a group within a group. Cut off all around from ingress from or egress to other groups. A sameness of type. The smug self-satisfaction of an inner measurement; a measurement by standards known within a limited group and not those of an unlimited, seeing, world. . . . Like the blind, blind mice. Mice whose eyes have been blinded.

Strange longing seizes hold of you. You wish yourself back where you can lay your dollar down and sit in a dollar seat to hear voices, strings, reeds that have lifted the World out, up, beyond things that have bodies and walls. Where you can marvel at new marbles and bronzes and flat colors that will make men forget that things exist in a flesh more often than in spirit. Where you can sink your body in a cushioned seat and sink your soul at the same time into a section of life set before you on the boards for a few hours.

You hear that up at New York this is to be seen; that, to be heard.

You decide the next train will take you there.

You decide the next second that that train will not take you, nor the next—nor the next for some time to come.

For you know that—being a woman—you cannot twice a month or twice a year, for that matter, break away to see or hear anything in a city that is supposed to see and hear too much.

That's being a woman. A woman of any color.

You decide that something is wrong with a world that stifles and chokes; that cuts off and stunts; hedging in, pressing down on eyes, ears and throat. Somehow all wrong.

You wonder how it happens there that—say five hundred miles from the Bay State—Anglo Saxon intelligence is so warped and stunted.

How judgment and discernment are bred out of the race. And what has become of discrimination? Discrimination of the right sort. Discrimination that the best minds have told you weighs shadows and nuances and spiritual differences before it catalogues. The kind they have taught you all of your life was best: that looks clearly past generalization and past appearance to dissect, to dig down to the real heart of matters. That casts aside rapid summary conclusions, drawn from primary inference as Daniel did the spiced meats.

Why can't they then perceive that there is a difference in the glance from a pair of eyes that look, mildly docile, at "white ladies" and those that, impersonally and perceptively—aware of distinctions—see only women who happen to be white?

Why do they see a colored woman only as a gross collection of desires, all uncontrolled, reaching out for their Apollos and the Quasimodos with avid indiscrimination?

Why unless you talk in staccato squawks—brittle as sea-shells—unless you "champ" gum—unless you cover two yards square when you laugh—unless your taste runs to violent colors—impossible perfumes and more impossible clothes—are you a feminine Caliban craving to pass for Ariel?

An empty imitation of an empty invitation. A mime; a sham; a copy-cat. A hollow re-echo. A froth, a foam. A fleck of the ashes of superficiality?

Everything you touch or taste now is like the flesh of an unripe persimmon.

. . . Do you need to be told what that is being . . . ?

Old ideas, old fundamentals seem worm-eaten, out-grown, worthless, bitter; fit for the scrap-heap of Wisdom.

What you had thought tangible and practical has turned out to be a collection of "blue-flower" theories.

If they have not discovered how to use their accumulation of facts, they are useless to you in Their world.

Every part of you becomes bitter.

But—"In Heaven's name, do not grow bitter. Be bigger than they are"—exhort white friends who have never had to draw breath in a Jim-Crow train. Who have never had petty putrid insult dragged over them—drawing blood—like pebbled sand on your body where the skin is tenderest. On your body where the skin is thinnest and tenderest.

You long to explode and hurt everything white; friendly; unfriendly. But you know that you cannot live with a chip on your shoulder even if you can manage a smile around your eyes—without getting steely and brittle and losing the softness that makes you a woman.

For chips make you bend your body to balance them. And once you bend, you lose your poise, your balance, and the chip gets into you. The real you. You get hard.

. . . And many things in you can ossify . . .

And you know, being a woman, you have to go about it gently and quietly, to find out and to discover just what is wrong. Just what can be done.

You see clearly that they have acquired things.

Money; money. Money to build with, money to destroy. Money to swim in. Money to drown in. Money.

An ascendancy of wisdom. An incalculable hoard of wisdom in all fields, in all things collected from all quarters of humanity.

A stupendous mass of things.

Things.

So, too, the Greeks . . . Things.

And the Romans. . . .

And you wonder and wonder why they have not discovered how to handle, deftly and skillfully, Wisdom, stored up for them—like the honey for the Gods on Olympus—since time unknown.

You wonder and you wonder until you wander out into Infinity, where—if it is to be found anywhere—Truth really exists.

The Greeks had possessions, culture. They were lost because they did not understand.

The Romans owned more than anyone else. Trampled under the heel of Vandals and Civilization, because they would not understand.

Greeks. Did not understand.

Romans. Would not understand.

"They." Will not understand.

So you find they have shut Wisdom up and have forgotten to find the key that will let her out. They have trapped, trammeled, lashed her to themselves with thews and thongs and theories. They have ransacked sea and earth and air to bring every treasure to her. But she sulks and will not work for a world with a whitish hue because it has snubbed her twin sister, Understanding.

You see clearly—off there is Infinity—Understanding. Standing alone, waiting for someone to really want her.

But she is so far out there is no way to snatch at her and drag her in.

So—being a woman—you can wait.

You must sit quietly without a chip. Not sodden—and weighted as if your feet were cast in the iron of your soul. Not wasting strength in enervating gestures as if two hundred years of bonds and whips had really tricked you into nervous uncertainty.

But quiet; quiet. Like Buddha—who brown like I am—sat entirely at ease, entirely sure of himself; motionless and knowing, a thousand years before the white man knew there was so very much difference between feet and hands.

Motionless on the outside. But inside?

Silent.

Still . . . "Perhaps Buddha is a woman."

So you too. Still; quiet; with a smile, ever so slight, at the eyes so that Life will flow into and not by you. And you can gather, as it passes, the essences, the overtones, the tints, the shadows; draw understanding to your self.

And then you can, when Time is ripe, swoop to your feet—at your full height—at a single gesture.

Ready to go where?

Why . . . Wherever God motions.

The Crisis (1925)

STERLING A. BROWN

Sterling Allen Brown was born on 1 May 1901 in Washington, D.C., where he went to the famous Dunbar High School. He attended Williams College as one of four black students (one in each class), was elected to Phi Beta Kappa in his junior year, and took his B.A. in 1922. The following year he earned an A.M. studying literature at Harvard, where his professors included the renowned Bliss Perry and George Lyman Kittredge ('92). He returned to Harvard in 1931-32, but decided not to proceed to a doctorate.

After brief teaching posts at Virginia Seminary and College in Lynchburg, Fisk University, and Lincoln University in Missouri, in 1929 he assumed a professorship at Howard University (where his father had taught). Aside from occasional visiting professorships, Brown continued his work at Howard long after his official 1969 retirement. He wrote literary criticism—including *Negro Poetry and Drama* and *The Negro in American Fiction*, both in 1937—and was the instigating senior editor of *The Negro Caravan* (1941), a mammoth anthology of black writing that remains a classic.

His own poetry earned him the label of "the new Negro folk-poet" from black scholar Alain Locke '08, Ph.D. '18. The despairing title poem of Brown's first collection, *Southern Road* (1932), is a good example, conjuring up the blues-flavored worksongs of convict gangs. His *Collected Poems* (1980) won the annual Lenore Marshall Prize for the outstanding book of poems published in the United States. In 1984 he was named the official poet laureate of the District of Columbia. In the same year Harvard, following the lead of eight other universities, bestowed an honorary Litt.D. degree on him, stating, "Deep-rooted in the Afro-American experience, his teaching and writing have invigorated the heartwood of American literature." An unusually effective reader, Brown recorded a good deal of his own poetry. And Haile Gerima's *After Winter*, a documentary film about Brown's life, had its premiere in Boston on 20 February 1986. The last surviving major writer of the New Negro Renaissance, Brown succumbed to leukemia in Takoma Park, Maryland, on 13 January 1989.

Sterling Brown in midcareer

I Visit Wren's Nest

For a gentler reminiscence of Atlanta's past, I went out to see "Wren's Nest," along with Griff Davis, a young photographer. This modest old home in West End, with many gables and gingerbread curly-cues, is a Mecca for American school children and their teachers, who want to see where the kindly Joel Chandler Harris created Uncle Remus, Brer Tortoise and Sister Cow.

Well, so did I: so I rang the front door bell. A little flaxenhaired girl answered. In response to my request to go through the house, she stood there with her blue eyes wide and, like Uncle Remus' Tar Baby, "she kept on sayin' nothin'." Then she skittered off. In a few minutes, her father, the caretaker, came to the door, hurriedly putting on a shirt.

I told him that we would like to visit the shrine. He started to open the screen door, and then noticed Griff. I had my hat on and he hadn't looked closely at me, but Griff is brown.

"Who's this boy?" he asked, staccato.

"He is Mr. Davis, of Atlanta University," I answered slowly.

"No," the man said. "Sorry, but I can't let you all come in. The Association has told me not to let in the colored."

I told him that I was writing a book, that at Harvard University in Massachusetts I had written research papers on Joel Chandler Harris, that I had a scholar's interest in Harris and his contribution to American literature, that Griff, Mr. Davis, was a serious student of photography, attempting to make camera studies of authentic Americans. I knew I wasn't going to get in, but I poured it on. I was thinking how the lonely lad Joel had hung around Negro cabins, none of them shut to him, listening to every wisp of talk, storing in his memory all the anecdotes and tricks of speech and song, piling up a rich compost as it were to produce those fine flowers that made his fame and fortune. So I poured it on. The caretaker's mouth was hanging open when I stopped, and Griff was grinning.

"I didn't make the rule," the caretaker complained. "Far as I'm concerned, it wouldn't make no difference. But the Association won't stand for it. They'd have my job."

He added that it would be all right to walk around the house, even to the gardens in the backyard. We declined the honor, but stopped at the pink-marble walk leading to the side. Upon each paving stone is printed the name of a Georgia author: Augustus Longstreet, Frank Stanton, Sidney Lanier, Thomas Holly Chivers.

"Now, take Chivers," I said pompously to Griff. The caretaker was on our heels, listening. "He was an unknown poet, of rare eccentric genius, much like, and quite influential upon Edgar [Allan] Poe. People in Georgia called him crazy, but I do not know that he was any crazier than the rest of them."

Griff turned to the caretaker, and asked, "I suppose it would be all right for me to take pictures?" The man thought it over, then, "I reckon so," he grunted, and left. As rapidly as Griff focussed the camera and worked those plates, he still could get only the front of Wren's Nest and the capacious rear of the caretaker, scrambling up the steps.

Phylon (1945)

Southern Road

Swing dat hammer—hunh—
Steady, bo';
Swing dat hammer—hunh—
Steady, bo';
Ain't no rush, bebby,
Long ways to go.

Burner tore his—hunh—
Black heart away;
Burner tore his—hunh—
Black heart away;
Got me life, bebby,
An' a day.

Gal's on Fifth Street—hunh—
Son done gone;
Gal's on Fifth Street—hunh—
Son done gone;
Wife's in de ward, bebby,
Babe's not bo'n.

My ole man died—hunh—
Cussin' me;
My ole man died—hunh—
Cussin me;
Ole lady rocks, bebby,
Huh misery.

Doubleshackled—hunh—
Guard behin';
Doubleshackled—hunh—
Guard behin';

Ball an' chain, bebby,
On my min'.

White man tells me—hunh—
Damn yo' soul;
White man tells me—hunh—
Damn yo' soul;
Got no need, bebby,
To be tole.

Chain gang nevah—hunh—
Let me go;
Chain gang nevah—hunh—
Let me go;
Po' los' boy, bebby,
Evahmo'. . . .

From *Southern Road* (1932)

COUNTÉE CULLEN

Countée Leroy Porter Cullen was born on 30 May 1903, the unproven claimants to place being Louisville, Baltimore, and New York City (the first seems the likeliest). We do not know who his natural parents were, but he was adopted as a teenager by a New York minister. He attended the mostly white De Witt Clinton High School, where he was editor-in-chief of the school paper and associate editor of its literary magazine. He took first prize in an oratorical competition, was vice-president of his senior class, and won election to the honor society with a 92-percent average. He had started writing poetry in grade school, and at 17 copped a first prize and national fame by penning "Life's Rendezvous" to counter the famous poem "I Have a Rendezvous With Death" by Alan Seeger (Harvard '10).

Entering New York University in 1922, Cullen majored in English literature, doing most of his work with Hyder Rollins, who held a Harvard Ph.D. and would accept a Harvard professorship in 1926. He minored in French, and also studied Latin, Greek, and German. Strongly influenced by Keats, and by the recent Pulitzer Prize winners Edwin Arlington Robinson and Edna St. Vincent Millay (she was the subject of his senior honors thesis), he won a host of national prizes, including the Witter Bynner Poetry Contest named for a poet from the Harvard class of 1902. "The Ballad of the Brown Girl" (1923) elicited from Harvard's balladry scholar, George Lyman Kittredge, the verdict that it was "an unusually successful example of poetical composition in the style of the 'popular ballad.'" "The Shroud of Color" (first published in the *American Mercury*, 1924) made a strong impact in the literary world.

After his 1925 graduation with a Phi Beta Kappa key (he was one of nine so honored out of a class of 102), Cullen spent the next year earning an A.M. degree at Harvard, where he particularly valued his study with Robert S. Hillyer ('17), who would a few years later win the Pulitzer Prize for his *Collected Verse*. His other professors included Kittredge and Irving Babbitt. During his first term in Cambridge, Cullen's first volume of poems, *Color*, appeared and garnered wide acclaim (the first of more than fifty reviews was in the *Harvard Crimson*, 21 October 1925), along with the Harmon Foundation Award.

Aside from poetry and critical essays, he collaborated on some theatrical projects, including a Broadway musical. In 1934 he prepared a new version of Euripides' *Medea*, with seven choruses set to music by Virgil Thomson (A.B. 1922, Mus.D. 1982), for the noted black actress Rose McClendon, whose illness aborted the production. Turning down black-college posts in the South, Cullen taught French and English at Frederick Douglass Junior High School in Harlem for a dozen years until hypertension and uremic poisoning led to his death in Sydeman Hospital on 9 January 1946. More than 3000 people attended his funeral in the Salem Methodist Episcopal Church.

The Shroud of Color

(For Llewellyn Ransom)[*]

"Lord, being dark," I said, "I cannot bear
The further touch of earth, the scented air;
Lord, being dark, forewilled to that despair
My color shrouds me in, I am as dirt
Beneath my brother's heel; there is a hurt
In all the simple joys which to a child
Are sweet; they are contaminate, defiled
By truths of wrongs the childish vision fails
To see; too great a cost this birth entails.
I strangle in this yoke drawn tighter than
The worth of bearing it, just to be man.
I am not brave enough to pay the price
In full; I lack the strength to sacrifice.
I who have burned my hands upon a star,
And climbed high hills at dawn to view the far
Illimitable wonderments of earth,
For whom all cups have dripped the wine of mirth,
For whom the sea has strained her honeyed throat

---

[*]Scholars have so far not succeeded in identifying Ransom.—Eds.

Countée Cullen as a high-school student in 1920

Cullen's gravestone in Woodlawn Cemetery, Bronx, N.Y.

Countée Cullen, wearing Phi Beta Kappa key, gives a reading in 1932.

Till all the world was sea, and I a boat
Unmoored, on what strange quest I willed to float;
Who wore a many-colored coat of dreams,
Thy gift, O Lord—I whom sun-dabbled streams
Have washed, whose bare brown thighs have held the sun
Incarcerate until his course was run,
I who considered man a high-perfected
Glass where loveliness could lie reflected,
Now that I sway athwart Truth's deep abyss,
Denuding man for what he was and is,
Shall breath and being so inveigle me
That I can damn my dreams to hell, and be
Content, each new-born day, anew to see
The streaming crimson vintage of my youth
Incarnadine the altar-slab of Truth?

Or hast Thou, Lord, somewhere I cannot see,
A lamb imprisoned in a bush for me?

Not so? Then let me render one by one
Thy gifts, while still they shine; some little sun
Yet gilds these thighs; my coat, albeit worn,
Still holds its colors fast; albeit torn,
My heart will laugh a little yet, if I
May win of Thee this grace, Lord: on this high
And sacrificial hill 'twixt earth and sky,
To dream still pure all that I loved, and die.
There is no other way to keep secure
My wild chimeras; grave-locked against the lure
Of Truth, the small hard teeth of worms, yet less
Envenomed than the mouth of Truth, will bless
Them into dust and happy nothingness.
Lord, Thou art God; and I, Lord, what am I
But dust? With dust my place. Lord, let me die."

Across the earth's warm, palpitating crust
I flung my body in embrace; I thrust
My mouth into the grass and sucked the dew,
Then gave it back in tears my anguish drew;
So hard I pressed against the ground, I felt

The smallest sand grain like a knife, and smelt
The next year's flowering; all this to speed
My body's dissolution, fain to feed
The worms. And so I groaned, and spent my strength
Until, all passion spent, I lay full length
And quivered like a flayed and bleeding thing.

So lay till lifted on a great black wing
That had no mate nor flesh-apparent trunk
To hamper it; with me all time had sunk
Into oblivion; when I awoke
The wing hung poised above two cliffs that broke
The bowels of the earth in twain, and cleft
The seas apart. Below, above, to left,
To right, I saw what no man saw before:
Earth, hell, and heaven; sinew, vein, and core.
All things that swim or walk or creep or fly,
All things that live and hunger, faint and die,
Were made majestic then and magnified
By sight so clearly purged and deified.
The smallest bug that crawls was taller than
A tree, the mustard seed loomed like a man.
The earth that writhes eternally with pain
Of birth, and woe of taking back her slain,
Laid bare her teeming bosom to my sight,
And all was struggle, gasping breath, and fight.
A blind worm here dug tunnels to the light,
And there a seed, racked with heroic pain,
Thrust eager tentacles to sun and rain;
It climbed; it died; the old love conquered me
To weep the blossom it would never be.
But here a bud won light; it burst and flowered
Into a rose whose beauty challenged, "Coward!"
There was no thing alive save only I
That held life in contempt and longed to die.
And still I writhed and moaned, "The curse, the curse,
Than animated death, can death be worse?"

"Dark child of sorrow, mine no less, what art
Of mine can make thee see and play thy part?

The key to all strange things is in thy heart."

What voice was this that coursed like liquid fire
Along my flesh, and turned my hair to wire?

I raised my burning eyes, beheld a field
All multitudinous with carnal yield,
A grim ensanguined mead whereon I saw
Evolve the ancient fundamental law
Of tooth and talon, fist and nail and claw.
There with the force of living, hostile hills
Whose clash the hemmed-in vale with clamor fills,
With greater din contended fierce majestic wills
Of beast with beast, of man with man, in strife
For love of what my heart despised, for life
That unto me at dawn was now a prayer
For night, at night a bloody heart-wrung tear
For day again; for *this*, these groans
From tangled flesh and interlockèd bones.
And no thing died that did not give
A testimony that it longed to live.
Man, strange composite of brute and god,
Pushed on, nor backward glanced where last he trod.
He seemed to mount a misty ladder flung
Pendant from a cloud, yet never gained a rung
But at his feet another tugged and clung.
My heart was still a pool of bitterness,
Would yield nought else, nought else confess.
I spoke (although no form was there
To see, I knew an ear was there to hear),
"Well, let them fight; they *can* whose flesh is fair."

Crisp lightning flashed; a wave of thunder shook
My wing; a pause, and then a speaking, "Look."

I scarce dared trust my ears or eyes for awe
Of what they heard, and dread of what they saw;
For, privileged beyond degree, this flesh
Beheld God and His heaven in the mesh
Of Lucifer's revolt, saw Lucifer

Glow like the sun, and like a dulcimer
I heard his sin-sweet voice break on the yell
Of God's great warriors: Gabriel,
Saint Clair and Michael, Israfel and Raphael.
And strange it was to see God with His back
Against a wall, to see Christ hew and hack
Till Lucifer, pressed by the mighty pair,
And losing inch by inch, clawed at the air
With fevered wings; then, lost beyond repair,
He tricked a mass of stars into his hair;
He filled his hands with stars, crying as he fell,
"A star's a star although it burns in hell."
So God was left to His divinity,
Omnipotent at that most costly fee.

There was a lesson here, but still the clod
In me was sycophant unto the rod,
And cried, "Why mock me thus? Am I a god?"

"One trial more: this failing, then I give
You leave to die; no further need to live."

Now suddenly a strange wild music smote
A chord long impotent in me; a note
Of jungles, primitive and subtle, throbbed
Against my echoing breast, and tom-toms sobbed
In every pulse-beat of my frame. The din
A hollow log bound with a python's skin
Can make wrought every nerve to ecstasy,
And I was wind and sky again, and sea,
And all sweet things that flourish, being free.

Till all at once the music changed its key.

And now it was of bitterness and death,
The cry the lash extorts, the broken breath
Of liberty enchained; and yet there ran
Through all a harmony of faith in man,
A knowledge all would end as it began.
All sights and sounds and aspects of my race

Accompanied this melody, kept pace
With it; with music all their hopes and hates
Were charged, not to be downed by all the fates.
And somehow it was borne upon my brain
How being dark, and living through the pain
Of it, is courage more than angels have. I knew
What storms and tumults lashed the tree that grew
This body that I was, this cringing *I*
That feared to contemplate a changing sky,
This I that grovelled, whining, "Let me die,"
While others struggled in Life's abattoir.
The cries of all dark people near or far
Were billowed over me, a mighty surge
Of suffering in which my puny grief must merge
And lose itself; I had no further claim to urge
For death; in shame I raised my dust-grimed head,
And though my lips moved not, God knew I said,
"Lord, not for what I saw in flesh or bone
Of fairer men; not raised on faith alone;
Lord, I will live persuaded by mine own.
I cannot play the recreant to these;
My spirit has come home, that sailed the doubtful seas."
With the whiz of a sword that severs space,
The wing dropped down at a dizzy pace,
And flung me on my hill flat on my face;
Flat on my face I lay defying pain,
Glad of the blood in my smallest vein,
And in my hands I clutched a loyal dream,
Still spitting fire, bright twist and coil and gleam,
And chiselled like a hound's white tooth.
"Oh, I will match you yet," I cried, "to truth."

Right glad I was to stoop to what I once had spurned,
Glad even unto tears; I laughed aloud; I turned
Upon my back, and though the tears for joy would run,
My sight was clear; I looked and saw the rising sun.

From *On These I Stand* (1925)

Excerpt from *The Medea of Euripides*: A New Version

CHORUS
(*Sing*)

WEEP FOR THE LITTLE LAMBS THAT DIE,
WEEP FOR THE EARLY-SLAIN,
WEEP FOR THE BRIDE SO SOON TO LIE
IN GOLDEN ROBES OF PAIN,
WEEP FOR MEDEA; WEEP FOR HER
WHO WIELDS THE FLASHING KNIFE;
WEEP THAT A MOTHER'S HAND SHOULD STIR
TO TAKE HER BABY'S LIFE.

(*The* TUTOR *and the* CHILDREN *return*)

TUTOR

Good news, my mistress, I have good news! Your worries are all over
now. All has happened just as you wished. Your little sons with their
fine gifts have won the princess. They are to stay in Corinth!

MEDEA

To stay in Corinth!

TUTOR

Why do you cry out as if in pain? This isn't the way I thought you
would receive such good news.

MEDEA

Good news! Good news! Indeed!

TUTOR

Have I stupidly said something I should not have said? Have I not brought you good news as I hoped to do?

MEDEA

You have only said what you had to say. I do not blame you.

TUTOR

Then why do you look so sad, mistress, and why do you cry?

MEDEA

I cry because I must. The gods and I have not done well.

TUTOR

Have courage, mistress. Now you can return to your own country. You will be happy there.

MEDEA

Before I go to mine I must send others to a further one.
(*She cries again*)

TUTOR

But you are not the only mother to be parted from her children. Some suffering is a part of every life, and should be borne patiently, as being the will of the gods.

MEDEA

I will be patient. I promise you I will. But go in now; get to your work. The children must still be cared for.
(*She turns to the children*)
O my sons, my sons, you have a place to live in and a home, but your unhappy mother may not live there with you. They are sending her

away before she can have a mother's full joy in you, before she sees you tall and strong, and married. I shall not be there to bless you on your wedding day. I have cared for you in vain, and toiled and worried, eating my heart out for you, bringing you into the world with shrieks of agony, and all in vain. Always I soothed my anguish with the thought of how one day you would tend me when old and past tending you, and how when I was dead you would fold my shriveled hands across my breast and bury me with honor. But that will never be. What can I hope for, parted from you, but a life lived out in misery and bitterness? When you no longer see your mother with your dear eyes, you will soon forget her! Why do you look at me like that? How can you smile, my little babies? What shall I do? Where shall I turn? My heart sinks as I look at you. When I see them like this, I grow weak as water clean through. My will is broken. I cannot do this thing!

(*Pause*)

Then I stand ridiculed; my foes are still unpunished. I must brace myself. To be tender now is to be a coward. Go, my children, go in; and let him who cannot bear to see the coming horror hide his face. My hand shall never shrink. But oh, my soul, how can you do this thing? Spare your sons, your own flesh, your very blood. In some friendly foreign land they may yet bring you peace and comfort. No, no—I will not leave them here to the mercy of their foes. They must die. There is no other way out. And since it must be so, let me who gave them their life take it from them. They were born to die today. I cannot change their destiny.

By now the burning chaplet blazes on my rival's head. By now she writhes, fast in the poisoned robe I wove for her. Dark is the path I tread but my foes shall tread a darker!

(*She turns to the children*)

And now, as your mother, I have a mother's last words for you, my children. Give me your little hands to kiss again, little hands so innocent of harm, dear little lips that I have often kissed and shall not kiss again forever. Oh, straight, slender bodies, frank open faces that I love! Do not fear! Your mother's blessings shall follow you to lighten up the land to which she sends you. Your father has made this world an evil place for you to stay. Farewell, small clinging hands! Soft, downy cheeks against my own, farewell! Go now. I cannot bear to look on you. It hurts me so! Ah, I know what a monstrous thing

I have to do, but rage has mastered me through and through, and routed reason in me.

FIRST WOMAN

Sometimes I think the happiest women are those who never had a child.

SECOND WOMAN

But the glad young voices ringing through the house!

FIRST WOMAN

Yes and the constant worries and all the little aches and pains!

SECOND WOMAN

But the joy of watching them, the little hands to hold, the little feet to guide.

FIRST WOMAN

The bitter we must eat that they may have the sweet!

From *The Medea and Some Poems* (1935)

Ralph Bunche in 1948

RALPH BUNCHE

Ralph Johnson Bunche was born in Detroit on 7 August 1904. Grandson of a slave, he was orphaned at twelve and thereafter cared for by his maternal grandmother in Los Angeles, where he was valedictorian of his high-school class. A gifted debater, he also won a four-year athletic scholarship to UCLA, where he played on three champion basketball teams. Despite part-time jobs, he wrote for the college paper, presided over the debating society, was sports editor of the yearbook, and a member of Phi Beta Kappa. He graduated *summa cum laude* in 1927.

Proceeding to Harvard, Bunche earned an A.M. in government in 1928 and began teaching political science at Howard University, soon becoming department chairman. He took several leaves for travel and research, completing a Ph.D. at Harvard in 1934. His dissertation on francophone Africa won the Tappan Prize as the best thesis in the social sciences. Bunche also laid important groundwork for Gunnar Myrdal's monumental *An American Dilemma* (1944).

From 1941 to 1944 Bunche was a research analyst for the Office of Strategic Services and then held a series of posts in the State Department. He helped draw up the charter of the United Nations, and joined the U.N. himself in 1946. His mediation in 1948-49 effected a cease-fire between the Israeli and Arab states, and he received an honorary LL.D. from Harvard and the Spingarn Medal in 1949. In 1950 he became the first black recipient of the Nobel Peace Prize.

In 1950 Bunche was appointed a professor in Harvard's Faculty of Arts and Sciences, but he resigned two years later without ever having taught, finding it impossible to extricate himself from continuing U.N. obligations. He did, however, later serve as a Harvard overseer (1959-65). Winning the Presidential Medal of Freedom in 1963, he rose to become Undersecretary General of the U.N., and amassed sixty-nine honorary degrees. He died in New York City on 9 December 1971, shortly after his retirement.

The Virtue of Color-Blindness

Habitually, as an American Negro, I am confronted with questions about the racial situation in the United States. People of the press, people in governments, people in the streets, always ask about it, and trying to answer the questions becomes quite a burden and a chore. But last summer, for a welcome change, I found that practically no one was asking me about the status of the Negro in the United States. That was because everyone was asking me about Senator McCarthy.

With your indulgence, I would like to recite just a few experiences —and I do this quite deliberately—covering most of the forty-nine years of my life, more than half of the time that has elapsed since the Emancipation Proclamation in 1863. I do this only because it may be revealing, because it will explain my own deep and continuing concern with this problem, and because perhaps it will throw some light on my thinking about the problem, which, in a nutshell, is that it is a sore burden to the entire nation and costly to every American whatever his color, wherever he resides, whether in New Orleans or in New York.

We may start with Detroit, my birthplace, where I spent the first ten years of my life. I came up as a child in Detroit with prejudice against another group—ironical, to be sure, but also typical in this milieu. The prejudice in Detroit in those days, which I inherited from the mores and folkways of the people of the community, was directed against the Italians, who were the immigrants then coming to Detroit and who were competing for jobs with the local inhabitants. Back in Detroit in 1914, one could observe all the stereotypes about the Italian population which are applied to any unwanted group. This has happened also in other parts of the country, up in New England, for example, where in the last century, the same sort of stereotypes applied to the Irish.

At that time in Detroit, there was little or no prejudice against Negroes because there were then not enough of us there. The Negro migration from the South came during the First World War. In fact, Detroit was so free of Negro prejudice in my childhood days that even the Y.M.C.A.'s were mixed. That in itself has an ironical significance. Later, they became segregated; but I learned to swim in a pool in a mixed Y.M.C.A. in Detroit.

My father was a barber, and one winter he got a job in Toledo, Ohio, so we moved to Toledo. There the feelings were very strong against the newly arriving Polish immigrants and there were community tensions. Later, we went for a winter to Knoxville, Tennessee. I think I was about six years old at the time. I've never been to Knoxville since. I imagine it is a very nice community, but I have only one impression of Knoxville, Tennessee, or rather, two. I relate it because it reveals how one experience of an unhealthy kind in a bad race-relations atmosphere can actually poison one's whole feeling. All I remember are these two things: First, that there were huge, delicious yams which grew in the red clay and which I liked very much. Secondly, that there was a park very close to where we lived into which I wandered one day and was promptly ordered out, because Negroes were not admitted. Whenever Knoxville has been mentioned in my presence in the intervening years, this early experience has been all that was registered in my mind about this community. This, obviously, is no healthy attitude for anyone to have. However, it is inescapable, because one's attitudes are based upon one's experiences and impressions.

Then we moved out West for my parents' health. We went to Albuquerque, New Mexico, and here again there was not much prejudice against Negroes, since they were so few in the community. There was very great feeling against Mexicans, however. As a matter of fact, one of my first direct experiences with racial prejudice was because my mother and I were probably mistaken for Mexicans. My mother took me to the Busy Bee Theater in Albuquerque in 1915. It was what we called in those days a "nickelodeon." My mother, crippled with rheumatism, took a seat in a middle row on the aisle. Very soon the usher came and tapped my mother on the shoulder and told her that he was very sorry but it was the rule of the house that Mexicans sit in the last row. My mother looked at him, and, in a most friendly way, thanked him for his kind consideration and said that the seats were quite comfortable and that she preferred to remain in them. We did remain in them, and that made quite an impression upon me as a youth.

Then we went out to Los Angeles. There we came in contact with prejudice against the Chinese and the Japanese, against the Mexican, and also against the Negro. In southern California in those days they drew no distinctions among minority groups in applying prejudice.

I recall one of my early experiences there. I had a newspaper route for one of the Los Angeles papers, and the newsboys were taken on an outing one day down to the beach, Venice or Santa Monica, as I recall. Two of us in the group were Negroes—Charles Matthews, now a prominent and highly successful attorney in Los Angeles, and myself. We had a very good time until we went to the bathhouses for the ocean bathing. There Matthews and I, because of our race, were met with refusal; we were not permitted to change. We had to sit outside the bathhouse until the other boys finished their swim. That made quite an impact upon me.

Later, I graduated from high school—Jefferson High School in Los Angeles. My high-school principal was a very fine man. I believe that although he had no prejudice he had never done much thinking about this problem. At my graduation, he came to me and said, quite sincerely, "We're sorry to see you go, Ralph. You know, we have never thought of you as a Negro."

I knew this was wrong, was incensed by it, but had not the words to express my feeling. But fortunately, my grandmother, who was a tiny woman of great spiritual strength and character, and who never lacked for words, was standing by and overheard this. Then in a very quiet way, for about five minutes, she lectured the principal of Jefferson High School, on what it means for a people to be proud of their origin and why we as Negroes were proud, were never apologetic, and that therefore, he was insulting not only her grandson, but the entire Negro race by saying that he had never thought of me as a Negro. After that there followed what perhaps was one of the longest and most profuse apologies any grandmother ever received for any reason whatsoever.

I remember, also, at U.C.L.A., how an early stand which the Provost of the university took had so much to do with determining the policy of that school, which has ever since been one of the very best in the country on the question of race relations. This was about 1923, when a Negro student, Leon Whittaker, was the Pacific Coast intercollegiate lightweight boxing champion. In those days, Stanford had what might be called an unwritten rule about not meeting Negroes in sports which involved direct personal contact. Their boxing team came down to meet U.C.L.A.'s. The Stanford coach announced that their lightweight boxer could not meet Whittaker, since Whittaker was a Negro. The U.C.L.A. coach this time was a little weak and substituted a white boxer for Whittaker, the Pacific Coast champion.

Unfortunately for the individual, but fortunately for the cause of democracy and the cause of racial justice, the U.C.L.A. white boy got the stuffings beaten out of him by the Stanford entrant. This incited the students of U.C.L.A. no little, because that was the decisive match, and they lost it to Stanford. Consequently, bright and early the next morning they were petitioning and circulating protests against the actions of the coach in making this substitution and thereby causing U.C.L.A. to lose the match and, also, causing one of our good students to get quite beaten up.

The Provost by noon of that day had a notice on the bulletin board in which he stated the simple principle on which the university would be run, namely, that there would be complete equality for all in the university community, irrespective of race or creed, that this principle would be observed by every teacher in the university, and anyone who could not act on that basis did not belong there. Very soon the boxing coach was out. That one act set the tone for this university, and has no little to do with the fact that in subsequent years Jackie Robinson, Kenny Washington and so many other Negroes have won distinction in that institution.

I might mention that chance may often be an important factor in hurdling racial barriers—for example the chance fact that a man cannot see very well. When I graduated from U.C.L.A. and went to Cambridge to do graduate work, I was given a letter by a man who ran a bookstore near the campus addressed to a friend of his who ran a bookstore in Cambridge. The intent was that I would use this letter to get my books at a discount in Cambridge. That was all. But when I got to Cambridge, I visited the bookshop and presented the letter to the owner—an extremely nearsighted man with heavy-lensed glasses. He pored over the letter, identified his friend's signature and said to me, "Sure, I'll give you a job." I had not come for a job, but I took it. Several weeks later, after the owner's wife had come into the shop and seen me, the owner called me aside and said, "Ralph, are you a Negro?" I replied affirmatively and expressed surprise that he did not know it. Explaining that he could not see well enough to tell, he said that had he known this originally he would not have hired me, since he would have thought that it would hurt his business. He found that it did not, however, and kept me on. Thus, the fact that a man may be a little blind can sometimes carry one over a racial obstacle. It is a pity that more people are not color blind in this respect. (1954)

From Foner, ed., *The Voice of Black America* (1972)

William H. Hastie ca. 1933

WILLIAM H. HASTIE

William Henry Hastie was born in Knoxville, Tennessee, on 17 November 1904, the only child of a college-educated father and a schoolteacher mother. He attended the celebrated Dunbar High School in Washington, D.C., finishing as class valedictorian and winning a scholarship to Amherst. One of four blacks in his class, he majored in mathematics and German, was elected to Phi Beta Kappa, and was graduated *magna cum laude* as valedictorian of the class of 1925. To earn money, he taught mathematics and science for two years at a manual-training school, and then entered Harvard Law School, where his high scholastic record earned him election to the *Law Review*. He received his degree with honors in 1930, followed by a Doctor of Juridical Science degree in 1933.

He joined the Washington firm of his second cousin Charles H. Houston (LL.B. '22, S.J.D. '23, and the first black on the *Harvard Law Review*), and taught intermittently at the Howard University Law School, becoming its dean in 1939. After a period as assistant solicitor in the Department of the Interior, he became the nation's first black federal judge, serving in the Virgin Islands (1937-39). During World War II he was an aide to the Secretary of War, but resigned in protest against the continuing segregation in the military—a public act of principle that was instrumental in winning him the Spingarn Medal in 1943. He returned to the Virgin Islands as its first black governor (1946-49). In 1949 he became the first black judge on a federal circuit court of appeals, being elevated to chief judge in 1968, and retiring to senior-judge status in 1971. Judge Hastie had received twenty-one honorary degrees (including an LL.D. from Harvard in 1975) at the time of his death from a heart attack in Philadelphia on 14 April 1976.

The Black Mystique Pitfall[1]

More than thirty-five years have passed since I first attended an annual convention of the NAACP. Thinking back, it is amazing that in the 1930s national and local leaders of this organization fought racism with such vigor, determination and enthusiasm. For at that time the prospect of much success was dim. Yet, then, as now, we ended each general conference session singing "march on till victory is won." And though the convention delegates were not as many as today we lifted every voice and sang loudly, and we meant what we sang.

We were regarded as militants and extremists because we refused to accept the notion of a racially segregated society and demanded radical change in the racist character of the American way of life. The NAACP was then regarded by many as both radical and impractical because it proposed to eliminate the whole complex of laws requiring or supporting racial segregation within a single generation.

Yet, during the last 25 years we have succeeded in outlawing the entire complex of legal requirements and prohibitions which imposed racial dis-crimination and segregation in almost every aspect of community life: in the armed services, in voting, in public education, in travel, in access to places of public accommodation, in access to public housing. The last major legal bastion of racism fell in 1967 when the Supreme Court ruled that a state cannot prohibit the marriage of a man and a woman because they are of different races.

Thus, for several years we have been able to say and to see that the legal order, which was grossly and pervasively racist 30 years ago, has become basically equalitarian and largely free of requirements or sanctions of racial segregation or discrimination. This comprehensive reshaping of the legal order has been one of the most remarkable achievements of any society in a relatively short period of time. The

[1]Text of address delivered by Judge Hastie at the NAACP 62nd Annual Convention in Minneapolis, July 7, 1971.

walls of Jericho have been breached on every side. And if the citadel of racism still has its defenders, we can be confident that, deprived of the protection of racist laws, racism is being overcome. That indeed has become our battle cry, our proud and confident song: "We Shall Overcome." Even a President of the United States, in an historic civil rights address to Congress and millions of television viewers calling for a comprehensive civil rights law, concluded with the clear, ringing and confident words, "we shall overcome."

Of course much remains to be done, much that the NAACP has been doing and is doing. The correction of law has been only the essential first campaign in a war against racism. A thousand battles remain to be won in every community to make the behavior of people conform with the equalitarian standards and mandates of our basic law. And from now on more of them must be fought outside of the courtroom than in lawsuits. You are fighting those battles. And encouraged by victories already won, you have every reason to look forward to greater and ever more numerous victories.

With such a background of past accomplishment and such prospect of future accomplishment in the war against racism, I, and I am sure many of you, have been surprised in recent years by the recrudescence of essentially defeatist policies and attitudes in members of the black community. I was not surprised a few years ago to hear a white South African educator try to convince an American audience that apartheid was good for both races in his country and would be good for both races here. But I have been amazed to hear voices of black Americans, including I am sorry to say numbers of young people, extolling the virtues of racial "separatism" as a desirable and potentially rewarding pattern for our future.

I told the gentleman from South Africa what I thought of his hideous views, apparently with the approval of an audience, mostly white. And now, I hope with your approval, I want to make some observations about black separatist notions in this country.

During the late 1960s, an alarming number of Negroes have tended uncritically to accept and encourage racial separatism in our country as a desirable and potentially rewarding pattern of American life. I state categorically that this trend must be halted and reversed, for it can lead only to greater bitterness and frustration and to even more inferior status than black Americans now experience.

Almost a hundred years ago, first by force and intimidation and somewhat later by segregation laws, the majority whites in the South and elsewhere succeeded in imposing racial separatism as a law-enforced pattern of post Civil War political, economic and social life. While this imposition was hateful to almost all Negroes it was not until the 1940s that a continuing drive, spearheaded by blacks and supported by an ever increasing number of whites, succeeded in making major breaches in the wall of separatist laws which kept most blacks out of the mainstream of American life. As already has been pointed out, by the 1960s practically all of this structure of laws sanctioning racial segregation had been destroyed. Thus many believed that the 1960s would see black America and much of white America, freed of racist laws, united in a climactic drive to eliminate from our society racist practices, behavior and patterns of thinking and living which still persisted after they were no longer required or encouraged by law.

At the same time, American Negroes have been migrating north and into cities. Fifty years ago, the majority of Negroes, poor, untrained and disinherited, lived in rural poverty. Millions, still poor, untrained and disinherited, have since moved into large cities. This black migration into the core of our cities has continued and accelerated and at the same time there has been unprecedented development of new residential areas in our outer cities and in suburbs beyond the cities. But access to most of this housing has been and even now, despite new fair housing laws tardily enacted, continues to be in fact inaccessible to most Negroes. Millions of whites have dispersed into new communities away from the center of our cities while millions of blacks, including most of the poor, untrained and disinherited, have concentrated in old and overcrowded center city ghettos. This distortion and prevention of normal population movement, probably more than anything else, has retarded the realization of a substantially integrated society which might otherwise have developed with the destruction of legal barriers. Instead, it has fostered the development of a deprived desperate subculture of poverty-stricken and all but hopeless black city dwellers. It also has spawned a new attitude toward separatism among many Negroes.

This is not to say that other factors have not been operating. Young blacks like young whites have become increasingly distrustful of, even cynical about the values of white society which tolerates so much poverty in the midst of extraordinary national affluence, which will spend lavishly for international war but only grudgingly for the domestic well-being of the disadvantaged, which spawned the white racists who murdered Martin Luther King, Medgar Evers and other less well known blacks and whites whose only wrong was aggressiveness in fighting racism. But the other side of the coin shows a black society that is no better in its aping of white materialism, in its accommodation of hucksters, hustlers and other operators as predatory and cynical as their white counterparts, in its spawn of sick violent men who murdered Malcolm X just as viciously as whites murdered Martin Luther King, and who continue to disfigure the black community with sporadic homicidal guerrilla strife among rival separatist groups.

Thus, revulsion against the vicious and indecent aspects of white society is no justification for glorifying and building a black society which in itself mirrors and at times intensifies the same evils. The only really better society of the future to which we can hopefully look forward and for which we can meaningfully work is a better total society in which present major evils, racism prominent among them, are substantially corrected.

Other blacks now reason that the black ghetto has become an ineradicable feature of American urban life. Accordingly, they have set out to glorify a separate subculture as a desirable base for community life and for developing black political and economic power and the human potential of black people generally. Listening to this siren song, too many young Negroes, particularly black college and university students, have conceived of their education as merely preparation for living in a black ghetto sub-structure and for the role of better exploiting the economic, political and humanistic potential of that subculture. Yet, the elimination of black ghettos during the next 25 years should be no more difficult than the elimination of racist laws during the last 25 years if enough people work diligently and purposefully to that end.

Of course, sensitive and concerned people should work as best they can to help make the life of the poor and untrained ghetto dwellers more rewarding, to relieve their economic plight and to mobilize their political power for effective self-help. But this should not blind us to the fact that the ghetto subculture is in itself stultifying and self-defeating. No one, least of all young people, should view it as something to be perpetuated. Rather, beyond ameliorating ghetto life, the basic direction and drive of effort should be toward bringing blacks fully into the mainstream of American life. Young black men and women in particular have the double opportunity of bringing themselves physically, psychologically, economically and culturally into that mainstream and at the same time concerning themselves with the plight of their less fortunate brothers. In summary, while ghetto life must be improved, this must be recognized as only a palliative, though a necessary one, in a period during which blacks and whites increase their efforts toward the elimination of the ghetto and the dispersal and integration of blacks within the total community.

Another consideration often underlies the disposition to accept and glorify racial separation. Life may be hard in the black community, but because the environment is familiar some find it more congenial than the unfamiliar large world where white strangers, many of them hostile, constitute the dominant majority. Moreover, one may become rather satisfied as a big fish in his familiar small dark pond yet feel insignificant, uncomfortable and even overwhelmed when thrown among all of the fish in the nearby mainstream of a deep, wide and rushing river. The psychology of withdrawal thus induced is understandable. But the future of the race, as of the world, belongs to the venturesome, not to the timid. The opportunities afforded by the state universities of Mississippi, Alabama, and Georgia would never have been opened to Negroes without the boldness, courage and willingness to face danger and discomfort which characterized the first blacks who enrolled there. The first black family in a neighborhood may not be made to feel at home. There may be real danger of physical harm to these trail-blazers. Yet, there always are a heroic few who will expose themselves in the vanguard. The older members of this audience remember that one of the early great victories of the NAACP occurred in the defense of a heroic little band of Detroit Negroes who successfully shot it out with a mob that had attacked them in a black home in a white neighborhood.

We also should face the fact that black ghettos never have afforded and never will afford worthwhile employment opportunities for more than a small percentage of the black community. This is not to dispute the desirability of more black ownership and operation of, and more black employment in, neighborhood businesses. Such highly visible enterprises and jobs in the neighborhood make for pride and dignity. And they represent economic opportunity and advancement for a relatively small number of people. But they offer no major solution to the problems of large-scale unemployment and under-employment of black people.

The major units of our economy will continue to be located elsewhere. Indeed, most people, regardless of color, don't want the noise and traffic and congestion of the centers of commerce and industry located next door to their homes. Thus, substantial upward mobility of the Negro toward more and better jobs is bound to carry him outside of the ghetto for employment and thus bring him more extensively and more closely in contact with whites, both co-workers and the public served by business and industry. And the higher each individual goes in the grade and type of his employment, the more he will have to succeed in an environment that is not predominantly black.

It follows that the earlier in his life that he learns to know and to cope effectively and confidently with an environment that is not black, the better prepared he will be for the future. I will never forget a conversation with Branch Rickey, several years after he opened the ranks of organized baseball to black players. He said that in his experience most black players entering the big leagues after attending school and playing as amateurs and semi-pros with and against whites experienced no unusual difficulty when they became major leaguers. The same, he said, was true of some to whom the big leagues represented their first experience in an environment that was not black. But, he added, all too many of this group with an exclusively black background tightened up and some of them never relaxed enough to succeed in performing up to their potential in the big leagues. To me this was one of the most scathing and tragic indictments of segregated learning and living that I ever had heard.

In Philadelphia, we have one of the best known and most successful projects to prepare disadvantaged blacks for employment and advancement in business and industry. Last night we paid well earned tribute to the black founder and leader of that enterprise, Rev. Leon Sullivan. In the course of this undertaking it has been found essential to spend long hours trying to equip people of the ghetto so that they can communicate and function effectively in a different environment and among people whose life-style is strange to them. The same problem exists, to a lesser degree, with many of us who, though more sophisticated, have had no opportunity to function except as members of a black community. I am all for black studies as important areas of learning which can contribute to pride, self-knowledge and self-esteem. But we have no less need for white studies which can help us to function more competently and usefully outside of the black community.

Then too, whites need the benefits of racially integrated living and learning. If blacks need to learn to be effective and at ease and able to communicate with whites in peer groups, a reciprocal need exists among whites. The opportunity to know blacks, to work with them and to gain respect for them as teachers and as fellow students is an important part of the white student's education. And at the same time many white students will acquire new interest in and understanding of the outlook and the problems of their black classmates. Of course this will not happen in every case. When I was in college, unfortunately there were some white students with whom I never exchanged even a pleasant "hello." But I certainly learned much from and about many students. And I hope that they learned some things of value from and about me. In the long run, it may well be that whites who have had no previous experience with fellow black students as members of peer groups or with blacks as competent teachers will be the greatest beneficiaries of unsegregated education. Ours will be a much better society when many white adults can look back at their childhood and say, "I loved my black teacher," rather than that ante-bellum condescension, "I loved my black mammy."

It seems appropriate at this point to comment upon another of the arguments we frequently hear from black apologists for racial separatism in the institutions of the community. The argument consists of two propositions: when whites impose segregation upon blacks, that is bad; but when blacks voluntarily choose to segregate themselves from whites, that somehow is good. And to make self-inflicted segregation at least sound better it is called "separatism" or more grandiosely "black nationalism."

I already have indicated that to me black racism is no better than white racism. For generations many Caucasians have glorified their whiteness, making a spurious virtue out of color and compensating for their own shortcomings by consoling themselves that at least they are white. Now many Negroes are practicing the same arrogant self-deception, glorifying their blackness, making a spurious virtue out of color and compensating for their shortcomings by shouting, "black is beautiful." To me, red or green is more beautiful than white or black. But this is an unimportant matter of taste. The serious thing is that racial mystique, with an overemphasis on racial differences and its attendant hostility toward other racial groups, is destructive of that sense of our common humanity and that willingness to make common cause for human betterment which whites and blacks so badly need. Any increased drawing apart of whites from blacks or blacks from whites in any institutional aspect of American life is self-defeating and harmful to all of us. It is not less harmful because some blacks say they want it that way.

I think the time is coming, within the life-span of many who are here today, when most whites and most blacks in America will rise above the superstition of caste and the feeling of racial superiority or inferiority. When that day comes, I will have no quarrel with blacks who, having won acceptance as equals, thereafter voluntarily choose to separate themselves from whites, just as some fine people now choose to withdraw into monasteries or to pursue their chosen way of life on a remote island in the South Pacific. But that day is not here yet. And the black separatist is helping to postpone its arrival by lending aid and encouragement to the white separatist in his losing fight to preserve caste as the pattern of American life. He is also blinding himself to the indignity of caste and the dreadful harm it does to blacks and whites alike by convincing himself that he likes it this way. I would have only compassion for the black separatist if he and the white separatist together were not perpetuating so much that is hurtful and hateful in American life.

My concluding observation, particularly addressed to separatists, is this. For too long in America whites have been up and blacks have been down. We are trying as never before to correct this racial disparity. In the process, whites must free themselves from false pride in their whiteness. And many of them are doing so. But it will not help for blacks, aping the worst characteristics of whites, to acquire false pride and arrogance in their blackness. Kenneth Clark, a very wise and thoughtful black American, made the essential point better than I can when he wrote:

"Nor can one build a solid pride on the quicksands of emotion, anger, rage, hatred—no matter how justifiable. Genuine pride—the pride that makes life worth the struggle with some hope of serenity— must come from solid personal achievement, from sensitivity and concern and respect for one's fellow man, from compassion and the willingness to struggle to give some substance to one's own life by trying to help others live with confidence in the possibility of positives. Pride, like humanity, is destroyed by one's insistence that he possesses it."

Let us face our problems and work for their solution in that spirit.

The Crisis (1971)

Rayford W. Logan in later years

RAYFORD W. LOGAN

Rayford Whittingham Logan, a butler's son, was born on 7 January 1897 in Washington, D.C., where he attended the Thaddeus Stevens School and the renowned M Street (later Dunbar) High School. At Williams College he was elected to Phi Beta Kappa, and received a B.A. in 1917 and an M.A. in 1929. During World War I he was a first lieutenant in the all-black 93rd Division, and remained abroad for several years to assist W.E.B. Du Bois in the work of the Pan-African Congress. At Harvard he earned a second M.A. in 1932 and a Ph.D. in history in 1936, profiting particularly from the guidance of professors Arthur Schlesinger Sr. and James Phinney Baxter III, as Du Bois had from that of A.B. Hart.

After teaching briefly at Dunbar High School, Logan headed the history departments of Virginia Union University (1925-30) and Atlanta University (1933-38). In 1938 he joined the faculty of Howard University, chairing its history department from 1942 until his retirement in 1965. He published many books on black history, and wrote the centennial history of Howard University. He received honorary doctorates from Williams (1965) and Howard (1972), was made a Commander of the National Order of Honor and Merit by Haiti (1941), and was the 1980 recipient of the Spingarn Medal. With a young colleague, he finished editing the invaluable *Dictionary of American Negro Biography* just before succumbing to a heart ailment in Washington on 4 November 1982.

The Confessions of an Unwilling Nordic

Negroes can attain only to a fixed level of education, acquire only a limited amount of wealth, travel only in certain degrees of latitude and longitude. If an individual is found out of these circumscribed milieux, he is not a Negro. He is an East Indian or a Brazilian, a Senegalese or a Tahitian, but not a Negro, and most certainly not an American Negro.

The following stories will strain the credulity of the readers of *The World Tomorrow* who, of course, have no preconceived ideas concerning Negroes. Remember, however, that an American Negro is the author, and that while he can imitate, he can not create. (See Lothrop Stoddard, Madison Grant, Imperial Wizard Evans, and other authorities.)

When I say that I am a Negro, I mean one of those who should not be able to "pass." Otherwise, there would be no point to this tale. My hair is what French people call *frisés*; my color, yellow. My features betray my African ancestry. In a southern city my brother, who can pass for a Nordic, was afraid to let me accompany him into a white restaurant. But it seems that I do not conform to some arbitrary conception of a Negro's speech, behavior, and dress. Through no fault of my own I have acquired an education superior to that of many of my lords and masters. I am a graduate of an old New England college—no, it is not Amherst—which prides itself on the number of high government officials, men of letters, and in the earlier days, soldiers of Christ that it has contributed to society. By osmosis, perhaps, I imbibed some of the learning and culture of this institution. As a result I have found myself in some very amusing, embarrassing, and edifying predicaments.

It was one of my favorite professors who first suggested what a dangerous anomaly I had become. At the close of a conversation concerning my future, he concluded:

"Upon whatever career you embark, always be colored."

"Why—," I looked at my hands and felt my hair. "Why, that should not be very difficult," I concluded with a puzzled laugh.

But it was. I had the first proof of my professor's perspicacity a few days after our conversation. While on the way to Washington to spend the Easter holidays of 1917, I left the train at North Philadelphia in order to stretch my legs. Upon returning, I found an enormous white man occupying most of the seat. With some difficulty I squeezed in beside him and pretended to sleep.

My fellow-traveler probably felt that there was no use to occupy the same seat unless you are going to talk. He interrupted my feigned slumbers by asking the name of some stream that we were passing. He appeared so totally ignorant of the geography of the section that I queried:

"Is this your first trip South?"

"No, this is my first trip North."

I eased off a little in my corner.

"My home is in Waco, Texas,"—I looked around for another seat—"I have just been up to the Quaker City on business."

"Is that so? I have a classmate from Waco, a fine chap,—."

"You don't say. I know his people well. I believe that his daddy is my wife's cousin. Say, he sure showed those folk up North how to play baseball, didn't he? . . . But it takes a lot of money to go there."

I did not deem it necessary to inform my corpulent friend that a scholarship made it possible for me to attend this ultra-exclusive school. By this time I was convinced that he had no idea that, perhaps for the first time in his life, he was riding with a colored man. I decided to sound him on the one subject about which I knew he could talk most fluently and authoritatively. Without too much abruptness I turned our conversation to lynching.

"We students of sociology are very much interested in this matter of lynching. Above all, we are trying to arrive at the reasons."

"Rape. All a 'nigger'"—I needed no further proof of his blissful ignorance—"thinks about is white women."

"But we up North are told that rape is responsible for only a comparatively small number of lynchings. I have read of one case in which the alleged cause was an argument about a mule."

"Hum . . . ('Alleged' seemed to be giving him some difficulty.) Maybe so. But you folks don't know 'niggers' as we do. All you know is what you read about 'em. I don't approve of lynching myself as a general rule, but I tell you we have to lynch one every now and then to keep 'em in their place. If we didn't they'd get so uppity that we couldn't handle them."

"I see. They must be making some progress then."

"Progress!" he snorted. "How can a darky make any progress? The curse of Ham is upon him. A 'nigger' won't ever be nothing but a 'nigger.' And the worst ones is them that's got white blood in 'em. (I was tempted to ask how they got it, but remembered in time that that was irrelevant.) The only 'niggers' that's ever amounted to anything is them that's got nothing but black blood. The only great 'darky' was Booker T. Washington, and he was coal black. *He* didn't have any high-falutin' ideas about sending a 'coon' to college."

"That hardly tallies with the opinion of our professor of American literature. He has frequently told us that one of the greatest stylists in America is Dr. Du Bois who, as you know, is almost white."

"Of course. That's due to the white blood in him."

This illuminating inconsistency inspired me to further questioning.

"What about voting? Do Negroes vote in Texas?"

"That depends. I make the 'niggers' on my farm vote for prohibition. When a 'darky' gets drunk, he don't want to work. When option is up, I line 'em up, march 'em to the polls and see that every damn one of 'em votes against liquor. But that is the only time I allow my 'niggers' to vote."

Deciding that I had learned enough and that I had listened at sufficient length to his insulting terms, I drifted off into the causes of the World War. We agreed that in the last analysis the conflict was a result of contending nationalities. This led my entertaining traveler to remark about the complexity of races in America. He himself had the blood of four or five peoples in his veins. Forseeing his question, I tried to avert it by concocting a story of an American boy whose English mother, born in India, had married in Turkey his French father, born in Martinique. This tickled him, but could not divert his thought.

"And what was the nationality of your ancestors?" For a moment I remembered my professor's admonition. But since we had not yet reached Baltimore and since there were still no other seats in the train, I quibbled.

"My case is almost as bad. My first name is German, my middle name, my mother's, is one of the oldest in England, and my last seems to be a favorite among the Irish saloon-keepers along Washington Street in Boston."

He chucked until the window rattled. Then we chatted about less dangerous things almost into Washington. As the train was pulling into Union Station, he gave me his card, told me that he was staying at the _____ Hotel with his cousin, the Representative from some district in Texas, and invited me to call to see him. I have often wondered whether he ever found from my classmate the identity of his inquisitive companion.

My next similar experience had for its setting the American hospital at Mailly, France. Probably no other colored officer had preceded me there, because this was in the early days of July, 1918. After the regulation bath, I found myself in a private room with a white orderly attending me. From the beginning, I realized that he never suspected that I was colored. Had he done so, the initial shock would have prevailed over his obligation to serve his superior. We Negroes have learned to look for that forced laugh, spontaneous irritation, or speechless amazement which many white men can not hide when they unexpectedly find themselves in the presence of their ubiquitous pest. Without an inquiring glance, my orderly set to work arranging my clothes, asking about my needs, giving me such information as would be helpful. I avoided conversation as much as possible, for I knew the only two subjects about which he was likely to talk: women and Negroes.

But he evidently thought it a part of his duties to help me beguile the time. One afternoon when he came to get the dishes, he asked to what regiment I had belonged. I told him, adding that it was a colored regiment. Instead of staring at me quizzically as I had expected, he ejaculated:

"Damn. Weren't you afraid of 'em? They say that them 'niggers' can fight like hell, but I wouldn't want to be with 'em. Didn't they ever try to bump you off?"

"Bump me off? What for?"

"Just 'cause you're white. I've heard it said that a white officer dassn't go in front of 'em up there at the front less the 'darkees' shoot 'em down from behind."

"But what do they want to kill them for? I don't know any who have been killed in our outfit."

"You're darned lucky then. Maybe you know how to treat them, but lemme tell you, I wouldn't want to be with 'em for all the *vin rouge* in France.—I guess they can guzzle plenty of cognyac, can't they?"

"No. Our soldiers are the same as any others."

"Well, they ain't got no chance if they ever come around here. We done told these frogs not to let one light in a cafe, and if we ever ketch a woman with one of 'em, we'll run her out of town. Why, these bloody idiots believe they've got tails like monkeys."

A call from another patient prevented him from continuing his revelations.

By this time I had decided never to disillusion any one who unbosomed himself to me so confidentially. At first I had wanted to "bawl out" the soldier for the use of words that are anathema to any self-respecting Negro. But the information obtained was well worth the price of my silence.

My most bewildering situation confronted me at Camp Pontanezen near Brest. To this day I do not know how the blunder occurred. I suppose, however, that the colonel commanding the casuals merely glanced at my record, found that I had considerable court-martial experience, spoke German and French fluently, and had a record at my previous camp of "excellent." It probably never dawned upon him that I was not white. Whatever may be the explanation, I was assigned to duty with a new convoy that had just come over from America to join the Army of Occupation in Germany.

I expected the order to be rescinded as soon as I reported to duty. But the commanding officer undoubtedly concluded that since I was attached to a white outfit I must be white. The situation became truly piquant the following day when the company commander called me to give these instructions:

"Mr.—, I am leaving for Paris at once. You will have complete charge of the company during my absence."

And so I am perhaps the only colored officer who actually commanded a white company in the A. E. F. For a week white shavetails, non-coms and "bucks" obeyed my orders with an alacrity that stupefied me. At no time did any one seem to suspect that an unwritten law of the American Army was being trampled under foot.

On the appointed day we prepared to entrain for Ehrenbreitstein. One white orderly was busy shining my shoes. Another was packing my bedding roll. In the midst of all this stir and confusion the captain came in from Paris and at the same time arrived orders from headquarters relieving me from duty with the regiment. The captain expressed sincere regret that I could not accompany them. I have never known whether the order was due to my being colored or a casual.

Some time afterwards I met the same captain while he was on leave in Paris. As soon as he saw me, he rushed up and kissed me on both cheeks.

"I certainly am sorry that they left you behind. That would have been a rich joke to have had a colored officer in a white outfit up in Germany. I swear I believe that I was the only one who knew the truth and I didn't care a rap."

Thus, the one person who apparently recognized the colored gentleman in the corded wood appreciated the joke too much to betray him.

After the war I decided to remain in France, where I would not, as I thought, run the risk of humiliating experiences. But I counted without the thousands of Americans who were roaming over Europe during those halcyon days when the German and Polish mark, the Austrian crown and the French franc were cascading toward zero.

One day in Vienna a woman, after eyeing me rather intently, approached and said in German:

"You have your Key?"

When she had verified in most minute detail my Phi Beta Kappa key, she informed me that her husband had been professor of German Literature at _____ University before the war. Without giving me an opportunity to express my delight at meeting a compatriot in such a distant land, she continued:

"Of course, I left America with my husband, who is a German. We are already planning to return—this was in 1921—since the feeling against us is rapidly declining. And we have no bitterness against you Americans. You were fooled into the war. The only thing that we can not forgive is your using 'niggers' against us. It was bad enough for the Frenchmen to use Africans, but to send 'darkies' from America, that was a crime against civilization. And for Woodrow Wilson to have committed such a folly! It was all right to use them as stevedores perhaps, but to have them kill white men! Is it a wonder that they did not revolt when they returned to America.

"And ever since the war, Vienna has been flooded with them. We are hardly able to live from hand to mouth while these jazz band players strut around in fur coats and diamonds. I even saw one the other day driving an automobile . . . It is positively disgusting the way the kids have gone crazy over them. You can see twenty or more following one every time he goes out in the street. And worst of all I have seen women dancing with them. It makes my blood run cold. We ought to form a society here to teach the 'darkies' that they have no more rights than in America. *I* am going back to America, where they know how to behave themselves."

Naturally, the richest yarn comes last. If it does not rank with Baron Münchhausen's best, I'm a prevaricator.

The stock exchange panic of April, 1920, found me "long" on dollars. The blow was such a severe one that my physician ordered me to Dax to take a rest cure. And so I went down to that delightful town on the Adour, as renowned for the stentorian voice of the train announcer as for the celebrities who come to take the baths in order to rid themselves of their real or fancied pains. Among the persons in the first class dining room were Mme. Poincaré and M. and Mme. Fallières. As far as I could judge there were no Americans. I felt free therefore to mingle with the guests, most of whom spoke French and German. I enjoyed the theatre, the mock bull fight, came down to dinner every evening in tuxedo, as did the other guests, had a bank telephone me the quotations from the Bourse, played bridge and billiards.

One evening as I was knocking the balls around waiting for dinner, a woman walked in.

"Would Madame like to play?" I inquired in French.

"Why, yes. I think that we have time for a short game, say twenty-five points."

The accent was not pure, but at the time my ear was not attuned sufficiently to distinguish the nationality of the person speaking. We had a rather exciting game, interspersing our shots with jokes about our ailments. The *Maître d'hôtel* announced dinner just as the last point was scored.

I laid aside my cue and stepped back with my most perfect European bow in order to allow my charming opponent to pass. But she had to satisfy her curiosity.

"Pardon me, but is the gentleman Polish?"

"Why, no, Madame, I am an American."

"You American? Whoever saw an American who looked like you? Besides," she changed suddenly to English, "you can't fool me. You may be able to fool these Europeans, but we Americans can recognize one another anywhere. Come now, there is no use in continuing your incognito. We all know that you are a Polish prince."

When I had recovered, I blurted:

"Since you are an American, you will certainly recognize an American Negro."

She nearly screamed with delight.

"You a 'nigger'! A 'nigger' here in Dax, staying at this hotel, speaking French better than I can, eating in the first class dining room while I eat in the second! That is the cleverest disguise I have ever heard in my life. A Polish prince passing for a 'nigger.' That is *too* funny."

Once, however, I had to establish my real identity in order to escape too tangible evidence of "conduct unbecoming an officer and a gentleman." Brest was likewise the scene of this episode. It came about in this way.

On July 4, 1919, an American officer, temporarily a victim of *eau-de-vie*, cognac and Pommery, threw a French flag from the window of a restaurant down into the *Rue de Siam*. "Old Gimlet Eye" had a harder time preventing a pitched battle between the French and Americans than he ever had chasing Chinese or bull-dozing Haitians. The feelings of the French, of course, remained extremely bitter.

As I was returning to camp one night shortly after this unfortunate incident, I passed four French sailors on the dimly lighted road. Without a word of warning one of them initiated me into a taste of Brittany mire. Fortunately, all four tried at the same time to pommel me. They made no effort to rob me. Their one desire seemed to be to commit assault and battery with the greatest degree of efficiency and thoroughness, and to use all possible variations of *"sale Américain," "sacré Américain,"* and others that I hope I misunderstood.

The effectiveness of their blows and the repetition of their oaths finally reminded me that I was not an American, but only a Negro. I told them so. I appealed to their friendship for Negroes. A punch on the nose and a jab to the ribs punctuated my statement and my appeal. Then, as one fist sought an unbruised spot on my face, I grabbed it and rubbed it over my hair.

"Tiens, he *is* colored. His hair is *frisés.* . . . *Mille pardons, mon ami* . . . We thought you were white."

Their apologies were profuse; their dismay touching. They escorted me back to camp singing "La Madelon."

I am opposed to segregation in any form. I am likewise opposed to class legislation of any description. But if Heflin or Blease succeeded in having passed a law requiring all anomalous Negroes to wear on their exterior garments and on the windshield of their automobile a sign, "colored," I should comply most willingly.

World Tomorrow (1927)

Leadbelly with his guitar ca. 1947

LEADBELLY

Huddie William Ledbetter was born outside Mooringsport, Louisiana, on 21 January 1885. He learned music from his mother (a choir director) and two musical uncles, and became known as the best guitarist and singer in the region by the age of 16. After his first marriage he moved to Texas, where he met the famous bluesman "Blind" Lemon Jefferson, who performed with him and taught him many songs.

Quick to anger, Ledbetter spent three stretches in prison for murder or assault (1918–25; 1930–34; 1939–40). It was during his second imprisonment that folklorists John and Alan Lomax discovered him while they were recording songs among Southern chaingangs. The musician acquired the nickname "Leadbelly" because, in Alan Lomax's words, "he had guts of steel and could outwork, outsing and outlast anybody else on a job."

Ledbetter accompanied the Lomaxes on a 6000-mile round of recording and performing, winding up in New York City and starting a professional career. He captivated both children and adults, and his visit to Harvard was followed by appearances on many college campuses. He had an unsurpassed ready repertory of some 500 songs of all types, many original with him. Fortunately, he recorded an enormous number of them for commercial release. He also did a series of radio programs in New York, and his singing graced a number of Hollywood films. Tennessee Williams, in his play *Orpheus Descending*, hailed Leadbelly as the "greatest man that ever lived on the twelve-string guitar," and the legendary Woody Guthrie called him "the best living folksinger."

Not long after a visit to Paris, Ledbetter succumbed to Lou Gehrig's disease in a New York hospital on 6 December 1949. He was the subject of a biographical novel, *The Midnight Special* (1971), by Richard Garvin and Edmond Addeo, and of an effective film biography, *Leadbelly* (1976), starring Roger E. Mosley and directed by the eminent black man-of-many-arts Gordon Parks.

Kenneth B. Murdock to John A. Lomax

Leverett House
Harvard University
Cambridge, Massachusetts

January 18, 1935

John A. Lomax, Esq.
Wilton, Connecticut

Dear Mr. Lomax:

I am delighted that there is a chance of getting you and Lead
Belly to come to Cambridge, and it will give me great pleasure to have
you here at Leverett House. We can get an audience for you of
undergraduates and faculty members, and I shall ask especially the
members of the English Department and of the Modern Language
Conference. Mr. Kittredge is an Associate of this House and will do
his best to be here, since he is very eager to hear Lead Belly.

It seems possible that if you were able to come, an afternoon
meeting, at which Lead Belly could sing, might be arranged in a small
room for a small group as part of a regular series of lectures given in
connection with a bequest of Mr. Gray for lectures on poetry. If this
were arranged, this meeting would be in the afternoon, and for it
there would be a fee of, I should suppose, about $50—possibly more.
Then, I should be delighted to have you dine with me and would plan
a meeting for the evening at Leverett House. Unfortunately the
Houses have no funds to pay lecturers or entertainers, but we should,
of course, be glad to have Lead Belly "pass his hat", and if there were
a fee for the afternoon performance your trip would not be entirely
unremunerative.

I have to be away from the first of February until the 9th. In the
next week Professor Copeland is reading in the House, and we find

ordinarily that one big event a week is enough. So far as I can tell now, however, the evening of the 18th, or 19th, or 20th, would be entirely all right, and I think that probably one of these afternoons could be arranged for the poetry meeting. If these dates are not convenient for you, what about the 25th, 26th, or 27th?

If you could possibly give me a choice of dates, it might make it a little easier to arrange both for the poetry meeting in the afternoon and might help to make sure that Mr. Kittredge could be present. He would be very much disappointed not to be here and tells me that he has very few engagements for February. However, if I could have a choice of dates to offer him, it would be more convenient.

I am hoping very much that all this can be arranged satisfactorily to you: the prospect seems to us a delightful one. Your recent book has aroused a great deal of interest among undergraduates here, and I know that they will be most appreciative of the opportunity to hear you speak and to hear Lead Belly sing. I am going away on the first of February, but I think if you can give me an idea of possible dates for you, we can arrange it all before that time.

Sincerely yours,

Kenneth B. Murdock
Master.

Negro Who Sung Way Out of Southern
Prisons Wins Two Harvard Audiences

Lead Belly and His 12-String Guitar Heard in Folk Songs of
South at Emerson Hall and Leverett House

Lead Belly, Negro minstrel who won his freedom from two Southern penitentiaries with his plaintive, husky voice accompanying him on his 12-string guitar, sang his way into the hearts of two Harvard audiences yesterday.

At Emerson Hall in the after-noon and at Leverett House in the evening, he performed before capacity crowds. The Cambridge intellectuals, and numerous English students, flocked to hear him illustrate the folk songs of the South.

He held them all, from Prof. George Lyman Kittredge to the lowliest freshman, spellbound with his primitive chants and his unique harmony. They heard more than folk songs, they heard the miracle voice of Lead Belly which has melted prison walls and wrung pardons from Governors.

He was introduced by John A. Lomax, Harvard, 1907, collector of early American ballads, to whose service the troubadour has devoted his life since Lomax maneuvered his release from the Louisiana Prison at Angola last Summer.

Past Behind Him

Lead Belly has put his past behind him. Gone are the days when he wandered about the Southland, a battered guitar slung over his shoulder and a long knife protruding from the hip pocket of his only pair of pants.

Today he is the chauffeur, servant and handy man of Mr. Lomax, and applies his energies especially to the guitar. He has forgotten the knife. He is well dressed, and he feels that the days when his toes protruded through his only pair of battered, rusty shoes are gone forever.

For his Cambridge debut he wore a colored shirt, red scarf, blue overalls, tan shoes, and silk socks. His guitar is new and polished, although it still has 12 strings, all of which he can set a-humming in a second.

At each appearance he played and sang for more than an hour, filling the halls with his powerful hoarse voice and vibrant music of his guitar. The applause justified his boast that he is the "King of the 12-string guitar players—the bestest in the world."

As he plays, his eyes are shut and his entire frame from head to toe rocks gently to and fro with his music.

Lead Belly's feet are a musical education in themselves. His left one beats the single tap from one end of a ballad to the other, while his right foot beats double, triple or quadruple time as occasion demands.

"If you don't think that's hard, try it yourself sometime," laughed Mr. Lomax. Several did and it is more than hard. It seems almost an impossible feat of muscular coordination.

He has a repertoire of 500 folk songs, ballads, adaptations of cowboy songs and chants. Many of them, he asserts, are of his own composition. Mr. Lomax has been unable to find any other sources for them.

They are mostly "sinful songs," which are distinguished from religious or spiritual songs by the Southern Negroes. Any song which lacks an ecclesiastical interpretation is a "sinful song."

Lead Belly himself has been sinful in the days when he handled a knife as aptly as he handles his guitar. Therein lies definite proof that he has composed at least two songs—one to Gov. Pat Neff of Texas, the other to Gov. O.K. Allen of his native Louisiana.

The former opened the gates of the Texas prison where Lead Belly was sent, sentenced to serve 35 years on a murder charge. The latter enabled him to quit the Louisiana prison where Mr. Lomax found him serving another extensive sentence for assault with intent to murder.

No Jazz in Ballads

There is but slight resemblance between his singing and that of the stage and radio Negro entertainers. There is a deep, primitive quality to Lead Belly's songs. He is really voicing the joys, sorrows and hopes of his race. There is no trace of jazz in his ballads and folk songs, but his "blues," which are quite different, posses[s] the basic foundations of American jazz.

As for his guitar, he can do more things to it than Max Baer did to Carnera.

The guitar was purchased in New York, after days of searching. It is not a common instrument.

"Twelve strings—It sounds like an eight-masted schooner," Prof. Robert Hillyer, one of the sponsors of his Harvard visit, remarked yesterday. Dean Kenneth B. Murdock and other members of the English department also encouraged the Cambridge visit of Lead Belly. Today Lead Belly and Mr. Lomax will return to their temporary home in Wilton, Conn.

Boston Globe (1935)

JOHN HOPE FRANKLIN

John Hope Franklin was born on 2 January 1915 in the tiny black Oklahoma town of Rentiesville, where his father was its postmaster and only lawyer. Both parents were college-educated and kept plenty of books at home. After the family moved to Tulsa, Franklin attended the all-black Booker T. Washington High School, where he was active in debating, singing, and trumpet-playing, and finished as class valedictorian in 1931. A scholarship plus odd jobs enabled him to attend Fisk University, where he found time to continue debating and singing in addition to serving as student-government president. Majoring in history, he received his B.A. *magna cum laude* in 1935. He pursued graduate work at Harvard, was a student of the famous historians Samuel Eliot Morison and Arthur M. Schlesinger Sr., and received his M.A. in 1936 and Ph.D. in 1941.

Starting in 1939 he taught history for four years at St. Augustine's College in North Carolina, moving to North Carolina College in Durham for another four years before accepting a professorship at Howard University in 1947. In 1949 he became the first Negro to read a paper before the Southern Historical Association, a body he would rise to head two decades later. He held visiting professorships at Harvard (1950), the University of Wisconsin (1952-53), and Cornell (1953), and in 1956 was persuaded to chair a feud-ridden department of 52 white historians at Brooklyn College—the first black to head any college department in the state. In 1964 he went to the University of Chicago and retired in 1982, when he accepted an invitation to a history chair at Duke University, shifting to its law school in 1985, where he has since remained.

Among his many books are *The Free Negro in North Carolina, 1790-1860* (1943); *From Slavery to Freedom: A History of Negro Americans* (1947), which quickly became the standard mainstream survey and reached its 6th edition in 1987; *The Militant South, 1800-1861* (1956), the first work by a black scholar to appear in the Harvard Historical Series since Du Bois' slave-trade volume 60 years earlier; *The Emancipation Proclamation* (1963), celebrating its topic's centennial; *A Southern Odyssey: Travelers in the Antebellum North* (1967), which won the Jules Landry Award; and *George Washington Williams: A Biography* (1985), which garnered the Clarence L. Holte Prize. Franklin

John Hope Franklin ca. 1960

also served for three years as national president of the United Chapters of Phi Beta Kappa. The recipient of a host of honors at home and abroad, he was named to the Oklahoma Hall of Fame in 1978 and holds honorary degrees (at last count) from 90 colleges and universities, including an LL.D. from Harvard in 1981. He is by common consent the foremost black historian of the past half-century.

Franklin's 1988 Charles Homer Haskins Lecture, which we excerpt below, is one in a series sponsored annually by the American Council of Learned Societies, and named for the Council's first chairman, who was, appropriately, an internationally renowned professor of history at Harvard (1902-31), dean of its Graduate School (1908-24), and one of Franklin's predecessors as president of the American Historical Association. Franklin included the Haskins lecture in his collection *Race and History: Selected Essays 1938-1988* (1989).

A Life of Learning

Since I was merely passing through [Fisk University] en route to law school, I had little interest in an undergraduate concentration. I thought of English, but the chairman of that department, from whom I took freshman English, discouraged me on the ground that I would never be able to command the English language. (Incidentally, he was a distinguished authority in American literature and specialized in the traditions of the Gullah-speaking people of the Sea Islands. I was vindicated some years later when he chaired the committee that awarded me the Bancroft Prize for the best article in the *Journal of Negro History*.) My decision to major in history was almost accidental. The chairman of that department, Theodore S. Currier, who was white, had come into that ill-fated course in contemporary civilization and had delivered the most exciting lectures I had ever heard. I decided to see and hear more of him.

During my sophomore year I took two courses with Professor Currier, and my deep interest in historical problems and the historical process and what he had to say was apparently noted by him. Soon we developed a close personal relationship that developed into a deep friendship. Soon, moreover, I made the fateful decision to give up my plan to study and practice law and to replace it with a plan to study, write, and teach history. My desire to learn more about the field resulted in his offering new courses, including seminars, largely for my benefit. He already entertained the hope that I would go to Harvard, where he had done his own graduate work [A.M. '28]. I had similar hopes, but in the mid-1930s with the Depression wreaking its havoc, it was unrealistic to entertain such hopes. With a respectable grade point average (that C+ prevented my graduating *summa cum laude*), and strong supporting letters from my professors, I applied for admission to the Harvard Graduate School of Arts and Sciences.

Harvard required that I take an aptitude test that must have been the forerunner to the Graduate Records Examination. It was administered at Vanderbilt University, just across town but on whose grounds I had never been. When I arrived at the appointed place and took my seat, the person in charge, presumably a professor, threw the examination at me, a gesture hardly calculated to give me a feeling of welcome or confidence. I took the examination but cannot imagine that my score was high. As I left the room a Negro custodian walked up to me and told me that in his many years of working there I was the only black person he had ever seen sitting in a room with white people. The record that Fisk made that year was more important. The Association of American Universities placed Fisk University on its approved list. On the basis of this new recognition of my alma mater, Harvard admitted me unconditionally. Apparently this was the first time it had given a student from a historically black institution an opportunity to pursue graduate studies without doing some undergraduate work at Harvard. The University declined, however, to risk a scholarship on me.

Admission to Harvard was one thing; getting there was quite another. My parents were unable to give me more than a very small amount of money and their good wishes. I was able to make it back to Nashville, where Ted Currier told me that money alone would not keep me out of Harvard. He went to a Nashville bank, borrowed $500, and sent me on my way.

Shortly after my arrival in Cambridge in September, 1935, I felt secure academically, financially, and socially. At Fisk I had even taken two modern foreign languages in order to meet Harvard's requirement, and in Currier's seminars I had learned how to write a research paper. Since I was secretary to the librarian at Fisk for four years, I had learned how to make the best use of reference materials, bibliographical aids, and manuscripts. Even when I met my advisor, Professor A. M. Schlesinger, Sr., I did not feel intimidated, and I was very much at ease with him while discussing my schedule and my plans. After I got a job washing dishes for my evening meal and another typing dissertations and lectures, a feeling of long-range solvency settled over me. Although I had a room with a Negro family that had taken in black students since the time of Charles Houston and Robert Weaver, I had extensive contact with white students who never showed the slightest condescension toward me. I set my own priorities, however, realizing that I had the burden of academic deficiencies dating back to secondary school. I had to prove to myself and to my professors that the Association of American Universities was justified in placing Fisk University on its approved list. I received the M.A. degree in nine months and won fellowships with which I completed the Ph.D. requirements.

There were few blacks at Harvard in those days. One was completing his work in French history as I entered. As in Noah's Ark, there were two in the law school, two in zoology, and two in the College. There was one in English and one in comparative literature; there were none in the Medical School, and none in the Business School.

The most traumatic social experience I had there was not racist but anti-semitic. I was quite active in the Henry Adams Club, made up of graduate students in United States History. I was appointed to serve on the committee to nominate officers for the coming year which, if one wanted to be hypersensitive, was a way of making certain that I would not be an officer. When I suggested the most active, brightest graduate student for president, the objection to him was that although he did not have some of the more reprehensible Jewish traits, he was still a Jew. I had never heard any person speak of another in such terms, and I lost respect not only for the person who made the statement but for the entire group that even tolerated such views. Most of the members of the club never received their degrees. The Jewish member became one of the most distinguished persons to get a degree in United States history from Harvard in the last half-century.

The course of study was satisfactory but far from extraordinary. Mark Hopkins was seldom on the other end of the log, and one had to fend for himself as best he could. I had no difficulty with such a regimen, although I felt that some of my fellow students needed more guidance than the University provided. In my presence, at the beginning of my second year, one of the department's outstanding professors verbally abused a student, visiting from another institution, and dismissed him from his office because the student's question was awkwardly phrased the first time around. Another professor confessed to me that a doctoral committee had failed a candidate because he did not *look* like a Harvard Ph.D. When the committee told him that he would have to study four more years before applying for reconsideration, the student was in the library the following morning to begin his four-year sentence. At that point, the chairman of the committee was compelled to inform the student that under no circumstances would he be permitted to continue his graduate studies there.

When I left Harvard in the spring of 1939 I knew that I did not wish to be in Cambridge another day. I had no desire to offend my advisor or the other members of my doctoral committee. I therefore respectfully declined suggestions that I seek further financial aid. It was time, I thought, to seek a teaching position and complete my dissertation *in absentia. . . .*

It was necessary, as a black historian, to have a personal agenda, as well as one dealing with more general matters, that involved a type of activism. I discovered this in the spring of 1939 when I arrived in Raleigh, North Carolina, to do research in the state archives, only to be informed by the director that in planning the building the architects did not anticipate that any Afro-Americans would be doing research there. Perhaps it was the astonishment that the director, a Yale Ph.D. in history, saw in my face that prompted him to make a proposition. If I would wait a week he would make some arrangements. When I remained silent, registering a profound disbelief, he cut the time in half. I waited from Monday to Thursday, and upon my return to the archives I was escorted to a small room outfitted with a table and chair which was to be my private office for the next four years. (I hasten to explain that it did not take four years to complete my dissertation. I completed it the following year, but continued to do research there as long as I was teaching at St. Augustine's College.) The director also presented me with keys to the manuscript collection to avoid requiring the white assistants to deliver manuscripts to me. That arrangement lasted only two weeks, when the white researchers, protesting discrimination, demanded keys to the manuscript collection for themselves. Rather than comply with their demands, the director relieved me of my keys and ordered the assistants to serve me.

Nothing illustrated the vagaries of policies and practices of racial segregation better than libraries and archives. In Raleigh alone, there were three different policies: the state library had two tables in the stacks set aside for the regular use of Negro readers. The state supreme court library had no segregation, while, as we have seen, the archives faced the matter as it arose. In Alabama and Tennessee, the state archives did not segregate readers, while Louisiana had a strict policy of excluding would-be Negro readers altogether. In the summer of 1945 I was permitted by the Louisiana director of archives to use the manuscript collection since the library was closed in observance of the victory of the United States over governmental tyranny and racial bigotry in Germany and Japan. As I have said elsewhere, pursuing Southern history was for me a strange career.

While World War II interrupted the careers of many young scholars, I experienced no such delay. At the same time, it raised in my mind the most profound questions about the sincerity of my country in fighting bigotry and tyranny abroad. And the answers to my questions shook my faith in the integrity of our country and its leaders. Being loath to fight with guns and grenades, in any case, I sought opportunities to serve in places where my training and skills could be utilized. When the United States entered the war in 1941 I had already received my doctorate. Since I knew that several men who had not been able to obtain their advanced degrees had signed on as historians in the War Department, I made application there. I was literally rebuffed without the Department giving me any serious consideration. In Raleigh, where I was living at the time, the Navy sent out a desperate appeal for men to do office work, and the successful ones would be given the rank of petty officer. When I answered the appeal, the recruiter told me that I had all the qualifications except color. I concluded that there was *no* emergency and told the recruiter how I felt. When my draft board ordered me to go to its staff physician for a blood test, I was not permitted to enter his office and was told to wait on a bench in the hall. When I refused and insisted to the draft board clerk that I receive decent treatment, she in turn insisted that the doctor see me forthwith, which he did. By this time, I concluded that the United States did not need me and did not deserve me. I spent the remainder of the war successfully outwitting my draft board, including taking a position at North

Carolina College for Negroes whose president was on the draft appeal board. Each time I think of these incidents, even now I feel nothing but shame for my country—not merely for what it did to me, but for what it did to the million black men and women who served in the armed forces under conditions of segregation and discrimination.

One had always to be mindful, moreover, that being a black scholar did not exempt one from the humiliations and indignities that a society with more than its share of bigots can heap upon a black person, regardless of education or even station in life. This became painfully clear when I went to Brooklyn College in 1956 as chairman of a department of fifty-two white historians. There was much fanfare accompanying my appointment, including a front-page story with picture in the *New York Times*. When I sought to purchase a home, however, not one of the thirty-odd realtors offering homes in the vicinity of Brooklyn College would show their properties. Consequently, I had to seek showings by owners who themselves offered their homes for sale. I got a few showings including one that we very much liked, but I did not have sufficient funds to make the purchase. My insurance company had proudly advertised that it had $50 million to lend to its policy holders who aspired to home ownership. My broker told me that the company would not make a loan to me because the house I wanted was several blocks beyond where blacks should live. I canceled my insurance and, with the help of my lawyer who was white, tried to obtain a bank loan. I was turned down by every New York bank except the one in Brooklyn where my attorney's father had connections. As we finally moved in after the hassles of more than a year, I estimated that I could have written a long article, perhaps even a small book, in the time expended on the search for housing. The high cost of racial discrimination is not merely a claim of the so-called radical left. It is as real as the rebuffs, the indignities, or the discriminations that many black people suffer.

Many years ago, when I was a fledgling historian, I decided that one way to make certain that the learning process would continue was to write different kinds of history, even as one remained in the same field. It was my opinion that one should write a monograph, a general work, a biography, a period piece, and edit some primary source and some work or works, perhaps by other authors, to promote an understanding of the field. I made no systematic effort to touch all the bases, as it were, but with the recent publication of my biography of George Washington Williams, I believe that I have touched them all. More recently, I have started the process all over again by doing research for a monograph on runaway slaves.

Another decision I made quite early was to explore new areas or fields, whenever possible, in order to maintain a lively, fresh approach to the teaching and writing of history. That is how I happened to get into Afro-American history, in which I never had a formal course, but which attracted a growing number of students of my generation and many more in later generations. It is remarkable how moving or even drifting into a field can affect one's entire life. More recently, I have become interested in women's history, and during the past winter I prepared and delivered three lectures under the general title of "Women, Blacks, and Equality, 1820-1988." I need not dwell on the fact that for me it was a very significant learning experience. Nor should it be necessary for me to assure you that despite the fact that I have learned much, I do not seek immortality by writing landmark essays and books in the field of women's history.

I have learned much from my colleagues both at home and abroad. The historical associations and other learned societies have instructed me at great length at their annual meetings, and five of them have given me an opportunity to teach and to lead by electing me as their president. Their journals have provided me with the most recent findings of scholars and they have graciously published some pieces of my own. Very early I learned that scholarship knows no national boundaries, and I have sought the friendship and collaboration of historians and scholars in many parts of the world. From the time that I taught at the Salzburg Seminar in American Studies in 1951, I have been a student and an advocate of the view that the exchange of ideas is more healthy and constructive than the exchange of bullets. This was especially true during my tenure on the Fulbright Board, as a member for seven years and as the chairman for three years. In such experiences one learns much about the common ground that the peoples of the world share. When we also learn that this country and the western world have no monopoly of goodness and truth or of skills and scholarship, we begin to appreciate the ingredients that are indispensable to making a better world. In a life of learning that is, perhaps, the greatest lesson of all. (1988)

From *Race and History: Selected Essays 1938-1988* (1989)

Muriel Snowden in 1981

MURIEL SNOWDEN

Muriel Sutherland Snowden was born in Orange, New Jersey, on 14 July 1916, one of three children of a dentist. She grew up in nearby Glen Ridge and was class valedictorian at its high school. She received her A.B. from Radcliffe in 1938 with a concentration in Romance Languages, but soon decided that her future lay in social work. From 1938 to 1943 she worked for a New Jersey welfare board, and then won a fellowship for graduate study in community organization and race relations at the New York School of Social Work. After a return to Cambridge in 1948 as executive director of the city's Civic Unity Committee, she and her husband Otto in 1949 conceived, founded, and directed Freedom House, Inc., a nationally renowned civic center in the heart of Boston's black community, for 35 years until their retirement in 1984 to become private consultants. Despite indefatigably throwing herself into an endless series of tasks promoting urban renewal and social betterment, Muriel Snowden made time to serve on countless committees and boards (she was the first black and only woman on the board of directors of the Shawmut Bank) and to teach community organization at Simmons College for more than a dozen years.

In 1972 she became the all-time top vote-getter for director of the Associated Harvard Alumni, and in 1977 was the first black woman elected to the Board of Overseers. She received many honors, including the College Alumnae Achievement Award from Radcliffe (1964), and honorary degrees from the University of Massachusetts at Amherst (1968) and from Boston College (1984). In 1987 she was the recipient of a $375,000 no-strings-attached "genius" grant from the MacArthur Foundation. She succumbed to cancer at her Boston home on 30 September 1988.

Right to Participate

Despite everything that came afterwards, my most vivid memory of
Radcliffe is of being denied access to a dormitory my freshman year.
It continues to rankle to this day—despite the fact that Radcliffe was
the only college to which I had applied; that I had graduated as valedictorian from one of the best public high schools in the country at
the time; that I had been admitted without examination under the
then existing "highest seventh plan" without the need for scholarship
assistance—[that] the Radcliffe administration focused on my race as
the rationale for concern about whether or not I would be "happy"
living in a dormitory.

For my mother, however, determined that I should not miss out
on the essence of college life, this was definitely a non-issue. For her,
the "quality" of my social life was our problem and not theirs; so after
being forced to live out my freshman year as a "day hop" commuting
from Belmont, I was finally assigned a room in Whitman Hall.

Thus, (I believe) as only the second Black woman in the history
of the college up until that time who had been "allowed" to live in a
dormitory, my life took on a somewhat different coloration from that
of other Black students who commuted the entire four years.

I remember those three years in Whitman as warm and happy
ones, where I shared with my dormitory mates the buzzing excitement
of the date one of them had with Joseph Kennedy, Jr.; the intense
dinner discussions about whether one should accept religious dogma
without question; gossipy sessions about sex, love, and marriage; the
agony of studying all night for exams; the secret champagne celebrations on the stairs after lights outs; and the anxiety of getting back to
the dorm by sign-in time.

Although I was to learn later that my presence sparked special
meetings about what would be the procedures should I decide to sign
up for the dorm dances, who would exchange dances with me and my
date, etc., there was very little open evidence of prejudice, hostility,

or discrimination. Life was easier for me as the result of growing up in an all-white community, attending all-white schools, being carefully nurtured in self-esteem and self-confidence by a close-knit family, and being shielded from the inevitable racial incidents that no Black family, no matter who they are, wholly escapes in this society.

In reality, I came to Radcliffe carefully wrapped in the cocoon of an "oreo," the nickname for those of us considered to be "black on the outside; white on the inside"—a living, breathing reflection of what whites thought Black people ought to be like.

However, even I had another life outside the dormitory. The Black Greek organizations at the time actively sought out the newcomers at the start of each year and provided us with the opportunity to meet students from other colleges around the New England area through the Interfraternal Council "mixers" (shades of today's students' Black Freshman Orientation?). Also, since I had been "properly" introduced to Boston's Black community by the couple with whom I had lived my freshman year, "racial isolation" did not become a problem.

Radcliffe did for me what college is supposed to do. It gave me time to grow up and to start finding out for myself who and what I was. From an educational point of view, though, I do not have that sense of challenging intellectual stimulation about which so many graduates rhapsodize. The excitement about "sitting at the feet of the masters" and finding direction through the guidance and encouragement of professors and tutors eluded me completely. As a matter of fact, I cannot now even recall the name of my tutor, an elderly gentleman who obviously could not have cared less about me or I about him.

Essentially, I found my way through the educational maze alone, choosing courses, deciding on a major (the wrong one), and ending up with an AB in Romance languages and literature rather than in sociology and social relations, where I really belonged. When I think about those days, the only names that come to mind are Pitirim Sorokin and Robert Merton, the eminent sociologists, who struck a responsive chord in my soul and jogged me out of my middle-class complacency, and the legendary [George Lyman] Kittredge under whom I did not study.

As much as I chafed at my liberal arts education as not being a "salable product," it has indeed provided me with the discipline and inner resources that have enriched my personal life so immeasurably. I continue to believe that Radcliffe should exist as Radcliffe in order to give women the space they require even if they are now something called "Harvard women."

Above all, I have Harvard and Radcliffe to thank for the degree that not only opened the door to my first job, but also has commanded the respect and attention I have needed over the years to promote the causes in which I so deeply believe.

There are undeniable pluses, but I have hopes that the day will come when I and other Black alumni/ae will be able to sing the Radcliffe and Harvard alma maters with a lump in the throat and nostalgic reverence for what "our" college meant to us. That will also be the day when the statistics will not show Black students opting for other educational institutions with a more sensitive and welcoming climate and where they will not have to pay the "oreo" price for acceptance.

To paraphrase the late Whitney Young, executive director of the National Urban League:

Look at us, we are here. We have our pride. We have our roots. We have our culture and rich heritage. We insist, we demand your recognition and your respect and our right to participate in those decisions which affect our lives and those of our children.

Radcliffe Quarterly (1986)

ELIZABETH FITZGERALD HOWARD

[Gertrude] Elizabeth Fitzgerald was born on 28 December 1927 in Baltimore, Maryland. Moving to the Boston area, she attended Brookline High School. At Radcliffe she concentrated in history and developed a lasting love of choral singing. She was elected secretary of the junior class and, the next year, president and class marshal (the first black in Radcliffe history to be so honored). After her graduation in 1948, she spent several years as a children's librarian at the Boston Public Library. Later at the University of Pittsburgh, she earned a Master of Library Science degree (1971), followed by a Ph.D. in the same field, with a dissertation on "The Reference Collection as a Resource for Religion Studies in Secondary Schools" (1977). Since 1978 she has been a professor of library science at the University of West Virginia in Morgantown. Her interest in the young is reflected in her study *America as Story: Historical Fiction for Secondary Schools* (1988) as well as her original fiction for children. Her recent book *Aunt Flossie's Hats (and Crab Cakes Later)* won a Parents' Choice Award.

Miss Radcliffe

Even for Radcliffe College, which for 69 years has gone about giving women the advantages of a Harvard education with little fuss and no feathers, Betty Fitzgerald was something special. In her freshman year, this sweet and seemingly shy Brookline, Mass., girl showed leadership ability and moved into extracurricular prominence by being elected to the board of administration of Briggs Hall, her dormitory. A member of the Student Assembly in her sophomore year, she went up to the Student Council in her junior year and was elected class secretary.

Elizabeth Fitzgerald Howard in midcareer

In December 1946, Betty was a Radcliffe representative at the organizing convention of the National Students Association in Chicago and a founder of the permanent NSA at Madison, Wis., the following summer. On the side she worked on the Radcliffe News and sang with the famous Choral Society. Last spring she was elected president of the senior class and, to double the honor, was chosen this year from a field of eleven candidates to be class marshal.

For any girl, Betty's extracurricular record would be considered distinguished. But though Radcliffe, traditionally reticent, was wisely matter-of-fact about it, there was one thing which made her even more noteworthy: Betty was a Negro, a fact not mentioned in any of the newspaper publicity. Daughter of a Harvard man, J. MacFarland Fitzgerald, and sister of the sophomore class vice president, the 20-year-old senior had risen in school politics on the strength of the popularity-winning personal charm and ability which had made her a success in Girls Latin School in Boston and Brookline High and later the biggest of campus "big wheels" at Radcliffe.

Last week Betty Fitzgerald's greatest collegiate moment came when, as class marshal, she headed the procession of 218 women who were awarded degrees at Radcliffe commencement exercises in Sanders Theater, Harvard. Although there had been Negro girls at Radcliffe since its founding in 1879, Betty was the first Negro to be either senior president or marshal. Her reaction: "The best part of it is that when my class returns for its 25th and biggest reunion in 1973, I lead the whole caboodle into Sanders Theater again."

Newsweek (1948)

Three Generations of a Black Radcliffe
and Harvard Family

PROLOGUE, APRIL, 1944

A Brookline High School senior snatches the letter from the postman
and tears it open. "It gives me great pleasure. . . ." Squeals and
shouts. Betty Fitzgerald has been admitted to Radcliffe College!

Her parents, John MacFarland and Bertha James Fitzgerald, have
been expecting this day. They had often turned to the photo album
page where two-year old Betty, in a bunny-eared snow suit, stood on
the steps of Whitman Hall in the Radcliffe Quadrangle. Mac
Fitzgerald had brought his family back to Boston from Baltimore in
the middle of the depression. Here, perhaps, there might be a job.
And here, at any rate, the public schools had renown and reputation.
And he would be near Harvard. Betty and her sister Barbara would
be able to go to Radcliffe. The years had rolled by, and if Fitzgerald
felt any disappointment in what Harvard had done for him he still
believed that for his daughters a Harvard education promised the
future. (Possibly Bertha was thinking about Harvard husbands for the
girls.)

What makes this scenario unique? Since 1636 there have been
generations of Harvard sons and grandsons. But Mac Fitzgerald was
different. He was from Baltimore and he was black. There are few
black families whose Harvard lineage stretches to three generations.
How did it all come about? What was it like to be a Negro student
in the 20s, the middle 40s, and early 50s? How has it been different
for a black student in the late 1970s and early/middle 80s? What does
Harvard mean to these three generations?

ACT ONE. PLACE: HARVARD YARD.
TIME: 1920.

John MacFarland Fitzgerald hadn't meant to go to Harvard. He
hadn't gone to school at all until his teens. Too frail, his parents felt,

so he had been tutored at home. He attended Howard Preparatory in Washington but the prep school folded. He spent one year at Howard University. But then Uncle Irving, his mother's brother, proposed that the two of them go into the chicken business. Mac Fitzgerald gave up college and invested in 500 chickens. But when winter came Uncle Irving heard the call of sunshine and went to Florida. Mac did not want to deal with the chickens by himself, so he sold them and applied to Harvard, Brown and Dartmouth. Harvard answered first.

Fitzgerald recalls that he lived in a Cambridge rooming house with other black students (including the famed lawyer Charles Houston; William Hastie, later governor of the Virgin Islands; Earl Brown, editor of *Life* magazine and a New York City councilman, et al.). Black students generally lived off campus, but occasionally one found his way to one of the Houses. For social life, Negro students sought out each other. Fitzgerald mentions one white student whom he knew quite well—Charles Poletti, later governor of New York—who had waited on tables in the Union.

Although Harvard was not unfriendly it was generally acknowledged that the people who really belonged were the children of the establishment. Negro students definitely were on the fringes, but Fitzgerald doesn't remember any real unpleasantness. Once a professor disallowed a display of innate racism by a student who referred in class to "a white lady and a colored woman." The student was silenced by the instructor, who intoned, "There isn't any such thing as a white lady. All women are women."

Although Booker T. Washington and W.E.B. Du Bois both had been guests in his parents' home, it was at Harvard that Mac Fitzgerald first became truly fired up by the struggle for rights of blacks. All Negro students were members of the Nile Club, a student-run organization that sponsored occasional lectures and social events. One memorable evening the speaker was Marcus Garvey, crusader for a separate black state. . . . [See earlier selection, "A Note on Marcus Garvey at Harvard."] The unbreakable and yet not always admitted bond between privileged middle-class blacks and their less fortunate brothers and sisters was indelibly impressed upon Fitzgerald . . . Fitzgerald took 11 courses in economics. But probably the most important lesson was Garvey's.

Fitzgerald soon found out that a Harvard AB was no guarantee of financial success. The business contacts that all white students took for granted were not there for Negroes. In the years that followed he worked variously in real estate and retailing, and tried writing, always struggling against the combination of recurrent ill health, bad luck and wrong skin color. (Sixty years later Fitzgerald's feelings for his alma mater are bitter-sweet.)

ACT TWO.
TIME: FALL, 1944.

Betty Fitzgerald took to Radcliffe as a mallard to the pond in Boston Gardens. She had not even applied anywhere else. Hadn't she been photographed on the steps of Whitman Hall at age two? But what was it like to be here in the 40's, one of less than a handful of Negro girls at Radcliffe and the only one in her class? Unlike Mac Fitzgerald, who knew who he was and where he was coming from, Betty was naive. She had always attended virtually all-white schools, so Radcliffe would not be anything new. Furthermore, she had been totally programmed to love the place. Her father had taught her to sing "Hit the Line for Harvard" and "O'er the Stands in Flaming Crimson" when she was in elementary school. She smiled at everyone and everyone smiled at her. If there were any racially motivated barbs flung her way—and surely there must have been—she just didn't notice. She sang with Choral, ran for and won class offices, including president of her class. She socialized with her Radcliffe classmates, but she dated only the handful of available black men at Harvard. Of course, there were other swains from the greater Boston area, one of whom chided her. "Why do you bother about being friends with these white girls? They'll forget all about you when you all leave here." Betty didn't agree.

In those days black students avoided the appearance of clinging together. The rule was to mix, to try to convince everyone that you were not any different. Betty Fitzgerald didn't feel any different. On retrospection, however, why was it that Dean Sherman dissuaded her from taking chemistry? She had an A from Brookline High. And why was she elected to all those offices? Was it partly a way for white students to assuage racist attitudes? That Betty was president and marshal caused much hoopla in the local press and even *Newsweek* magazine. Fancy, a Negro student! But for Fitz at the time it was all glory. Short-lived glory, though, when it came to job hunting. Radcliffe was not a very career-oriented place in those days, and while that was all right for the privileged, it was not immediately satisfactory for the young women who would have to work after college. What to do but sign up for the Radcliffe typing and shorthand course. After a summer of odd-job typing and a fruitless foray to New York for something in publishing, a suggestion from Miss Stedman led to a filing job at the Boston Public Library. Hardly the goal of a Radcliffe education, but it was a step. But a Radcliffe education did prove to be a foundation for future career aspirations. Betty now has a PhD in Library Science from the University of Pittsburgh and teaches children's and young adult literature at West Virginia University.

Betty's sister, Barbara, entered Radcliffe in the Class of '51. She graduated with no clear career goals. But after being an instructor with the Bell System and a high school Latin teacher, she is now a nurse practitioner at Upstate Medical Center in Syracuse, N.Y.

Most of Betty's black friends from Boston have gone either to Boston University or south to Howard or Fisk. Perhaps they thought it odd that she and her sister Barbara '51 were going to Radcliffe. Betty and Barbara both selected Harvard husbands. Betty married Lawrence C. Howard, PhD '56, who is professor and former dean at the Graduate School of Public and International Affairs at the University of Pittsburgh. Barbara married Otey M. Scruggs, PhD '58, who is professor of history at Syracuse University.

ACT THREE. SCENE ONE.
PLACE: COMSTOCK HALL. TIME: SEPTEMBER, 1975.

Jane Elizabeth Howard, eldest daughter of Betty Fitzgerald and Lawrence C. Howard, whispers, "Bye, Mom," and walks down the hall to the Comstock living room without looking back, leaving Betty to swallow the lump in her throat and to muse about the fulfillment of a foreordained plan. In her early high-school years, Jane had been determined to study ballet somewhere. Then at 15 she accompanied her parents to the 25th reunion of the class of '48, where a highlight was the daring college-y antic of sneaking a swim in the Adams House pool. By the time Jane was ready for college, Radcliffe-Harvard was her first choice. She knew she wanted to go to law school.

The world was vastly different, without and within Radcliffe. Coeducational living and equal access for women had occurred. Young women knew for certain that they would be planning for careers. And Harvard had embarked on a serious campaign to attract black students, and had succeeded in greatly increasing the number who attended. Moreover, black students had definite theories on how to take on Harvard.

Instead of trying to blend in, they developed an all-encompassing sense of community. Black students congregated together at the dining room tables and nodded greetings to each other as they passed on the street. The community was not an open one. The black students who led more integrated lives were largely ostracized by the rest. Few whites were able to penetrate their closed ranks.

Jane enthusiastically immersed herself in this environment. She had black roommates, started a Third World dance troupe, joined the Black Students' Association (successor to the Nile Club) and lived in one of the Houses with a large black population. She says it was refreshing to be part of a crowd, in contrast to the isolation she had experienced at her small Pittsburgh prep school. For Jane, " . . . it was like coming home." Her immersion in the black world at Harvard raised her awareness of who she was, and she became highly politicized. Now, five years later, she says that the experience made it possible for her to have white friends again.

The pressure to get good grades for graduate school caused black students to help and bolster each other. At the black senior dinner dance on the evening of Commencement in 1979, each graduate's name was called by the M.C., who announced which business, law, or medical school he or she would be attending. They had made the most of Harvard and their theme song rocked the Currier dining room: "Ain't no stopping us now!" Jane Elizabeth Howard '79 finished Harvard Law School in 1982, and is now married to Clarence A. (Gus) Martin '78, Duquesne Law School '81. Both are working in Washington, D.C., where Jane is an associate with the law firm of Covington and Burling, and Gus is legislative assistant to Cong. Charles Rangel (D-N.Y.).

ACT THREE. SCENE TWO.

Mac Fitzgerald's grandson, Jeffrey Scruggs, son of Barbara Fitzgerald and Otey M. Scruggs PhD '58, might have gone to baseball camp at the end of his junior year of high school in Syracuse. But, as he said to a friend, "The colleges aren't interested in baseball." So he spent the summer as a research associate at The Roswell Memorial Cancer Research Institute in Buffalo. Salutatorian and most valuable player,

Jeff arrived at Harvard with the Class of 1985. He says that things are different now for black students even from the way they were when his cousin Jane was an undergraduate. The trend of the '80s is integrationist. "You can be friends with whomever you're friends with," he says. "No longer do you look for a black table in the dining room." The college rooming policy assigns freshmen to the Yard in mixed batches. There is at least an effort to prevent concentrating a large number of blacks in one House. Jeff says that most blacks are in a rooming group with at least one other black. "The ultra preppy blacks associate more with just whites." Many black students come from nearly all-white high schools and are accustomed to being in integrated situations. There seems to be little stigma attached to interracial dating.

All in all, Jeff senses there is more openness and ease in the '80s. Perhaps black students no longer feel so strongly that they have to prove anything? An economics major, Jeff has also taken a number of Afro-American Studies courses. He does wonder about the scarcity of black varsity athletes and black faculty. However, being surrounded by talented, motivated young blacks is a new experience for Jeff Scruggs, and as a result he feels that being at Harvard has made him more black than he was—and values this as one of the pluses in being here. He also feels very secure about his future. Ain't no stopping us now!

Radcliffe Quarterly (1984)

[Editors' note: Jeffrey Matthew Scruggs received his A.B. *cum laude* in 1985, and his M.B.A. with distinction from the Harvard Business School in 1991.]

Harold Scott, age 22, as King Lear in 1958

Harold Scott in 1976

HAROLD R. SCOTT

Harold Russell Scott Jr. was born in Morristown, New Jersey, on 6 September 1935. He attended Phillips Exeter Academy, majored in English at Harvard, and received his degree in 1957. As an undergraduate he demonstrated astonishing versatility as an actor in roles ranging from the adolescent Boy in Tennessee Williams' *The Purification* to the elderly Duke of York in Shakespeare's *Richard II*, and including the title parts in Sophocles' *Oedipus Rex* and O'Neill's *Emperor Jones* along with the dancing role of Paris in *The Golden Apple* and the singing role of Jupiter in Offenbach's *Orpheus in Hades*. Within a year of his graduation a highly praised production of Shakespeare's *King Lear* was mounted especially for him, in which he played the octogenarian monarch at 22 (a feat previously accomplished only by England's famed William Devlin). A few months later he appeared in Genet's *Deathwatch* in New York, which brought him a 1959 Obie Award for his "distinguished performance."

He was invited to become a member of the original company of the Lincoln Center Repertory Theatre in 1964, and began a career in directing in 1966. Since then he has combined acting and directing on Broadway, off Broadway, at regional theatres throughout the country, and at more than a dozen universities, with occasional stints as teacher, lecturer, and producer. In Shakespeare he has played Macbeth, Othello, Hotspur, Claudius, Ariel, and Brutus, and performed the leading roles in the American premieres of works by Wole Soyinka. For five summers he was actor and director at the O'Neill Memorial Theater Center, and for two seasons artistic director of Cincinnati's Playhouse-in-the-Park. At Harvard's Loeb Drama Center, he has directed Genet's *The Blacks*, Beckett's *Waiting for Godot*, Pinter's *The Birthday Party*, and *Indians* by Arthur Kopit '59. In 1972 the New England Theatre Conference bestowed a special award on Scott for excellence as actor, director, and teacher. His records include James Weldon Johnson's *God's Trombones*, along with more than thirty "talking books" for the American Foundation for the Blind. In 1980 Scott joined the faculty of Rutgers University, where he is now professor of theatre and head of the graduate directing program, while continuing to direct in New York and elsewhere.

Harvard and the Performing Arts:
"How Long, O Lord . . . ?"

Here we are twenty years later. And those of us who left Harvard
determined to pursue a life in the performing arts are still the bastard
children of an institution that has never embraced the concept that
performing is a respectable occupation for more than extracurricular
hours. Would that one could say that it was merely a *twenty*-year-old
problem!

Actors, dancers, and often singers and other musicians have a
rather pathetic history where respectability, or even acceptance or
acknowledgement as responsible beings, is concerned. Performers in
general are thought of as emotionally unstable, financially irresponsible, morally depraved, and not too bright. Fascinating to watch, either
clinically or vicariously, but somehow dangerous to be around. Not
quite suitable for use in the home, much less the community.

It is significant that to this day we in the performing arts still refer
to ourselves affectionately, but with an unfortunate modicum of self-
abnegation, as "gypsies." This is the mythic life-style that has been
delegated to us. How tragic that Harvard insists on perpetuating that
myth. It is an annoyance and an embarrassment.

It is also an irony when one considers how "star"-oriented we have
become as a nation. John Kennedy was the first President in my
memory to be described by the media as having the indefinable
charisma of a movie star. How doubly ironic that he was also a
Harvard graduate. And, one might add parenthetically, a better actor
has never graced the White House.

Somehow that description seems to have a pejorative connotation
when applied to a President, doesn't it? I can feel some of you
thinking: *How dare he desecrate the memory of a great man by calling
him an actor?* But what is an actor?

To paraphrase Tennessee Williams, an actor brings you reality in
the form of an illusion. Through his craft he moves you emotionally;
he stimulates your thought; he commands your attention by his voice,
his speech, his carriage; and if totally successful, he gives you comfort

and security by the ease, grace, and power with which he executes his skills.

What does a President, a diplomat, a politician, a lawyer, a minister do? Or rather, what is it that we wish or hope a President will do when we cast our ballot? Is it not really one and the same thing?

It is always assumed that a performer's world is one of make-believe. Pretending to be someone else. In fact, the performer's world is one of truth on the most profound and often painful level. We are observers of truth. We are purveyors of truth. When the performance does not ring true you can be almost guaranteed that the actor will be panned and the play will close. As Hamlet states in his address to the players, it is the actor's job "to hold, as 'twere, the mirror up to nature."

It is interesting to note with the advent of television and other mass-oriented media how important "performance" has become. Elections have been lost because a candidate did not present a convincing "image." Nixon's heavy beard and close eyebrows were thought to make him look untrustworthy; corrective makeup was immediately introduced. Kennedy's wardrobe was chicly tailored with suppressed waists and elevated shoulders; that's costuming. Jimmy Carter's hair is not cut; it is styled. The White House is no longer redecorated; it is designed with the care and precision of a Hollywood set. When a President's vocal delivery has been too monotonous or regional speech patterns too extreme, in come the voice and speech therapists to modify the image, theoretically so that all Americans can relate to him. And always a director is present to show him how to use the camera as he reads his text. I think the metaphor is complete.

In short, all of our lives are performances of sorts. Why does Harvard still persist in refusing to train people to deal with these realities of performance as a valid occupation?

One reads the *Crimson:* "Committee on Theatre Recommends Against Establishing Drama Department at Harvard . . . One student opposed establishing a drama department because 'drama departments attract hacks.'" (The chairman of this committee is a professor of ancient and modern history.) One reads the *Radcliffe Quarterly*: "For about ten years the arts at Radcliffe consisted of a program called Sports, Dance, and Recreation, offered by the Radcliffe Physical Education Department." One reads *The Harvard Independent*: "Being an actor at Harvard is one of the most difficult things one could be. The directors here think that if you're serious about acting you wouldn't be at Harvard, and if you are serious, you won't get any better since this is no place to learn." These quotations are from 1976 publications. They could just as well have been written in 1956, which I understand is now referred to as the core of The Golden Age of Theater at Harvard. "Nothing has changed, John Brown, nothing has changed," wrote Stephen Vincent Benét. We have been brainwashed.

One still hears the same perverse argument I heard as a freshman: If Harvard has a theater department, would she have produced as many deeply talented, prominent artists as she has? My answer is YES, probably more. Sand in the oyster is not the only way to produce a pearl.

About a year ago, I received a letter from Robert Anderson, probably best known to you as the author of *Tea and Sympathy.* He is also the chairman of the Board of Overseers' Committee to *Visit* the Loeb Drama Center. (Note the verb. The italics are mine.) It was a pitch for funds and included what Anderson described as "an incomplete list of Harvard and Radcliffe graduates who have gone on to work in the performing arts." I was shocked at some of the important names that appeared on that list. I had no idea that they were Harvard graduates, and yet I was one. I was also shocked at some of the glaring omissions. But then how could the list be complete when we have no departmental affiliation with the university? In my anger I did not respond.

Two more brief observations. In 1972 I was appointed to the Harvard faculty to teach a seminar in acting and to direct a production on the Loeb mainstage. What to do with me? How can you appoint a man to a faculty that has no department to embrace him? A title was invented. I was appointed "Visiting Stage Director" (note the verb again) and given a proper officer's card, #1-82168, valid through 10-72. At last I was official as an artist at Harvard, even temporarily. I cherish that red and white plastic card, even to this day. But what is that title, and what is Mr. Anderson's committee? One cannot be an instructor, much less a professor, nor even chairman of a committee of a building, a nondepartment. But obviously the need for such appointments is there somewhere.

More recently, I was elected a director of the Associated Harvard Alumni, a great honor. I attended my first meeting last fall and looked at the predominance of lawyers, judges, scholars, and bank presidents that surrounded me. No MFA or PhD or any other initials or symbols could precede or follow my name to distinguish my status, even if I had wanted it, and I didn't particularly want it. However, I feel that decision should have been mine, not the university's.

Oh Harvard, you glorious, perverse, stubborn conservative, you. You have learned to accept women, blacks, Jews, and a few other pushy minorities. In addition, you have hidden a few longhaired, bearded scientists in their laboratories. You have been forced to admit the existence of Gay Liberation and even to grapple with transsexualism in your tenured closet. Why is the performing artist and the reality of his dignity such a threat?

We live in an age when Ronald Reagan nearly won the Republican presidential nomination, Pearl Bailey is a delegate to the UN, and Shirley Temple Black has been a major diplomat—to name but a few performers turned politicians. We live in an age when former mayors John Lindsay and Carl Stokes dish out our morning and evening news—to name but two politicians turned performers.

We have all heard of the George Pierce Baker odyssey ad nauseam. That was 1925. We know that the Yale School of Drama is now one of the most dynamic arts institutions in the country. What kind of revolution will it require to make Harvard finally see the importance of providing a training ground for the performing arts? We as individuals have given Harvard the artists. When will she give us back the simple dignity of a title we have earned and that the world at large recognizes as valuable? We are your performing artists. Celebrate us. Do not hide us in "incomplete lists."

Bernard Shaw closes his masterwork, *St. Joan*, with these beautiful and prophetic words: "O God that madest this beautiful earth, when will it be ready to receive Thy saints? How long, O Lord, how long?" The performing artist may not be a saint, if indeed there are any saints left in our midst, but he can bring you beauty and truth with grace and style, intelligence, and imagination—and that's a bold word in these computerized times.

From *Harvard College Class of 1957 20th Anniversary Report* (1977)

[Editors' postscript: It is of course impossible to gauge precisely what impact this and similar pleas had on the University community. But it is important to note that three years later Harvard decided to import the Yale Repertory Theatre's company and house it in the

Loeb Drama Center as the American Repertory Theatre. In addition, Harvard began in the fall of 1980 to offer for credit a group of courses in "dramatic arts" that included the study of acting, directing, and designing.]

William Melvin Kelley in 1965

WILLIAM MELVIN KELLEY

William Melvin Kelley Jr. was born in New York City on 1 November 1937. After attending the private Fieldston School, he spent parts of five years at Harvard (Class of '60) but left before completing his degree. An English concentrator, he studied with novelist John Hawkes and three-time Pulitzer Prize winner Archibald MacLeish. His short story "The Poker Party," published in the *Harvard Advocate*, won the Dana Reed Prize as the best piece of undergraduate writing.

Kelley's novels range from the Faulknerian *A Different Drummer* (1962), which won two awards, to the Joycean *Dunfords Travels Everywheres* (1970), which brought him another award. From his collection of short stories, *Dancers on the Shore* (1964), Langston Hughes chose "The Only Man on Liberty Street" for inclusion in *The Best Short Stories by Negro Writers* (1967). "The Ivy League Negro," which Kelley wrote for *Esquire* (August 1963), drew much comment.

Kelley's writing has also appeared in *Negro Digest*, *Saturday Evening Post*, the *New York Times Magazine*, *Mademoiselle*, and other periodicals, and in numerous anthologies. We reprint his contribution to "Black Power: A Discussion," for which the *Partisan Review* solicited 12 brief statements in 1968. His short story "My Next to Last Hit" appears here for the first time. Kelley has spent some time teaching college in this country and abroad, and much time living in foreign locales. In addition to writing, he has been active as a photographer and sign maker. Currently he is a member of the Department of Creative Writing at Sarah Lawrence College.

Black Power

Is it still necessary, in 1968, to discuss the differences between the two peoples, African and European, who inhabit the United States?

I thought everybody accepted those differences. I thought that everybody knew the difference between James Brown and Elvis Presley, or Willie Mays and Mickey Mantle, or the waltz and the guaguanco, or the Temptations and the Beatles, or Leontyne Price and Joan Sutherland, or Duke Ellington and Aaron Copland or even old Nat Turner and Mr. Jefferson Davis. And so I did not think we had to leaf back to Chapter One. But we do.

Please, sir, we are different, sir.

Our ancestors came from Africa, yours from Europe. Our ancestors did not want to come to the United States, yours did. Once we arrived in the United States, yes, we both worked—but separated from each other. We did not mix. You remained, essentially, a European people. We remained an African people.

We remained African because in Africa we had possessed a complex and highly-developed oral tradition. Knowledge—of the past, of the environment, artistic traditions, philosophy, myth, cuisine—was passed from one generation to the next, orally.

For the most part, we did not have written languages, books. You had books, libraries, where knowledge of the past, the environment, artistic traditions, philosophy, myth and even cuisine was boxed, packaged, stacked, catalogued, categorized, entombed and enshrined. In books. You must have money to get into such places, to study books, to buy books. Everybody cannot do it.

Many more people talk than write. Many more people hear and see than read. And we, those of us whose ancestors came from Africa, we had, still have, an oral tradition.

Unlike many immigrants, we did not suffer the shock of being separated, by English, from languages which were both oral and written. We were torn only from spoken cultures.

We missed the sounds of each of our languages, but the content, its meanings, stayed with us. An important aspect of our African cultures was the strong emphasis on Improvisation. Improvisation, in many different forms, is common to all of Africa.

In the United States, we improvised. An African, a grown man, taken in battle or kidnapped, marched to the coast in chains, forced onto a ship, carried across an ocean, unloaded, sold and told, finally, that he must pick somebody else's cotton, such a man had better improvise.

He did. We all did. We improvised on English. We improvised on Christianity. We improvised on European dress. We improvised on European instruments. We improvised on European games.

Orally. An African woman may have learned to cook her owner's dinner the way he liked it, but when she cooked her own food, she added a little pepper, as she had done in Africa. And that's the food she fed her children, or the African children she was feeding. And she taught the girls to cook that way, the old way. And those girls taught their girls. Orally. To our day.

We talked. We improvised. And our ancestors came from Africa. That is why you cannot compare James Brown to Elvis Presley, or the Temptations to the Beatles, or Duke Ellington to Aaron Copland, or even the Black Power Movement to the Abolitionists and the Anarchists.

We are different.

Partisan Review (1968)

My Next to Last Hit by "C. C. Johnson"

My next to last hit got very personal in several ways. And everybody in the Business knows he can't let the hit get personal. One messes up, makes mistakes. I find I do better work when I don't care, but just do it dispassionately. If my Mom hadn't named me Calvin Coolidge Johnson, she could have named me Cooley, most really meaning Coldly—the way I do everything I do. Ask anybody if Cooley doesn't mean Dry Ice.

I doubt I could have gotten very far in the Business if I had conducted myself in a passionate manner. Generally Reupeons didn't trust Africamericans. Many of them didn't like to have us around at all. Some maintain that niggers lack courage and loyalty, that we talk too much. I broke many barriers in those areas. But I'll confess I think I progressed in the Business because I knew the Daon from childhood days, even before I worked in his father's bakery on White Plains Avenue in the Bronx, New York. The Daon and I grew up on the same block.

Back in the Hiroshima summer of 1945, to pinpoint it exactly, I needed a job badly. Pop had died a few years before, leaving Mom with me and my five-year-old brother, Hondo. A couple of kids had died between him and me. So at age fifteen I began to look for a serious job, not just for extra but for ordinary. I went in and out of every Negro-owned store in Williamsbridge, from 233rd Street to Gun Hill Road, from Bronxwood Avenue to the Bronx River, even tried the A&P, Safeway and Grand Union, but couldn't find anything, no deliveryboy or packer or sweeper needed.

One night going home to Barnes Avenue, I said to myself, Why not try Mr. Capeurtao. Every time I went in there, he saw me, recognized my soul (his words, not mine), I could see it in his eyes. Such white men do exist; take George Washington. Mr. Capeurtao always asked after my progress in school. I always did well and told him so and he always behaved like it truly pleased him; he'd give me a pastry or sometimes a small pie. So that night, stifling tremors of fear in anticipation of talking about Money with a white man, expecting him to say No, but willing to try, in I stepped.

I found Mr. Capeurtao engaged in conversation with his son, Roff the Cowboy Capeurtao, the future Daon. He'd gotten the nickname Cowboy because as a child he'd often expressed the desire to go west to become one. At seventeen he actually did it and spent two years in Texas. But something happened and he returned to the Bronx. The nickname stuck, but only men who knew him for years, like myself, dared mention it.

I don't remember that they conversed about anything of great criminal importance, just Mr. Capeurtao—robust in his baker's whites, whitehaired but brown as a walnut, his face baked by years of looking into a flaming oven—behind the counter passing the time of day with his middle son, Roff.

And in I stepped, halting two paces just inside the front door of the shop, by the cookie section. They stood near the back of the rectangular store, near the bread. "Hello, Mr. Capeurtao." I took one step closer. "What d'you know, Roff?"

Roff's head swiveled slowly toward me like the turret of a tank. In his midtwenties, he still worked as a pianomover with his uncle and also delivered baked goods for his father, which he used as a cover for Hookers on Wheels. He had two mattresses on the floor of the back of the bakery truck, and two females to fill them. He could still wring a human neck like a chicken's with his bare hairy hands. He had none of his father's craftsman's elegance, but took after his mother's people, no insult intended. They came from the southernmost region of Reupeo. Few read or wrote.

"You got money, Cooley? Gimme some."

"Shoosh, Roff, you stand in the presence of a scholar." Mr. Capeurtao softly tapped his son's forehead across the counter. "Good evening, young Cooley."

I had hoped to find him alone, which happened sometimes, in the late afternoon just us two in the bakery. But the store clock read eight-twenty and I didn't have a speech worked out for this contingency, felt disheartened, then angry with myself that I hadn't shown more foresight. "Mr. Capeurtao?"

"Yes, Cooley?"

Behind me, the door opened. I turned to see—saw a shotgun's barrel sneaking out from under a blue wool coat, coming up like an erection, right into my face. I dropped to a crouch and went for the icepick in my back pocket which I'd started to carry when I roamed around the city at night. A fool filled with myself and my problems, I thought the gunman had come for me. I lunged low at the open wool coat, plunged my icepick into the scrotum and testicles, heard a man scream and a gunshot. The bullet entering the gunman's brain caused graymatter and bonechips to spray me as we landed on the floor, me sprawled atop the twitching, dying man. I rolled off him. He died.

"Nice pickwork, Cooley." Roff holstered his smoking Leurgo .357 and leaned over to inspect the corpse's face. "Teach yourself that stuff?"

I opened my mouth, started to shiver. The wooden handle of my icepick stood up from the dead man's groin. I'd thought the gunman had come for me, to bring me more grief and woe. At fifteen, I realize now, I already felt hunted.

"Hey, Pop, call the cops." Using a handkerchief, Roff extracted the icepick, carefully wrapped it and put it into his inside coat pocket. "Get a new one, Cooley."

"But Roff," Mr. Capeurtao objected softly. "He's from the Smepriroa Faction—"

"I said call the cops, Pop." Roff swiveled his cold eyes on me. "Prick tried to stick us up and I plugged him. Right, Cooley?"

When the cops came, Roff the future Daon embroidered it a bit. "Officer Callahan, you should see this kid in action. He fought for my father like his own. This gunman woulda got away with the whole store if this kid didn't protect us. Such bravery should go in the News no less." After they took away the body, he gave me a $100 bill and a bag of groceries and sent me home, telling me to keep shut up and report for work at six in the morning.

So I went to work for Mr. Capeurtao before and after school and learned the baker's trade. In the daytime, I continued at high school, graduating in June 1948 with Honors. Every so often, I'd do a job for Roff the future Daon, mostly collecting numbers receipts from the Brothers allied with him, occasionally beating up guys, once sticking an icepick through some man's palm, though I didn't do my first legitimate hit till after I returned to the city from Harvard in 1953 when no opportunities opened up.

Perhaps it seems strange to recount how I first joined with Capeurtao and Sons, took up baking and other Business, so near to the end of my story. But the reason for this arrangement rests in the personal nature of this next to last assignment, first for the Daon and subsequently for myself. As I stated earlier, though my first assignments gave me some personal satisfaction, since they involved avenging the assassination of Mr. Capeurtao, still I could maintain the necessary detachment, do the work efficiently and exit in peace. But this hit turned weird and personal from the second Roff Capeurtao the Daon came into the bakery, which I had run for him since the death of his father and after that section of the Bronx went from Reupeoamerican to Africamerican.

"Come in back, Cooley." The Daon hadn't even waited for his bodyguards, Laon and Saom, solid like two brass bookends, to check the premises. He rolled by me, an armored vehicle in the best worsted, through the swinging doors into the oven room. "Wants to bug out my broads . . . " The doors deadened his utterance.

I nodded at Laon, his chief protector. "Which ones?"

"The holes went on strike."

"On strike?" I put down a tray of cookies I'd just brought to the front of the shop. "Next you'll say they formed a union." I'd started to despise unions when I found out how easily we corrupted them.

"Laughing at me?" Laon scowled, his gun hand twitching. He resented my close relationship with the Daon. "Huh?"

"I better get in back."

"Yaoh."

I went in the oven room.

". . . wants to bug out my broads' brains." The Daon had removed his overcoat and jacket, stood in naked bulletproof vest and trousers. "Tell me about this Hamilton Dapper."

I had to think a moment. Hamilton Dapper. TV Host. Political pundit. Syndicated columnist. Media Analyst. Professional feminist. Television spokesperson for at least one financial institution. A prepschool old boy and former Ivyleaguer. Scion of a wealthy cracker (i.e. WASP) family. Friend of Presidents. World traveler. Sometime war correspondent, but only if the war played well to the dinner audience. Theater critic. Book reviewer. Roff the Daon could hardly have missed him as a fellow citizen of his time and place, but except for political fundraisers they lived in two different orbits. And even at political fundraisers, Daon Roff Capeurtao and Mediamond Hamilton Dapper sat in two different sections, the Daon in the shadows, Dapper in the spotlight.

"He has a couple of TV shows, Daon."

"I want that you smash him." He gave the order like a man switching a channel with a handheld remote control unit. "Give you ten thousand."

My heart made my chest quake. Already I didn't like the feel of this assignment. But I couldn't just say No. "How much in the front, Daon?"

"What's wrong, Cooley? Think I'll screw you?"

"You might." At moments like these in the Business, a man could speak honestly, but always respectfully. "You still didn't give back my icepick."

"Smart black son of a saint!" His face cracked into a smile. "How's your Mom doing?"

I couldn't tell if he'd just threatened my mother, so I gave a neutral reply. "She's in good health."

"May she live many more years." He gave me a quick strange look, all hardness, in an instant dropping away. "I never told you about me and your mom. Does she still sit on the porch and read? One day Pop beat me good with the belt for spilling a basket of bread. Fists too. I ran out the house and down the block. Saw your mom on the porch reading. So I ran up on the porch. Begged her to save me from Pop. Your little mom! So here comes Pop. A belt in one hand and a broom handle in the other. Roff, get down here! I shit my short pants. Musta been maybe eleven. But she stood up to him. You don't supposed to beat'im that way Mr. Cap. He said, Yes, Mrs. Johnson. Walked me back home." The Daon stopped.

I dared a question. "He ever beat you again?"

"Definitely." He snorted. "When we got home, he broke my jaw."

I remembered then the real topic under discussion. "With respect, Daon, Hamilton Dapper leads a very public life." I had other reservations too.

"What d'you want? Public place or private?"

The Daon really wanted Hamilton Dapper dead. Usually the assignment came in a package. Time and place and manner. The Daon had gone deep into Specialization. A rare Capeurtao had attended Harvard Business School and the Daon listened to him. "Private."

"Easy. We got a hole in his office. What else?" He sensed my hesitation, my weakness.

"With respect, Daon, what does he have to do with our Business?"

I'd stepped over a line. Troops did not question the motives of the Daon. You did not want to question his motive because then you would know it, too. It would become your motive, or it wouldn't. Either way, knowing the Daon's motive made you less efficient. You messed up.

The Daon reached out and tapped my forehead with his forefinger. "He bugs my broads' brains with his bulldung. You know you start a revolt with women."

"Laon told me the holes went on strike." I still couldn't conjure up his motive. "Dapper's into one of them?"

"That Dapper had three holes on his show one morning. Now they call themselves High Rise Hookers, want double their fee, and free cocaine. So smash him, Cooley. I'll toss in the icepick."

I couldn't say No, at least not to his face. Not that I continued to believe the icepick could materially connect me to a longforgotten murder which all concerned preferred to list as a foiled robbery attempt. Rather because for several years, I'd actually believed that it did. And by the time, one chimelike evening skeed on cocaine and cold as dry ice, it occurred to me that the Daon had run a beautiful game on my mind, I had well embarked on my Business career. Besides, I liked baking.

The icepick meant nothing as evidence. The Daon's bullet had surely killed the man in the blue wool coat, not my instrument in his scrotum. But the icepick symbolized our attachment. The Daon had seen the killer in me and brought it forth. Harvard only put the polish on the killer. Now the killer hesitated.

He clutched my right earlobe with his left hand. "Hear this, I make you judge. And if you decide, execute! If not, I can get somebody else."

The Daon told me an address. I'd report there at two the next afternoon, bringing my own weapon. The Business would get me into Hamilton Dapper. I might kill him in his bed. Or in his garage. Or taking a piss in the executive washroom. I might end up as his caddy and finish him on the back nine. One man I sold a poisoned pork sausage at a street fair, an out-on-loan assignment. Most of the time, they'd slip me into a man as a deliveryboy. Several times, I've delivered Death in a brown paper bag, especially when the Business wanted to muscle into Entertainment.

At two the next afternoon, I reported for duty. The man there gave me a pair of overalls, on the back of which he'd stenciled

SMITH CARPETING CO. I perceived the plan immediately, the maintenanceman gambit. I'd used the class structure and racism often to gain access to prohibited places. A few years ago, an Africamerican dressed in clean coveralls and carrying a toolkit could get into any downtown Manhattan building. Day or night. Nowadays it takes more ingenuity to penetrate places.

After I dressed, I checked my weapon, a revolver with a silencer. I fired off a shot to make sure it worked. I hadn't spent much for the revolver, having bought a halfdozen on a recent trip to the South. I'd paid a lot for the silencer which I always took away with me. Actually, I rather dislike the sound of firearms; a silent weapon would provide a breakthrough for our profession. In another age, I'd have used knives exclusively. The revolver I usually left at the scene of the crime, where it could tell the police nothing. Sometimes it might even lead investigators to rule the death a suicide.

Tooting some cocaine, I tried to make myself into a guided missile, a mind thing I do like an actor's sense memory. I imagine myself as a missile already fired and homing in on my target. Nothing can call me back. I see myself whirling burrowing smashing into through skin fat muscle bone, emerging on the other side in a shower of blood, escaping with the life of my target.

This time I had some difficulty getting myself into a mood to wipe out Hamilton Dapper. The assignment had gotten too personal, ironically because the Daon wanted him squashed not for something really personal, a brother killed or a territory seized, but for causing his highpriced prostitutes to think. I'd never before heard of his ordering an assassination over an idea. I consider that kind of killing closer to politics. What people thought did not usually concern him, only what they did. People made laws against drug selling and taking, against gambling, prostitution and murder, then broke all the laws. The Daon respected only the law of human behavior. What did a man want and how badly did he want it? Would he kill for it? I heard him ask such questions on several occasions of men with whom he had contradictions. But first he would ask, How much does he want? Then he'd want to know how much pain the man could endure. He had only four weapons. Money. Fear. Pain. Death. With due respect for his criminal mind, I knew that Death did not work well on Ideas. Especially if the Idea had value, and even if it didn't.

I pride myself on my logic, but found myself engaged in an illogical enterprise. Finally I resolved to wait and see. The Daon had made me judge after all. I didn't have to tell him what I really thought. I could just say that I hadn't found Hamilton Dapper alone.

I left for Dapper Enterprises at three-thirty and walked crosstown. I wondered if anybody passing could imagine that I might take someone's life within the hour. Sometimes Death comes that close and we don't even know it.

At Dapper Enterprises, in a townhouse he owned in the East Sixties, the hole had made an appointment for Mr. Skippy Smith from Smith Carpeting to restaple the carpet in Mr. Dapper's office. During the night, vandals had broken in and slightly wrecked the place, pulling up the carpet as if looking for hidden riches. The receptionist told me this while I waited to get in. "Mr. Dapper's willing to endure the upset for one day, no more. Reasonable overtime won't bother us, if you finish tonight."

"Yes, ma'am," I said politely. I had a few years on her, but I knew my role. "Definitely will finish tonight."

I sat for fifteen minutes, as the receptionist (I wondered if she was the hole) took phone calls and ran little errands. She had a cute way of bouncing her first few steps getting up from her desk, a folded note clamped between thumb and index finger. I liked watching her little life dance.

The fifth time she left her desk, I stood and walked into the bowels of the set-up. I carried my toolkit past cubicles and corners where young people, mostly female, talked on phones or hunched over reading matter or stared off into space. The females staring off into space seemed to have the more attractive work places, provocative and evocative clippings and photos tacked to their walls, flowers on their desks. The thick smug carpets made my steps silent. I didn't know which office held Hamilton Dapper, but I knew enough about office hierarchy to guess correctly. I followed the power vibration right to his door, finding it slightly open. I put on workgloves and knocked softly, then entered.

Hamilton Dapper looked at me over his halflens reading glasses. "You came to fix the rug." He sounded disappointed. "Will it be unpleasantly noisy?"

"I work silently, Mr. Dapper." I reset the door, slightly open, where he'd had it. The vandals (I imagined younger clones of Laon and Saom gleefully going about destruction) had torn a sixteen-by-four foot section of carpet from the floor in front of Hamilton Dapper's desk and piled it in a corner near the wall-to-ceiling bookshelves. I began to untangle it and spread it onto the naked wood floor.

He sat at an electric typewriter, staring at the humming machine. He typed, then stopped, then typed again and didn't seem pleased with what he'd written. He made more noise at his work than I did at mine.

"Now I'm gonna try the gun, Mr. Dapper." I opened my toolkit and took out the giant stapler. "If it makes too much noise, I'll come back tomorrow."

"O god, no! Do it now and be done."

I started stapling in the corner further away from him and where some passing female couldn't see me. The rug muffled the thump of steel spike into wood floor. "This okay, Mr. Dapper?"

He typed to the end of his sentence. "You said what?" He typed another sentence. "O yes."

I returned to my stapling, getting into the work. I didn't enjoy it as much as baking, but if I had to make a living at it, I wouldn't mind. I got some satisfaction from seeing the carpet going down smooth and blue. I'd almost finished when I became aware that I didn't hear his typewriter clattering. I looked up.

Hamilton Dapper sat back, smoking a cigarette, studying me. "Do I know you from some place?"

I looked him dead in the eye. "That depends on the place, Mr. Dapper." I shot the last staple into the floor.

"Stop that a minute. Let me get a good look at you." He indicated a black wooden armchair facing his desk, the official patented Harvard chair. Every suite of rooms at Harvard contained one for each man. When he left, he had the right to buy it. Everybody has a hustle.

I sat facing him.

"It seems I met you a long time ago." He studied me some more. "I see the face I know in the face I see." I saw that he liked the sentence he'd just created. "Did you ever work in Cambridge?"

"England?" I toyed with him a bit, way ahead of him now.

He shook his head. "Massachusetts. Near Boston. You couldn't have gone to Harvard."

"Why not?" I enjoyed the flicker of shock in his eyes. "Class of fifty-three."

"No shitting! Well, I'll be a horse's ass."

After that, we got down. I got interested in him. And I thought he got interested in me. His office transformed itself into a room in Adams House at Harvard, back in the early fifties when the Africamerican knew his place and the Euramerican too.

Me at Harvard. Talking to some young high class WASPs about Life, meaning Money and Power. We hardly ever talked about Sex. Back then they didn't even allow females into a man's room after seven p.m. on weekdays. A Harvardman had to get his snatch before dinner. But no man talked about it. So the B.S. ran to Money and Power. Come to think of it, we didn't talk too much about Money either. Pop had worn out his heart and left some insurance. I had a scholarship. And I worked on the Dorm Crew, cleaning toilets with a brush. I could charge necessities like records and clothes at the Coop. Every so often, the Capeurtaos sent me a couple hundred. So Money didn't bother me.

Power. We talked about Power. Assuming we would have it (even naïve brown me) and attended Harvard to learn how to wield it. The Fine Art of Ruling Others. Assuming that admission to Harvard signified permission to have and wield Power. They gave you a diploma when you got in! Even if you didn't get a degree, you didn't go away emptyhanded. You'd already reached the upperclass. Obviously the gods had smiled. And if the gods smiled on a man, Cooley—my Pop would say—not only would a man get rich, he would get smart. It followed then if a man had money for more than one generation that smartness would stack up like interest, becoming wisdom.

My Pop (b.1894-d.1942) had prepared me to meet an American nobility at Harvard. Somewhere back in Georgia before he ran away from childhood, Pop must have met a cracker who blew his mind, combining the stature of George Washington (who grew hemp and loved walnuts) with the brilliance of Thomas Jefferson (who grew ideas and loved sweet Sally Hemings), an android of Gary Cooper with the streetsmarts of Humphrey Bogart.

Evenings in the early forties, Pop and I'd sit at the yellow kitchen table, opening and munching walnuts. He told me about one WASP he met in Chicago who gave him a job just because Pop had courage enough to ask for it. Pop had never done accounting work before but had confidence in his math, and said so, and the man had gone for it. Got the job. Did well. Till the Big (1917) War opened the drafted Pop went to France to tend the Cavalry's horses. Never saw combat. Saw France sweeping up horse shit. Years later, he still couldn't talk about it. I had to find out about it from Mom.

Poor uptight Pop, he expected great things of the WASP. If dealt with patiently and tactfully, he'd do righteously. Once he accepted our humanity, he'd do well by us. He'd pay us our back wages. He'd brag to the world about our accomplishments. How he couldn't have built America without us. How the partnership between the English-man (doing the planning) and the African (doing the plotting) resulted in a pie big enough to feed the wretched and poor runaways of Europe.

"We've been in America longer than anybody but the English," Pop stressed, early as I can remember. "And before most of them." Pop disregarded the original People, displaying racism in regard to them.

Pop raised me to trust the WASP, who mostly came straight. Either he hated you or he loved you, but never fibbed about it. If he called you nigger behind your back, he called you nigger to your face. Especially if you worked for him. Now I found myself in earnest conversation with one of the exalted WASPs of my time. If he knew, Pop's chest would swell with pride.

I began to genuinely enjoy my conversation with Hamilton Dapper, and the pleasant memories it stirred up. Then a strange thing happened. We had conversed for fifteen minutes on the general state of the world, when I decided to get more specific, and so asked him about the state of the nation, as seen from his lofty perch, and its chances of survival.

His blue eyes looked into my brown two, then his voice said, just simple and quiet: "I don't know, Skippy."

"You don't know. A great idea tottering on the edge of the historical dustbin and you tell me you don't know if we'll make it or not?"

He looked at me across his typewriter, his eyes sorrowful and sheepish. "You needn't bother to heap recrimination on me. Your people certainly haven't fulfilled their responsibilities as citizens. You rarely vote."

"You folks rarely vote your ownselves," I responded.

"Everybody's bored," he said.

"Everybody's bored," I agreed. "Even black folks are bored. If you don't have the latest attachment for your TV, forget it. Vote today? That means they'll keep breaking into my TV tonight. But in a class and race society, which you admit we have here despite great progress, it's the responsibility of your class and race not to get bored. If you're born with all the breaks, you have a responsibility to your subjects. Even the Bible says that."

Hamilton Dapper shrugged, sighed, took a puff on his cigarette. Silence dropped her veil over his office. After a time, I asked him if he'd met anybody lately would make a good President.

"You see, Skippy, what it takes a man to get elected President practically makes it impossible for a good President to get elected. We get our good Presidents by accident. Who would've thought that Teddy or Harry would turn out so well? Only George Washington fulfilled our expectations. But by the end of his terms, the people disliked him. He actually wanted to free his slaves, and finally did. They didn't like him very much in Virginia."

"But no one on the horizon?" He shook his head. "No one has any grasp or vision. Perhaps one doesn't need it. The Senate and the Supreme Court run the country by now. So everything takes a long time and comes out looking like a camel. Meanwhile, we all slide down hill."

"It's a bloody mess." Hamilton Dapper lit a new cigarette. "What would you do about it?"

"If I knew I'd be the President's valet, whispering advice while I helped him with his hairpiece. But I do notice you folks always do the same thing. Complicate and mystify. Throw money at problems. Form a committee. Why not be brave enough to simplify? Especially your class. The ruling class. Set a new tone. Enough yachts already. Give us a good example of diligence and frugality. Never having known poverty, you can't imagine how demoralizing it gets for the poor man to watch you folks going through your wasteful changes. You give your subjects no choice but to believe you either incompetent or corrupt." Never scold a WASP, Pop had taught. He doesn't take scolding well. He thinks it means you don't like him. "Nothing personal, you understand."

"I understand." Hamilton Dapper peeped at his wristwatch. "But you misunderstand one essential point, Skippy. My class isn't raised to rule. We don't consider you our subjects. We're merely raised to be polite and to say bright things at cocktail parties. We have no class or race consciousness." He stood and extended his hand, blue eyes bright. "I guess you'd better get on with your work now. Me too."

I removed my right glove, but grabbed his right wrist with my gloved left hand and gripped it tight, at the same time reaching into my coveralls for my weapon. When he saw the pistol, he tried to squirm away, giving me his right temple for a target. Before he could utter a syllable, I put a bullet into his brain, silent as a puff of wind. The staple gun had made more racket.

Dead, he slumped back into his chair, his head thudding forward onto his typewriter. Blood leaked out onto his halfdone page.

I put my glove back on and wiped the pistol clean of fingerprints and removed the silencer. Then I pressed the pistol into his right hand, his smoking hand. I found the cigarette he'd just lit and mashed it out, then gathered up my toolkit and stepped out of his office. A few females glanced up, but seeing me and not Hamilton Dapper, returned to their reading and phonecalls. I closed the door behind me.

"The man says not to disturb him for a few hours," I told the receptionist. "The staple gun made too much noise, so he got behind in his work. But I finished the job, so you can drop the check in the mail."

"Fine." She smiled, but through me. "Look for it around the first of the month."

Next day the tabloids crowed the news. Even the Times mentioned it, though it made short shrift of Hamilton Dapper on its Obit page. TV HOST TAKES OWN LIFE. Typewritten Note Expresses Pessimism. Recent Divorce Seen as Contributing to Despondency. Bugged out her brain too. Roff the Daon amazing perceptions about people. "Talented as hell, but never a very stable character. He had everything, money, power and position, but none of it made him happy," continued Mr. Lipshutt, longtime associate and agent of the deceased. "Some men are just naturally morose. Maybe it goes with the talent." Reached at the home of her mother, the former Mrs. Dapper broke down on receiving the devastating news she had not heard before. "It can't be true, just can't!" she shrieked. "It must be some macabre trick. Ham always did have a sick sense of humor. You wait. He'll turn up in a few days, the bastard!" Wonder if she gets any dough now. But the Herald has obtained a copy of his bloodstained last testament to the world. His head fell, thud! Drip. Drop. It reads in part: "These recent revelations recall to remembrance my oft-used wheelbarrow image. Only now it turns out the wheelbarrow we approach in Hell costs seven times its real value. And may not even last until we get to Hell. Every day we receive more evidence that our society hurdles headlong toward self destruction. We all know it. We complain. But we don't change our ways."

It all made interesting reading on my flight to Colombia, where I went the next day for some rest and recreation. In the following days I did little but read accounts of it in Englishlanguage periodicals coming in from the U.S. I'd snort fine cocaine, then sit by the pool ogling the young bodies and reading about the Dapper Suicide. By the time it faded to the back pages and into the Beyond, I knew the time had come to return to the Bronx and my baking.

(1988)

Archie Epps in 1970

Herbert Denton in 1965

THE AFRICAN AND AFRO-AMERICAN SOCIETY
CONTROVERSY

In the spring term of 1963, black students held informal meetings with a view to establishing an official organization, the Association of African and Afro-American Students. In late April, they adopted a constitution; but on 6 May the Harvard Council for Undergraduate Affairs voted against approval, 14-5, because of the "discriminatory membership clause." On 9 May, the *Crimson* printed a letter from Archie C. Epps, then a graduate student. This was followed by an editorial advocating recognition, along with a series of four dissenting editorials, of which we reprint the last. In October, the AAAAS appealed to the administration for formal recognition. After several postponements and some rewording of the membership clause, the faculty voted approval in December.

Archie Calvin Epps III was born in Lake Charles, Louisiana, on 19 May 1937. Following his B.A. from Talladega College in 1958, he earned a Bachelor of Divinity degree from Harvard in 1961. After six years as assistant dean of the College, he was in 1970 named Dean of Students, a post he still holds. He also served as assistant conductor of the Harvard Glee Club from 1964 to 1967, and as a trustee of the Boston Symphony Orchestra.

The Mail   May 9, 1963

AFRICANS AND AFRO-AMERICANS

To the Editors of the Crimson:
The line of argument put forth by the African and Afro-American

students is strange to many. The argument is that the "association has not defined itself in racial terms by using the phrase 'African and Afro-American,' and that the group's members considered race unimportant to their membership clause." Opponents on the HCUA [Harvard Council for Undergraduate Affairs] said the group was "racially discriminatory because in practice it would not admit whites."

The white race is one of many races. It is significant therefore that the HCUA did not say the Association would discriminate against Chinese or Arabs, but only against the white race. The spokesman for the Association, Mr. [Ayi Kwei] Armah, said, "The terms African and Afro-American cover many races including Arabs and persons of partial European descent." This means there is no discrimination on the basis of race. There is no discrimination on the basis of color or creed: Armah pointed out that Africans and Afro-Americans include "people who are more white than black"; the Association is not a religious organization.

I suspect that the difficulty for the HCUA and other persons arises in part from the way in which the Association has chosen to define itself and to select its members. The basis of the definition is that the members have a special relation to Africa, namely, that all of the members have ancestors who were from Africa or the members themselves are from Africa or both. Incidentally, the ruling elite of South Africa has by its own assertion pure European ancestry and consequently would exclude itself from the Association by definition.

If the proposed association were to be called "The European and Euro-American Association," would this group be discriminatory against Afro-Americans? Manifestly not. Most of the members of the group known as Afro-Americans have noticeable traces of European ancestry, e.g., the great variations in skin color. Therefore the inclusion of one race, the European, may exclude others, e.g., the Chinese, but it does not follow that it will exclude them all.

The HCUA argument that the Association would be racially discriminatory contains a pivotal fallacy: It assumes that geographical areas are racially homogeneous. The Association would include many races but not all. The position of the Association is that no matter whomever you will find in it, you will find the African and the Afro-American.

Are those who have proposed the formation of the Association to be held responsible for the fact that there are other people who are not Africans? Are they responsible because others do not have the choice to join or not to join the Association because they are white? On the other hand, would the HCUA and the Administration deny the right of these students to make a choice which is not available to persons who are "purely" white? Are Africans and Afro-Americans to be denied the freedom to associate as Harvard and Radcliffe students because they are not white?

These students are asked to give up the freedom within the University which goes with the right and the fact of being different. A principle is here involved which challenges the presumption that one race must be omnipresent and that it shall be the "yardstick" by which the freedom of non-white races will be determined.

Archie C. Epps III, 1G

Harvard Crimson

Herbert Howard Denton Jr. was born in Muncie, Indiana, on 10 July 1943. He grew up in Little Rock, Arkansas, where his father was principal of a black elementary school. A scholarship helped him finish his secondary education at the Windsor Mountain School in Lenox, Massachusetts, where he was class valedictorian. At Harvard he served on the editorial board of the *Crimson*, while majoring in American history and earning his 1965 A.B. with honors. In 1966 he joined the staff of the *Washington Post*; and, after an Army tour of duty in Vietnam (where he received the Bronze Star) he did local reporting and rose to city editor in 1976. In 1980 he joined the national staff, and in 1983 began a two-year stint as foreign correspondent in Lebanon. He then opened the paper's Canadian bureau in Toronto, where he succumbed to AIDS on 29 April 1989.

On the Other Hand   May 14, 1963

AFRO-AMERICANS

Some time ago, one of the founders of the newly-organized African and Afro-American Association invited me to join his group. He argued that existing groups working for Negro rights cannot effectively cope with Negro problems because of the influence of white members. His central point was that whites, however good their intentions, can never fully understand the situation and aspirations of Negroes because, by virtue of their being white, they cannot share, fully and directly, in the experience of Negroes in a white-dominated society. They can only feel vicariously what Negroes feel directly, and, consequently, their approach must contain distortions which severely limit their ability to contribute to Negro endeavors.

He carried his argument a step further: not only are whites *qua* whites inherently excluded from an understanding of Negro problems, but Negroes *qua* Negroes—whether of American or African origin— have in common an indefinable "experience of oppression" which in some essential sense binds them together as a racial group. They stand apart from other groups which have been oppressed, and yet remain somehow together despite their disparate national origins and the differences between colonial rule and American bigotry as styles of oppression.

While one might agree that American Negroes have some things in common to justify their association in an exclusive group, the idea of an international unity with African Negroes seems far more dubious, particularly when it is argued that the unifying "experience of oppression" somehow does not apply to non-Negro groups which have been persecuted. Apart from the color of their skins, what arguments can be adduced for a unity which implies that the experience of being oppressed *as a Negro* (whatever the actual character of the oppression) is essentially different from the experience of being oppressed because one belongs to some other minority group?

While this notion seems to be gaining fairly wide acceptance in some quarters, there seem to be strong and unanswered objections to it. Unless one adheres to some notion of a racial unconscious, it would seem that the experience of each individual consists of what happens to him within his own concrete social and cultural situation. The tribulations of his ancestors three hundred years ago become relevant only insofar as they are reflected in his personal situation, or insofar as he is taught to believe them emotionally important regardless of his own position. Hence it would seem that what matters for the Afro-American "unity of oppression" is not a common "Negritude," but rather the degree to which the environmental situations of African and American Negroes are parallel.

Considered objectively, and without recourse to the somewhat obscurantist idea that whites and Negroes are intrinsically incapable of understanding one another (an idea which is always assumed, never demonstrated), the notion of an Afro-American Negro unity which transcends all other ties is extremely questionable, to say the least. African Negroes have come from a social environment which is still by and large tribal and industrially undeveloped, and a political situation in which absolute colonial rule and rigid racial paternalism were until recently completely predominant. Their sympathies often tend to lie with Marxist notions of forced economic development, and with the conception of racially founded nationalist hegemony. The situation of American Negroes is quite different. Centuries removed from tribal roots, they live in an industrialized society in which the idea of equality, while hardly realized in concrete terms, has been almost universally accepted as an ethical norm towards which society must, will and can move. The personal experiences of African and American Negroes—and, in particular, the ways in which oppression has been experienced—cannot but reflect these striking differences in their social, economic, and political circumstances. It is difficult to see what overriding bond of experience American Negroes have with Africans which ties them closer to Africa than to their native land, or should cause them to reject equally close collaboration with other groups which have been oppressed.

In the final analysis, the argument for American and African unity rests on the undemonstrable—and perhaps slightly paranoid—act of pure faith which asserts *a priori* that whites and Negroes *per se* cannot understand one another nor collaborate in an atmosphere of equality and mutual respect. One thing is certain: the surest way to prevent equality is to convince everyone of such a thesis. Paranoid presuppo-- sitions rapidly become self-fulfilling prophecies. The ideal of equality is not refuted; it is merely rendered historically impossible by ideologies which generate racial distrust.

One must question the desirability of encouraging such ideas— which may be understandable in the context of African experience—in a country where ethical norms and historical progress point in the opposite direction. The question becomes even sharper when one notes that a principal strategy of conversion to these ideas is to allege that those Negroes whose experience has led them to different conclu- sions have "sold out" to the *ofay* "enemy": to call them "Uncle Toms" and arouse, through emotional ideologizing, a sense of guilt designed to lead them to positions which, in an atmosphere less charged emo- tionally, might be wholly inconsistent with their personal experience and ethical norms.

One must further question the desirability of fostering such a psy- chological pattern within the Harvard environment. Negro students coming to the University are likely to be overwhelmed with the idea, promoted by the only "official" Negro organization on campus, that even the most liberal and interesting white students they may meet cannot possibly understand them, and may even be hypocrites—that the only place they are truly among friends is in an all-Negro organization strongly influenced by Black Nationalism. Such an outcome drastically curtails their ability to benefit from the central Harvard experience of association with and exposure to the broadest possible spectrum of people, ideas and movements. One may seriously ask whether an organization which so functions is in anyway compatible with the educational ideals of this University.

Whether or not the College should recognize the African and Afro-American Association, despite its explicit racial discrimination, remains an open question. The moral objection to discrimination is not that it involves making distinctions between people, but that the racial distinctions involved are rationally indefensible and lead to social evil. The most relevant criterion in evaluating the AAAA would thus seem to be, not the legalistic implications of its membership clause, but the effect the group will have upon the concrete educational experience of an important number of undergraduates —whether it will, in fact, lead to social evil within the Harvard community. The Association's representatives have not, so far, presented any cogent, rationally outlined arguments to this point. Barring the explicit adoption of an across-the-board *laissez-faire* policy of University recognition, perhaps the College authorities should hold the AAAA charter in abeyance until the club's representatives have clarified their position on this question.

Herbert H. Denton, Jr.

(The above represents the opinion of a minority of the Editorial Board.)

Harvard Crimson

Malcolm X addressing a Harlem rally in 1963

MALCOLM X

Born Malcolm Little on 19 May 1925 in Omaha, Nebraska, the self-educated Black Muslim minister became famous as Malcolm X. He was assassinated in New York on 21 February 1965. The visits of Malcolm X came at important turning points in his intellectual development. He came to Harvard to give speeches on three separate and significant occasions: once in 1961, when he was deeply in his Black Muslim period; in March 1964, when he had just resigned from the Black Muslims; and in December 1964, soon after he had returned from an extensive trip to Africa, two months before his assassination, and in the midst of the period of his partial acceptance of racial integration. One of the most compelling themes in Malcolm X's literature is the explicit sense of exile felt by Black Americans which he articulated so well. This theme lay at the surface of nearly all his Harvard speeches. He often seemed so surprised by the rough treatment that blacks had received at the hands of whites. And in these moments his rhetoric stands with the great rhetoric of all literature that comes from the everlasting struggle of men and women to be free.

It has become clear since his death that Malcolm X was the most effective exponent of the black nationalist strategy and a man, strangely enough, whose very being may be more integral to the American experience of his generation than any other man's, white or black. Because Malcolm X was so completely a man of words, it is in his speeches that he must be found, and in no other single group of speeches can his development as man and thinker be so clearly seen than in those he delivered at Harvard.

—Archie Epps

The Leverett House
Forum of
March 18, 1964[1]

Archie Epps, Moderator

Academicians and laymen have often thought of Negro radicalism or
nationalism in terms of pathology. In other words, Negro personalities
in radical movements are thought to be abnormal, or shysters, or
freaks of some sort. Accordingly, Negro radicalism is conceived of as
the fervent product of systematic and protracted frustration; its ideology, a pathological response to economic, social, and cultural discrimination. The Negro radical movement is never credited with meaning
what it says. Its pronouncements are interpreted rather than heard.
None of its arguments is accorded the courtesy one gives reality.
They are tolerated as the angry response of Negroes to white rejection. It is perhaps more nearly correct that what is often thought
absurd about Negro radicalism turns out to be logical conclusions to
a line of reasoning and experience which are unknown and beyond the
imagination of most observers who are not themselves Negro. Negro
radicalism is, rather, the spontaneous and articulated answer of some
Negroes to real problems little appreciated by timid and peaceful
souls.

It is nearer the truth, no doubt, that some of you have come to
see and hear Malcolm X only to observe what you think is his curious
pathology. Surely some have come for the reason one would attend
a circus—to watch the dancing bear. To be sure, revolutions, and this
one, are full of the inadequacies of men and of their pathologies; but,
on the other hand, revolutions give rise to profound meditation on the
problem of evil and on the place of man in society. Specifically,
revolutions demonstrate in the clamor of men the economic forces of
the age; their molding of society and politics, of men in the mass and
individual man; and the powerful reaction of all these forces on the
social environment at one of those rare moments when society is at
a boiling point, fluid and therefore discernible to man. The conflicts
of this revolutionary age in America enable us, I think, to see the very
bones of American society. And it is no doubt incumbent on students
and academicians, indeed, on all men to reconsider Negro radicalism,

Negro movements, and all social history in light of discovering the social reality which is contained in them.

The speaker this evening is Mr. Malcolm X, who lives in New York State and is at this time Minister of Moslem Mosque, Incorporated.

MALCOLM X: Nineteen hundred sixty-four will probably be the most explosive year that America has yet witnessed on the racial front; primarily because the black people of this country during 1963 saw nothing but failure behind every effort they made to get what the country was supposedly on record for. Today the black people in this country have become frustrated, disenchanted, disillusioned and probably more set for action now than ever before—not the kind of action that has been set out for them in the past by some of their supposedly liberal white friends, but the kind of action that will get some kind of immediate results. As the moderator has pointed out, the time that we're living in now and that we are facing now is not an era where one who is oppressed is looking toward the oppressor to give him some system or form of logic or reason. What is logical to the oppressor isn't logical to the oppressed. And what is reason to the oppressor isn't reason to the oppressed. The black people in this country are beginning to realize that what sounds reasonable to those who exploit us doesn't sound reasonable to us. There just has to be a new system of reason and logic devised by us who are at the bottom, if we want to get some results in this struggle that is called "the Negro revolution."

Not only is it going to be an explosive year on the racial front; it is going to be an explosive year on the political front. This year it will be impossible to separate one from the other. The politicking of the politicians in 1964 will probably do more to bring about racial explosion than any other factor, because this country has been under the rule of the politicians. When they want to get elected to office they come into the so-called Negro community and make a lot of promises that they don't intend to keep. This feeds the hopes of the people in our community, and after the politicians have gotten what they are looking for, they turn their back on the people of our community. This has happened time and time again. The only difference between then and now is that there is a different element in the community; whereas in the past the people of our community were patient and polite, long-suffering and willing to listen to what *you* call reason, 1964 has produced an element of people who are no longer willing to listen to what you call reason. As I said, what's reasonable to you has long since ceased to be reasonable to us. And it will be these false promises made by the politicians that will bring about the BOOM.

During the few moments that I have I hope that we can chat in an informal way, because I find that when you are discussing things that are very "touchy," sometimes it's best to be informal. And where white people are concerned, it has been my experience that they are extremely intelligent on most subjects until it comes to race. When you get to the racial issue in this country, the whites lose all their intelligence. They become very subjective, and they want to tell us how it should be solved. It's like Jesse James going to tell the Marshal how he should come after him for the crime that Jesse committed.

I am not a politician. I'm not even a student of politics. I'm not a Democrat. I'm not a Republican. I don't even consider myself an American. If I could consider myself an American, we wouldn't even have any problem. It would be solved. Many of you get indignant when you hear a black man stand up and say, "No, I'm not an American." I see whites who have the audacity, I should say the nerve, to think that a black man is radical and extremist, subversive and seditious if he says, "No, I'm not an American." But at the same time, these same whites have to admit that this man has a problem.

I don't come here tonight to speak to you as a Democrat or a Republican or an American or anything that *you* want me to be. I'm speaking as what I am: one of twenty-two million black people in this country who are victims of your democratic system. They're the victims of the Democratic politicians, the victims of the Republican politicians. They're actually the victims of what you call democracy. So I stand here tonight speaking as a victim of what you call democracy. And you can understand what I'm saying if you realize it's being said through the mouth of a victim; the mouth of one of the oppressed, not through the mouth and eyes of the oppressor. But if you think we're sitting in the same chair or standing on the same platform, then you won't understand what I'm talking about. You'd expect me to stand up here and say what you would say if you were standing up here. And I'd have to be out of my mind.

Whenever one is viewing this political system through the eyes of a victim, he sees something different. But today these twenty-two million black people who are the victims of American democracy, whether you realize it or not, are viewing your democracy with new eyes. Yesterday our people used to look upon the American system as an American dream. But the black people today are beginning to realize that it is an American nightmare. What is a dream to you is a nightmare to us. What is hope to you has long since become hopeless to our people. And as this attitude develops, not so much on Sugar Hill [in Harlem]—although it's there too—but in the ghetto, in the alley where the masses of our people live . . . there you have a new situation on your hands. There's a new political consciousness developing among our people in this country. In the past, we weren't conscious of the political maneuvering that goes on in this country, which exploits our people politically. We knew something was wrong, but we weren't conscious of what it was. Today there's a tendency on the part of this new generation of black people (who have been born and are growing up in this country) to look at the thing not as they wish it were, but as it actually is. And their ability to look at the situation as it is, is what is primarily responsible for the ever-increasing sense of frustration and hopelessness that exists in the so-called Negro community today.

Beside becoming politically conscious, you'll find that our people are also becoming more aware of the strategic position that they occupy politically. In the past, they weren't. Just the right to vote was considered something. But today the so-called Negroes are beginning to realize that they occupy a very strategic position. They realize what the new trends are and all of the new political tendencies.

During recent years at election time, when the Governor was running for office, there was call for a recount of votes here in Massachusetts. In Rhode Island it was the same way—in Minnesota, the same thing. Within American politics there is now such a similarity between the two parties that in elections the race is usually close enough to permit almost any single block to swing it one way or the other. Not only is this true in city, county, and state elections, but it's also true in the national elections, as witness the close race between President Kennedy and Nixon a few years back. And everyone admits that it was the strategic vote of the so-called Negro in this country that put the Kennedy administration in Washington. The position in the political structure of the so-called Negro has become so strategic that whenever any kind of election rolls around now, the politicians are out there trying to win the Negro vote. In trying to win the Negro vote, they make a whole lot of promises and build up his hopes. But they always build him up for a letdown. By being constantly built up for a letdown, the Negro is now becoming very angry at the white man. And in his anger the Muslims come along and talk to him. Yet instead of the white man blaming himself for the anger of the Negro, he again has the audacity to blame us. When we warn you how angry the Negro is becoming, you, instead of thanking us for giving you a little warning, try to accuse us of stirring up the Negro. Don't you know that if your house is on fire and I come to warn you that your house is burning, you shouldn't accuse me of setting the fire! Thank me rather for letting you know what's happening, or what's going to happen, before it's too late.

When these new trends develop in the so-called Negro in America, making the so-called Negro aware of his strategic position politically, he becomes aware too of what he's not getting in return. He realizes that his vote puts the governor in office, or the mayor in office, or the president in office. But he's beginning to see also that although his vote is the vital factor that determines who will sit in these seats, the last one those politicians try to help is the so-called Negro.

Proof of which: Everyone admits that it was the Negro vote that put Kennedy in the White House. Yet four years have passed and the present administration is just now getting around to civil rights legislation. In its fourth year of office it finally passes some kind of civil rights legislation, designed supposedly to solve the problem of the so-called Negro. Yet that voting element offered decisive support in the national election. I only cite this to show the hypocrisy on the part of the white man in America, whether he be down South or whether he be up here in the North.

Democrats, now after they've been in the White House awhile, use an alibi for not having kept their promise to the Negroes who voted for them. They say, "Well, we can't get this passed or we can't get that passed." The present make-up of the Congress is 257 Democrats and only 177 Republicans. Now how can a party of Democrats that received practically the full support of the so-called Negroes of this country and control nearly two-thirds of the seats in Congress give the Negro an excuse for not getting some kind of legislation passed to solve the Negro problem? Where the senators are concerned, there are 67 Democrats and only 33 Republicans; yet these Democrats are going to try to pass the buck to the Republicans after the Negro has put the Democrats in office. Now I'm not siding with either Democrats or Republicans. I'm just pointing out the deceit on the part of both when it comes to dealing with the Negro. Although the Negro vote put the Democratic Party where it is, the Democratic Party gives the Negro nothing; and the Democrats offer as an excuse that the fault lies with the Dixie-crats. What do you call them—Dixie-crats or Dixo-crats or Demo-Dixo-crats!

Look at the shrewd deceptive manner in which they deal with the Negro. A Dixo-crat is a Democrat. You can call them by whatever name you wish, but you have never seen a situation where the Dixie-crats kick the Democrats out of the party. Rather the Democrats kick the Dixie-crats out of their party if there is ever any cleavage. You oftentimes find the Dixie-crats "cussing out" the Democrats, but you never find the Democrats disassociating themselves from the Dixie-crats. They are together and they use this shrewd maneuvering to trick the Negro. Now there are some young Negroes appearing on the scene, and it is time for those who call themselves Democrats to realize that when the Negro looks at a Democrat, he sees a Democrat. Whether you call him a Dixo-Democrat or a Demo-Dixie-crat, he's the same thing.

One of the reasons that these Dixie-crats occupy such a powerful position in Washington, D.C., is that they have seniority. By reason of their seniority and primarily because they have denied the local Negro his right to vote, they hold sway over key committees in Washington. You call it a system based on democracy, yet you can't deny that the most powerful men in this government are from the South. The only reason they're in positions of power is because the Negroes in their area are deprived of their constitutional right to vote. But the Constitution says that when at any time the people of a given area are denied their right to vote, the representatives of that area are supposed to be expelled from their seat. You don't need any new legislation; it's right in front of you already. The only reason the politicians want new legislation is to use it to further trick the Negro. All they have to do is to go by that thing they call the Constitution. It needs no more bills, it needs no more amendments, it needs no more anything. All it needs is a little sincere application.

As with the South, the North knows its own by-pass for the Constitution, which goes by the name of "gerrymandering." Some fellows gain control in the so-called Negro community and then change voting lines every time the Negro begins to get too powerful numerically. The technique is different from that in Mississippi. There is no denying the Negro the right to vote outright, as in Mississippi. The Northern way is more shrewd and subtle; but whether victim of the Northern way or the Southern method, the Negro ends up with no political power whatsoever. Now, I may not be putting this in language which you're used to, but I'm quite sure that you get the point. Whenever you give the Negro in the South the right to vote, it will mean an automatic change in the entire representation from the South. Were he able to exercise his right, some of the most powerful and influential figures in Washington, D.C., would not now be in the Capitol. A large Negro vote would change the foreign policy as well as the domestic policy of this government. Therefore the only valid approach toward revolutionizing American policy is to give to the Negro his right to vote. Once that is done, the entire future course of things must change.

I might say this is how we look at it—how the victims look at it, a very crude and what you might call pessimistic view. But I should rather prefer it as a realistic view. Now what is our approach towards solving this? Many of you have probably just recently read that I am no longer an active member in the Nation of Islam, although I am myself still a Muslim. My religion is still Islam, and I still credit the Honorable Elijah Muhammad with being responsible for everything I know and everything I am. In New York we have recently founded the Muslim Mosque, Incorporated, which has as its base the religion of Islam, the religion of Islam because we have found that this religion creates more unity among our people than any other type of philosophy can do. At the same time the religion of Islam is more successful in eliminating the vices that exist in the so-called Negro community, which destroy the moral fiber of the so-called Negro community.

So with this religious base, the difference between the Muslim Mosque, Incorporated, and the Nation of Islam is probably this: We have as our political philosophy, Black Nationalism; as our economic philosophy, Black Nationalism; and as our social philosophy, Black Nationalism. We believe that the religion of Islam combined with Black Nationalism is all that is needed to solve the problem that exists in the so-called Negro community. Why?

The only real solution to our problem, just as the Honorable Elijah Muhammad has taught us, is to go back to our homeland and to live among our own people and develop it so we'll have an independent nation of our own. I still believe this. But that is a long-range program. And while our people are getting set to go back home, we have to live here in the meantime. So in the Honorable Elijah Muhammad's long-range program, there's also a short-range program: the political philosophy which teaches us that the black man should control the politics of his own community. When the black man controls the politics and the politicians in his own community, he can then make them produce what is good for the community. For when a politician in the so-called Negro community is controlled by a political machine outside, seldom will that politician ever do what is necessary to bring up the standard of living or to solve the problems that exist in that community. So our political philosophy is designed to bring together the so-called Negroes and to re-educate them to the importance of politics in concrete betterment, so that they may know what they should be getting from their politicians in addition to a promise. Once the political control of the so-called Negro community is in the hands of the so-called Negro, then it is possible for us to do something towards correcting the evils and the ills that exist there.

Our economic philosophy of Black Nationalism means that instead of our spending the rest of our lives begging the white man for a job, our people should be re-educated to the science of economics and the part that it plays in our community. We should be taught just the basic fundamentals: that whenever you take money out of the neighborhood and spend it in another neighborhood, the neighborhood in which you spend it gets richer and richer, and the neighborhood from which you take it gets poorer and poorer. This creates a ghetto, as now exists in every so-called Negro community in this country. If the Negro isn't spending his money downtown with what we call "the man," "the man" is himself right in the Negro community. All the stores are run by the white man, who takes the money out of the community as soon as the sun sets. We have to teach our people the importance of where to spend their dollars and the importance of establishing and owning businesses. Thereby we can create employment for ourselves, instead of having to wait to boycott your stores and businesses to demand that you give us a job. Whenever the majority of our people begin to think along such lines, you'll find that we ourselves can best solve our problems. Instead of having to wait for someone to come out of your neighborhood into our neighborhood to tackle these problems for us, we ourselves may solve them.

The social philosophy of Black Nationalism says that we must eliminate the vices and evils that exist in our society, and that we must stress the cultural roots of our forefathers, that will lend dignity and make the black man cease to be ashamed of himself. We have to teach our people something about our cultural roots. We have to teach them something of their glorious civilizations before they were kidnapped by your grandfathers and brought over to this country. Once our people are taught about the glorious civilization that existed on the African continent, they won't any longer be ashamed of who they are. We will reach back and link ourselves to those roots, and this will make the feeling of dignity come into us; we will feel that as we lived in times gone by, we can in like manner today. If we had civilizations, cultures, societies, and nations hundreds of years ago, before you came and kidnapped us and brought us here, so we can have the same today. The restoration of our cultural roots and history will restore dignity to the black people in this country. Then we shall be satisfied in our own social circles; then we won't be trying to force ourselves into your social circles. So the social philosophy of Black Nationalism doesn't in any way involve any anti-anything. However, it does restore to the man who is being taunted his own self-respect. And the day that we are successful in making the black man respect himself as much as he now admires you, he will no longer be breathing down your neck every time you go buy a house somewhere to get away from him.

That is the political, social, and economic philosophy of Black Nationalism, and in order to bring it about, the program that we have in the Muslim Mosque, Incorporated, places an accent on youth. We are issuing a call for students across the country, from coast to coast, to launch a new study of the problem—not a study that is in any way guided or influenced by adults, but a study of their own. Thus we can get a new analysis of the problem, a more realistic analysis. After this new study and more realistic analysis, we are going to ask those same students (by students I mean young people, who having less of a stake to lose, are more flexible and can be more objective) for a new approach to the problem.

Already we have begun to get responses from so-called Negro students from coast to coast, who aren't actually religiously inclined, but who are nonetheless strongly sympathetic to the approach used by Black Nationalism, whether it be social, economic, or political. And with this new approach and with these new ideas we think that we may open up a new era here in this country. As that era begins to spread, people in this country—instead of sticking under your nose or crying for civil rights—will begin to expand their civil rights plea to a plea for human rights. And once the so-called Negro in this country forgets the whole civil rights issue and begins to realize that human rights are far more important and broad than civil rights, he won't be going to Washington, D.C., anymore, to beg Uncle Sam for civil rights. He will take his plea for human rights to the United Nations. There won't be a violation of civil rights anymore. It will be a violation of human rights. Now at this moment, the governments that are in the United Nations can't step in, can't involve themselves with America's domestic policy. But the day the black man turns from civil rights to human rights, he will take his case into the halls of the United Nations in the same manner as the people in Angola, whose human rights have been violated by the Portuguese in South Africa.

You'll find that you are entering an era now where the black man in this country has ceased to think domestically, or within the bounds of the United States, and he's beginning to see that this is a world-wide issue and that he needs help from outside. We need help from our brothers in Africa who have won their independence. And when we begin to show them our thinking has expanded to an international scale, they will step in and help us, and you'll find that Uncle Sam will be in a most embarrassing position. So the only way Uncle Sam can stop us is to get some civil rights passed—right now! For if he can't take care of his domestic dirt, it's going to be put before the eyes of the world. Then you'll find that you'll have nobody on your side, whatsoever, other than, perhaps, a few of those Uncle Toms—and they've already out-lived their time. . . .

MODERATOR: I suggest we follow this format: We will have reactions and responses to what Malcolm X has said from the members of the panel, then give Malcolm X a chance to discuss their views.

The first member of the panel to address us will be Professor James Q. Wilson, who has written an important book about Negro politics in Chicago. At present, Professor Wilson is Associate Professor of Government at Harvard and also Director of the Joint Center for Urban Studies [M.I.T. and Harvard].

JAMES Q. WILSON: Malcolm X, Ladies and Gentlemen. It is impossible not to be impressed with the conviction, the sincerity, the force and the vigor of the man who has just spoken to you. He is protesting against outrages he feels keenly. They are real outrages.

They are outrages, echoes of which can be found throughout American history, echoes raised by white and Negro voices alike.

The American political system, I suppose, is unique in many ways. One way it is unique is that it has a built-in resistance to fundamental, far-reaching change. This resistance to fundamental change has frustrated the efforts of people through two centuries of our history to achieve a fundamental social revolution short of force of arms. The system is, I believe, as Malcolm X has said, based on the *politics of hope*—hopes which politicians do not intend to realize. I think the reason is not because politicians are wicked men, and certainly not because they are more wicked than all of us, but because there is something inherent in the system which, on the one hand, induces them to offer promises and, on the other hand, prevents them from keeping them. We have had Populists, Socialists, Trotskyites, Greenbackers, and urban reformers, who for two centuries have railed against the system and this system has refused fundamentally to change—refused fundamentally to change for a variety of reasons. The chief reason, I suppose, is because politics in the long run has always paid off; that is, the politics of hope holds out to people in the long run the prospect, however dim and however uncertain, of freedom and of jobs and opportunity. And enough people have received these so that eventually their energies have been sapped and their enthusiasms converted.

The question, of course, is whether the politics of hope will work in this era when men such as Malcolm X are leading a new kind of social revolution in America. In the 1930s we used to say, with a note of relief in our voices, that there was no genuine Negro radical movement. There was no wholesale commitment of the Negroes to the Communist Party, because at that time there was no educated Negro middle class to provide the ideological cadres of such a revolutionary commitment. When the middle class was born, we pundits used to say, they would find the revolutionary consciousness in the event of a depression. Well, the revolutionary consciousness is now emerging, but not from the Negro middle class. The latter has been carried away with the politics of hope. I think Malcolm X would say it has been nicely "bought off" by the system. The revolutionary consciousness, we now find, is not a product of the middle class, but of the Negro lower class and of the young people, who have formed a kind of alliance unique in American politics, which proposes to change fundamentally the system in the direction of basic goals seen in visionary terms—which means they will be imperfectly realized.

A second question is how the American system will respond to this demand for fundamental change. The balance of power theory so long fashionable in discussions of the Negro vote is not true. The Negroes do not hold the balance of power in American politics for the same reason that no other single identifiable group holds the balance of power. And the reason that none of them do is that all of them do. The reason that all of them do is that American politics is so fragmented, so decentralized into bits and pieces of authority, so widely distributed over the constitutional landscape, that at any point in time almost any group can say with some plausibility that it contributed to the success of that politician. There is no national mandate. There is no national consensus. There is no politics in which one voice and one vote is the marginal voice, the marginal vote that decides the election.

The balance of power theory has been put to the test by third-party movements throughout our history, and the record has been a record of failure. No third party, with maybe one or two exceptions (which perhaps I tend to forget but conveniently ignore), has changed the outcome of any election in American history. No third party has ever become a major party. No third party, except for Teddy Roosevelt's Bullmoosers, has ever become a second party. Only four ever received any electoral votes, and only three of these won as much as ten percent of the popular vote. To be sure many of them were counted out by politicians when the ballot box was not so sacrosanct as it is today. Very few have ever won seats in Congress, and none have ever changed an election so far as we can be certain. One of the reasons why the balance of power theory has not contributed to the influence of third parties is because many groups within the two-party system can claim a whole share in this balance. It is true that in eight major northern industrial states, which together hold two hundred and ten electoral votes in the electoral college, the Negro vote for the Democratic candidate for President in 1960 was larger than the margin by which he defeated his Republican opponent in those states. Does this mean that Negroes are responsible for his victory? It means they were only if you take into equal account that Catholics in those eight states also cast votes for the Democratic candidate in excess of plurality, that the Jews cast ballots in excess of plurality, young people and perhaps even college professors, God help us, cast ballots in excess of plurality. All these groups can say with equal plausibility that they hold the balance of power.

Gerrymandering is not the reason. There are many cities today in which Negroes are represented almost in proportion to their population. It is usually those cities which have shown the least progress in the direction of civil rights. Chicago has seven Negroes in the city council and nine Negroes in the state legislature. They are represented not precisely but nearly in accordance with their population. Yet Chicago and Illinois have been the slowest in taking any steps in the direction of major civil rights legislation. Negroes in New York are under-represented in politics. Yet this state has done far more for the Negro. Why? Because civil rights legislation by and large has not been aimed at capturing the Negro vote. The Negro vote could already be taken for granted by the Democratic Party. The civil rights legislation was therefore aimed at capturing the vote which was uncommitted, that independent vote which changes from election to election. And that was a vote of "supposedly liberal white friends" of the Negro, to use the former speaker's words.

It is fashionable today for Negroes to dislike and distrust their supposedly liberal white friends. It is just as fashionable for their supposedly liberal white friends to dislike and distrust themselves, for we are going through a period of anxiety in which we doubt our own capacity for action. We want something done collectively, but we cannot bring ourselves to act collectively. So we engage dubiously in personal relationships with students who need our help in Roxbury. The white liberal with his reticence, self-consciousness, and introspection today reflects precisely the same concern and the same charges the previous speaker has thrown at us. He does not need to indict us. We've indicted ourselves, and we know it. The question is where do we move in a system of this kind? John F. Kennedy did not ignore the promises he made to all the other groups that hold the balance of power. The trouble is that those promises canceled out each other. And this is not said in criticism of Kennedy. It is stated as characteristic of the system, and the question is how do you propose to change this? And is the change worthwhile? Perhaps it is; I don't know because I'm not a Negro, thank God. And perhaps from their point of view it is. I'm skeptical, but I remain open, I think, to persuasion. It is not deceitful Southern Democrats with civil rights filibustering who keep this legislation out of existence. The party label is about as meaningless as Malcolm X has so graphically pointed out.

Whether putting Negroes in office would change the *politics of hope* to the *politics of reality* is the real question. There are Negroes in office in almost every city and state of any consequence in the United States today. (I automatically exclude Mississippi.) What difference does this make? I don't know, but it's certainly not dramatic.

The white politicians cannot change the system. They've tried. I recall one time when there was a third party movement, an effort to capture certain key positions in the American political system and hold them long enough to force certain fundamental changes. In 1912 the Socialist Party in the United States captured six percent of the presidential vote. Almost nine hundred thousand people voted for its candidate for president. They elected fifty-six mayors, one hundred and sixty councilmen, one hundred and forty-five aldermen, eighteen state representatives, and two state senators. There were over one thousand Socialist Party members holding office in the United States at the time. They printed fourteen daily newspapers and two hundred ninety-eight weekly newspapers. They had one hundred eighteen thousand dues-paying members. And where is the Socialist Party today?

The Negro Party, if that is what is being proposed this evening, is not going to have precisely this outcome. Socialists can be lost in the American melting pot because the mark of their identity is carried inwardly and not outwardly. Negroes cannot be lost in this system because the mark of their identity is carried outward for all to see, for all time. The question is: Even though the spirit and the people and the movement continue to exist, what will happen if the strategy is a separatist strategy, a third-party strategy or even a strategy within a party to capture a party's leadership?

Is a separatist strategy going to accomplish as much as those nonparty, and in some cases nonlegal, methods by which the system is challenged directly by students sitting-in, lying-in, kneeling-in, walking-in, or whatever? This attacks the system in the one place where it is vulnerable—its conscience, its slow, belated, fuzzy but existent conscience. When you start to play the political game, then you're playing the game where the conscience is not involved for most people, because the political game is one which people believe must be interpreted and explained in cynical terms ... cynical, because they know it hasn't made any difference in the past; cynical, because they distrust the motives that go into politics and know that the best things in life, from their point of view, come from extra-political sources.

MODERATOR: The second speaker this evening will be Dr. Martin L. Kilson. Dr. Kilson is Lecturer on Government at Harvard, and will soon publish his first book, *Political Change in a West African State*.

MARTIN KILSON: When I was working out my notes for this evening, I thought that I would be the only one on this panel who would end up being rather pessimistic and somewhat cynical about things, because I am rather pessimistic about things, and what I have to say begins on a pessimistic note and ends on a pessimistic note.

Now the first negative note that I want to begin on is essentially about the way we modern Americans go about political things in a modern social-cultural system. It seems to me that the whole American political experiment and experience and process always reflected what one would call a certain kind of madness. By this I mean there has always been a certain kind of emphasis upon the politically mundane and the politically vile as a means of staking a claim for one's self or for one's group in the mainstream of American society. Thus, for instance, the Irish, the Italians, and all of the other nineteenth century white immigrant groups fashioned quite consciously what, I think, can be called in a general way thoroughly corrupt, parochial political arrangements, in order to wrest out status and prestige and influence from the established patricians, Protestant elite groups; and through this to enter into the mainstream of American social life. We're told now that these white immigrants have quite succeeded. They have made it, so we are told; but unfortunately, the political arrangements they fashioned in order to succeed still persist at all levels of the American political system, and it is my feeling that they are about to strangle us all, including the sycamores on Memorial Drive. What is more, these mundane, corrupt, inefficient methods of allocating the resources of a modern society cannot really begin to handle the problem which the Negro confronts.

Then there came the Negro. Of course we came in the early 1900s from the South with great migration movements to the North and to the cities—what some thought to be the promised land. As former slaves, and therefore with immeasurably weaker positions in material and physical capacity for making way in an urban context, significantly few of these new Negroes could really fashion any meaningful stake in the mainstream of American society. But some, as the early middle-class Negroes, did attempt to fashion a stake in the mainstream, and, curiously enough, in close relationship with the corrupt political institutions created by the immigrant groups; who, indeed, tended to look upon the Negro as something less than a man. And so this peculiar kind of relationship between the early Negro middle class and national and state politicians appeared always to me a very curious kind of business. We're told too that this ten to fifteen or twenty percent of Negroes who have fashioned some kind of stake in American society have also "made it."

However, there remains the mass of Negroes who, it seems, were in a small sense not so lucky. For even they, I think, still wanted to establish an estate in the American material heaven. And in a sense, why not? At their own level of cheap and exploited labor and human souls, they essentially contributed as much to the development of the American mainstream as any other group. In some respects, they contributed more than many groups. And this brings me to the question of the evening: the question of Black Nationalist politics and the conception of it which is now being propounded and organized by our speaker, Mr. Malcolm X.

Now it seems quite frankly that as another means of fashioning a foothold, a stake for the Negro in the American mainstream, the Black Nationalist, or any other black racist political proposition, is essentially as mundane and as vile as the institutions used successfully by the white immigrants. Yet, I think that the peculiar madness in American society has left the great mass of Negroes no really significant alternative method.

What is the method behind this kind of Black Nationalist proposition? I am myself totally willing to grant a good part of the description by Malcolm X and others of the position and experience of the Negro in American society. From such experiences has emerged a deep-seated frustration on the part of most Negroes as well as an ambivalent, love-hate complex, as it were, toward the white American majority. It is this frustration and complex upon which Malcolm X's Black Nationalist proposition must either stand or fall. Now, one can certainly query this business in more particular terms, and I do query it. But my thinking is that this is hardly a useful exercise, for as has been indicated, the Black Nationalist method is, at its own level of experience, as "ethical" as techniques used by immigrant groups. In other words, self-styled maneuvering is basically a legitimate part of this curious madness I have in mind as being so characteristic of the American political experiment. Therefore, it seems to me that the really important question, at least from a social scientist's point of view, is whether or not Mr. Malcolm X's Black Nationalist proposition, or any other Black Nationalist proposition, can, in fact, make a greater claim for the Negroes in the American mainstream. Now Mr. X is necessarily optimistic on this point, or he wouldn't be in business. But I myself am rather pessimistic on the question. But I hasten to assure Mr. X that my pessimism doesn't stem from any kind of unconscious wish that his Black Nationalist method would fail. It rather stems from my own reading of the complex and terrible plight that most Negroes encounter today. And it also stems from my reading of the past circumstances and forces that gave rise to the first (at least organizationally successful) Black Nationalist proposition at the end of World War I (1918-1925)—the Garvey Movement.

Now for one thing, I am convinced that among the seventy-five percent of Negro Americans whom we can safely call the Negro masses—that is, the poor and the downtrodden—there remains still some room for an effective Black Nationalist political appeal. Indeed, the political history of the urban Negro in this century, as I read it, reveals that only the black racist appeal has ever been able to effectively mobilize around political and social action any significant portion of the Negro American population. This is precisely what Marcus Garvey and his *Universal Negro Improvement Association* demonstrated, even though at the level of concrete contributions to the resolution of the Negro problem it contributed, I think, essentially very little. But today, in the middle of the twentieth century, any Black Nationalist political group confronts the evident fact that the circumstances which facilitated the Garvey movement have been significantly altered within the social structure of the urban Negro. Now I do not mean, of course, that the basic caste relationship of the Negro to the over-all white American society has been significantly altered. This relationship is basically the same as it has been for one century. What I do have in mind concerns the characteristics involved in the urban social structure of Negro society.

At the end of World War I it was interesting to note that urban Negro society was evolving basically along lines comparable to that of other groups. That is to say, it had an expanding structure of voluntary associations, which were slowly but surely meeting some of the basic day-to-day needs and problems of the urbanized mass. All the facts which I know reveal that the Garvey movement evolved within the framework of this expanding infrastructure of Negro voluntary associations, especially among the Negro masses. Even among the early small middle-class elements, some important middle-class personalities finally went over to the Garvey movement—people like Emmet J. Scott. Scott was an eminent Uncle Tom. He was a private secretary to Booker T. Washington, and upon Booker T. Washington's death inherited the whole structure of influence of that man; with that Scott became a partisan of the Garvey movement. But essentially, there were very few people this high up in the middle class who went over to the Garvey movement.

Today, however, you have a very different situation. With the exception of that twenty or twenty-five percent of middle-class Negroes who have some kind of stake in American society, who "have it made," for most Negroes this emergent and lively social structure of voluntary associations no longer prevails. The Great Depression dealt a deadly blow to all spheres of the social structure of the urban Negro masses. And today this structure stands in essentially permanent disintegration. In fact, I wonder if we cannot put it in the category of social pathology. But not in the sense in which Mr. Epps was talking earlier. By social pathology I mean something which is disintegrated permanently, in a state of flux, incoherent, and all the rest . . . Data on all spheres of the poor urban Negro social structure attest to this. Church attendance among poor Negroes is essentially nonexistent. The family structure is so weak, so fluid, as to be meaningless; and the same holds true for almost any index of effective meaningful social structure among the seventy percent of poor urban Negroes.

What is equally significant is the manner in which the American system impinges upon this poor Negro social structure; and how it has done nothing but intensify this state of social pathology or of permanent social disintegration. For instance, all indices of social and economic well-being find seventy percent of the Negro population at rock bottom. Economic recessions of the forties, fifties, and of the sixties have played havoc with this population, hitting it at a rate normally two or three times that of the rest of the population. In some urban centers in the past fifteen years, where one finds a heavy Negro concentration, unemployment has stood at twenty-five percent and more of the adult male population. Thus, I myself cannot help questioning whether a Black Nationalist proposition can be successful in this state of tragic and terrible social disintegration. Frankly it is beyond comprehension that the Nation of Islam, Mr. X's movement, or any other exclusively racist proposition could in and of itself even begin to contribute a drop in the bucket. Nor do I think that the politically mundane and the politically vile methods which the white immigrants have bequeathed us can handle the job. In fact, I myself can see no basic, lasting, or meaningful resolution to the terrible plight of most Negroes within the present political arrangements and modes of thought that the American market place of political ideas has given us.

MODERATOR: Mr. X, I wonder if you'd like to reply to either Professor Wilson or Dr. Kilson.

MALCOLM X: As I said in my opening statement, I'm not a student of politics nor a politician, but I did learn a lot listening to the speakers. [Mr. Wilson] pointed out very decisively that politics won't solve the problem . . . this is what I got out of what he said . . . the politicians can't do it. In fact I can see now why the Honorable Elijah Muhammad said that complete separation is the only answer. For what I got from what he was saying is that Uncle Sam sees no hope within his political system of solving this problem that has become so complex that you can hardly even describe it. And this is why I said that we are issuing a call to youth, primarily, to get some new ideas and a new direction. The adults are more confused than the problem itself. It will take a whole generation of new people to approach this problem.

I would not like to leave the impression that I have ever, in any way, proposed a Negro party. Whoever entertains that thought is very much misinformed. We have never at any time advocated any kind of Negro party. The idea that I have been trying to convey is that Black Nationalism is our political philosophy. I didn't mention "party." By Black Nationalism I meant a political philosophy that makes the black man more conscious of the importance of his doing something to control his own destiny. The political philosophy maintained now by most black people in this country seems to me to leave their destiny in the hands of someone who doesn't even look like them. So, you see, the political philosophy of Black Nationalism has nothing to do with party. It is designed to make the black man develop some kind of consciousness or awareness of the importance of his shaping his own future, instead of leaving it to some segregationists in Washington, D.C., who come from the North as well as from the South. In pointing out that we are putting an accent on youth, we wish to let you know that our minds are wide open. We don't think we have the answer, but we are open-minded enough to try to seek the answer not from these old hicks, whom I think have gone astray, but from the youth. For the young may approach the problem from a new slant and perhaps come up with something that nobody else has thought of yet.

In reply to Dr. Kilson, who pointed out how Marcus Garvey failed: Marcus Garvey failed only because his movement was infiltrated by Uncle Toms, sent in by the government as well as by other bodies to maneuver him into a position wherein the government might have him sent to Atlanta, Georgia, put in a penitentiary, then deported, and his movement destroyed. But Marcus Garvey never failed. Marcus Garvey was the one who gave a sense of dignity to the black people in this country. He organized one of the largest mass movements that ever existed in this country; and his entire philosophy of organizing and attracting Negroes was based on going-back-to-Africa, which proves that the only mass movement which ever caught on in this country was designed to appeal to what the masses really felt. More of them then preferred to go back home than to stay here in this country and continue to beg the power structure for something they knew they would never get. Garvey did not fail. Indeed, it was Marcus Garvey's philosophy that inspired the Nkrumah fight for the independence of Ghana from the colonialism that was imposed on it by England. It is also the same Black Nationalism that has been spreading throughout Africa and that has brought about the emergence of the present independent African states. Garvey never failed. Garvey planted the seed which has popped up in Africa—everywhere you look! And although they're still trying to stamp it out in Angola, in South Africa, and in other places, you will soon be able to see for yourselves whether or not Garvey failed. He may have failed in America, but he didn't fail in Africa; and when Africa succeeds, you'll find that you have a new situation on your hands here in America.

I can't abide anyone referring to Black Nationalism as any kind of racism. Whenever white people get together they don't call it racism. The European Common Market is for Europeans; it excludes everyone else. In that case you don't call it racism; all the numerous blocks and groups and syndicates and cliques that the Western nations have formed are never referred to as racist. But when we dark people want to form some kind of united effort to solve our problem, either you or somebody you have brainwashed comes up with "racism." We don't call it racism; we call it brotherhood. To note just one more small point: it is true that a large middle-class group of so-called Negroes has developed in this country, and you may think that these Negroes are satisfied or that they want to stay here because they have a "stake." This is the popular misconception. The middle-class Negro in this country is almost more frustrated, disillusioned, and disenchanted than the Negro in the alley. Why? The Negro in the alley does not even think about integrating with you because he knows that he hasn't enough money to go where you are in control. So it doesn't enter his mind; he's less frustrated when he knows it's impossible. But this middle-class Negro, sharp as a tack with his Harvard accent and with his pocket full of your money, thinks he should be able to go everywhere. Indeed, he should be able to go everywhere, so he will try.

MODERATOR: I will take questions from the floor.

STUDENT QUESTION: I have a question for Mr. Malcolm X. What is your view of the *Freedom Now Party,* which is certainly a third party movement? How do you feel about this alternative way of solving the Negro problem?

MALCOLM X: I have met Negroes of the *Freedom Now Party,* all of whom seem to be very militant. They are young and militant and less likely to compromise. For these reasons it offers more hope than other alternatives being dangled in front of the so-called Negro. I couldn't say I would endorse the *Freedom Now Party,* but my mind is wide open to anything that will help gain progress. In addition, members of the *Freedom Now Party* seem to be more flexible than members of the Democratic and Republican parties. I don't think anything can be worse than the Democrats and Republicans.

STUDENT QUESTION: Mr. Malcolm X, do you support a bloody revolution and, if not, what kind do you have in mind, especially when the Negro is at a numerical disadvantage?

MALCOLM X: Don't tell me about a six-to-one disadvantage. I agree it is a six-to-one disadvantage when you think in terms of America. But in the world the nonwhite people have you at an eleven-to-one disadvantage. We black people consider ourselves a part of that vast body of dark people who outnumber the whites, and we don't regard ourselves as a minority.

STUDENT QUESTION: Mr. Malcolm X, you said the type of civil rights agitation we see now has not altered the morality of white people. Could you comment on that?

MALCOLM X: When exposed to the methods of civil rights groups, whites remain complacent. You couldn't appeal to their ethical sense or their sense of legality. But, on the other hand, when they hear the analysis of the Honorable Elijah Muhammad, whites become more sharply attuned to the problem. You can appeal to what intelligence whites have. Let the black man speak his mind so that the white man really knows how he feels. At the same time, let the white man speak his mind. Let everyone put his facts on the table. Once you put the facts on the table, it's possible to arrive at a solution.

The civil rights movement has put the white man in a position where he has to take a stand contrary to his intelligence. Many whites who do not support integration are afraid to say so when face to face with a Negro for fear the Negro will call him a bigot or a racist. So that even though a white in his intelligence can see that this forced integration will never work, he's afraid to say this to a black man; whereas if the white could speak his mind to the black man, he might wake that man up. My contention is that the approach used by the Honorable Elijah Muhammad is more realistic. A white man can speak his mind to a Muslim, and a Muslim is going to speak his mind to a white man. Once you establish this honest, sincere, realistic communication, you'll get a solution to the problem. But don't you give me that you love me and make me do the same thinking when there's nothing in our backgrounds nor anything around us which in any way gives either of us reason to love each other. Let's be real!

MR. WILSON: Your skill at numbers is accurate . . . If you want to add Cleveland and St. Louis to the list, I would double the argument in spades . . . (Laughter) There was no pun intended. It seems to me that more progress is found in states with a lower proportion of Negroes . . .

MODERATOR: Malcolm X, would you like to comment?

MALCOLM X: No, I don't think I'd better. I don't know whether to comment on spades or . . . (laughter). But you can see why I believe in separation.

Malcolm X and Martin Kilson also had a very funny exchange. Malcolm X had made the point earlier that middle-class Negroes and Negro intellectuals really distrusted whites as much as the more frank and courageous Negroes he knew. These well-established Negroes told him things in the "closet" which would surprise the whites, he reported. Mr. Kilson, who is a Negro, and Malcolm X had an exchange on just this assessment of the well-established Negro. Malcolm X had just commented on Kilson's speech, and a question had suggested that Mr. Kilson had not really said what he believed. The questioner went on to ask from what vantage point did Mr. Kilson speak.

MR. KILSON: As Malcolm X has suggested to you . . . it's not so easy for a Negro intellectual to discuss these problems, as you may expect. I happen to be an academic and as such I adhere to certain canons of observation and discourse, and of behavior. But [I am an] academic who is quite conscious of being a Negro, and rather proud of it. When you ask me from what vantage point I speak, I [must tell you] that I speak from whatever that vantage point is [which permits me] to effectively integrate the difficult position of being both an intellectual and a Negro. I can't satisfy everybody in what I say. Essentially, therefore, I [am] very individualistic about such matters. I seek essentially to satisfy Martin Kilson. (Applause)

MALCOLM X: May I comment on his comment? (Laughter)

Well, he is actually proving my point that this middle-class Negro is more frustrated than anybody else.

If you were able to hear one of them in the closet, with none of you around, you would . . . realize how serious this problem is.

You can't be an individual; no black man in this country can be an individual. Dr. Ralph Bunche, an internationally recognized and respected diplomat, was segregated in Atlanta, Georgia.

MR. KILSON: I must comment! Here I think Malcolm is perfectly right. I'm not under the illusion that with respect to white society I can be an individual in the sense that he has in mind. I'm a Negro with respect to white society. But I still argue that an intellectual has certain functions to perform and carries a certain kind of burden. Let me also say in my own self-defense that I am not one who says one thing in public and another thing in the closet.

MALCOLM X: I am happy that I have found a Negro intellectual who will come out of the closet. (Laughter and applause)

From *Malcolm X: Speeches at Harvard* (1968)

[1]The Leverett House Forum was an interesting event. Most of Malcolm X's performances on public platforms with opponents had seemed to me, at least, sort of public rituals: Malcolm X would give the Black Muslim line and the opponent would disclaim any interest whatsoever in the weight of the Malcolm X position and would certainly not consider it an alternate popular Negro strategy. It was my duty as moderator of the Leverett Forum to try and arrange a more honest and hopefully productive public meeting. My colleagues, Martin Kilson and James Q. Wilson, were most coöperative in this regard. They agreed to participate in the Forum. And, what was most important, I knew they took the subject of Negro affairs seriously both from a personal and intellectual point of view.

The manuscript you have here is almost complete except for the question and answer period. I have left out a paragraph of mine in the introduction which seemed redundant. Some criticism might be made of my choice of the questions and answers. Most were actually more exciting and even hilarious than the ones included here. For example, this exchange between Mr. Wilson and Malcolm X, with a play on the word "spade," a colloquial ghetto term for Negro, had everyone in stitches. Mr. Wilson was responding to a question as to whether a greater proportionate Negro population in a city did manifest itself in actual progress for the group.

James Alan McPherson in 1968

JAMES ALAN McPHERSON

James Alan McPherson was born in Savannah, Georgia, on 16 September 1943. Working as a dining-car waiter during the summer, he earned a B.A. in English and history from Morris Brown College in 1965. Recruited by Harvard Law School, he financed his Cambridge studies in part as janitor of an apartment house next door to the *Harvard Crimson* building, and received his LL.B in 1968. Like Archibald MacLeish, he went from a Harvard law degree to a distinguished career in creative writing. *Hue and Cry*, a volume of short stories, appeared in 1969 and won the National Institute of Arts and Letters Award in literature. A second collection, *Elbow Room*, was published in 1977 and won both the National Book Award and the Pulitzer Prize. In 1976, McPherson and Miller Williams published *Railroad: Trains and Train People in American Culture*.

McPherson earned an M.F.A. degree from the University of Iowa in 1971. He served short terms teaching on the Santa Cruz campus of the University of California and at Morgan State University, with a stint as teacher of fiction writing at the Harvard Summer School in 1972. He was a professor in the English department of the University of Virginia from 1976 to 1981, when he moved to the University of Iowa and its famous Writers' Workshop, where he remains. He has received a Rockefeller grant and a Guggenheim Fellowship; and in 1981 he was honored with a five-year "genius" grant from the MacArthur Foundation.

On Becoming an American Writer

In 1974, during the last months of the Nixon Administration, I lived in San Francisco, California. My public reason for leaving the East and going there was that my wife had been admitted to the San

Francisco Medical Center School of Nursing, but my private reason for going was that San Francisco would be a very good place for working and for walking. Actually, during that time San Francisco was not that pleasant a place. We lived in a section of the city called the Sunset District, but it rained almost every day. During the late spring Patricia Hearst helped to rob a bank a few blocks from our apartment, a psychopath called "the Zebra Killer" was terrorizing the city, and the mayor seemed about to declare martial law. Periodically the FBI would come to my apartment with pictures of the suspected bank robbers. Agents came several times, until it began to dawn on me that they had become slightly interested in why, of all the people in a working-class neighborhood, I alone sat at home every day. They never asked any questions on this point, and I never volunteered that I was trying to keep my sanity by working very hard on a book dealing with the relationship between folklore and technology in nineteenth-century America.

In the late fall of the same year a friend came out from the East to give a talk in Sacramento. I drove there to meet him, and then drove him back to San Francisco. This was an older black man, one whom I respect a great deal, but during our drive an argument developed between us. His major worry was the recession, but eventually his focus shifted to people in my age group and our failures. There were a great many of these, and he listed them point by point. He said, while we drove through a gloomy evening rain, "When the smoke clears and you start counting, I'll bet you won't find that many more black doctors, lawyers, accountants, engineers, dentists. . . ." The list went on. He remonstrated a bit more, and said, "White people are very generous. When they start a thing they usually finish it. But after all this chaos, imagine how mad and tired they must be. Back in the fifties, when this thing started, they must have known anything could happen. They must have said, 'Well, we'd better settle in and hold on tight. Here come the niggers.'" During the eighteen months I spent in San Francisco, this was the only personal encounter that really made me mad.

In recent years I have realized that my friend, whom I now respect even more, was speaking from the perspective of a tactician. He viewed the situation in strict bread-and-butter terms: a commitment had been made to redefine the meaning of democracy in this country, certain opportunities had been provided, and people like him were watching to see what would be made of those opportunities and the freedom they provided. From his point of view, it was simply a matter of fulfilling a contractual obligation: taking full advantage of the educational opportunities that had been offered to achieve middle-class status in one of the professions. But from my point of view, one that I never shared with him, it was not that simple. Perhaps it was because of the differences in our generations and experiences. Or perhaps it was because each new generation, of black people at least, has to redefine itself even while it attempts to grasp the new opportunities, explore the new freedom. I can speak for no one but myself, yet maybe in trying to preserve the uniqueness of my experience, as I tried to do in *Elbow Room*, I can begin to set the record straight for my friend, for myself, and for the sake of the record itself.

In 1954, when *Brown v. Board of Education* was decided, I was eleven years old. I lived in a lower-class black community in Savannah, Georgia, attended segregated public schools, and knew no white people socially. I can't remember thinking of this last fact as a disadvantage, but I do know that early on I was being conditioned to believe that I was not *supposed* to know any white people on social terms. In our town the children of the black middle class were expected to aspire to certain traditional occupations; the children of the poor were expected not to cause too much trouble.

There was in those days a very subtle, but real, social distinction based on gradations of color, and I can remember the additional strain under which darker-skinned poor people lived. But there was also a great deal of optimism, shared by all levels of the black community. Besides a certain reverence for the benign intentions of the federal government, there was a belief in the idea of progress, nourished, I think now, by the determination of older people not to pass on to the next generation too many stories about racial conflict, their own frustrations and failures. They censored a great deal. It was as if they had made basic and binding agreements with themselves, or with their ancestors, that for the consideration represented by their silence on certain points they expected to receive, from either Providence or a munificent federal government, some future service or remuneration, the form of which would be left to the beneficiaries of their silence. Lawyers would call this a contract with a condition precedent. And maybe because they did tell us less than they knew, many of us were less informed than we might have been. On the other hand, because of this same silence many of us remained free enough of the influence of negative stories to take chances, be ridiculous, perhaps even try to form our own positive stories out of whatever our own experiences provided. Though ours was a limited world, it was one rich in possibilities for the future.

If I had to account for my life from segregated Savannah to this place and point in time, I would probably have to say that the contract would be no bad metaphor. I am reminded of Sir Henry Maine's observation that the progress of society is from status to contract. Although he was writing about the development of English common law, the reverse of his generalization is most applicable to my situation: I am the beneficiary of a number of contracts, most of them between the federal government and the institutions of society, intended to provide people like me with a certain status.

I recall that in 1960, for example, something called the National Defense Student Loan Program went into effect, and I found out that by my agreeing to repay a loan plus some little interest, the federal government would back my enrollment in a small Negro college in Georgia. When I was a freshman at that college, disagreement over a seniority clause between the Hotel & Restaurant Employees and Bartenders Union and the Great Northern Railway Company, in St. Paul, Minnesota, caused management to begin recruiting temporary summer help. Before I was nineteen I was encouraged to move from a segregated Negro college in the South and through that very beautiful part of the country that lies between Chicago and the Pacific Northwest. That year—1962—the World's Fair was in Seattle, and it was a magnificently diverse panorama for a young man to see. Almost every nation on earth was represented in some way, and at the center of the fair was the Space Needle. The theme of the United States exhibit, as I recall, was drawn from Whitman's *Leaves of Grass*: "Conquering, holding, daring, venturing as we go the unknown ways."

When I returned to the South, in the midst of all the civil rights activity, I saw a poster advertising a creative-writing contest sponsored by *Reader's Digest* and the United Negro College Fund. To enter the contest I had to learn to write and type. The first story I wrote was lost (and very badly typed); but the second, written in 1965, although badly typed, was awarded first prize by Edward Weeks and his staff at the *Atlantic Monthly*. That same year I was offered the opportunity to enter Harvard Law School. During my second year at law school, a third-year man named Dave Marston (who was in a contest with Attorney General Griffin Bell earlier this year [1978]) offered me, through a very conservative white fellow student from Texas, the opportunity to take over his old job as a janitor in one of the apartment buildings in Cambridge. There I had the solitude, and the encouragement, to begin writing seriously. Offering my services in that building was probably the best contract I ever made.

I have not recalled all the above to sing my own praises or to evoke the black American version of the Horatio Alger myth. I have recited these facts as a way of indicating the haphazard nature of events during that ten-year period. I am the product of a contractual process. To put it simply, the 1960s were a crazy time. Opportunities seemed to materialize out of thin air; and if you were lucky, if you were in the right place at the right time, certain contractual benefits just naturally accrued. You were assured of a certain status; you could become a doctor, a lawyer, a dentist, an accountant, an engineer. Achieving these things was easy, if you applied yourself.

But a very hard price was extracted. It seems to me now, from the perspective provided by age and distance, that certain institutional forces, acting impersonally, threw together black peasants and white aristocrats, people who operated on the plane of the intellect and people who valued the perspective of the folk. There were people who were frightened, threatened, and felt inferior; there were light-skinned people who called themselves "black" and darker-skinned people who could remember when this term had been used negatively; there were idealists and opportunists, people who seemed to want to be exploited and people who delighted in exploiting them. Old identities were thrown off, of necessity, but there were not many new ones of a positive nature to be assumed. People from backgrounds like my own, those from the South, while content with the new opportunities, found themselves trying to make sense of the growing diversity of friendships, of their increasing familiarity with the various political areas of the country, of the obvious differences between their values and those of their parents. We *were* becoming doctors, lawyers, dentists, engineers; but at the same time our experiences forced us to begin thinking of ourselves in new and different ways. We never wanted to be "white," but we never wanted to be "black" either. And back during that period there was the feeling that we could be whatever we wanted. But, we discovered, unless we joined a group, subscribed to some ideology, accepted some provisional identity, there was no contractual process for defining and stabilizing what it was we wanted to be. We also found that this was an individual problem, and in order to confront it one had to go inside one's self.

Now I want to return to my personal experience, to one of the contracts that took me from segregated Savannah to the Seattle World's Fair. There were many things about my earliest experiences that I liked and wanted to preserve, despite the fact that these things took place in a context of segregation; and there were a great many things I liked about the vision of all those nations interacting at the World's Fair. But the two seemed to belong to separate realities, to represent two different world views. Similarly, there were some things I liked about many of the dining-car waiters with whom I worked, and some things I liked about people like Dave Marston whom I met in law school. Some of these people and their values were called "black" and some were called "white," and I learned very quickly that all of us tend to wall ourselves off from experiences different from our own by assigning to these terms greater significance than they should have. Moreover, I found that trying to maintain friendships with, say, a politically conservative white Texan, a liberal-to-radical classmate of Scottish-Italian background, my oldest black friends, and even members of my own family introduced psychological contradictions that became tense and painful as the political climate shifted. There were no contracts covering such friendships and such feelings, and in order to keep the friends and maintain the feelings I had to force myself to find a basis other than race on which such contradictory urgings could be synthesized. I discovered that I had to find, first of all, an identity as a writer, and then I had to express what I knew or felt in such a way that I could make something whole out of a necessarily fragmented experience.

While in San Francisco, I saw in the image of the nineteenth-century American locomotive a possible cultural symbol that could represent my folk origins and their values, as well as the values of all the people I had seen at the World's Fair. During that same time, unconsciously, I was also beginning to see that the American language, in its flexibility and variety of idioms, could at least approximate some of the contradictory feelings that had resulted from my experience. Once again, I could not find any contractual guarantee that this would be the most appropriate and rewarding way to hold myself, and my experience, together. I think now there are no such contracts.

I quoted earlier a generalization by Sir Henry Maine to the effect that human society is a matter of movement from status to contract. Actually, I have never read Sir Henry Maine. I lifted his statement from a book by a man named Henry Allen Moe—a great book called

The Power of Freedom. In that book, in an essay entitled "The Future of Liberal Arts Education," Moe goes on to say that a next step, one that goes beyond contract, is now necessary, but that no one seems to know what that next step should be. Certain trends suggest that it may well be a reversion to status. But if this happens it will be a tragedy of major proportions, because most of the people in the world are waiting for some nation, some people, to provide the model for the next step. And somehow I felt, while writing the last stories in *Elbow Room*, that the condition precedent the old folks in my hometown wanted in exchange for their censoring was not just status of a conventional kind. I want to think that after having waited so long, after having seen so much, they must have at least expected some new stories that would no longer have to be censored to come out of our experience. I felt that if anything, the long experience of segregation could be looked on as a period of preparation for a next step. Those of us who are black and who have had to defend our humanity should be obliged to continue defending it, on higher and higher levels—not of power, which is a kind of tragic trap, but on higher levels of consciousness.

All of this is being said in retrospect, and I am quite aware that I am rationalizing many complex and contradictory feelings. Nevertheless, I do know that early on, during my second year of law school, I became conscious of a model of identity that might help me transcend, at least in my thinking, a provisional or racial identity. In a class in American constitutional law taught by Paul Freund, I began to play with the idea that the Fourteenth Amendment was not just a legislative instrument devised to give former slaves legal equality with other Americans. Looking at the slow but steady way in which the basic guarantees of the Bill of Rights had, through judicial interpretation, been incorporated into the clauses of that amendment, I began to see the outlines of a new identity.

You will recall that the first line of Section 1 of the Fourteenth Amendment makes an all-inclusive definition of citizenship: "All persons born or naturalized in the United States and subject to the jurisdiction thereof, are citizens of the United States. . . ." The rights guaranteed to such a citizen had themselves traveled from the provinces to the World's Fair: from the trial and error of early Anglo-Saxon folk rituals to the rights of freemen established by the Magna Carta, to their slow incorporation into early American colonial charters, and from these charters (especially George Mason's Virginia

Declaration of Rights) into the U.S. Constitution as its first ten amendments. Indeed, these same rights had served as the basis for the Charter of the United Nations. I saw that through the protean uses made of the Fourteenth Amendment, in the gradual elaboration of basic rights to be protected by federal authority, an outline of something much more complex than "black" and "white" had been begun.

It was many years before I was to go to the Library of Congress and read the brief of the lawyer-novelist Albion W. Tourgée in the famous case *Plessy v. Ferguson.* Argued in 1896 before the United States Supreme Court, Tourgée's brief was the first meaningful attempt to breathe life into the amendment. I will quote here part of his brief, which is a very beautiful piece of literature.

This provision of Section 1 of the Fourteenth Amendment *creates a new* citizenship of the United States embracing *new* rights, privileges and immunities, derivable in a *new* manner, controlled by *new* authority, having a *new* scope and extent, depending on national authority for its existence and looking to national power for its preservation.

Although Tourgée lost the argument before the Supreme Court, his model of citizenship—and it is not a racial one—is still the most radical idea to come out of American constitutional law. He provided the outline, the clothing, if you will, for a new level of status. What he was proposing in 1896, I think, was that each United States citizen would attempt to approximate the ideals of the nation, be on at least conversant terms with all its diversity, carry the mainstream of the culture inside himself. As an American, by trying to wear these clothes he would be a synthesis of high and low, black and white, city and country, provincial and universal. If he could live with these contradictions, he would be simply a representative American.

This was the model I was aiming for in my book of stories. It can be achieved with or without intermarriage, but it will cost a great many mistakes and a lot of pain. It is, finally, a product of culture and not of race. And achieving it will require that one be conscious of America's culture and the complexity of all its people. As I tried to point out, such a perspective would provide a minefield of delicious ironies. Why, for example, should black Americans raised in Southern culture *not* find that some of their responses are geared to country music? How else, except in terms of cultural diversity, am I to account for the white friend in Boston who taught me much of what I know about black American music? Or the white friend in Virginia who, besides developing a homegrown aesthetic he calls "crackertude," knows more about black American folklore than most black people? Or the possibility that many black people in Los Angeles have been just as much influenced by Hollywood's "star system" of the forties and fifties as they have been by society's response to the color of their skins? I wrote about people like these in *Elbow Room* because they interested me, and because they help support my belief that most of us are products of much more complex cultural influences than we suppose.

What I have said above will make little sense until certain contradictions in the nation's background are faced up to, until personal identities are allowed to partake of the complexity of the country's history as well as of its culture. Last year, a very imaginative black comedian named Richard Pryor appeared briefly on national television in his own show. He offended a great many people, and his show was canceled after only a few weeks. But I remember one episode that may emphasize my own group's confusion about its historical experience. This was a satiric takeoff on the popular television movie *Roots*, and Pryor played an African tribal historian who was selling trinkets and impromptu history to black American tourists. One tourist, a middle-class man, approached the tribal historian and said, "I want you to tell me who my great-great-granddaddy was." The African handed him a picture. The black American looked at it and said, "But that's a *white* man!" The tribal historian said, "That's right." Then the tourist said, "Well, I want you to tell me where I'm from." The historian looked hard at him and said, "You're from Cleveland, nigger." I think I was trying very hard in my book to say the same thing, but not just to black people.

Today I am not the lawyer my friend in San Francisco thought I should be, but this is the record I wanted to represent to him that rainy evening back in 1974. It may illustrate why the terms of my acceptance of society's offer had to be modified. I am now a writer, a person who has to learn to live with contradictions, frustrations and doubts. Still, I have another quote that sustains me, this one from a book called *The Tragic Sense of Life*, by a Spanish philosopher named Miguel de Unamuno. In a chapter called "Don Quixote Today," Unamuno asks, "How is it that among the words the English have borrowed from our language there is to be found this word *desperado*?"

And he answers himself: "It is despair, and despair alone, that begets heroic hope, absurd hope, mad hope."

I believe that the United States is complex enough to induce that sort of despair that begets heroic hope. I believe that if one can experience its diversity, touch a variety of its people, laugh at its craziness, distill wisdom from its tragedies, and attempt to synthesize all this inside oneself without going crazy, one will have earned the right to call oneself "citizen of the United States," even though one is not quite a lawyer, doctor, engineer, or accountant. If nothing else, one will have learned a few new stories and, most important, one will have begun on that necessary movement from contract to the next step, from province to the World's Fair, from a hopeless person to a desperado. I wrote about my first uncertain steps in this direction in *Elbow Room* because I have benefited from all the contracts, I have exhausted all the contracts, and at present it is the only new direction I know.

Atlantic (1978)

THE FOUNDING OF THE AFRO-AMERICAN STUDIES DEPARTMENT

The Crisis of 1969

LAWRENCE E. EICHEL

"I think, and it wouldn't be unfair to say before this body and before the world, that at one time this week we had the power to seriously disrupt this university . . ."
Skip Griffin, President of Afro
[Leslie F. Griffin Jr., '70]

On April 9, 1968, a year to the day before the seizure of University Hall, 80 black students stood alone on the steps of Memorial Church. Inside the church, President Pusey led more than 1200 mourners, all but a handful of them white, in eulogizing Martin Luther King, slain five days before in Memphis. Outside, the members of the Association of African and Afro-American Students (Afro) commemorated Dr. King in their own way, with demands on Harvard, made in the spirit of the movement for which King had stood. Inside, the President spoke of the man, not of the movement: "We are not met here to prove anything or to assert anything—certainly not to demand anything; but rather simply to honor a great man and a great citizen," a man who "never came among us but as a man of God." To the students assembled outside, Dr. King had been something more than a man of God; he had been a black man. "If they come out of there with tears in their eyes," said Jeff Howard ['69, Ph.D. '80], then President of Afro, as he pointed to the church, "we want it to be plain that we don't want their tears. We want black people to have a place here at Harvard." The place of the black man at Harvard was far from the President's mind as he spoke; he praised the tactics, not the goals of Dr. King. For Afro, the occasion demanded a reaffirmation of the black revolution. Skip Griffin, soon to become Afro's president, reserved judgment on the white man's service inside: "If they're really sorry, they'll change this school." That same day, Afro issued "Four Requests on *Fair* Harvard"; the issue of Black Studies had finally come to the nation's oldest university.

On Thursday evening, April 17, 1969, Afro found itself alone again. The Faculty had deferred a decision on Afro's Black Studies demand until the following week. The community as a whole, clearly, would vote the next day to end the strike, despite the fact that the Faculty had left the issue of Black Studies unresolved.

Most of the Faculty did not understand what the fuss was all about. They thought that they had disposed of the sensitive question of Afro-American Studies in February by their endorsement of the substantive recommendations of *The Report of the Faculty Committee on African and Afro-American Studies*, popularly known as the *Rosovsky Report*.[1] Harvard Afro had hailed the *Report* as a landmark in student-faculty cooperation. To understand why the blacks' exhilaration in February had turned to threats of militant confrontation in April is a long and complicated story that requires a brief study of the black man's recent history at Harvard.

Harvard Afro was created in April, 1963, to "promote mutual understanding between African and Afro-American students, to provide ourselves a voice in the community . . . and to develop the leadership capable of effectively coping with the various problems of our peoples." Membership in the new organization was to be "open to African and Afro-American students currently enrolled." In May, Afro sought recognition as an official campus activity. But to many white liberals at Harvard in the spring of 1963, the notion of an organization for black students only was completely unpalatable. Harvard's student Council on Undergraduate Activities reflected this sentiment by voting to deny recognition to Afro, citing Afro's

---

[1]The *Report* was written by a nine-member Faculty committee, chaired by Henry Rosovsky, Professor of Economics.

membership clause as "discriminatory." The Council's action provoked heated debate on campus until November when a Faculty committee moved to confront the issue. The committee also rejected Afro's bid, stating that the Faculty was "unwilling at this critical time to put the weight of Harvard's approval behind the principle of racial separatism and exclusion." Finally, in December, eight months after the controversy had begun, Afro was recognized on the same standing as the exclusive "final clubs": it was entitled to admit members by "invitation only."

During the first few years of its existence, Afro was little more than a social and cultural group to which black students could come to discuss ideas like black nationalism, ideas that were still taboo for general consumption. As the number of blacks at Harvard increased, and as the civil rights mentality began to be replaced on campus by an emphasis on black power and black pride, the blacks gained confidence in their ability to "make it" at the university. They asserted their identity openly by eating together at the first "soul table" in the freshman dining hall. They published the *Harvard Journal of Negro Affairs*, a periodical in which black men wrote about black subjects for the entire academic community. Not until after the assassination of Dr. King, however, did the controversial idea emerge that it was a black student's duty to devote his primary extracurricular energies to Afro. Only then did Afro become an active political organization.

Another factor that contributed to Afro's changing nature was Harvard's intensified recruiting efforts in ghetto neighborhoods of America's largest cities, especially in the preceding two years. In the past, Harvard's few blacks had come from a limited number of established families. Young militants, fiercely proud of their identity, now brought a new political consciousness to Afro.

Although the issue of Black Studies,[2] an issue which has become a *sine qua non* for most student confrontations, was not broached at Harvard until April, 1968, the leadership of Afro had spent much time during the previous seven months talking, without progress, to faculty and administrators about making the Harvard curriculum more relevant to black people. After the public expression of the "Four Requests on *Fair* Harvard" in the demonstration after the King assas-

---

[2]Members of Afro generally prefer the term "Afro-American Studies" to "Black Studies." We shall use the terms interchangeably.

sination, the effective channels of communication, for which Afro had been searching, suddenly materialized. Two days after the publication of the demands, Dean of Admissions Chase Peterson ['52, MD '56] met with Afro and explained his plans, to Afro's satisfaction, for the class of 1973 (in fact, for the class of '73, Harvard accepted 109 blacks out of a total of 1360 acceptances; 96 enrolled; 51 blacks were enrolled in the class of '72). Action on the other requests was more complex and longer in coming. Conferences between Afro and Dean [Franklin] Ford's staff resulted in the appointment of the Rosovsky Committee. The Committee was charged with several responsibilities, including the establishment of a program leading to the A.B. degree in Afro-American Studies. The announcement of a new course, "The Afro-American Experience," came a week later.

The Rosovsky Committee worked throughout the fall. Its report was released on January 20, 1969; perfunctory Faculty endorsement followed on February 11.[3] Abiding by the letter of the *Report*, Dean Ford appointed a Standing Committee on Afro-American Studies, consisting of seven faculty members and no students. The dean himself chaired the Committee, which would govern the Black Studies program.

Included in the *Report*'s recommendations was the suggestion that men and women, with "considerable competence and national reputations" in aspects of the black experience, should be offered faculty appointments even if they lack "normal academic credentials." A search committee composed of three faculty and three student members was established immediately to hunt for qualified faculty members. The university wanted to make a degree in Black Studies available to the class of '72, then freshmen.

But perhaps more important than the actual substance of the *Rosovsky Report* was an intangible entity that would be known during the crisis as "the spirit" of the *Report*. Professor Rosovsky described that spirit to the Faculty:

The word that should be stressed is cooperative. It was a cooperative venture on the part of everyone who participated in the program.

---

[3]The 51-page document covered four topics: the quality of black student life at Harvard, Afro-American Studies, African Studies, and the recruitment and financing of black graduate students.

Two members of Afro, Ernest "Chico" Wilson ['70] and Octavia Hudson ['71, Ph.D. '79] attended every meeting of the Rosovsky Committee while it was formulating the *Report*. Wilson and Miss Hudson were offered voting rights during the deliberations; they refused. Faculty members met constantly with other black students and twice with the full executive committee of Afro. The Rosovsky Committee set up these extraordinary arrangements because they recognized the special expertise which black students would bring to the task of establishing a program dealing with the black experience. Even though the final draft of the *Report* did not contain all that the black students had sought, the spirit of the *Report* prevailed. With the kind of informal consultation that had brought about the *Report*, the remaining problems could be worked out, despite the absence of student members on the Standing Committee. But between February 11 and April 9, that scheme of informal consultation broke down.

When the newly appointed Standing Committee assembled on the morning of March 5, Dan Fox, Assistant Professor of History, mentioned the need to draw up the outline of a Black Studies major. The Committee decided to adopt the recommendation of the *Rosovsky Report*:

The most feasible way to make such a degree program possible for this class may be to conceive the program as a combination of Afro-American Studies and an existing concentration. The Committee would offer colloquia and possibly tutorial for the evaluation of students in these combined programs. We emphasize that this is not necessarily the final form the undergraduate degree program will have.

That very afternoon, on behalf of the Committee, Fox's secretaries put this program for the class of '72 into suitably dry bureaucratic jargon. At a meeting of the search committee later the same day, Fox told the committee's three student members—Chico Wilson, Bob Hall [Robert L. Hall, '69], and Craig Watson ['72]—that a "tentative and temporary" decision had been made. What Fox meant by "temporary" was that those freshmen who entered the program in April would not be bound to fulfill the "tentative" degree requirements if the program were revised in the next year. What Wilson, Hall, and Watson understood by "temporary" was that the Standing Committee had not yet formulated the final plan to present to prospective concentrators. They were wrong. Fox thought that by informing the student members of the search committee he was in fact informing all of Afro. "I assumed that they were accountable as well as representative," he observed later. Wilson thought that Fox's vague description of the proposed program meant the information was not definitive and, therefore, "not the kind of thing you talk about to outsiders," not even to other members of Afro. Thus, the information meant for all black students never got past Wilson, Hall, and Watson.

Later, Henry Rosovsky would assure his fellow professors that there had been "no betrayal of any kind" by the Standing Committee. "We were doing in April exactly what we said we were going to be doing in the *Report.*" But the Standing Committee had departed from the spirit of the *Report.* It had dealt with the delicate issue of the program for Harvard's first recipients of a degree in Afro-American Studies in a closed, unresponsive manner. With the benefit of similar hindsight, Chico Wilson was prepared to admit that the misunderstanding might well have been an administrative foul-up, but, he added, "administrative foul-ups are driving this university straight to hell."

The spirit of cooperation that had taken a full year to build would be destroyed on one morning in April.[4]

In late March, Dan Fox called up Burris Young, Assistant Dean of Freshmen, to set a time for the meeting for prospective concentrators in Afro-American Studies. By sheer coincidence, Young suggested the evening of April 9.

That meeting took place April 9 as scheduled, just across Quincy Street from the locked gates of Harvard Yard. At the gathering, outlines of a three-year program for current freshmen were distributed. Entitled *Afro-American Studies Combined with One Allied Field*, the outline described what, by normal Harvard standards, seemed an

---

[4]On other fronts, Afro was developing an increasingly militant style of involvement in campus issues. In December, Afro's Radcliffe members staged a sit-in in the office of President Mary Bunting to push for a more vigorous black recruiting effort. In February, 85 Afro members and sympathizers disrupted the opening meeting of a Design School course entitled "An End to Urban Violence." The seminar on "the architecture of urban peace" seemed to Afro as decent an academic discipline as "studying target practice." The course was scrapped; the professor and Afro leaders worked out a new topic.

unduly heavy set of requirements for an undergraduate degree. Many members of Afro had always found the idea of combining Black Studies with another field to be more than slightly insulting. Later, in the crisis, Fran [Francesta E.] Farmer ['71, J.D. '74], a black Radcliffe sophomore, would explain this feeling:

This communique presupposes that Afro-American Studies is less than a legitimate and valid intellectual endeavor. We reject this notion. Afro-American Studies needs no prop from so-called allied fields.

Members of the Afro leadership were never shown the outline.

Lee [A.] Daniels ['71], a black sophomore, first saw the plan shortly before 7:00 A.M. in Harvard Yard on the morning of April 10, after he and other members of Afro had watched the police clear the demonstrators out of University Hall. Like every student who saw the bust, Daniels was angered by what he had seen, but when he saw the outline for the Black Studies program, he was furious. In the minutes after the police left the Yard, the question of who was responsible for the bust was in everyone's minds. A similar question seemed equally applicable to the program in Black Studies which Daniels held in his hands: Who had made the decision? Who had been consulted?

As the situation in the Yard cooled, Daniels returned to his room. He wanted to call members of the Standing Committee; he wanted an explanation. When he entered the room he found Bob Hall of the search committee lying semiconscious on the bed. Hall was bleeding from a nightstick wound he had suffered while watching the bust. Ignoring Hall for the moment, Daniels called Dan Fox whom he knew to be involved in the freshman program. He found Fox's explanation of the program unsatisfactory and reported to the leaders of Afro. Copies of the Afro-American Studies outline were Xeroxed, along with an announcement:

Brothers and sisters—We are being *sold* out!
There is a meeting—*1:00 P.M. at PBH.* Please be there!

That leaflet touched off 12 days of virtually round-the-clock meetings for Afro at Phillips Brooks House (PBH), beginning April 10.

Initially, the police, not Black Studies, were the primary topic of discussion. Bob Hall was not the only black bystander clubbed in the bust. Mark [D.] Smith ['72] had been standing in front of Matthews

Hall, watching the operation when a policeman came racing across the Yard in pursuit of a small group of white students who had escaped University Hall. Somehow, the policeman ended up striking Smith instead. To Afro, this incident was a clear example of the racism of white police.

The blacks at that first April 10 meeting considered themselves to be on strike against the use of police and the beatings of Hall and Smith. The members of Afro were angry; they were ready to do anything. Even the possibility of taking over a building was considered. If the blacks had seized a building, they would have taken guns with them, to protect themselves from "white racist cops." But few blacks were yet prepared to do battle with police. Someone asked, "How many of you know how to use guns?" Few did, and the idea was dropped.

Characteristic of the mood in that meeting was "A Personal Statement," written by "three concerned black students." For the authors of the statement, Black Studies was already an issue of highest priority. "Black students *must tell* the university what Afro-American Studies is to be at Harvard." They spoke of the possibility of future militant action if the moderate and SDS strikes failed to provoke constructive responses:

Black students should then move to occupy University Hall, or another suitable site and present the university with a list and description of our demands as regards Afro-American Studies, African Studies, as well as the university's involvement in the community.

It is self-evident that if the administration moves against members of the Black community at Harvard in the same brutal fashion that it used against white dissenters, Black students would not accept it. Black students would be forced to call on their brothers in the greater Boston area for moral-and-other support. Should storm troopers be used against us, we must retaliate in kind.

Meanwhile, within the Afro organization, a process of significant political change was taking place, a process that Dan Fox would label a *coup*. The three members of the search committee—Wilson, Hall, and Watson—had been Afro's representatives to the Faculty. These students were responsible for informing Afro of the actions of the Standing Committee, to give warning *before* unfavorable decisions were reached. In as much as communication between the Standing Committee and the three blacks had broken down, Wilson, Hall, and

Watson had failed to perform their delegated duties. They would not be entrusted with leadership positions during the black strike.

This failure of the negotiators discredited the whole idea of negotiations. Confrontation represented a more appealing and potentially more productive course of action.

By Friday, Afro had focused its attention on its relationship with the rest of the students. Skip Griffin spoke at the Memorial Church Group rally, announcing the blacks' support of the strike on the moderates' demands but urging that SDS [Students for a Democratic Society] not be abandoned. During the day, Afro sent representatives to examine the University Road apartments and the Affiliated Hospitals site in Mission Hill, to check out the substance of the SDS demands. The representatives were satisfied, and Afro announced its support of the SDS demands "because they are based on fact."

Since the Standing Committee's program in Black Studies had been found unacceptable, Afro decided to take advantage of the situation and propose an alternative structure of the Standing Committee for the Faculty's immediate consideration. The blacks elected a ten-member strike steering committee to make short-run strategy decisions and to draft a proposal that would give students control over the Black Studies program.

While waiting for the expiration of the three-day moderate strike, Afro joined SDS in some delicate political maneuvering. On Saturday morning, April 12, a member of the SDS strike steering committee informed Skip Griffin, Afro president, that SDS had decided to offer Afro two seats on its 15-man steering committee. Griffin never contemplated a binding alliance with SDS, but he agreed to send Lee Daniels and Suzanne Lynn ['71] as observers to their steering committee meeting on the third floor of Emerson Hall. One SDS member asked the Afro representatives to outline the terms on which Afro would agree to join forces with SDS. Daniels and Miss Lynn told their hosts that an endorsement of Afro's demand for a meaningful Black Studies program was the absolute minimum. Their statement triggered a heated debate among the members of SDS. Jared Israel, a member of PL [Progressive Labor Party], called Black Studies a "very bourgeois" demand. He argued that Afro was not revolutionary, that the blacks merely wanted to get their own place in the power structure. Insulted and impatient, the blacks left the meeting with no commitments and further convinced that cooperation with SDS was impossible.

The inability of Afro and SDS to agree on a joint strike demonstrated the very real differences between white and black student radicals at Harvard. Despite their occasional use of militant tactics and style, Harvard's black radicals were reformers. Harvard's white radicals saw themselves as revolutionaries, seeking victories on "substantive" issues, while building a movement designed to overthrow "the system." This contrast led the groups to take fundamentally different approaches to problems. In the aftermath of the King assassination, Afro sought four specific changes directly affecting black students at Harvard. SDS talked in terms of developing strategies to combat racism and demanded an end to the oppression of black-ghetto dwellers by the forces of law and order. Members of Afro felt that SDS's casual use of words like "racism" indicated a lack of knowledge and genuine concern for the problems of the black man in America. "We just don't trust SDS," explained one black student. "It's just a group feeling. We supported their demands but not them."

The issue of restructuring the university revealed the essential difference in outlook between Afro and SDS. As a member of Afro told SDS:

The issue of restructuring is very important to us as black students. The reason we're in the mess we are now, the reason the Standing Committee on Afro-American Studies was able to hand us that piece of bullshit they did a few nights ago is because they had the sole power to decide what Afro-American Studies was going to be . . . we feel that such a thing cannot happen again and we plan to incorporate into our demand structural reforms so that it can never happen again. We're going to have power over how the Black Studies program is set up.

Members of SDS, on the other hand, were suspicious of restructuring. As long as the present economic system remained, they reasoned, marginal changes in the decision-making process would be unlikely to affect outcomes substantially. Student representatives would be co-opted by the system. Discussions on restructuring consumed long periods of time and distracted attention from the original demands. No quick, decisive, movement-building victories could be won on restructuring.

Afro also disagreed with SDS on the value of a Black Studies program. According to Afro, a Black Studies department served the black revolution (and thus all blacks) by increasing black awareness and by training community organizers. But the WSA [Worker Student Alliance Caucus]-PL Faction of SDS viewed Black Studies as a "bad" demand, postponing the revolution by pacifying the blacks, who were viewed as potentially the most revolutionary sector of the society. The WSA leaflet, "Fight to Win," made the following critique of Afro's request for representation on a Faculty committee:

A movement for black student power, like white or any student power, builds a bourgeois attitude toward workers. That movement teaches students to play games with the rulers for a bigger slice of stolen pie. The bourgeoisie hopes to *mistrain black students as it's long done with whites*, using them later to hold down the magnificent struggles of black working people.

Nonetheless, SDS, attempting to expand its base while keeping its politics pure, invited Afro to offer a proposal for Black Studies to the general membership of SDS. That opportunity came at an SDS meeting Sunday night, April 13, just after Afro had finished a draft of the Black Studies proposal. After an hour of discussion, 1200 supporters of the SDS position made Black Studies the eighth demand by a virtually unanimous vote. SDS hoped that the blacks would now join the white radicals, but Afro never again participated formally in SDS activities. Afro had used SDS to increase student awareness of and support for Afro's own demand.

Afro met again Monday morning. The first mass meeting was set to convene at 1:30. The consensus was that Afro would have to remain on strike until the Black Studies issue had been settled, regardless of what course of action the majority of the university community chose to follow. Afro decided to attend the mass meeting anyway, hoping to gain further support from the huge crowd expected. Members were instructed to "yell as loud as you can," on voice votes at the stadium. In order to exert pressure on the Faculty, Afro also decided to conduct several demonstrations before the mass meeting. Shortly before noon, the blacks started off en masse from PBH toward the stadium, but there were to be a few stops along the way.

First stop: University Hall. F. Skiddy von Stade ['38], Dean of Freshmen, met the demonstrators on the steps of the building and invited them upstairs to the Faculty Room. There, Skip Griffin presented their Black Studies proposal, completed the night before, to von Stade, who was filling in for Dean Ford. The group then headed for its second stop: the Registrar's Office. To emphasize the intensity of their emotion, the black students demanded and received applications for withdrawal from the university. Then the group went back through the Yard to the Freshman Union for lunch. Since Saturday night, the members of Afro had been eating most of their meals as a bloc as a gesture of solidarity and for the "protection" of the group. Finally, at 1:30, the group marched over to Soldiers Field. With more than 5000 people already in the stadium, the blacks dramatically continued their march into the stands and onto the uppermost row of seats. As soon as they seated themselves, they stood up, began to clap rhythmically, and changed to a current rhythm-and-blues tune:

Hey, hey! We're all on strike! One time. STRIKE!
Hey, hey! We're all on strike! Two times. STRIKE!STRIKE!
Hey, hey! We're all on strike! Three times. STRIKE!STRIKE!STRIKE!

"Back to the trees, jungle bunnies!" yelled a voice from below, but the insult went unheeded.

After the mass meeting voted a three-day extension of the strike, Afro decided to leaflet the Faculty meeting on Tuesday. Representatives distributed copies of their proposal on the future form of the Standing Committee on Afro-American Studies to most of the professors, but they were not granted entrance to the meeting. President Pusey promised to give them a hearing at the Thursday session.

On Wednesday, April 16, Afro put Wes [Wesley] Profit ['69] and Jeff Howard, both seniors, in charge of the presentation to the Faculty. First, they had to find a Faculty member to introduce Afro's proposal to the meeting. Profit and Howard received a positive response from professors Stanley Cavell and John Rawls, members of the Philosophy Department, who agreed to handle the *pro forma* responsibilities of moving and seconding their resolution.

The proposal that Profit and Howard discussed with Cavell and Rawls had four major sections. Part one would guarantee that a Black Studies program would "embody an interdisciplinary approach," that curriculum standards would be flexible enough "to allow courses that are radical both in subject matter and approach." Part two would give the Committee full powers over faculty appointments. Part three would assure it of an independent budget. This recommendation would supplement the Standing Committee with a temporary governing board of Afro members, concentrators in the field, and faculty members. This governing board would have the totally unprecedented power to review faculty candidates for tenure in the department. Never before had students been given any formal role in the tenure process. Cavell and Rawls worked through Wednesday night and into Thursday morning on a draft of the Afro proposal, omitting the clause that gave students power over faculty appointments. In so doing, they changed the motion's numbering system, a change that would be one of the many sources of confusion on the floor of the Faculty meeting.

The third special meeting of the Faculty of Arts and Sciences had lasted over three hours before the subject of Black Studies was discussed. In formulating the agenda for the April 17 meeting, Dean [Edward] Mason [acting Dean of Faculty, 16 Apr.-20 May '69] had thought that Black Studies was "clearly third priority," below the Committee of Fifteen elections and ROTC [Reserve Officers' Training Corps]. Only after the meeting did he realize how hot an issue it had become.

Jeff Howard presented the organization's case to the Faculty. "We are here," he began, "in a spirit of cooperation." He summarized the history of Afro-American Studies at Harvard, assuring the Faculty that the new Afro motion was not a repudiation of the *Rosovsky Report*, but only "a friendly amendment concerning the implementation of that report." The original program for the Black Studies major had precipitated the crisis, but "the possibility of such mistakes cannot be removed until students are adequately represented in bodies making decisions concerning them. We come here neither belligerent nor rigid," Howard concluded, "but our backs are against the wall."

A few minutes later, Henry Rosovsky donned his black, horn-rimmed reading glasses and approached a floor microphone. He explained his view of the misunderstanding: "Students did not play an active role in the formulation of the major, because, first of all, time pressure to get a multifaceted and rich program rolling was extreme." Besides, he said, "The efforts of this spring are highly transitory." Rosovsky expressed his opinion that the Afro proposal went far beyond the *Rosovsky Report*. Wes Profit replied that the *Report* had stressed cooperation; events had shown that institutional structures were required to assure that such cooperation took place.

Stanley Cavell had been working without sleep on the Afro

motion for the last 24 hours. The popular philosophy professor was in no condition to address the Faculty. He did so anyway. From this moment on, the meeting moved quickly toward a state of chaos. Cavell explained the background of the proposal, read it hurriedly, and without clarification. While Cavell rambled on irrelevantly, the meeting was in a state of tragicomic bedlam. Faculty members were scurrying in the aisles, comparing copies of the apparently identical Cavell draft and the Afro motion distributed two days before. They besieged Cavell with a barrage of questions. Then Professor Anthony Oettinger got to the microphone. "Mr. President," he began, "I have the feeling that I have lost all comprehension of what is going on [applause]. What on earth is going on? I simply do not understand it except that I know a lot of people are angry. We'd better find out a little bit more about what's going on. I move we table this."

"No, let's have it read again!" shouted a liberal voice from the back rows.

"Well, there is a motion on the ... Is there some way that we can ..." Oettinger groped for words. "Have you made a motion, Professor Cavell?"

Cavell's answer was something less than direct: "I call the question, Mr. President."

"On what?" rejoined Oettinger.

The meeting stumbled along until Oscar Handlin, quivering with rage, reached the microphone to request adjournment:

The Faculty has been in session for well over four hours. It has considered a variety of questions. It is now being asked to make a change which alters the fundamental practices of this Faculty and one which, in all earnestness, will *prejudice* the future of this department. I don't have *any* doubts in my mind but that the changes of the order that are now suggested will make it *increasingly* difficult to attract scholars of the first order to come here. I can not see how the Faculty at six-ten can now begin fully to consider this issue.

First the Faculty voted to extend debate; still, few professors were able to understand what was going on. Finally, a 239 to 150 vote postponed discussion of the Afro proposal until Tuesday, April 22, five long days away.

Without waiting for formal adjournment, Wes Profit and Jeff Howard hustled off to PBH where yet another Afro meeting was scheduled to convene. The evening of April 17, 1969, would be one of the longest and most anxious nights in Harvard history. Afro was very, very angry.

The meeting in PBH was long, bitter, and stormy. To the more militant members of Afro, the Faculty meeting had demonstrated the deeply racist nature of the university's almost totally white Faculty. The professors had dealt with a demand of white students (ROTC), had given the Afro issue only token attention, and then had "adjourned for cocktails" without reaching a decision. For the less militant members, the Faculty meeting had been equally revealing. Some degree of confusion on the Faculty's part would have been understandable. But their insulting and almost total ignorance of the subject indicated that few Faculty members had even read the *Rosovsky Report* by which all of them swore. For the militants, the obvious tactic was dramatic and immediate confrontation. For the less militant, the solution was to educate the faculty, to give them one more opportunity to reach an intelligent decision. If that decision were still unacceptable, the militants would have their way.

"Folks were just letting off steam," said one black looking back at the night of April 17. Groups of blacks left PBH periodically and marched through the Yard, chanting and singing, lighting bonfires, and generally making their presence felt. Rumors flew around the campus. Afro was planning to seize University Hall, the Computing Center, or Widener Library.[5] Outside PBH, knots of reporters huddled together, waiting to follow the blacks if they seized a building. At one point during the evening, a black student emerged from PBH and strolled over to the reporters. He stopped. "Really up-tight, aren't you?" He turned and walked back to PBH.

About midnight, the meeting adjourned with a compromise decision. Afro would take over University Hall for three hours the next morning to talk with professors: "We want to make it perfectly clear that this is the last talking we will do with the Faculty. It would

---

[5]Had Afro, or any group for that matter, tried to enter Widener Library, they would have been astonished to find a small contingent of Faculty members confronting them, asking them not to damage any of the 8,000,000 volumes in the building. Anticipating the anger of Afro that night, several Faculty members, including law professor Archibald Cox, feared for the safety of the library's irreplaceable volumes. They set up an all-night guard that remained on duty for several evenings and were ready to do so again.

be an understatement to say that we were outraged by what happened at the Faculty meeting. It added insult to longstanding injury." One Afro member called Dean Mason to inform him of Afro's plans. Hoping to avoid a confrontation, Mason invited Afro to hold such a session. Early the next morning, the dean called several dozen professors, urging them to attend and to spread the word to their colleagues.

The Faculty Room of University Hall had been put to unprecedented uses during the crisis, but none so curious as "office hours." A few minutes after 9:00 A.M., about 80 black students arrived. Skip Griffin, dressed in work jacket, jeans, and his ever-present wire-rimmed sunglasses, sat in what was customarily President Pusey's chair and propped his feet on the ancient and massive mahogany table. About 80 Faculty members filtered in and out of the room throughout the morning. After the session had begun, Henry Rosovsky, the man whose name had been synonymous with Black Studies at Harvard, entered. One black student recognized him immediately: "What you did yesterday [referring to his speech to the Faculty]—that was the cheapest thing you ever did in your life."

"Office hours" marked the introduction of a new character into the black drama: Professor of Sociology Alex Inkeles. Inkeles sympathized with many of the proposals suggested in the Cavell motion of April 17. But he found the motion vague in its terminology and uninformed in its examination of the process of granting tenure. Inkeles prefaced his own specific proposals with a brief speech, offering his services to achieve the goals set forth by Afro. The majority of the black students said that they did not want a faculty member writing a resolution for them, but Inkeles assured Afro that his services were nonetheless very much available.

The purpose of "office hours" was for Afro to provide information for the faculty, not to negotiate with them. At noon, Skip Griffin lifted his legs off the table and got up to leave. Some faculty members asked that Afro stay so that the two groups might find more common ground. "Office hours are over," Griffin replied. "We've got nothing more to talk about. This was an educational session for *you* about *our* proposal. We're leaving." And they left.

If nothing else, "office hours" had shown Afro that their current resolution was unacceptable in language and perhaps in substance to most Faculty members. The Afro proposal would have to be rewritten. But many blacks were fed up with debating over the selection of words for the sensitive ears of the faculty. The blacks were also unhappy with the student body as a whole. At the second mass meeting, Friday afternoon, the community had voted to suspend the strike despite the fact that the Black Studies issue remained unresolved. Afro planned to stay on strike until the Faculty reached its verdict.

Afro's strike steering committee convened early Saturday morning, April 19, to rewrite the legislation. After spending most of the day in the agonizing process of writing a document by committee, the blacks emerged with a draft to be presented to all of Afro Sunday afternoon. But there would be other proposals as well.

Sunday morning, two Afro members met Alex Inkeles at his house in an effort to work out a mutually acceptable resolution. They returned to the Afro meeting with a second and somewhat different suggestion for the governance of the Black Studies program at Harvard.

Meanwhile, another small group of blacks had drawn up a third draft which they felt combined the best points of the original Afro and original Inkeles proposals.

None of these three resolutions could command the support of the group that assembled at PBH Sunday afternoon. All that the members of Afro could agree on was the establishment of a special committee to write a fourth draft. Two emotional meetings, two more proposals, and 30 hours later, Afro finally gave its approval to a document that had been voted on line-by-line by the entire membership of the organization.

With the hitherto elusive consensus solidly formed around a precise proposal, Afro turned Monday night to questions of tactics for the Tuesday afternoon Faculty meeting that would pass judgment on Afro's case. Skip Griffin, Myles Lynk, Jeff Howard, Wes Profit, and Clarence [L.] James ['72, left after freshman year] were chosen to address the meeting and to answer questions about specific points. All other members were asked to listen to the meeting in the lobby of the Loeb, where they would be available for immediate consultation. The frustrated and exhausted blacks decided that any attempt by the Faculty to amend, add to, or delete from their handiwork would be considered a "No" vote. If the Faculty did vote "No," Afro would meet early Tuesday evening to consider militant action. And the blacks expected a "No" vote.

By Sunday evening, Alex Inkeles knew that Afro had chosen not to support his motion. Spurned by the constituency of his first choice, Inkeles sought a new source of support: the Faculty itself. He spent Sunday night calling the members of the original Rosovsky Committee and representatives of both the liberal and conservative caucuses, asking them to meet Monday in University Hall. This emergency session assembled promptly at 9:00 A.M. and began to debate over what kind of compromise the Faculty could in clear conscience offer to Afro. Inkeles painstakingly reworked his motion until he had the endorsement of most members of the Rosovsky Committee and of Dean Mason. The only reservation came from Professor Ernest May of the conservative caucus.

Inkeles used Monday evening to deliver copies of his final proposal to Afro and to both caucuses. His meeting with representatives of Afro produced nothing; Afro was on the verge of reaching its own consensus and had no use for yet another proposal. The liberal faculty caucus received Inkeles enthusiastically and committed its votes to his motion. The conservatives were less enthusiastic; they reluctantly consented to endorse the motion, if it were amended to delete all mention of Afro per se. The conservatives did not object to giving representation to black students, only to giving it explicitly to members of a political organization, such as Afro.

Faculty members started arriving at the Loeb just before 4:00 P.M. Tuesday afternoon. They filed through the crowd of 70 blacks in the lobby and picked up copies of two resolutions: one was presented by Inkeles, the other by Afro. Both motions would expand the Standing Committee, the program's temporary governing board, to include three members of Afro and three students majoring in Black Studies. But while the Inkeles motion gave students equal representation, it also reduced drastically the power of that body. Students would have no control over faculty or curricula. Afro also demanded equal student representation in the permanent governance of the program. Inkeles would allow no students in such positions, guaranteeing that student power would be relatively harmless and absolutely temporary.

At the Faculty meeting the two motions would be considered separately.[6] Both Mason and Pusey agreed that it was essential to

---

[6]During the crisis, the Faculty had considered several motions simultaneously. Before the April 22 meeting, the President had announced his intention to return to the Faculty's rules that called for disposing of motions one at a time.

give the Afro motion a full hearing, and, therefore, they put it first on the agenda. Alan Heimert, Master of Eliot House, introduced the resolution; and Zeph Stewart, Master of Lowell House, rose to second it. As a member of the Standing Committee, Stewart spoke knowledgeably about the specific origins of Afro's grievances:

Having collaborated through every part of Professor Rosovsky's report and having been assured that they would continue to do so especially in the devising of the program, how could the black students feel that anything less than a complete breach of faith had occurred? How could they feel any trust in the further functioning of a mechanism which had betrayed them so soon and might betray them again?

Afro's demand, Stewart argued, was a special case, and "not merely another part of the movement of violent protest and disruption by which the university is being racked." As a result, "the Faculty must go as far as reason and generosity will allow to meet the proposals of a specially qualified group which sincerely believes in the reasonableness and justice of what they ask."

When Stewart had finished, President Pusey recognized Myles Lynk, the first of Afro's speakers.

Black people, students or otherwise, know more about what a Black Studies program could be than most members of this Harvard Faculty. And because a university community should be less concerned with past precedents that are inadequate to the present than with constructive change applicable to the future, the Afro proposal should be passed because it best meets the needs of the Afro-American Studies Department. It must be passed if black people are to maintain faith in this segment of white America. And I believe that it will be passed, as you gentlemen are honorable men.

Skip Griffin, Afro's president, followed Lynk with a reminder about "my brothers and sisters who wait outside":

I think, and it wouldn't be unfair to say before this body and before the world, that at one time this week we had the power to seriously disrupt this university, and I don't think we used it because that wasn't our goal, our goal was a meaningful Black Studies program. I think we held off because we wanted just such a program . . . Not to make a decision in favor of the proposal that we have put here before you is to commit a serious mistake, to perhaps play a part in creating a tragic situation which this university may never be able to recover from [hisses]. I just hope that you would consider seriously the gravity of the situation before acting.

Many members of the Faculty saw Griffin's remarks as a threat.

Next, it was the opposition's turn. Ernest May, the first of three history professors who would speak against the Afro resolution, stepped to a microphone near the front of the theater. As much as he wanted to support the blacks, May said, he could not do so for three reasons. First, he saw a danger in giving students the right to recommend candidates for faculty appointment, not because students were irresponsible but because they were untrained. Second, granting such powers to blacks would set a precedent; students in all departments would demand similar privileges. Third, May feared that outstanding scholars would not come to Harvard if their careers were made dependent on student opinion.

Laurence Wylie, Professor of the Civilization of France, rebutted May's argument over the question of precedent involved. Wylie argued that the history of Harvard contained precedents for almost anything. "It's like the Bible," he said, "you can find anything you want in it."

During the course of the debate, the blacks accepted two minor amendments. One changed the description of courses in the Afro motion from "radical and relevant" to "innovative." The other subjected the entire Black Studies program to a full review by the Faculty during the 1971-72 academic year. Neither amendment, the blacks felt, weakened the substance of their motion: "We still feel that we have the chance of making a good department here and that department will stand any test this Faculty cares to give it."

At 6:00 P.M., it was time for the Faculty to decide. A voice vote proved inconclusive.

"All in favor, please rise," the President asked. "All opposed." It was still too close to call. The President asked for a head count.

While the counting proceeded, the members of Afro in the lobby huddled nervously around their transistor radios. Moments later, the verdict came.

"The motion is carried by a vote of two fifty-one for, one fifty-eight against . . ."

In the lobby outside, the blacks were ecstatic. Their shout drowned out the voice of the President inside the theater. Shaking hands of sympathetic professors as they left, the five Afro spokesmen hurried from the theater to join the party outside. It was an electric moment.

Jeff Howard was elated. "It's a hell of a victory and we're all very happy with it. This is a great victory not only for Afro, but for this university. It's going to recreate a trust that was failing, and I hope that together the faculty and students can move on and take control of this university."

And all over Cambridge that evening, while Afro celebrated, concerned members of the Harvard community breathed a collective sigh of relief.

The Faculty's extraordinary vote provoked several questions. All of Harvard wondered what would have happened had the Faculty passed the Inkeles motion or no new motion at all. Later, Myles Lynk had some answers:

The effect of the rejection of the Afro proposal would have outweighed the acceptance of the Inkeles proposal. We were prepared to take militant action but it would have been an indication of frustration, out of anger. If the Faculty had rejected our proposal, it would have been a slap in the face. Therefore, we would slap them back.

"Militant action" might have meant the seizure of a building, and, in the wake of the Cornell incident the previous weekend, that might have meant an armed takeover. Militant action might have meant individual "acts of sabotage" (as one black called them), such as withdrawing from the college or urging potential freshmen not to come to Harvard.

Perhaps no group was so surprised by the outcome of the April 22 meeting as the Faculty itself. Why had the Faculty taken this radical step? Certainly, fear was an element in the vote. Just one day before, professors had seen in the *New York Times* the frightening picture of armed black students leaving a seized building at Cornell. They could easily visualize the same thing happening in Cambridge. Skip Griffin's speech to the Faculty and the intimidating presence of 70 Afro members in the lobby must have made that threat even more real.[7] But Afro also appealed to the Faculty's sense of reason and

---

[7]On the day after the vote, the *Crimson* showed one black student leaving the theater with a meat cleaver in hand. [See photo below by Timothy G. Carlson '71—Eds.]

fairness; for the most part Afro's presentation was clear, calm, and rational, even in the Faculty's own terms. Clearly, some faculty members were convinced that the Standing Committee had broken its brittle covenant of faith with the blacks. Others wanted to restore a sense of community to Harvard by dramatically reasserting their faith in a group of students. Finally, the actual vote showed a preponderance of natural scientists voting in favor of the Afro resolution. Natural scientists, always suspicious of social scientists, were prepared to endorse such academic experimentation precisely because they considered Black Studies to be less than a legitimate field of intellectual endeavor.

On the evening of April 22, however, one crucial fact made all this speculation seem remote and unimportant. The last major threat of violence on campus had been overcome. For everyone except SDS, the crisis was over.

From Eichel, Jost, Luskin and Neustadt, *The Harvard Strike* (1970)

Students cross Brattle Street on leaving faculty meeting in Loeb Drama Center on 22 April 1969 (photograph by Timothy G. Carlson '71).

Excerpt from the "Rosovsky Report,"

January 20, 1969

The Faculty Committee on African and Afro-American Studies has made the following major recommendations:

1) Among black students there is a strong and definite desire for creation of a social and cultural center for black students. Such a center is conceived as something of a counterpart to Hillel House, the Newman Center, or the International Center. It is recommended that the Dean urge all appropriate elements of the University to use their good offices in securing and financing a building and providing continued support to the activities of such a social and cultural center.

2) We recommend that the University create a standing Faculty Committee on degrees in Afro-American Studies to develop and supervise a combined major in this field. This degree should be available to students in the class of 1972, and the most feasible way to make such a degree possible is to start the program as a combination of Afro-American Studies and an existing concentration.

3) A central point of the Faculty Committee's work should be the establishment of a Center for Afro-American Studies. The purpose of this institution would be to provide intellectual leadership, a physical locale and sufficient material resources for consideration of all aspects of the Afro-American experience.

4) We recommend that the University establish a co-ordinating Committee on African Studies to oversee the future increase and stabilization of courses in this area.

5) At present black enrollment in the graduate school is very

small. It is recommended that GSAS make a major recruitment effort, and in addition, that it set aside fifteen to twenty fellowships a year for black students who possess the potential to become scholars of the first rank.

Faculty and administrative review of these recommendations is a matter of urgency.   Hopefully, their implementation will also be accomplished as quickly as possible. While our report—as all university committee reports—necessarily uses many unspecific terms and qualifiers typical of institutional language, it would be tragic if this obscured the sense of urgency felt by the Committee and by our witnesses.

We know that the adoption of our recommendations would cost Harvard a great deal of money. However, that is true of nearly all projects and programs. The real issue is one of intellectual and social priorities.   We believe that our area of concern should have no difficulty in moving near the top of any priority list. A special fund drive in support of the Committee's recommendations would be a most appropriate step.

Respectfully submitted,

> C. T. W. CURLE
> DANIEL M. FOX
> GEORGE W. GOETHALS
> ALAN HEIMERT
> H. STUART HUGHES
> MARTIN L. KILSON, JR.
> GARY T. MARX
> J. W. M. WHITING
> HENRY ROSOVSKY, *Chairman*

Faculty Vote of April 22, 1969

At a meeting of the Faculty of Arts and Sciences on April 22, 1969 the following votes were passed:

VOTED: That Station WHRB be given permission to broadcast live the meeting of April 22, 1969 and to rebroadcast the meeting in its entirety, with the provision that any speaker who wishes not to make his statements public may so announce and his statements will not be broadcast.

VOTED: I. That the Faculty intends the Afro-American Studies Program to be a department, interdisciplinary in nature, offering a standard field of concentration. At the same time, the Faculty urges that other departments enrich their course offerings in Afro-American studies as well. This field of concentration shall be made available to students in the class of 1972.

II. That to aid in the development of the Afro-American Studies Department the Standing Committee shall have the following functions:
A. To oversee expansion of library resources in the Afro-American Studies field,
B. To develop the Afro-American Research Institute,
C. To solicit funds for Departmental Chairs,
D. To work towards a greater-Boston consortium of university Afro-American resources,
E. To seek out and hire immediately, temporary consultants knowledgeable in Afro-American Studies and personally involved in the Afro-American experience to assist in the development of this program,

F. To nominate the first four to six appointments in the department, two of which must be tenured.

That the Standing Committee on Afro-American Studies shall be expanded to include three students chosen by the Association of African and Afro-American Students at Harvard and Radcliffe and three students chosen from and by potential concentrators in the field. These students will have full voting rights on the Committee and will be guaranteed funds for summer work in developing this program. When the two permanent appointments to the Department have been nominated and appointed, and sufficient faculty members have been secured to constitute the Executive Committee described below, the Standing Committee will be dissolved.

III. That responsibility for this field of concentration shall be vested initially in an Executive Committee to be established as soon as the first four members of the Department have been appointed and have taken up their duties. This Committee will consist of four members of the Department faculty, two students elected by the Association of African and Afro-American Students at Harvard and Radcliffe, and two students elected by concentrators in the field of Afro-American Studies. When formed, this Committee will assume all of the responsibilities of the Standing Committee except item F, paragraph II above. When the Standing Committee is dissolved, item F, paragraph II, will also be subsumed by the Executive Committee. This Committee will also be responsible for curriculum development, standards, and course requirements in Afro-American Studies. Courses should be innovative and relevant both in subject matter and approach. The initial committee will function through the academic year 1971-72. At an appropriate time during that year this Faculty in consultation with the committee will review all aspects of the program and make recommendations as to the membership, operating rules, and responsibilities of the permanent Executive Committee.

IV. That official discussion of concentration requirements and curriculum development be suspended until the Executive Committee is formed.

_____

ROBERT SHENTON, *Secretary*

Muriel Morisey Spence in 1986

Herbert Nickens in 1969

Godfred Otuteye in 1971

THE 1969 YEARBOOK

In Harvard's *Yearbook 333*, honoring the Class of 1969, the editors included a special section presenting essays by eight black students. Of these we here reprint three—two by seniors and one by a sophomore.

A Feminine Hell

MURIEL MORISEY SPENCE

Muriel Morisey Spence was born in Greensboro, North Carolina, on 7 September 1947, attended school in Philadelphia, and was a history concentrator at Radcliffe, from which she was graduated in 1969. After short stints as a teacher in Boston and a journalist in Washington, she worked in several capacities for Congressman Walter Fauntroy, the House Judiciary Committee, the Black Women's Community Development Foundation, and Representative Shirley Chisholm, during which time Spence earned a J.D. degree from Georgetown University Law Center. Following her graduation in 1977, she lectured in Africa under the auspices of the U.S. Information Agency. From 1978 to 1983 she was an attorney in the U.S. Department of Justice, receiving a Special Commendation Award from the Attorney General for "outstanding service" to the Civil Rights Division. In 1983 she joined the legal staff of the American Civil Liberties Union, and in 1985 returned to Harvard as Director of Policy Analysis in the Office of Government, Community and Public Affairs, serving also as Lecturer on Education and on the board of freshman advisors and the Law School Committee on Student Services. She joined the law faculty of Temple University in 1991.

The relationship of any Radcliffe student to Radcliffe's deans, advisors, residents, etc. is about as close as the relationship of a Harvard student to Nathan Pusey. To the problems of adjustment each Cliffie must work out her own solutions, but in doing so the black Cliffie is faced with a greater psychological challenge than her white counterpart can possibly be. There are definite factors about Radcliffe and its policy towards black students which have contributed to the problems faced here. Both the admissions procedure and the realities of Radcliffe's relation to Harvard work to intensify the distances between the black Radcliffe student and her Harvard counterpart, and to make even more strained and difficult her attempt to define her roles as campus political activist and as woman. Radcliffe does not yet understand her black students, and Harvard does not yet know what to do with its women, and as a result the black Cliffie does not yet know what to do with herself.

Radcliffe does not yet understand her black students. The admissions policy works on blacks in much the same way that it does whites. The old cliché that Cliffies tend to be as a group more intellectual, better prepared academically, and more frequently from middle and upper income families than Harvard men is borne out by four years of careful though informal observation. Looking at the four classes in Radcliffe at any one time, one is tempted to say that we are not chosen for the same reasons as the men at all. The discrepancies are too real to be accidental.

Harvard's blacks are a surprisingly heterogeneous group. What they do have in common in each case, whether because of middle class advantages of schooling, genuine brilliance, or rare and extraordinary personal qualities, is something which appeals to the white liberal and makes him feel that he sees the potential for leadership and success in the old Harvard manner.

The senior looks at seven classes of Cliffies and wonders what in the world we are supposed to be headed for. Surely the admissions board does not expect to create a generation of black Radcliffe Club presidents, women's college deans, research scientists, and community leaders. Even more surely they cannot be projecting us into the role of black housewife and family mainstay. Perhaps at some earlier point it would have been reasonable to expect black counterparts for the standard Radcliffe success stories. But today such expectations are at best outdated, and at worst indicative of a serious insensitivity to what has been happening lately in the black community. The admissions policy which chose the classes through 1972 has been basically the same as the one which chose the one or two blacks per class in the previous few decades. Part of the meaning of this fall's confrontation between black students and the Radcliffe administration was an attempt to communicate the need for revised admissions criteria. It will be interesting to see what difference this confrontation will make.

The problems the black Cliffie faces not only are the result of the selection process, but also reflect a strained and somewhat segregated life throughout the year. As is similarly the case for our white counterparts, black Cliffies find that being "up there" at the Cliffe creates physical barriers to meeting and relating to men in a natural and relaxed setting. There was a time when people assumed that Afro was a kind of social club, where black students talked politics, but more often got together and partied a lot. This has not been true for at least the four academic years the seniors have experienced. It is in fact indicative of the seriousness of the dilemma that the degree to which a Cliffie is deeply involved in the activities of Afro seems to be inversely proportional to her chances for a full and meaningful social life with blacks at Harvard.

There are different ways which each individual finds to approach this problem, but each is in itself a sacrifice where none should be necessary. Some thrust themselves fully into the political struggle, apparently on an equal footing with the men. But very few who make this decision would deny that they feel deeply and painfully the need for a real sense of femininity as well. However, those who pursue the fulfillment of their femininity cannot deny that their social life is very much dependent upon political activity. That is to say that without being at least somewhat active in Afro, one's social life is stifled. Striking the balance between the two is a problem for which a viable solution is rarely found.

The black Cliffie lives in a unique world, carrying much more than her own weight in the activities of the black students on campus, and at the same time cheated in many ways of a meaningful yet genuinely feminine role in the total community of black students. Hopefully this situation is a temporary one. Today, however, it is at best a greater psychological challenge than one usually bargains for and at worst a kind of particularly feminine hell.

It makes extra demands (like the combined expectations of making serious intellectual contributions while never interfering with the growing dominance of the black man). It requires sacrifices, and worst of all, it seems nearly impossible for the black Cliffie to find both emotional and intellectual fulfillment as a woman. The dilemma of the black Cliffie is a source of severe frustration and anger.

Most black students at Radcliffe see their society as the black one which is awakening to itself and its endless possibilities for growth and development. We wish to fulfill our personal needs and make our social contribution within the context of that black community. Unless the preparation for those goals can be better achieved at Radcliffe than seems possible to many here now, Radcliffe and its black students will continue to fail each other. Radcliffe does not yet understand her black students, and Harvard does not yet know what to do with its women, and as a result the black Cliffie does not yet know what to do with herself.

From *Harvard Yearbook* (1969)

Travels with Charlie: In Search of Afro-America

HERBERT W. NICKENS

Herbert Wallace Nickens was born on 28 December 1947 in Washington, D.C., where he attended St. John's College High School. At Harvard he concentrated in biology, was an assistant editor of the *Harvard Journal of Negro Affairs*, and received his A.B. in 1969. In 1973 he earned both M.D. and M.A. degrees at the University of Pennsylvania. Following a psychiatric residency at Yale, he pursued graduate work in sociology and taught at the University of Pennsylvania. In 1982 he began working on problems of aging for the National Institute of Mental Health, and in 1986 became Director of Minority Health in the Public Health Service. At the end of 1988 he took office in Washington as Vice-President of the Association of American Medical Colleges, dealing especially with minority health.

For Harvard's black community the Class of 1969 was one of transition. Black enrollment reached a critical mass. The decline of integrationism and the growth of militancy and black consciousness on campus responded to and paralleled that in society as a whole. Our awareness had advanced to the point that the fact of our blackness was an issue, but few of us knew what to do about it. Being black exacerbated the already difficult freshman adjustment in addition to raising questions all its own. We not only had to learn to live with strangers, but with white strangers whose attitudes toward us were rarely indifferent to our color. We often bore the burden of being cultural and anthropological curiosities: inspected, sometimes devaluated, frequently overvalued, but never regarded in absence of the black conversion factor. We found ourselves spread-eagled between black and white, each culture offering its own values, aspirations, life-styles, and rewards.

To appreciate what it has meant to be black at Harvard over these last four years, it is necessary to see that the transition from integrationism to black power was not merely a change of politics, but had profound implications for one's life as a whole; what has happened to the black seniors is missed unless the ambivalences of being black in white America are constantly kept in mind.

One such ambivalence was manifested early in our freshman year. For some, comfort was derived from the "soul table" in the Union. Many felt that to be themselves, to be regarded simply as a person, they needed to be in the company of other blacks. Others, however, would not sit there. For them this was a re-segregation, a step backwards, contrary to what they had come to Harvard to accomplish. But, the either/or character of this action did not reflect the mixed state of our minds. Most of us felt both ways about eating only with blacks. We felt similarly mixed about other aspects of Harvard life.

Since black freshmen were rarely assigned to live together almost all of us faced the problem of getting along with whites in close quarters. The major problem was bridging the cultural gulf: problems of communication frequently were substantial. I have often heard friends remark, "I like him, but I get tired of having to explain things, and myself." Though one might say that this interchange is part of the richness of the Harvard experience, the divisions between black and white are too deep to support such a judgment.

All too frequently, the cultural interchange was one-way. It is a fact of life in America that while blacks have had to absorb the dominant white culture in order to function, whites have had no such reciprocal need. Some of us began to feel like the "local curiosity shop," which might have been all right if we had been foreign students who are frequently surrounded by those ignorant of their culture, constantly called upon to explain it. But our foreignness was contradictory because we were ostensibly in our own country. White interest in us usually reflected insensitivity and obtuseness rather than sympathy and curiosity.

Despite these difficulties, meaningful relationships were often achieved, usually between a sensitive white and a tolerant black. Thus, when it came time for us to move from the Yard many of us chose white roommates. Sometimes, however, it was less because of friendship than because we were too self-conscious to seek out actively other blacks. It would have seemed too separatist, not then acceptable. At this time most of us still wanted to be a Harvard man as we saw him modelled for us by other students and by tradition.

It was probably in the area of dating that our ability to copy Harvard models ran into the most conflict. One of the first things we noticed about our sister school was that there was a dearth of "sisters." Not only were there only a half dozen black Radcliffe students in our class, but there really wasn't a significant number of black women in the other schools Harvard men ordinarily plunder. The obvious solution, then, was to date whites.

Dating whites solved one problem but created others. Though many meaningful interracial relationships developed, the tendency was strong for blacks and whites to relate to each other with an extensive set of predetermined responses, which when coupled with external social factors further complicated the already difficult process of two people getting to know one another.

Our society is hostile to interracial unions, and so are parents. This tended to cast a pall on all such dates. Mixed couples are very much caught between two worlds. If a couple wished to go somewhere outside the Square there was the likelihood that they would be stared at, and the small but real possibility that they could be insulted or even attacked. If they wanted to go to a party there was always the question of whose . . . black parties were quite different from white ones.

Not to be ignored were other factors which plagued the establishment of genuine relationships. Many of the unions were a form of experimentation. For many students interracial dating had been impossible because of inavailability, parental opposition, or, depending on where one lived, fear for your life. For many white women, dating blacks was a way of proclaiming their liberalism, and served as a mechanism for rebellion against their parents and society. Added to this was the allure of the "black buck" factor, the myth of the black males' sexual superiority. Not surprisingly, there was also operating on black men a sexual myth, that of the "white goddess" which sees white women as the ultimate sexual prize. Dating was a problem. There were too few "sisters," too many myths . . . the anxiety of defining self deepened.

Traditionally, we had been taught to value conventional self-improvement. "Get the diploma," we had been told. Our people have always thought of education as a key to enable us to escape our origins or, in some cases, to perpetuate them, but in any case to flee our blackness, to wear a "white collar," to eke out the security and stability that seemed so precious. Some of us sought invisibility . . . many were only semi-involved in "civil-rights." The majority of us, however, had not even begun to seek a real commitment to blackness from ourselves, much less from institutions and organizations.

In time we began to receive fallout from Southern summer experiences; Stokely announced that SNCC was henceforth black, might get violent, and sent the blue-eyed legions of summer freedom fighters home. The burgeoning concept of black power suggested to us that black striving for the white life style reflected empty values, a misdirection of energy, and a denial of the embryo self within us that was not to be compromised, but asserted. We began to suspect that becoming a black white man was not "making it" after all. We paused mid-stride on the way to co-optation. As the calls for relevance became more strident we were forced into an increasingly difficult position, and black power's counter-ethos left none of us untouched. It was, however, the assassination of Martin Luther King that ultimately served to alienate and fuse black students in a cohesive, self-conscious community.

Dr. King was killed in the Spring of our junior year. This was the watershed of race relations at Harvard. Such was the stature and meaning of the man. He was the symbol and the leader of "revolution by the rules." He was God-fearing and nonviolent. Many who had sought to avoid the pain of being black in our society were caught up short. The defenses which all of us had erected to escape the loneliness of social consciousness were seriously weakened in the face of this devastating evidence. Dr. King died because he threatened to alter the social order. None of us felt that he was killed by a small group of conspirators. His murder was only made possible by a pathological environment hostile to all black people. This realization snapped us from somnambulism. We felt alone and we felt revulsion.

Black students sought the support and comfort of their brothers and sisters. We became acutely aware that the number of black men and women at Harvard had increased. The meeting that was held following Dr. King's death was attended by over a hundred students, many of whom had not previously been involved politically or socially with the main body of blacks on campus. In addition to the political effects of this meeting, and those that followed, there was a social reorientation.

The Class of 1969's center of gravity had shifted toward Blackness; individuals are distributed variously along the spectrum, but a change is discernible in nearly all. We have suffered and survived a crisis-ridden period of transition in search of a more viable social identity. If we want black roommates we choose them, and whites are beginning to ask themselves about their own racism rather than query us about "Negritude." Now when the myths surrounding us are most vivid, and opportunities for social maneuvering and sexual manipulation are greatest, we find them least satisfying. We are weary of bankrupt values and dead-end desires. We share a sense of mission even in our interrelations and a dream for which there is no model in the society around us. Black people are seriously interested in loving themselves and one another.

From *Harvard Yearbook* (1969)

Part of a Longer Story

GODFRED PEHUER OTUTEYE

Godfred Pehuer Otuteye was born on 6 June 1949 in Akplabanya, Ghana, and prepared for college at the Adisadel School 140 miles away in the city of Cape Coast. At Harvard he concentrated in applied mathematics and was also associate editor of the *Harvard Journal of Afro-American Affairs*. After being graduated with honors in 1971, he attended the Harvard Business School for one year, eventually completing his M.B.A. degree at the University of Southern California in 1974. In 1974 he began working for the Union Bank in the Los Angeles area, and served as Vice-President in charge of commercial loans from 1977 to 1982. After a year as chief financial officer for the Brinderson Corporation, he became Vice-President and chief financial officer for Micro D, Inc. in 1983, being promoted to Senior Vice-President in 1985. In 1988 he assumed responsibility for the company's international operations.

All of Harvard was engulfed in one of those tar-dark, glue-thick winter nights; the porch lamps struggled helplessly against the encircling gloom. The only audible sounds, besides the traffic, came from the tired protests of what must have been an ancient typewriter irritated at being called to duty this late hour of the night. It was hot inside, most of the heat coming from the tension that our debate had created. The air was as tense as the skin of a tom-tom when wet. What had started as a harmless exploration into the causes and early developments of the Vietnam War had degenerated into subjective emotional outbursts, accusations and counter-accusations about the C.I.A., foreign aid, and race.

"If Americans are as bad as you say they are," he accused me, "why did you accept their scholarship offer? It is American money from the pockets of voluntary donors and the taxpayer. Tell me, to what advantage is it to the United States to offer assistance to hundreds of foreign students like you?"

I related this incident to put on record my full awareness of the resentment that Americans feel towards aliens who justly or unjustly criticize United States adventures abroad as well as social inequities here at home. In what follows I am going to concern myself mainly with Harvard University, and although Harvard is not the U.S. there are those who love it too. It is my hope that they will read in these remarks more than just cynicism and ingratitude. Finally, in these introductory remarks, I wish to emphasize that the views expressed here are mine alone and not the consensus of African undergraduates at Harvard.

The scene was the Freshmen Union—it was Orientation Week for the class of '71. Parents and their sons were chattering about Tom this and Dick that who did not make it to Harvard. I gathered that Harvard was unfamiliar to some of them as it was to me. But there was an important difference. They were Americans and regardless of where they came from they could talk about Boys' State, summer jobs or cherry pie. I was an outsider—even the names of some of the items on the menu tempted me to go fasting. I remember writing to a friend to tell him how much "living chlorophyll" we were being fed daily. During one meal I was asked by a guy I had just met to come meet a student from Liberia. My heart soared. I was delighted at the prospect of meeting an African student at last. It turned out that the "Liberian" in question was not a Liberian at all. His father had worked in that country for a long time as a missionary and he had lived there many years too. After the usual hi-how-are-you and a handshake, he looked me up and down the way a frustrated cop would look at an intractable petty criminal:

"I hope you will go back to your country when you are through," he said seriously.

"I'm planning to."

"Yeah? That's what you all say when you first come here. I knew one kid right from the jungles; he came to the States on scholarship, got his degree and then instead of going back to the jungle where his people needed him, he stayed on in the States to work . . . and he was right from the jungles . . . !"

He shrugged and gesticulated helplessly as if to say "I cannot understand you people." This lecture which I had neither requested nor expected just about blew my mind. I turned and walked away to carry my tray back to the conveyor belt. It would not have been so bad if I had not already gotten sick and tired of hearing that same nauseating litany from certain Harvard officials and others including a salesman at the Coop who on learning from me that I was interested in mathematics looked at me hard as though my head needed fixing and said:

"You ought to be in biology or nutrition, you know. I have a friend in your country who wrote to say that the greatest problem facing your people is malnutrition. Your people need healthy bodies before they can study mathematics."

In later months I was to encounter the same mentality in many more people in the Harvard Community. They seem to know exactly why African students come to the United States and they are ever ready to volunteer much verbiage and insult to keep them from going astray. Here is a skeleton of their line of thought: Africa is ignorant, sick, coup-ridden, wallowing in a mud of poverty, underfed and unable to rule itself even badly. The African student, especially if he is at Harvard, being a promising member of a small elite comes to the U.S. to soak up, like a sponge, the technological civilization and pluralistic democracy for which America is famous. Then he goes back to his country and with this miracle water he transforms a brown barren backward land into green prosperity and the space age. Specific instances of this kind of attitude towards African students are many and varied. I will just mention one example as an illustration:

I sat at lunch with the headmaster of one of the prestigious prep schools in this area. He had come to Harvard to do a brief study on behalf of the Harvard Board of Overseers. We talked about student power and campus confrontations during which time he maintained adamantly that college students were too young and fickle to be trusted with the kinds of responsibilities that they wanted to share with professional administrators. The only digression from this topic (the ROTC debate was raging at the time) was a brief mention on his part of Kwame Nkrumah. He told me how he had heard of Nkrumah as oppressor of the Ghanaian people and one who wasted, squandered and mismanaged his country's resources. I knew where he got his misinformation (from the American Press) and I tried in vain to give him a more balanced picture of what happened in Ghana under Nkrumah. His put-on tough approach annoyed me as he seemed to be saying that he had all the answers. Suddenly he asked if I was in government.

"No," I replied without volunteering my field of concentration.

"In any case, you will go back to your country and become a great leader and all your ideas, you will have picked up at Harvard," he concluded with a nod and a conspiratorial grin. I excused myself and went away to class, irritated and amused at the same time. As far as he was concerned, I had it made because I came to Harvard!

The record has it that the majority of African leaders who had their university education in the United States ended up being strong advocates of all that falls under the umbrella term "African socialism," which some Americans have christened communism. Although it is not communism, African socialism is a far cry from American democracy, and as far as I know it was not taught as a political science in the American colleges these leaders went to. The point here is not to dispute Harvard's potential as a reliable incubator producing top-notch leaders and leadership. Indeed one of my complaints against Harvard is that it is too elitist in its admissions policies, a fact which gives its students a false sense of self-importance. Be that as it may, the point here is to expose a basic fallacy in the reasoning outlined above, that what is good for America should be at least as good for Africa!

There is no doubt that Africa today is in a mighty state of flux; nothing seems to have much stability in politics and government. (Much however remains stable. The vast majority of Africans still live away from urban centers with traditions and customs that have offered stony resistance to all threats of change.) Coups and counter-coups, civil war and border disputes have occurred with alarming frequency. Here again some people like Senator Allen J. Ellender of Louisiana know exactly why: in contradiction of all history, current affairs and common sense, he suggested a few years ago that African political instability exists because Africans were not yet mature enough for self-determination. To Ellender, who was obviously at a complete loss in the face of what he saw in Africa, this pat formula explains "the white man's burden." Others may not be quite so candid as Ellender but they have their doubts too.

I would like to suggest to such people that Africa is quite a different phenomenon than the United States. The political question "which way Africa?" does not have for an answer the simple alternatives, the political left or right. I do not agree with the man who called a radio program to spill his political ignorance: "There are two forms of government: American and communist." In fact, the way for Africa may not be either of these. I hope it is not. Frantz Fanon, one of the most formidable writers on the colonial experience, has warned African nations against imitating Europe or worse still, others who have imitated Europe. That, he argued, would be catastrophe. But neither is communism the panacea for Africa's ills; in fact there are no panaceas. Africans want and Africa must have a form of government that is harmonious with African institutions and socio-economic factors.

For example, some short-sighted western sociologists have blasted our extended family system as suffocative of individual initiative. They refuse to see that the extended family has done things for its members which the father-mother-children arrangement can never hope to match. Orphanages are unheard-of in traditional African society; neither are there many old people who live all alone. Any African government that does not take account of this social institution or of widespread polygamy may not see tomorrow.

Anyone who has been following events on the African continent is aware that the African people have consistently rejected foreign doctrines that were hastily transplanted into their midst. What all this means for the African student at Harvard is that he has a whole lot to unlearn on his return home. No realist can hope to build Africa from blueprints drawn up in Cambridge, Mass. This point becomes all the more significant when one realizes how backward Harvard is with respect to African Affairs.

The Rosovsky Committee in its report wrote: "African Studies at Harvard—unlike Afro-American Studies—has had the advantage of *satisfactory and congenial growth* within established disciplines" (emphasis my own). The evidence offered in support of this bold claim is shaky, to say the least. A few historical collections here and a few marginal courses there is all that constitutes Harvard's African Studies program, if one may call it that. The truth is that there is a dearth of knowledge on Africa in the Harvard Community as a whole.

The reason is partly historical. Africa, for many western people, has always been the source of cheap labor, mineral resources like uranium and gold, timber and agricultural products. Nothing else except wild tropical jungles. Talk of African civilizations, history and culture is as recent as today. Another possible explanation for Harvard's backwardness with respect to African Studies is that so much is changing so fast in Africa that those who are only marginally interested in African affairs get left behind.

There is an even more pathetic side to this bad situation. The average Harvard student, with the aid of the mass media, is positively misinformed about Africa and its people. I am always wary of using words like "tribe" because of what it connotes to the American mind. A lot of these people just do not care to check the validity of what they hear and read. I wonder how many Harvard students ever listen to African radio stations broadcasting daily to the North American continent. Of course, I am aware of efforts to acquaint students with Africa, such as V.T.A., BROTHER, and the International Ministry at Harvard. The fact still remains that many Harvard students conceive of Africa, in the words of David E. Apter, as a land of "dense jungle or arid plateaus, pestilent swamps and miasmic mists, all under a sweltering sun which always shines, even when it is raining." It is barely a decade ago that a Ghanaian jazz musician visiting the United States was asked if Africans lived in trees.

"Yes," he replied, "and your ambassador lives in the tallest tree."

African Studies has not had "satisfactory growth" at Harvard. Whether this is "congenial" is a question that Harvard must face. Personally, I do not think it is. As a leader in American education Harvard, with the resources it commands, can and should lead the way in opening up Africa *from the inside* to American students, professors and the American people in general. By "from the inside" I mean that opportunities should be created for Harvard students to see Africa from the African's point of view.

For example, Americans are generally and officially averse to polygamy. It is difficult to see how someone with this bias can present polygamy in a fair light. I remember a conversation with two American girls who got upset when I talked sympathetically of polygamy. What they and many others do not seem to realize is that the main difference between polygamous societies and American monogamy is one of vocabulary: what the African calls second or third wife the American calls mistress. This is not a defense of polygamy.

I believe that the student and faculty exchange programs between Harvard and African universities is one effective way to approach the problem. There are quite a few Africans in Harvard's graduate schools, but these numbers can be expanded. African professors should be invited to Harvard as guest lecturers for a year, and vice versa. There are a number of young promising African writers whom Harvard can invite here as writers-in-residence. They can then teach seminars in the Houses where they live. It should be possible for Harvard students with strong interests in Africa to spend a year or summer studying at an African university for credit. With careful planning and coordination a program of this sort would not cost too much money, nor would it inconvenience the administrations of the universities involved.

There is need for a more vigorous push for courses in Africa than was recommended in the Rosovsky report. This raises the question of shortage of American professors in the field. I would hate to see Harvard "buy" professors away from African colleges. The best plan may be to allow Harvard graduate students in African Studies to spend two years or so working at an African university. This has been done in isolated cases for students interested in economic development in countries like Pakistan. A more formal arrangement with African universities would help the situation enormously. I am not advocating this push for African Studies because the lack thereof strikes me as "a negative judgment by Harvard university on the importance of these areas of knowledge and research." That may or may not be so. My concern here is to draw attention to what is, in essence, mere lip service paid to African Studies.

I may mention that there is a comic side to this ignorance of Africa as well. I still remember the coed who refused to believe that there is not "Thanksgiving" in Africa. She thought Africans must be missing the greatest fun in the world. Somebody else asked me last summer if we have 4th of July celebrations in Africa! Then there are those who believe anything you tell them. An African freshman at another Ivy League College went to buy some liquor and found himself confronted by the law.

"May I see your ID, sir?" he was asked.

"What's that?"

It was the manager's turn to be surprised. Slowly he explained, after learning where my friend was from.

"Oh yeah." Kojo said cooly, "You see, in Africa we don't have birth certificates but I was told I was born in the year of the Great Fire, and that was a long time ago." Kojo got his liquor and has been buying there regularly ever since.

Being black at Harvard is like being nine feet tall. People always want to know what the atmosphere is like up there. They query you about the New York school strike, Planning 113b, the Rosovsky Committee, and Afro, all in one breath. They are "concerned" about the separatist tendencies of some black students who like to sit together at meals. What do you think? They do not seem to see that most white students follow definite sitting patterns at meals. I know some students who have gotten addicted to specific tables in our dining hall.

Black admissions is another perennial issue: "What's all this noise about minimum quotas? Isn't it unreasonable? What if the Poles, the Jews, the Italians, the Irish, the Armenians and everybody else demanded quotas to Harvard?" "Why don't you date white girls?" These and a zillion others are thrown at you at every opportunity. The black experience is perceived as uniform, thus every black student must feel the same way about all issues that affect his race directly. Hence when Prof. Martin Kilson writes a letter to the *Crimson* that disagrees with statements made by black student leaders there is wild commotion. "What do you think? Certainly Kilson must be right." The students are dismissed as emotional militants who have crucified reason and resurrected confrontation and force as the only means of solving campus problems.

It is a gross understatement to say that this state of affairs is intolerable or sickening. Many a time I have had to kill a question with a put down to save myself the loss of time and energy that past fruitless discussions of "the problem" have cost me. It is not that the questions are not legitimate. They are, and I am willing to discuss them with anyone genuinely interested. However, they are generally ill-posed by white students. You are queried as though you should be capable of reading other black men's minds. Take the example of the white student who complained to me about a black student leader who "acted hostile" to him when he (the white student) once approached him. What did I think of it? Nothing. Can't a black man be an individual?

Another problem with these questions is that the same people ask them continually. Apparently black students do not think about anything else! To those who are quick to point out that even if these questions are ill-posed, they come from people who are genuinely curious, let me say that when you are being accosted, as is often the case with race issues, it is irrelevant what the motives of your assailant are. The world is too full of examples of destructive actions which were initiated with good intentions for black students to accommodate what is an unpleasant situation.

I once had the misfortune of being, for a while, the advisee of a man who had no advice to give, and who was not interested in giving whatever else he had. Once, when I turned in my study card for his signature, he inspected it and told me that my course selection was "too tough." Would I drop Physics 12 and take Humanities 3 instead? I said "no." That blew his cool for some reason. He told me my SAT scores were not spectacular and that I should take it easy. This was Harvard. By this time he had crossed out Physics 12 and written "Hum. 3" in red ink above it and went on to sign the card. I went ahead and took the physics course anyway. At the end of the term he congratulated me on my grades (they were not really that good) adding: "I did not think you could handle it. I clearly underestimated your ability." Faced with a situation such as this it should be understandable why some black students request that they be assigned to black tutors. In fairness to the "adviser system" I must admit that I have received very useful advice informally from one white gentleman affiliated with the Admissions Office. He has never told me what to do. He simply tells me what the alternatives are and what it costs to choose one rather than the other. I make the decision and, in this respect at least, he is treating me as an individual and not as his conception of a black man from Africa.

How about relations between African students and their black American counterparts? Let me point out at the outset that no matter how many dashikis they may wear, black Americans are not Africans who happen to be in the United States; they are Americans even if in the minds of some people the content of that word amounts to something other than what it connotes for white America. As such there is a definite cultural difference between the African and his black American brother, although we share a common heritage.

One sometimes catches black American students interpreting African happenings under the presuppositions of western philosophy. Who can blame them? Then there are those among them whose conception of Africa is about as mythical as Tarzan. Africa was the land of mighty kingdoms, Ghana, Mali, Zimbabwe, to mention a few, till it was plundered and balkanized by evil white men. This is true but there were weak African kingdoms too; there were tribal scuffles, divisions, dissension and destruction. What I am suggesting is that it is wrong to say that if the African was not a savage (Tarzan) he must be a mighty angel of a man. No, the African is human.

Since Malcolm X (Marcus Garvey was born ahead of his time), black Americans and black Africans have been working together to reestablish those broken historical and cultural links that now lie buried in the Atlantic sea bed and the plantations of the South. This is happening at Harvard too. African students have worked on the Ad Hoc Committee of black students. I have had numerous informal discussions with black students about African governments, politics, schools, customs and traditions right down to the popular high-life dance. In Atlanta, Georgia, last summer I was warmly received by all the black folks I met. The West Side of that city, for all its Americanness, was very much like some parts of Accra. In short, to borrow from Kwame Nkrumah's words, both black Americans and black Africans realize that the freedom of black people anywhere in the world is meaningless unless it is linked with the total liberation of black people everywhere.

It is possible that there are as many African experiences at Harvard as there are African students in the college. The foregoing is only part of a longer story. As we do in Ghana, some day I shall tell the rest over plenty of roasted cocoyams and plantains.

Tswa manyeaba.*

From *Harvard Yearbook* (1969)

[*A solemn greeting of farewell—Eds.]

Ernest J. Wilson III in 1970

ERNEST J. WILSON III

Ernest James Wilson III was born on 3 May 1948 in Washington, D.C., where he attended the Capitol Page School. At Harvard he was business manager of the *Harvard Journal of Negro Affairs*, and edited its special issue on "The Black Press." A concentrator in government, he received his A.B. in 1970. Pursuing graduate studies in Berkeley at the University of California, he earned his M.A. in 1973 and Ph.D. in political science in 1978. For a time he served as legislative assistant to Congressman Charles Diggs Jr., and in 1974 was the first-prize winner in the first Du Bois Essay Awards established by *Black Scholar* magazine. A specialist in the oil market, he has traveled and lectured in Europe, Africa and Latin America, and been an energy consultant for the World Bank and the U.S. Departments of State and Interior. From 1977 to 1981 he was on the faculty of the University of Pennsylvania. Since then he has been a professor of political science at the University of Michigan, where he also became Director of the Center for Research on Economic Development in the fall of 1988.

The Reform of Tradition, the Tradition of Reform

Two influences, outside of the family, did the most to form my character. The first was the educational and religious enthusiasm at Howard University, Washington, D.C., where my father was professor of Latin, and where I lived on the campus from birth until I entered Harvard. The second great influence was the atmosphere of tolerance, justice, and truth at Harvard. Endeavoring not to swerve under the stress from the principles thus engendered, sometimes to the detriment of material and official advancement, has been the greatest satisfaction of my life.

This quotation from my grand-uncle, Harvard class of 1897, expresses at least two interesting elements relevant to this essay. First, it acknowledges the formative role that Harvard College can play in an individual's life. This is a traditional refrain in the writing of black and white college graduates—Harvard shaped their lives.

Seventy years later, the black student experience at Harvard College put a twist on this refrain. For in the mid to late 1960s we changed Harvard as Harvard changed us. In our own selective acceptance and rejection of the traditional Harvard experience, my fellow students and I challenged Harvard in unprecedented ways, and in the process we changed the scholarly structure of the University.

Some of us were also guided by the second element of Eugene Gregory's class report—his firm grounding in autonomous Afro-American values and the supports provided by an indigenous black institution—Howard University. These values of cultural autonomy and worth also informed our own time at Harvard College.

In my freshman year there was no Department of Afro-American Studies, no Du Bois Institute, no cultural center for black students. Racial issues were not high on the priority of the University administration. The subject of Afro-America was not widely treated in the traditional disciplines and departments. My freshman year there were few black students in leadership positions in major campus-wide organizations. In other words black campus life was not unlike what it had been in the 1930s when Ralph Bunche was a student, or, for that matter, when W.E.B. Du Bois was a student in the late 19th century. When Du Bois and others wrote of their lives at Harvard they usually described themselves as black refugees to fair Harvard. They came; they studied what the University offered; they left. Harvard in those years admitted the occasional black student, but it did not admit the study of black life and culture as an important and legitimate element of the curriculum. This was the Harvard I found in 1966. By the end of the 1960s, these conditions were to change.

I have elsewhere described the political and institutional history of Afro-American studies at Harvard [*Harvard Magazine*, Sept.-Oct. 1981]. Here, I want to indulge the personal side of that history and to indicate some of the personal motivations and values that led at least one undergraduate into student activism. In my own case these values include an assumption of the validity of Afro-American life and culture, and that their study was a high calling. With this came another family-instilled value—a strong belief that excellence in scholarship could, and should, be combined with intellectual activism. Third, I benefitted in my student days from a long familiarity with university life.

Through the decade of the 1960s dozens of white and black students participated in challenges to fair Harvard's traditional sense of itself and they pressed to make Harvard more open to the scholarly examination of gender and race. Many found common purpose to press for educational reform. They came from a variety of places and from different backgrounds. They were motivated by a variety of personal and political reasons.

In my freshman year (1966), I often sensed more than a whiff of condescension toward black students. Some whites acted as if we were a black tabula rasa ready to be filled with New England education and high culture. Others caricatured us as the carriers of the culture of James Brown; any interest in the written word, or in Beethoven, was somehow disappointing and inauthentic. Then in 1967 and 1968 the black rebellions in the cities and the upsurge in nationalism and activism among black students created conditions ripe for a black student movement at Harvard, as at other colleges and universities.

What we accepted and what we rejected during this highly politicized period reflected the personal history that each of us brought to the institution. Many black students eventually seized on similar political values, usually reformist and nationalist; all took different roads to get there. My own experience at Harvard certainly reflected my personal—and family—history. Some of the values and interests that I brought from home Harvard positively reinforced—intellectual curiosity, delight in a spirited and partisan argument, a breadth of experiences, social and political engagement. Some skills and outlooks I learned for the first time. However, other personal values Harvard denied—especially the validity and autonomy of Afro-American cultural life, and the importance of studying it. Nonetheless, I strengthened my commitment to these values as I struggled to give them a reality and meaning within the University. Indeed, struggling against the rejection of values that I took to be self-evident became an important part of my Cambridge education.

I grew up on the campus of Howard University in Washington, D.C., born in Freedman's Hospital, living in campus housing. Each day I walked through the center of the campus, past the clustered classroom buildings named for Frederick Douglass and Sojourner

Truth, and under the imposing if familiar presence of Founder's Library, to attend Lucretia Mott School, the segregated elementary school just catercornered from Freedman's on Fourth Street. My young world was well contained on the campus, and Howard University was home. I had a proprietary feel for the place, and as a child I felt it was (almost literally) my own and my home. My father worked in the new red brick administration building overlooking Benjamin Banneker School just across Georgia Avenue. My maternal great-grandfather was in Howard's first graduating class of five students and later taught there; my maternal grandfather taught Latin and English, and co-founded the Howard University Players, the first drama society. In the 1940s my father studied at Howard with E. Franklin Frazier, Alain Locke ['08], [William] Leo Hansberry [A.M. '32] and Rayford Logan [Ph.D. '36]. And into the 1960s, siblings and assorted cousins passed through its gates. University life for me was immediate and personal.

In that community, and around our warm and constantly crowded kitchen table, came professors and poets and students and friends (for example, poet-professor Sterling Brown [A.M. '23], my grandfather's student and friend, and my father's teacher and friend). Discussions were debates and all were engaged, enthusiastic and loud. My father led discussions that ranged from Negro spirituals to Nietzsche, and an important constant was the everpresent threat and fact of racial inequality in a racist society. That external threat, and the values of my extended family, meant that learning and scholarship were from the earliest days tied to social relevance. Howard University had a mission—to better the race through medicine, through law, through philosophy. It was to demonstrate too that black people could excel. Relevance did not mean any less excellence. On the contrary. Our best scholars devoted themselves to superior social and natural science, and to moral uplift.

If I felt proprietary about Howard University, and if it nourished in me a strongly critical sense of committed learning, I felt somewhat the same way about Harvard University. Not in an immediate sense, but as a place I was familiar with but hadn't yet visited. My maternal grandfather, T. Montgomery Gregory, was a member of the Harvard class of 1910, a friend of John Reed and Walter Lippmann, to whom he introduced me in 1966. He was active on the debating team and a lifelong loyal son of Harvard. His son [Thomas Montgomery Gregory, Jr.] was a member of the class of '44, and his older brother,

Eugene, was in the class of 1897.

It was assumed that after high school I would follow one part of the family tradition and become the fourth member of the family to go to Harvard. I would take with me a tradition of critical thinking, a predisposition to teach, a familiarity with university life, and an abiding belief in the importance of studying Afro-American life. All of this helped me, I now believe, in helping to bring Afro-American studies to Harvard.

As an underclassman at Harvard, I felt a mixture of sheer delight and naïve surprise. The former was promoted by the enormous wealth of things to do and learn in Cambridge—lectures, recitals, and plays, people to talk to and to listen to. The surprise (and several years later, as race relations deteriorated nationally, outrage) flowed from the invisibility of the things I took for granted at home—the disciplined and serious and sustained study of black culture, politics, and life.

Part of that struggle between 1966 and 1970 involved me and other undergraduates as negotiators with a not inconsiderable array of faculty, administrators, overseers and alumni. Those of us on the negotiating team (most notably Robert Hall ['69], now professor of history at University of Maryland, who also grew up on a college campus and had experiences similar to my own; Francesta Farmer ['71], President of Crossroads Africa; business executive Craig Watson ['72]; and Harlan Dalton ['69], on the Yale Law School faculty) drew up lists of those from whom we expected opposition, and support, and we visited each in turn to lobby and to discuss the merits of bringing Afro-American Studies to Harvard.

In retrospect, we had a lot of gall even to attempt such changes; we were just wet-behind-the-ears undergraduates. Part of the hubris came from our feeling that, at last, history was going our way. We knew that we were riding the crest of a wave. With Nina Simone singing that all of us were "young, gifted and black," we felt our newly assertive blackness was not just an extra burden, as it was for many of our predecessors, but also at times a decided social benefit. And after all, cities were literally burning over the question of black equality; and the real heroes of the black revolt, courageous black students in the Deep South, were engaged in far less genteel and more dangerous battles at Ol' Miss and Texas Southern. For us, pressing for Afro-American Studies in Cambridge seemed the least we could do. And the excitement of creating something new, scholarly and socially relevant was exhilarating.

Part of my own self-confidence came from my earlier experiences as a page in the U.S. Supreme Court between 1963 and my graduation from high school in 1966. During those three and a half years, I met senators and congressmen on a regular basis, lunched with Chief Justice Warren, met President Johnson and Vice President Humphrey, and got to know many in the Washington diplomatic community. Fortunately, some of these contacts were substantive and not merely ceremonial, and I gradually assumed that talking to one's elders, including putatively distinguished ones, was not in the least unusual.

Washington and the Page School were good preparation in other ways. While enjoying a successful high-school career in a student body that, like Capitol Hill as a whole in those days, was entirely dominated by southern whites, I was able to sustain my close friendships with friends in my northwest Washington neighborhood. Nor did being a page prevent me from joining the "Free DC" movement led by activist Marion Barry, or other progressive causes. I also developed life-long friends in Washington's diplomatic community. I relished the rich multicultural life of the city, and I was determined to continue that life in Cambridge. Thus, while I was very active in and head of several campus black-student organizations and publications, I also joined the *Harvard Lampoon*, wrote for the *Crimson*, ate at the Signet, was elected a Class Marshal and joined one of Harvard's final clubs [the Fly], well-known locally for its splendid spring garden parties.

All of this seems very neat and tidy in retrospect, and I suppose I view it as such today. But re-reading my diaries and journals from that period I can also see it in a different light. I recall feeling the demands and pulls from different directions by different communities. In the late 1960s bigoted nationalist students would taunt and insult other black students walking across the Yard with a white friend. I refused to be taunted, or a taunter. Nonetheless, the pressures to conform to narrow and preconceived notions of racial or social categories were intense. I and others resisted as best we could.

Harvard did not teach me these particular "balancing" skills, but it certainly sharpened them. Harvard reinforced my love of politics and of the intellectual life, and, however imperfectly, showed me that the intellectual life and the life of commitment can, with effort and imagination, be combined.

I left Harvard with the usual complement of new intellectual skills and classroom learning. I also learned valuable lessons about institutional change. Black students in this topsy-turvy time did succeed in expanding the realm of the possible and opening new possibilities for choice in the College and the University. We helped to legitimate and expand the study of Afro-American life at the University.

In retrospect, I also left Cambridge somewhat naïve about the resilience of big institutions and their ability to follow their own worn paths, and the manifold ways that institutions resist and thwart change. Inertia, racism, and unhealthy elitism proved harder to change than we as undergraduates realized. Forcing choices into seemingly choiceless conditions still does not guarantee that the choices made will be the most desirable ones. The imperfect and odd choices that all parties made in the early days of the Afro-American Studies Program and the Du Bois Institute at Harvard, including some that students made, are cases in point.

The Harvard I left in 1970 (and revisited in 1980 as a Fellow at the Kennedy School of Government) is different from the one I found in 1966. Now there is a niche in which interested black and white faculty and students can more easily find programs and materials on black life in America. They can also find an even more precious present than that which those of us in that time tried to leave behind— the institutional and intellectual legitimacy of studying black life without fear of being mocked or marginalized. That struggle is not yet completely won at Harvard or at other universities. It is, however, an important beginning that we bequeath to students and scholars who follow us. I am confident they will continue the tradition.

(1989)

UP FROM HARVARD

A Guide

for

BLACK GRADUATES

OG & CP

1969

Cover of 42-page career guide for Harvard blacks, prepared by black student Eric L. Jones '70 for the Office for Graduate and Career Plans in 1969.

EMORY J. WEST

Emory Junior West was born on 5 February 1950 and grew up in Miami, where he attended the Dorsey Junior High School and Miami Central High School. At Harvard he won two Hatch Prizes for his poetry, which appeared in the *Advocate* and the *Harvard Journal of Afro-American Affairs*. His ardent interest in the early history of blacks at Harvard yielded two exhibits in Widener Library and two articles in the *Harvard Bulletin* (November 1971; May 1972). In 1972 he received his A.B. in anthropology *cum laude*, and proceeded to an M.A. at Berkeley in 1973 and a certificate in health-care administration from George Washington University in 1977. For some years he was a research associate and later a project director in policy analysis for the National Urban League in Washington, D.C. He also held a fellowship at M.I.T., where he concerned himself with housing and community-development problems facing blacks.

Harvard and the Black Man, 1636-1850

The religious beliefs of the Puritans shaped the society of seventeenth-century New England and provided the initiative that founded many American institutions. Harvard College was one such institution. Slavery was another.

It was only two years from the founding of the College, in 1636, to the New England beginnings of the slave trade. The importation of a few slaves by Captain William Pierce in the Salem ship Desire, in December 1638, was a simple start; but the slave trade developed a system that brought great wealth and the necessary leisure for cultural and intellectual leadership to New England. The "peculiar institution" of slavery was not only accepted as custom. It also had legal sanction.

"In the Body of Liberties of 1741, Massachusetts gave slavery, as well as servitude, statutory recognition," writes the Black historian Lorenzo J. Greene in *The Negro in Colonial New England*. "The wealth and culture of Newport and Boston reflected to a great extent the 'golden harvest' reaped from the Negro traffic." Massachusetts, with Boston as its chief port, was the center of the slave trade in seventeenth-century New England. Harvard, a few miles upriver from Boston, was involved very early in slavery.

Many of the prominent families of Boston had one or two slaves as servants and handymen. Increase Mather, Puritan minister, statesman, and President of Harvard (1685-1701), was a slave-master. Greene notes that "prominent persons of good standing like Benjamin Wadsworth, President of Harvard College [1725-1737] might even be permitted to pay the first installment a month or so after the slave was delivered." Slavery was a primary supportive factor in the development of Boston's elite.

Harvard reaped its share of the "golden harvest" early, in the direct form of labor provided to the College, and the indirect form of financial support from Massachusetts residents and English merchants. The first record of the presence of a Black man at Harvard . . . appears in the *Confession of Mistress Eaton*, written in 1639: "For the Moor his lying in Sam. Hough's sheet and pillow-bier, it hath a truth in it: he did so one time, and it gave Sam. Hough just cause of offence." Samuel F. Batchelder, in *Bits of Harvard History* (1924), poses some important questions—in an offensive manner—about this passage:

What ebony face with rolling white eyeballs grins sheepishly at us from this mildewed page? Who was this blackamoor who surreptitiously helped himself to beer and (possibly under its influence) made so free of little Sam Hough's bed? Have we not here the first darkey "scout" of Harvard, progenitor of the whole tribe of college coons and great-grandfather of all Memorial Hall waiters? What fluky breeze of fortune wafted this dusky child of nature from a languorous coral strand to the grim confines of Calvinistic Cambridge? Were colored brethren already hanging round the Square looking for odd jobs ere that classic forum had become clearly distinguishable from the encircling wilderness? And if the Moor slept in Sam Hough's pillow-bier, then by the shade of Othello (who used a pillow for quite a different purpose), where did Sam sleep? We must fill in the picture for ourselves. History in its surviving fragments offers us no further aid, and tradition, still so young as to be inarticulate, avails us no whit.

In answer to Batchelder's questions, we can say that the "fluky breeze" was the slave trade, and that this Black man may have been the first to serve in a labor force that would be vital to the maintenance of Harvard College.

In accord with its Puritan beginnings, the Harvard of the seventeenth and eighteenth centuries probably felt that the cleaning of its halls was a fitting occupation for a Black man. But it was not receptive to the idea of any Black man walking those halls as a student. Writes Lorenzo J. Greene,

According to the racial philosophy of the Puritans, Negroes and Indians were an inferior race whom God had given them as part of their inheritance. Not only was the Negro regarded as a sub-species, but as late as 1773 a member of the graduating class of Harvard University, debating the legality of enslaving the Africans, justified the institution partly on the ground that the Negro was a "conglomerate of child, idiot, and madman."

The customs of New Englanders operated to keep Blacks in their place, and to prevent them from attaining freedom of thought and association—two important prerequisites of higher education. Greene points out that the power of custom was effectively invoked by the Reverend Gurdon Saltonstall, A.B. 1684, an ancestor in the longest continuous lineage of Harvard graduates:

Saltonstall successfully convinced the court that despite Abda's white blood, the child had the same status as the mother. Although Saltonstall admitted that there was no law specifically providing for the enslavement of mulattoes, he added that the custom of enslaving them had the same force as law. This case was extremely important because it set a legal precedent for holding mulattoes in bondage.

Such paternalism toward Blacks was shared (and fostered by) many benefactors and graduates of Harvard College; they in turn exercised great influence on the thought of colonial New England. There was always fear among whites that the Blacks might violently resist their enslavers. Rulings in 1656 and 1693 prevented Blacks from receiving military training in Massachusetts; the second included Blacks and Indians in a privileged class with "members of the Council, the representatives . . . secretary, justice of the peace, President, fellow students and servants of Harvard College," who were excused from military training. This may have been a privilege for the others, but it was not intended as such for the Blacks.

There was an increasing effort to pacify feelings of resentment and rebellion, by indoctrinating the Black man to accept his condition of slavery. "During the period between 1730 and the Revolution, many Negroes were baptized and accepted into the churches of their masters," writes Greene. "Since colonial New England was over-whelmingly Congregationalist, a majority of the slaves became members in the churches of that denomination." Led by Cotton Mather, the Congregationalists made progress in converting slaves to Christianity, and the duty of the slave to love and obey his master. There were special classes for slaves, and they were allowed to sit in the gallery of the church on Sunday (seating was arranged according to social status, and the gallery was the lowest position). "Even in the galleries Negroes were not always tolerated," notes Greene. "The Corporation of Harvard College objected to their sitting in the gallery of the First Parish Church at Cambridge in 1756."

Yet slaves in New England demonstrated their ability in many ways. They showed business acumen in trading, and managing the businesses of their enslavers. Some used their knowledge of roots and herbs, and became medical practitioners; others served as apprentices to physicians. As pressmen, Blacks aided in printing some of the first newspapers in New England. Literary talent found expression in the stories and poetry of Lucy Terry, slave of Ensign Ebenezer Wells of Deerfield. Phillis Wheatley's poetry was widely acclaimed in New England and London (one of her poems is addressed to the students of Harvard College). [See p. 10.] Such achievements contradicted the generally held assumption that Blacks, by nature, were intellectually inferior to whites. As an educational institution, Harvard seems to have shared in these assumptions, a posture that now appears as irrational, racist, and defensive.

Whites were willing to use the services of Black men, but not to offer them the educational, political, and social opportunities available to others in the society. When the Revolutionary War began, free Blacks joined ranks with white men in Cambridge. Congress approved the arrangement, but attempted to restrict the practice. The Revolu-tion was a battle for freedom and self-determination, yet while some Blacks were freed as compensation for their services in war, they were still denied self-determination.

In spite of the lowly positions reserved for them, free Blacks achieved distinction and some success. At Harvard, they took advantage of openings that followed the Revolution, and influenced the institution significantly. But although Blacks provided valued services, proved capable of scholastic achievement, and demonstrated loyalty to Harvard, its educational doors remained closed to them. Hereditary distinctions among students had been abolished in admissions requirements in 1773; but the power of custom remained operative, and hereditary distinctions were still made between Black and white.

For nearly a century after the Revolution, Black men served Harvard students as "scouts." Every elite student had one, until the system was superseded by regular janitorial service in 1879. One scout, Charles Lenox, began by selling pies and cakes; he was a conscientious man who served the College by making loans to students and professors. William Emmons, who peddled pickles and a drink called egg pop, was renowned for his eloquence.[1] He printed some of his addresses on standard topics, and sold them alongside his pop and pickles. A Black man named Lewis sold home-brewed beer of two varieties, spruce and ginger. Which was spruce and which was ginger was a common topic of debate, wrote James Russell Lowell in his *Fireside Travels: Cambridge Thirty Years Ago.* Lewis seemed to be the only one who could discern, but he coaxed his customers into purchasing with gratifying courtesy.

Around the beginning of the nineteenth century, Black men had begun taking more initiative to free themselves from white domination. In New England, these endeavors were most evident in Boston, which had the largest population of Blacks. In *The Education of the Negro Prior to 1861* the Black historian Carter G. Woodson, Ph.D. '12, surveys some of these efforts:

In 1798 a separate school for colored children, under the charge of Elisha Sylvester, a white man, was established in that city in the house of Primus Hall, a Negro of very good standing. Two years later sixty-six free blacks of that city petitioned the school, but the citizens in a special town meeting called to consider the question refused to grant this request. Undaunted by this refusal, the patrons of the special school established in the house of

---

[1] When a mock honorary degree was conferred on Emmons by the Med. Fac., an undergraduate burlesque of a learned society, the citation read: Guglielmus Emmons, Praenominatus Pickleius, Qui Orator Eloquentissimus Nostrae Aetatis, Poma, Nuces, Panem-Zingiberis [gingerbread], Suas Orationes, Egg-Popque Vendit. D.M. Med. Fac. Honorarius.

Primus Hall, employed Brown and [Williams] of Harvard College as instructors, until 1806.

The school was moved to the recently completed African Meeting House on Belknap Street in 1806 and remained there until 1835, when a school building was erected with funds contributed by Abiel Smith. A Black man named Prince Saunders, former diplomatic official of Emperor Christophe of Haiti, was brought to Boston by Professor William Ellery Channing of Harvard, and became instructor of the school in 1809. John B. Russwurm [an 1826 Black graduate of Bowdoin] was also an instructor for a time.

Black men established successful businesses—barber shops, clothing shops, gymnasiums. In 1831, at a convention in Philadelphia, plans were made to establish a College for Colored Youth in New Haven. This brought intense opposition from the Mayor, Common Council, and Yale College, and suggestions from Boston that the college be located there. The city's merchants saw benefits from proposed commercial dealings with the West Indies, and the Massachusetts Colonization Society saw an opportunity to help the recently founded Colony of Liberia. The people of Boston seemed amiable, but they had self-interest at heart. There is no indication that they genuinely intended to extend liberty and justice to Blacks. One objection to having the college in New Haven had been incipient rivalry between Blacks and white youth at Yale. The sort of reaction Blacks might have expected from Harvard students is suggested by this excerpt from the diary *Charleston Goes to Harvard*, written on June 13, 1831:

. . . After retiring to my room, about 10 o'clock the sound of distant music broke upon my ear. It was the New York black band, returning from Fresh Pond, where, I understood, they had been spending the afternoon. They were persuaded to come into the College yard, and after playing "the coal-black Rose," and some other tunes of the same cast, much to our edification, and having collected a hat full of cents, they wheeled about and marched out again. It was amusing, or rather ridiculous, to see these "niggers," tall and short, blowing away with their thick lips as if their lives depended upon the force with which they produced the sounds. A black band is no new thing to me, who was accustomed to see nothing but black bands in Charleston.

The diarist's amusement obscures the fact that he was writing in a time of mounting turbulence. In [1829], a free Black named David Walker had appealed to Black men to arm themselves and throw off their oppressors. This helped fuel the Black movement for self-determination. In 1831, William Lloyd Garrison started his abolitionist newspaper, *The Liberator*, which was to arouse public opinion through-out the nation. Reaction followed quickly. There were demands that Walker be murdered, and *The Liberator* banned. The situation was serious and tragic.

In Freedom's Birthplace, by John Daniels, reveals how Boston's mayor, Josiah Quincy, replied to these demands:

. . . as a result of his inquiries he found the paper had only an "insignificant countenance and support" in the community, and that it "had not made, nor was likely to make converts among the respectable classes." He said he had "ferreted out the paper and its editor, that his office was an obscure hole, his only visible auxiliary a Negro boy and his supporters a very few insignificant persons of all colors."

Quincy became President of Harvard in 1829. "He was one of the first . . . among northern men to denounce the slave-holding interest as a rising and dangerous tyranny" (Bush: *The Harvard Presidency*). The anti-slavery movement that Quincy had deemed insignificant as mayor was to grow and cause conflict at Harvard.

An early manifestation involved the Reverend Henry Ware, A.B. 1812, a Divinity School professor who founded an anti-slavery society. The Boston press demanded that he be fired; students ridiculed him and pelted him with nuts. Ware was considered damaging to the University, but Quincy, espousing academic freedom, refused to fire him.

Near the end of Quincy's presidency, the case of Beverly Williams promised to force the issue of educational access to Harvard for Blacks. In a letter to Quincy written August 16, 1844, W. A. Stearns, chairman of the School Committee of Harvard College, discussed the overabundance of applicants to Hopkins Classical School (founded primarily to prepare boys for Harvard). One of the applicants was Beverly Williams, "a ward of the Reverend Mr. Parker's in Cambridge Port. Williams is a colored boy, but a bright scholar and of unexceptionable character." Williams was accepted at Hopkins and might have entered Harvard with the Class of 1851, but he died of consumption on July 17, 1847.

There is no way of knowing whether Williams would have been accepted at Harvard. His attendance at Hopkins was an anomaly, and it would have been so at Harvard. On April 4, 1847, Mr. J. Cowles of Georgia had written Edward Everett, then President of the College, inquiring about the possibility of Williams being admitted. Cowles was perturbed: his son would be entering in the same class, he said, and he was considering sending two more sons within another year. On April 13, Everett wrote Cowles that it was uncertain whether Williams's friends intended to offer him for admission, but that he would certainly be fitted to attend—whereas Cowles' son Henry was so academically deficient that he could not be admitted under any conditions.

Everett's reply probably reflected his convictions about Africans' capacity for intellectual achievement, as well as his regard for the principle of academic freedom, so staunchly supported by Quincy in the Ware case. Everett favored returning Blacks to Africa, but in a speech delivered in 1853 to the American Colonization Society, he spoke highly of Blacks' potential for intellectual attainment. As examples, he cited Paul Cuffe, the first Black separatist, and Beverly Williams.

In 1848, members of the U.S. House of Representatives had heard another testimonial to Williams's excellence of character and scholarship. John Gorham Palfrey—proponent of the New England conscience, former Dean of the Harvard Divinity School, editor and statesman—had astounded the House by speaking of Williams as a "charming boy" who had attended classes with his son and was fit to continue on to Harvard. Palfrey offended the sensibilities of the Congress by applauding too graciously the moral and intellectual qualities of Williams. Andrew Johnson, who was to become President after Lincoln's assassination, checked Palfrey by appealing to the white man's ultimate logic: "Would the gentleman from Massachusetts be willing to see that interesting, talented, charming Negro boy become the married companion of his own daughter?" The next day, Johnson assured Palfrey that he had intended no offense, but wanted to establish that men of honor, discrimination, and high morality would accept a gifted Negro like Beverly Williams in theory, but not entirely in practice.

When Black students were finally permitted at Harvard, it was not at the College but at the Medical School. Three Black men were there for a few months in 1850-51, and one may have been there earlier. Not until 1865 did the College open its doors to a Black.

For the most part, students, professors, and administrators were guilty of supporting or tolerating the degradation of African peoples.

Harvard, after all, was an elite institution in a society that generally condoned human bondage for political, economic, and social reasons. The rationale that slavery was justified by the natural inferiority of Africans to Anglo-Saxons—prevalent since the beginning—seems to have remained an accepted position at the Harvard of the 1840s and 50s.

Harvard Bulletin (1971)

[See also Emory J. West, "Harvard's First Black Graduates: 1865-1890," *Harvard Bulletin* 74 (May 1972): 24-28.—Eds.]

Andrea Lee in 1984

ANDREA LEE

Andrea Nancy Lee was born in Philadelphia on 27 April 1953, and prepared for college at the Baldwin School for Girls in nearby Bryn Mawr. Majoring in English, she was graduated *magna cum laude* from Radcliffe College in 1974 and received an A.M. there in Comparative Literature in 1978. A writer for the *New Yorker*, she is best known for her report *Russian Journal* (1981), which won the Jean Stein Award from the American Academy and Institute of Arts and Letters; and for her novel *Sarah Phillips* (1984), from which the chapter "Fine Points" is here reprinted. Andrea Lee has for some time lived in Italy, and is currently writing another novel.

Fine Points

One great thing about Margaret was that she wore exactly the same size clothing that I did, an excellent quality in a roommate; she had, however, completely different taste, with an inclination toward plunging necklines, crimson tights, and minidresses in big, bold Scandinavian prints. My own wardrobe ran to jeans and black turtle-necks, odd little somber-colored tunics that I felt made me look like a wood nymph, and short pleated skirts that seemed to me to convey a sexy *jeune fille* air worthy of Claudine at school. "You literary types are always trying to look understated," Margaret would say whenever she saw me dressed for a seminar, for an *Advocate* meeting, or for a date. She was a chemistry major from Wellesley, Massachusetts, an avid lacrosse player with a terrific figure and a pair of unabashed blue eyes that revealed a forceful, stubborn nature—Margaret could keep an argument going for days. She adored fresh air and loathed reticence and ambiguity, and she had little patience with a roommate who, languid from lack of exercise, spent weeks reworking a four-word line of poetry.

"It's a question of fine points," I would retort loftily, though I had only a vague idea of what that might mean.

Margaret and I got along well for young women with such different souls. We spent a lot of time together in our cramped dormitory suite, squabbling comfortably over clothes and discussing romance—the one subject on which we were, to some extent, in agreement. The suite was on the fourth floor of Currier House; it consisted of two tiny rooms, a bathroom we'd decorated for a giggle with pinups of the bustiest *Playboy* Playmates we could find, and a kitchenette filled with moldy oranges stolen from the cafeteria. Our windows faced east, toward the corner of Garden and Linnaean streets—a lovely view, really, with the Observatory woods, the flat-bottomed, whale-shaped clouds that came sailing down from Maine, and the tall, somber Cambridge houses back of the trees.

In the winter of 1973, our junior year at Harvard, on afternoons when Margaret was back from the lab and I was supposed to be at my desk reading Donne and Herbert for seminar or writing poetry for Professor Hawks's versification class, we would hang out in Margaret's room and drink oolong tea, which Margaret brewed so black it became a kind of solvent. Lounging on Margaret's bed, below a periodic table she'd tacked up on the wall, we'd complain at length about our boyfriends. These young men, a couple of blameless seniors from Adams and Dunster Houses, were certainly ardent and attentive, but they bored us because they seemed appropriate. We yearned, in concert, to replace them with unsuitable men—an array of Gothic-novel types who didn't seem at all hackneyed to Margaret and me. (Margaret, the scientist, had in fact a positively Brontëesque conception of the ideal man.) We envisioned liaisons with millionaires the age of our fathers, with alcoholic journalists, with moody filmmakers addicted to uppers; Margaret's particular thing was depraved European nobility. A few years earlier it might have been possible for me to find the necessary thrill simply in going out with white boys, the forbidden fruit of my mother's generation; but in the arty circles I frequented at Harvard, such pairings were just about required, if one was to cut any dash at all.

What our fantasies boiled down to was that Margaret and I, in the age-old female student tradition, ended up angling for members of the faculty.

"It's just a question of days before Dr. Bellemere tumbles," said Margaret one afternoon. (She flirted shamelessly with her adviser, but for some reason could not bring herself to call him by his first name— Don.) "And *then*, what naughty delights!"

As a matter of fact, I was the one who first was offered the chance to taste those delights. In February a genuine instructor —Geoffrey Knacker, who had taught my seminar on metaphysical poetry the previous semester, and who shared an apartment in Central Square with Millicent Tunney, another junior faculty member—asked me to meet him for a cup of coffee. Margaret sat cross-legged on my bed while I got dressed for the date—we were to meet at six at the Café Pamplona—and grew snappish when I refused the loan of a pair of red tights. She told me that if I hid my light under a bushel, I wouldn't even get him to kiss me. I didn't listen to her. I was busy making myself look as beautiful and mysterious as I could, and when I had slicked my hair back into a bun, rimmed my eyes with dark pencil, and put on a severe gray dress with a pair of black high heels I had bought in a thrift shop, even Margaret had to applaud the result.

"If Hopalong calls, tell him I'm riding in the Tour de France," I said. Hopalong Cassidy was the name we had privately given my boyfriend, who had what I thought was an unnecessarily jaunty gait.

"You're a cold, hard thing," said Margaret in an approving tone.

I owned a rather rubbed-looking sealskin jacket that had belonged to my mother; when I had wrapped it around me, waved goodbye to the girl who stood studying behind the bells desk of the dormitory, and stepped outside into the February twilight, I had an agreeable feeling of satisfaction about the way I looked, and an agitated romantic feeling about the meeting to come. "Perhaps I'm in love," I thought, though in fact I could barely remember what Geoffrey Knacker looked like.

It was ten minutes to six. I walked down Garden Street toward Cambridge Common, listening to the unaccustomed click of my high heels on the brick sidewalk, slippery with melted snow and patches of dirty ice. In the darkness around me, students riding bicycles or walking with book bags were returning to dinner from classes in Harvard Yard. The sky over the dark buildings and narrow streets was a deep lustrous blue, streaked at the edges with pinkish light, and the air was cold and damp. Near Follen Street a small battered

Datsun was trying unsuccessfully to park between a jacked-up Riviera and a Volvo plastered with psychedelic stickers. The sound of grinding gears made me think of the time during my sophomore year when a precursor of my boyfriend Hopalong had gotten very stoned at the Dartmouth game and had pursued me along Garden Street by backing up his car for a whole block, all the while declaiming the words from the Temptations' song "My Girl." The incident had infuriated me at the time, but now I thought of it as something gay and romantic, the sort of thing that happened constantly to a woman destined to exercise a fatal influence upon men.

My feeling of agitation increased as I approached the Common. The usual shouts and guffaws were coming from the war monument in the middle, where Cambridge townies liked to hang around smoking dope and drinking wine, but they seemed far away. I looked through the rows of leafless maples at the university towers and traffic lights clustering ahead of me, and felt an unreasonable, blissful happiness to be walking in high heels and a fur coat on a clear evening to a meeting with a man who was likely to mean trouble—the kind of trouble that mothers and magazine articles particularly warned against. I felt a bit like Anna Karenina, burning with a sinful glow; and as if someone beside me in the darkness had spoken a few passionate, muted words, it seemed to me that I was ravishingly beautiful. I began to pretend that someone *was* walking with me: a lover who didn't resemble my boyfriend, or even Geoffrey Knacker. This imaginary lover, in fact, didn't have much of any appearance at all, only a compelling simplicity of character that granted every dangerous wish I had ever had. As I walked through the Common, giving a wide berth to the monument, where two long-haired girls were giggling beside a guy who looked like Jimi Hendrix, I crooked my fingers very slightly inside the pocket of my fur jacket, as if I were holding hands with someone. And then I did something I never afterward admitted to anyone, not even Margaret: I recited a poem to my invisible companion—Donne's "The Flea."

By the time I got to the Pamplona, I had almost forgotten Geoffrey Knacker, who rose from his tiny table to greet me, with an air of being slightly startled by my appearance. He was a tall, thin man with a mournful, rather handsome face and gray halfmoons of skin under his eyes; in the white-tiled, low-ceilinged interior of the Pamplona, surrounded by graduate students chatting over cappuccino, he appeared curiously yellowish and misanthropic, as if he'd lived most

of his life in a remote tropical outpost. He helped me with my coat
and I ordered an ice cream. Then the two of us began to talk, rather
constrainedly, about metaphysical poetry until Geoffrey began paying
me heavy-handed compliments.

"I always felt that behind your reserved manner in class was a rare
sensitivity of nature," he said, giving me a slow, gloomy smile, and I,
who had been attracted by just that smile in the seminar, found myself
filled not with rapture but with an inexplicable annoyance. It
occurred to me that this meeting was just like a coffee date with any
callow comp lit major, who would begin by throwing out portentous
hints about his ideal woman and end, ritually, by suggesting we drop
mescaline and swim nude in the Adams House pool. I tried to think
of the romantic fact that Geoffrey Knacker was an instructor, and that
both of us were flouting lovers in order to meet, but all I could seem
to feel was irritation at a flat, straw-colored mole that Geoffrey had
where his jaw met his neck, and at the way that as he talked, he
joined the tips of his fingers together and pumped them in and out in
a tiny bellowslike motion. We were sitting at an inconspicuous table
in a corner, but it seemed to me, in my hypersensitive state, that all
the other students in the Pamplona could see the mole and the
working fingertips, and were laughing discreetly at them.

As I rattled my spoon in my ice-cream dish, some demon prompted me to say, "But certainly you must have seen hundreds of
exceptional students in all your years as a teacher." "Hundreds?"
repeated Geoffrey Knacker in an injured tone. "Why, no. I finished
my dissertation three years ago. I am only thirty-one."

We didn't really have much to say to each other. It was clear, in
fact, that our initial attraction had become puzzling and abortive, and
that this meeting was one of those muted social disasters that can be
devastating if one cares. I didn't care much; nor, it seemed, did
Geoffrey Knacker. We shook hands and parted outside the Pamplona
without even the polite device of mentioning plans to get in touch.
When he zipped up his jacket and, with one last unhappy smile,
trudged off in his L.L. Bean boots toward Central Square, I clicked off
back to Radcliffe in my high heels, feeling positively elated. Geoffrey
Knacker, I decided, was a bore, but the *fact* of Geoffrey Knacker was
exciting. As I came into Harvard Square and threaded my way
through the slush and evening traffic on Massachusetts Avenue, the
romantic sensation I'd had while walking through the Common
returned to me in full force. I seemed, agreeably, to be taking up the

strands of an interrupted idyll, and in my right palm, deep in the pocket of the fur jacket, was the pleasant tickling feeling that denoted the grasp of my imaginary lover.

When I got back to the suite, Margaret was working on a problem sheet for Chem 105, and her boyfriend—a young man with such an earnest, childlike gaze that we'd nicknamed him Christopher Robin —was seated cross-legged on her bed, using a metal mesh contraption to sift seeds and stems out of an ounce of grass he'd just bought. (One of Margaret's complaints about him was his methodical attitude toward sex and drugs.) "Oo-la-la—very thirties," said Christopher Robin, giving my outfit the old once-over, and then Margaret dragged me into the bathroom.

"Well, what happened?" she demanded, locking the door, turning on both faucets, and settling herself on the sink counter under the enormous bosom of one of the Playmates we'd pinned up. "He must have kissed you—or did you fall into bed together? You're absolutely beaming."

"Knacker was actually kind of a fizzle," I said. "But it was fun anyway."

"Idiot child," said Margaret. "Take off that coat—you've wasted it. I knew you should have worn red stockings."

When I tried to explain myself, she leaned back against the bathroom mirror, closed her eyes, and giggled so that the frame of the mirror shook. "My artistic roommate," she said. "The woman of epiphanies. You're going to kill me with your fine points."

A few weeks later Margaret was dancing to a Stones tape at a party in a converted airplane factory up near MIT when she ran into her adviser, Dr. Bellemere, whom she at last succeeded in calling Don. Bellemere, who was a post-doc a bit older than Geoffrey Knacker, and who fluttered hearts all through the chem labs with his leather vest and Buffalo Bill mustache, had had a lot of the punch, which was a Techie grape-juice concoction laced with acid. He led Margaret out of the strobe lights into a dark corner of the loft, kissed her passionately, and told her he spent every lab session thinking about her legs. A triumph for Margaret—except that she inexplicably discovered a preference for Christopher Robin, and so the thing with Bellemere went no further, except for a bit of embarrassment in lab.

"But there was something really solid there—a kiss, not just daydreams," Margaret told me pointedly when we discussed it later. For a change, we were sitting among the scattered books and papers of my room while I packed my book bag to go down and visit Hopalong at Adams House.

"I don't think the two situations were so different," I said. "I'm afraid, sweetheart, that whatever we try to do, in our two different ways, we end up being just a couple of nice girls."

"Oh, I hope not!" said Margaret, flopping backward on the bed. "But anyway," she went on stubbornly after a minute, "a real kiss is better than an imaginary one."

And she thumped her booted feet on my bedspread for emphasis.

I wanted to contradict her, but then I remembered how bullheaded and tenacious Margaret could be in an argument, how tiresomely withholding of her oolong tea and the little English butter biscuits that her mother sent her, and that I loved. In the end I just raised my eyebrows with the air of one to whom has been granted higher knowledge, and kept my mouth shut.

From *Sarah Phillips* (1984)

LEIGH JACKSON

Leigh Alexandra Jackson was born on 29 October 1960 in Washington, D.C., where she prepared for college at the Sidwell Friends School. At Radcliffe she concentrated in philosophy and received her degree in 1982. For a while she worked in New York City for the Columbia University Press and for an advertising firm, and later took graduate courses at Stanford University. Returning to Washington, she served from 1986 to 1988 as assistant editor and book editor of the fledgling *American Visions*, a magazine of Afro-American culture. In the summer of 1988 she began writing for the *Washington Post*, moving in 1990 to the *Philadelphia Daily News*.

Your Poet Is on Television

I had long wanted to meet her. When I was in high school, I devoured her poems. They were exuberant, odd, written only as a true nose-thumber would write them. The words she chose were phonetic and sassy parodies of grammatical propriety: wuz for was; cuz for because; i for I.

Interest became an obsession. I clipped articles and interviews and bits of poems, pressing the papers between the pages of a book, like a prom corsage. I copied her phrases and outrageous spelling into my notebook with meticulous reverence and a favorite pen. I memorized all the words to the Smokey Robinson songs she quoted so lovingly.

And I wondered at her pictures. There were few blacks like her in the demurely privileged Washington, D.C. neighborhood where I grew up. The sons and daughters of first-generation comfort, we shunned flamboyance and controversy. We learned to hold onto our privileges as our parents had gained them: cautiously, quietly, carefully.

But there she was. Photographers snapped her onstage in

rainbow-colored outfits or reading before throngs of open-mouthed admirers. Her hair flowed as freely as her syntax. It curled around her brown face in thick, coppery dreads, and a brass nose-ring sparkled amid her freckles.

There were the stories about her that I loved. The rumors of weekend Concorde flights to Paris. Of witheringly smart debates with retrograde men, unapologetic and suspicious men whose criticisms I couldn't quite understand.

She was the writer I hoped to be, and I took this fascination with me to Harvard, packed it up with my clock radio and prep-school yearbook, with my dog-eared copy of Jean Toomer's *Cane* and my French primer, with my Temptations albums and my violin.

Like many of my black classmates, I groped for a sturdy but pliable sense of my blackness, one that would accommodate both a general history of oppression and our specific cases of Harvard-fed opportunity. It wasn't easy.

We shared hardworking parents, many of whom even attended the same black colleges and segregated high schools; we shared connections to southern towns—spiritual hometowns—from which parents or grandparents came; we shared favorite singing groups, dishes that cropped up on family dinner tables; and we shared our Harvard education.

Who knew what this new mixture, this recombinant history would mean? Who knew what the creature that embodied these seemingly contradictory experiences would look like?

We didn't, and we searched each others' faces nervously for signs of that perfect embodiment of Harvard and black. And we searched our own mirrors for flaws, imbalances in the Harvard/black equation. But there was no paradigm, no one example. Black came in such rich varieties at Harvard. There was the swan-necked dancer, the smooth-talking Chicago outrage, the quietly ambitious pre-med, the sweetly pious Mississippian. There was the Detroit actor with his red painter's pants, the charming Republican, the soft midwestern architecture student who nodded off during meals, like a dormouse. Together, we defied history and yet challenged each other to meet its standards of blackness. We teased each other about dancing prowess and diction, grades of hair and choices of girlfriends.

No, it wasn't easy. Few could disentangle this particular angst from the knotty anxieties that seemed to plague all students: Am I smart enough? Am I disciplined enough? What do I want to do with my life?

Throughout that first year, I clung to my poet, wore her defiant words like an amulet.

When I heard she was coming to read at a nearby school, I summoned the courage to approach the professor who invited her. "Well, why don't you come to dinner with us?" he asked. I decided I would write about her for the newspaper, do for her, I hoped, what she had done for me: animate some quivering, nascent emotions; awe.

The night I was to meet her, I dressed up in my tweed skirt and loafers and met her at the downtown hotel. She was splendidly draped in a spotted leopard blouse, bright turquoise cowboy boots and feather earrings that brushed her cheeks.

She was beautiful but strangely quiet. We struggled through dinner; I, counting the greenbeans on my plate and she, jingling her bracelets with every emphatic shake of her hand.

Dinner swallowed but not tasted, I followed her to the university dining hall where she was to read. Students, perched on couches and crumpled on the floor, straightened their spines as she began to read. Her hand balled into a fist that swung before her like a pendulum, she beat out the meter of her verse. She spoke softly but fiercely. The audience gasped quietly after each poem.

When she finished, the professor led her to a sofa where she could receive her admirers. I crept up to her. "Could we sit together for a few minutes to talk?"

"What do you mean, talk?" she shouted. "You had your chance." Her bracelets jingled on her arm as she waved her finger at me. The room fell silent—except for the tinny sound of those bangles. My face felt hot and sweaty. I backed away from her, into the snack table, into the students clustered around the celery sticks and port salut cheese.

"Excuse me," I mumbled and fled, back to my dorm room, back to Harvard.

My roommate, a sloe-eyed pre-law student from Tennessee, greeted me. She had filled our room with the blue haze of a pressing comb, the biting smell of slightly seared flesh. I coughed.

"Your poet is on television," she said. She paused, as though to say something, and then returned to her hair.

I turned to the TV. There was my poet, talking and gesturing with a familiar energy. The colors of those exotic, wonderful clothes were gone, turned black and white by the picture. I couldn't make out what she was discussing, but I turned the set off.

(1988)

Christopher Edley in 1991

Derrick Bell in 1971

THE GREENBERG-CHAMBERS INCIDENT
HARVARD LAW SCHOOL, 1982-83

Third World Coalition Letter

May 24, 1982

To the Harvard Law School Community:

The Third World Coalition of Harvard Law School feels strongly that the course created and taught by former Harvard Law School professor Derrick Bell, Constitutional Law and Minority Issues, should continue to be instructed by a Third World professor. This course is concerned with the legal system and Third World people in the United States and, therefore, it is extremely important that it be taught by an instructor who can identify and empathize with the social, cultural, economic, and political experiences of the Third World community.

The Law School community would greatly benefit if Third World professors were brought to the School. Third World instructors would bring much needed diversity to the faculty, as well as improve and further the Law School's academic and scholarly pursuits. The lack of Third World professors at Harvard Law School is not due to a vacuum of qualified Third World legal professionals, but rather to the institution's inadequate search methods and the biased criteria it uses to judge prospective Third World faculty candidates. There are many Third World lawyers, judges, and professors who possess the academic skills and talent to teach at Harvard Law School.

The Third World Coalition will urge the members of its constituent organizations to boycott Constitutional Law and Minority Issues for the following reasons: (1) the extremely low number of Third World professors at the Law School, (2) the appropriateness of a Third World instructor to teach the Constitutional Law and Minority Issues course, (3) the availability of qualified Third World legal professionals to teach this course in particular and teach at the Law School in general, and (4) the inadequate efforts of Harvard Law School to find these professionals and the biased criteria it uses to judge prospective Third World faculty candidates.

The lack of a Third World professor to teach Constitutional Law and Minority Issues is a manifestation of the larger problem of Third World appointments to the Harvard Law School faculty. In fact, the entire appointments problem is part of a larger affirmative action problem that exists at Harvard Law School. The Law School also has significant affirmative action problems in admissions and the hiring of Third World administrators. These affirmative action problems can only be solved if the institution is willing to change some of its structure and procedures. An excellent way to begin addressing these problems would be with the affirmative action proposals which the Third World Coalition has already introduced to Dean [James] Vorenberg and various faculty members.

The frustrations of Third World students with affirmative action problems at the Law School is at its highest level since any of us in the Third World Coalition have been here. A forum must be provided where faculty, administrators, and students can come together and reasonably discuss solutions to the problem. If such a forum is not provided, we fear that frustrations and antagonisms will only increase.

The Third World Coaliton

James Vorenberg Letter

Office of the Dean
Harvard Law School
Cambridge, MA

July 21, 1982

Dear Second and Third Year Students:

You have received today a set of materials from the School that included a new two-hour course on Racial Discrimination and Civil Rights taught by Julius Chambers and Jack Greenberg. A course description and biographical notes on the instructors are attached. This course has been added since Preliminary Registration. There is some further information relating to the course that I feel you should know.

Late in the spring the Executive Committee of the Black Law Students Association and the Third World Coalition decided to recommend a boycott of the course. I enclose the letter from Muhammad Kenyatta, BLSA's President, to Julius Chambers and the Coalition's statement setting forth their respective reasons for the boycott. I also enclose letters from Messrs. Chambers and Greenberg responding to Mr. Kenyatta's letter.

I fully understand and support the desire to increase the number of minority teachers at the School. The faculty is committed to this goal and is actively pursuing it. I am very pleased that since the end of classes a black lawyer has accepted, effective next summer, the School's offer of an assistant professorship, and I am hopeful that our offer to another black lawyer will be accepted. We will continue these efforts, and I hope and expect that BLSA and the Coalition will continue to press for progress.

However, I believe that to boycott a course on racial discrimination, because part of it is taught by a white lawyer, is wrong in principle and works against, not for, shared goals of racial and social justice. To boycott a course about fighting discrimination, because there are not more minority teachers at the School, seems inconsistent with the purpose sought. And I believe the suggestion in the BLSA letter that Mr. Greenberg's views and his continuing as Director of the NAACP Legal Defense Fund warrant an organized boycott aimed at keeping students from taking this course is inconsistent with important principles of academic freedom.

It is important to bear in mind who these two instructors are. Both men—one black and one white—have devoted their working lives to using the legal system to fight for the rights of black people. We are very pleased that we have arranged to have them teach at Harvard, because we believe there are many students who will welcome the opportunity to use the Winter Term to explore litigation strategy and skills with two of the nation's most experienced and effective civil rights litigators. They have also been successful law teachers.

I hope that between now and Registration in September each of you will read the attached materials carefully and will decide for yourself whether to take advantage of this opportunity.

I apologize for intruding on your summer, which I hope is going well for you.

Sincerely,

James Vorenberg
Dean

Black and White at Harvard

MUHAMMAD KENYATTA

Regarding the appointment of Jack Greenberg to teach minority
issues at Harvard, we are not protesting Greenberg's race [Aug. 23].
Black students and others are lobbying for desegregation of the
virtually all-white faculty at Harvard Law. At issue is the rectitude of
affirmative action as a remedy for racially exclusive hiring patterns.
If Harvard and its defenders can convince the American people that
affirmative action equals anti-white racism, then every affirmative
action policy at any school or workplace is in jeopardy. If this issue
has "no validity" to Jack Greenberg, what must be questioned is not
his color but his competence to represent critical black interests.

Muhammad Kenyatta, President
Harvard Black Law Students Association
Harvard Law School
Cambridge, Mass.

Time (September 27, 1982)

[Muhammad Isaiah Kenyatta (1944-92), A.B. (Williams) 1981, received his
J.D. from Harvard in 1984.—Eds.]

The Boycott at Harvard:
Should Teaching Be Colorblind?

CHRISTOPHER EDLEY JR.

Christopher Fairfield Edley Jr. was born in Boston on 13 January 1953. After receiving a B.A. from Swarthmore College in 1973, he followed in his father's footsteps by entering Harvard Law School, where he had the honor of being elected to the *Harvard Law Review* and earned his J.D. *cum laude* in 1978. Simultaneously he garnered a Master of Public Policy degree from Harvard's Kennedy School of Government. Follow government jobs in Washington, D.C., he accepted appointment to the Harvard Law School faculty in 1981, receiving tenure in 1987.

Yes, it's preposterous on it's face: black students at Harvard Law School boycotting a civil rights course to be taught by two visiting superstar civil rights attorneys, because one of the attorneys is white. The uproar from all over has been remarkable to those of us who are always surprised to see how much attention the real world pays to events in Cambridge. But as you might imagine, things are more complicated than they appear.

First, my abbreviated version of the "facts." For several years, Harvard's first tenured black law professor taught a successful course on race, racism and the law. But when Derrick Bell left in December 1980 to become dean of Oregon's law school, black students and some others began pressing the faculty to ensure both that Bell's course be continued in some manner and that the one black who was left among some 65 professors did not remain in solitary splendor. No problem, so far. Within a couple of months, in the spring of 1981, the faculty's continuing but desultory hiring process actually produced offers to three young blacks. I accepted; the other two needed more time to think.

So, this past year, my first as an untenured assistant professor, there were two of us on the faculty. There was no course analogous to Bell's, but others covered some of that material. Throughout the year, students became increasingly concerned that there was no convincing faculty commitment either to the course or to minority hiring. Of the two minority job offers still outstanding, one person foolishly decided to go teach at Yale, and the other continued to play hard to get—the students were, as always, told virtually nothing about what was going on. And the faculty had a series of discussions about having visitors teach a course on race, but those discussions occurred rather late in the year, leaving little maneuvering room for the dean and his advisers to solve the course coverage problem for this coming year.

Ultimately, the faculty approved a list of possible visiting instructors to teach the course during the school's intensive January semester, in which a full course is compressed into three weeks, meeting every day and occupying the students' full credit load for that mini-semester. (It's often a more practical teaching schedule for visiting teachers with regular employment elsewhere, like judges and lawyers.) Dean James Vorenberg, himself a member of the board of the NAACP Legal Defense and Education Fund (LDF), asked Julius LeVonne Chambers, LDF president, to teach the course. Chambers, who is black, is a legendary figure among civil rights attorneys of this or any generation, having handled countless major cases, including several landmark Supreme Court cases. Chambers considered, but decided his schedule would not allow him to take on the whole burden, and suggested that Jack Greenberg, who is white, be appointed to teach the course jointly. Greenberg, director-counsel of LDF, has been the chief executive officer of LDF since succeeding Thurgood Marshall in 1962 and, like Chambers, has been a major figure in civil rights litigation since the dawn of the modern movement. The dean agreed to the package deal, and many of us were excited at the prospect of a course covering four areas that these two towering figures have been absolutely central in shaping: school desegregation, voting rights, capital punishment and employment rights. The plot thickens.

Meanwhile, on the appointments front, the school announced a slew of white male appointments for the coming year, with no apparent progress on minority hiring. By the end of the spring, the Chambers-Greenberg package was arranged, but when the black students heard about it, many of them were dismayed. There were several reactions—and remember that this is a collection of some 140 people, not a monolithic political cell: anger that the best the faculty seemed able or willing to do on the hiring front was to appoint a temporary visitor, Chambers, who is avowedly uninterested in being considered for a regular professorial appointment; anger that there was no solution to the problem of finding a regular faculty member to teach a course on race and the law, only this stop-gap measure for 1982-83; anger that the school felt it necessary to hire a white instructor for a course black students felt was a particularly natural target for minority hiring, and which they felt would be more suited to their needs if taught by a minority instructor (more on this later).

After internal discussions, the Black Law Students Association decided to organize a boycott of the Chambers-Greenberg course for early September when students return to Cambridge and register for their full year of courses. But this all occurred as May exams were getting under way, and there was no time for it to develop into a great cause for the whole community. There was, however, time for the faculty to think about the boycott and the reasons BLSA gave for it. Their reaction was to focus on BLSA's personalized attack on Greenberg and his participation in the course, attacks that many on the faculty feel violated basic principles of academic freedom as well as the liberal integrationist ethic—the idea that someone otherwise superbly qualified to teach a course should be barred because of ideology or especially race is anathema.

Beyond this, however, the manner in which the students framed their justification for a boycott did little to call attention to their essential objections: hiring part-time people is an unacceptable way of dealing with the need for more minority faculty members and for course offerings concerning problems of race. A further argument, admittedly more problematic to many, is that a course on racism taught by a white will probably be different from a similar course taught by a black; the students want at least the latter, and will not settle for the former alone—nor, they insisted, for the Chambers-Greenberg joint venture, which they viewed as a half-measure.

All of this became a matter of public discussion when the dean sent a mid-summer letter to the entire student body that, in a sense, warned them that this controversy would await them in September. He enclosed the basic exchange of correspondence between BLSA, Chambers and Greenberg.

It is important to discern what this controversy is *not* about. It is not, despite ill-considered words by some students, about whether Chambers and Greenberg have done great things for civilization or are capable of teaching an inspiring course: anyone who would doubt these propositions is just stupid, in my view, and should be ignored. Nor is it a controversy about race as a criterion for selecting faculty members in the abstract, because no one I have spoken to at Harvard argues that certain subjects should be taught *only* by people with a particular complexion, ethnicity, political persuasion or configuration of reproductive organs. And finally, this is not a controversy about either the need for more than two minority professors at the huge Harvard Law School, or the need for courses concerned with problems of minorities. On all of these matters, there is consensus if not unanimity. That is a tribute to all of the members of that community, and certainly could not have been said a few short years ago. (In late spring, by the way, the unanswered minority job offer was finally accepted, and an offer was made to an additional person, who has all but accepted. So it now seems likely that in 1983-84 the number of minority faculty will double from two to four. Students have yet to be fully informed about the details of these developments.)

There is, however, an important debate about whether race should be a *consideration* when the school matches instructors to course offerings. It is not dissimilar to the question of assigning minority and white reporters to different stories at a newspaper, or matching Foreign Service officers to diplomatic posts. Do the precepts of academic freedom and liberalism mean that curricular and teaching decisions should be colorblind?

Well, ideally, but not now. Du Bois was right about the continuing importance of race in this century, and students and practitioners of law should be among the first to recognize that. Race remains a useful proxy for a whole collection of experiences, aspirations and sensitivities, in at least as strong a way as anyone's ethnic heritage or professional experiences shape the way he understands and explains life. It's not just a matter of having a particular slant on things; it's a question of what kind of glasses you've been wearing as the years roll by.

There is no question that I teach administrative law the way I do in part because of my experiences in government and my training as a policy analyst; a colleague teaches corporate finance the way he does in part because his many years of experience as a practitioner give him a perspective on what is really important in the field, and how it should be handled. There is a familiar expression: "you are what you eat." It is similarly true that we teach what we have lived, and this may be particularly true in a field like law, which is, after all, about life and how it is or ought to be ordered.

Greenberg and Chambers have been idols of mine since I was a very small kid. Many is the night I've paced around tangled in frustration because it seems so incredibly unlikely that in my life I will be able to make anything remotely approaching the magnitude of their contribution to the cause of justice for black Americans. But it is undeniable, though ironic, that despite their accomplishments race still matters a great deal. And for some subjects, the courses will probably be different, and certainly be *perceived* as being different, when taught by a white rather than a black. Both courses could be valuable. Both, for now, may be necessary.

Washington Post (August 18, 1982)

A Question of Credentials

DERRICK BELL JR.

Derrick Albert Bell Jr. was born in Pittsburgh on 6 November 1930. He received an A.B. in political science from Duquesne University in 1952, and an LL.B. from the University of Pittsburgh Law School in 1957. Following several jobs in government and with the NAACP, he became lecturer at the Harvard Law School in 1969. Since 1971 he has been professor of law, except for 1981-85, when he was dean of the University of Oregon Law School. He was named to the Weld Chair in 1989, and holds honorary degrees from Tougaloo College, Northeastern University, and Mercy College.

Denigration by much of the white community appears to be the usual price of progress by blacks in this country. Harvard's black law students are learning this curious racial fact of life first hand in the wake of the latest in a decade-long effort to convince the faculty of the country's most prestigious law school to hire more black and other minority law teachers.

In recent weeks, newspapers across the country have enlivened their pages during the summer doldrums with reports that Harvard's black students plan to boycott a civil rights course next year in order to protest the school's hiring of a white civil rights lawyer to teach the course. Without bothering to interview student leaders, editorial writers have condemned the boycott as reverse racism.

Belated Intensity

In general, the media have adopted a self-righteous stance against this supposed discrimination by blacks that, if leveled with equal intensity against white racism, might have eliminated that evil long ago. But there is a special joy, motivated by guilt, that comes to whites when they can interpret actions by the black victims of racism as somehow small manifestations of the massive discrimination they have committed or condoned since the country's birth.

It was not a happy summer for boycott proponents, but there may be a lesson in another recent news story reporting that the late Jackie Robinson had been honored at Cooperstown, New York, for his pivotal role in breaking the color line in professional baseball. Perhaps the message from Cooperstown to Cambridge is that Harvard's affirmative action policies will continue to raise fears about loss of the vaunted Harvard quality until the Law School can locate and hire academic equivalents of Jackie Robinson.

Last year, the country's best-known law school caused consternation in some circles when the student-run *Law Review* decided to consider race as a factor in selecting its membership. The *Law Review*'s action was frankly intended to increase the small number of blacks and other minorities who have served on the prestigious legal periodical's staff.

Critics of the decision predicted a fall to mediocrity of one of the last institutions in which applicants for membership were judged strictly on their grades and the quality of unsigned writing samples. For their part, black law students, the supposed beneficiaries of the plan, viewed it as a patronizing means of protecting with a thin veneer of tokenism a selection system that favors students who come from elite, upper-class backgrounds. Both sides agreed that the *Review* should have more black students, but how qualified applicants were to be determined was the critical issue.

In the most recent controversy, Harvard's Black Law Student Association and a Third World Coalition of minority law students have called for a boycott of a racial discrimination course primarily to protest what seemed unacceptably slow progress in locating and offering full-time teaching positions to black lawyers. The students were disappointed that Harvard did not use the civil rights course opening to hire and take a close look at a black teacher who might later be considered for a permanent faculty position.

During the summer, the Law School announced that one black lawyer had accepted an offer to join the regular faculty in 1983-84, and another black lawyer has been given an offer for the same year. If they both come, the number of regular black faculty would increase from two to four. It seems safe to assume that minority-student persistence played more than a minor role in this faculty recruitment effort.

In retrospect, it may not have been tactically wise for the black students to frankly indicate displeasure with the two well-known civil rights lawyers hired to teach a civil rights course during the Winter Term. They have taken their lumps for their candor, and it is now appropriate to examine more carefully and calmly the basis for their concerns.

Specifically, the black students believe that the two appointees, Jack Greenberg and Julius Chambers, who are, respectively, the director counsel and president of the Board of the NAACP Legal Defense and Educational Fund, Inc., are too committed to the civil rights goals of the 1950s to effectively delineate contemporary racial issues in the law for black students.

Request for Turnover

Again, the issue is qualifications. Both Greenberg and Chambers have exemplary records in civil rights litigation, but the students question the Legal Defense Fund's litigation priorities in recent years. They also express the view that while Greenberg's contributions to civil rights have been great, he should long since have recognized the symbolic value of his position to the black community and turned over the leadership post to a black lawyer. Jim Lorenz, a white lawyer who helped start the highly successful California Rural Legal Assistance program in the 1960s, turned over his director's position after a few years to a Mexican-American lawyer for precisely this reason.

Civil rights organizations generally have integrated staffs, but virtually all of them, including the major Jewish groups, are led by members of the minority the organization was established to serve. The value of such leadership for blacks is not merely symbolic. When Thurgood Marshall was director of the Legal Defense Fund, black lawyers around the country, but particularly the South, placed his photograph in a prominent spot in their offices as a reminder to clients that black lawyers could and did handle cases competently and gain victories in the court.

We now know that dozens of editorial writers and, we must assume, a substantial portion of the literate citizenry, take strong exception to the black students' evaluation of Greenberg's value to civil rights and his potential as a teacher. That the students also objected to Julius Chambers raised far less comment.

The phenomenon is not new. There is a tendency to elevate whites who have done substantial service in the civil rights cause to a quasi-sacred status that is beyond criticism, at least by blacks. These individuals are heroes to whites. They have done for blacks what blacks have not been able to do for themselves. They are proof that not all whites are racist. Blacks should show a proper respect for their accomplishments undiluted by petty carping over the details of their performance.

When the black law students ignored this unwritten rule of racial conduct, they incurred this summer that character of public outrage which Frederick Douglass experienced in the 19th century when he dared to suggest that the assistance of white Abolitionists, while much-appreciated, did not entitle them to an unchallenged leadership role in the movement to end slavery.

Qualifications at Issue

But while self-appointed defenders of Jack Greenberg's civil rights credentials were taking blind-side shots at the students all summer, the real issue remained qualifications. Harvard officials insist that they are searching for qualified, minority faculty, and Dean James Vorenberg reportedly told the students that he would prefer "an excellent white teacher" for the civil rights course over a "mediocre black one." No one can disagree with the dean's preferences, but obviously, the black students define excellence and mediocrity very differently from the way their dean does.

One could wish that ability in the classroom could be determined as clearly and as directly as it is on the playing field. When Jackie Robinson finally made it to the major leagues, his outstanding performance, as measured by his batting average, bases stolen, and fielding plays made, left no room for debate about qualifications. Robinson was a super-star, and his consistently outstanding play ended all reasonable argument about the inferiority of blacks in professional sports.

But there are few performance statistics in law school teaching. Faculty are hired, in the main, based on potential, and potential is determined in large part by where the applicant went to law school and how well he or she performed there. The law school equivalent of Jackie Robinson who lacked these credentials, in the absence of vigorous insistence by black students, would likely not get a second look from Harvard.

It should be said that Harvard has done about as well in hiring minority law teachers as most other mainly-white law schools. Like other schools, Harvard ended generations of all-white-male teaching staffs in the late 1960s in response to the rather vigorous protest activities of minority students, aided by the effective support of some faculty members.

In 1969, after a dozen years of litigation and administrative experience with both private and government civil rights agencies, I became the first black on the Harvard Law School's permanent faculty. Granted tenure in 1971, I taught there for eleven years, and developed a civil rights course based on my law text, "Race, Racism, and American Law." While I taught other courses in the Constitutional Law area, my major contribution was in the law of race, the area of both my practice and life experience.

My academic record, good grades and a law review editorship at the University of Pittsburgh Law School, ordinarily would not have gained me much consideration for a faculty position at Harvard, where qualifications include extraordinary grades from Harvard or another major law school, a clerkship on the U.S. Supreme Court, and perhaps a few years at one of the country's prestigious law firms.

Fallen Barriers

There is a strong presumption that applicants with credentials of this character have teaching and scholarly potential. Because there are no longer any overt racial barriers at Harvard, some faculty believe it is as wrong to consider race as a positive qualification in hiring teachers as it was to use it as an excuse to bar blacks like Jackie Robinson from professional sports.

But legal education is more complicated than baseball. Race can create as legitimate a presumption as a judicial clerkship in filling a teaching position intended to interpret to law students the impact of racial discrimination on the law and lawyering. The special and quite valuable perspective on law and life in this country that a black person can provide is not limited to civil rights issues, as Supreme Court Justice Thurgood Marshall's thundering dissents have proven over the years.

Quite often during my years at Harvard, my views on policy matters differed substantially from those held by my colleagues. While my minority positions seldom prevailed, I like to think they made possible a fuller discussion of issues than would otherwise have been possible. Is it only fortuitous that Prof. Chris Edley's *Washington Post* Op-ed piece provided almost the only enlightened comment on the black student boycott published this summer?

Stymied Efforts

My efforts at Harvard to recruit more blacks with backgrounds similar to mine were stymied by faculty who preferred to wait for applicants with academic credentials like their own, but who just happened to be black. Blacks with high-level academic credentials do exist. Understandably, some prefer the far more lucrative life of big-law-firm practice to teaching.

Three blacks with outstanding academic credentials were hired, and two were tenured, at Harvard during the years after I arrived. The first was Prof. Clyde Ferguson, an expert in civil procedure and international law. The second, Harry Edwards, is now a federal judge on the U.S. Court of Appeals for the District of Columbia. A third, Christopher Edley Jr., was one of the handful of blacks who served on the *Harvard Law Review*, and last year joined the faculty as an assistant professor.

But neither Ferguson nor Edley is currently a specialist in civil rights law. After I left Harvard at the end of 1980, some 500 students petitioned the school to hire someone to "teach Derrick Bell's civil rights course." They specifically requested that a black teacher be hired for the course.

Unique Insidiousness

As two of the more than 150 black students put it in a letter to the dean in March, 1982, "While the Civil Rights movement or experience has touched many, we feel strongly that the course we seek should be taught by a professor who has personally experienced the unique insidiousness of racism in the United States."

Rather clearly, the request is not reverse racism. It is a call for a teacher whose credentials include experiences in and with American racism similar to those the students have already suffered. Unless there is a miraculous racial reform quite soon, these students as lawyers, and their black clients, will likely have to face such experiences for the remainder of their lives.

Harvard's black students do not wish to decide who should be hired to teach there. This is properly a faculty responsibility. They do not even begrudge the subtle but real ego gratification that must come when Harvard faculty select new teachers with credentials quite like their own. Obviously, some persons with outstanding academic records become good teachers and some do not. Similarly, not every black lawyer can bring to the classroom the insights and understanding the students seek. But some clearly can. They are needed, and a civil rights course is an ideal means to test that ability.

Index of Success

The correlation between good grades and academic success is not so close that the school should reject the students' suggestion that at least one civil rights teacher, in a school with so large a faculty, should have experienced, as well as worked to end, racial discrimination. The racial outlook for Harvard's black students, and for that matter, the country, is not so bright that there is no need for a teacher who in the context of an academic offering is able to speak in depth and detail about the contradictions and dilemmas that will come with black professional status.

Indeed, early in the course, this teacher might try to explain why a society which, after sanctioning centuries of slavery and the most debilitating policies of racial discrimination, needs to believe that the deep racial injustices it has condoned may best be cured by convincing black victims that what they and theirs have experienced has no significance, and surely is not the credentialing equivalent of straight-A grades in a mainstream, mainly white law school.

Harvard Law Record (1982)

Farah Griffin in 1985

FARAH GRIFFIN

Farah Jasmine Griffin was born in Philadelphia on 23 February 1963, and prepared for college at the Baldwin School for Girls in Bryn Mawr, Pennsylvania. As an undergraduate she was a reporter for the *Harvard Crimson* and was also active in several black organizations. She received her degree in 1985 with honors in History and Literature. Following a period as research associate for Judge A. Leon Higginbotham Jr. in Philadelphia, she embarked on a Ph.D. program in American Studies at Yale in the fall of 1986. She received a fellowship from the American Association of University Women to complete a dissertation on migration and urbanization in African-American culture and obtained her doctorate in 1992.

On Hair and Harvard

Upon entering Holworthy 22 in the fall of 1981, I wandered into the bathroom and confronted a big, old, white urinal. This building was not erected with me in mind, I thought. So, after three weeks of daily confrontations with that contraption and all that it came to represent for me, I left one institution of education and acculturation—Harvard, in search of another—an old-fashioned black hairshop.

I found *Lucielle's* in the not yet gentrified South End. Wherever I've traveled in this country, I've been able to find places like this, where funk, jazz, rhythm and blues or gospel emanate from well-equipped sound systems, or old radios, and where next door there's a fried chicken joint, on the corner a Chinese take-out place, and across the street a bar. *Lucielle's* was no different, but it was special because it was my first. After three weeks at Harvard it felt good to hear the heartfelt laughter and melodic voices of black women. The place reminded me of my grandmother's kitchen and that was criterion enough for me. Lucielle was a small honey-brown woman of about sixty years or so who coddled me, called me baby and fussed over "all that thick, beautiful hair on your head, Child!"

Poor, black and female, I sought out black beauticians in search of my sanity for the next four years: men and women, young, old, gay, straight, conservative, radical, even a few evangelists featured in this motley crew that reaffirmed my value as a thinking, feeling, and growing young woman. Through hours of press and curls (no chemicals, thank you), cuts, trims, and braids I sat and prepared for another two weeks of Harvard. We would talk about politics, sex, relationships and God. After one of these sessions I always returned to Cambridge feeling relaxed and renewed.

If hairshops were places where I established my equilibrium, Harvard was the place where it was again shattered. For me this was both a triumph and a tragedy. Harvard was a sea of contradictions. On the one hand, I sat in a lecture given by a noted historian who painted a portrait of the Old South, sentimental and full of little "playful pickaninnies" (those were his words); on the other hand, I came to know and love "my professor" Nathan Huggins, who taught me to begin taking myself seriously as an intellectual and to be committed to establishing African-American subject matter as material worthy of scholarly inquiry.

In the journal entries I kept for my History and Literature sophomore tutorial I found myself engaged in a written debate with one of my tutors. In response to my frustration over the dearth of black authors on his syllabus, he wrote that he was forced by time to limit his selection to major American authors. "Henry James, my dear, is major because people like you have made him so," I thought. When I asked this same tutor if I could write my paper on Du Bois' *The Souls of Black Folk*, he said no because he had never read Du Bois.

In contrast, I also met an exciting recently arrived professor who brought such energy, enthusiasm and dedication to his teaching of African-American literature that he inspired me to want to stimulate a group of students the way he stimulated me. He made me want to teach, to write and he and Professor Huggins encouraged me to pursue graduate study. Their confidence in my intellectual abilities sustained me in much the same way as did those Thursday afternoons in hairshops.

At Harvard, a reader of my senior thesis complained of my failure to place Frances Harper, a 19th-century black novelist, poet, essayist and political activist, in the context of larger white women's movements. In fact, I thought the thesis was problematic because I spent so much time placing Harper in this context that I neglected to deal with her in the depth she so well deserved. Our differing perceptions of the weakness of the essay reflected our different understandings of Harper's significance as a historical figure.

Between 1981 and 1985, the deconstructionist literary critic Barbara Johnson was the only Harvard professor doing work on black women. However, through the various lectures, dinners and master's teas sponsored by the Afro-American Studies Department, Radcliffe, and interested individuals, I met Toni Morrison, Alice Walker, and Paule Marshall. At Radcliffe, where the Black Women's Oral History Project was underway, I came into contact with scholars of the newly emerging field of Black Women's Studies: Valerie Smith, Deborah McDowell and Linda Perkins were all fellows at the Bunting Institute during my years in Cambridge. During a lecture give by Perkins at the end of my freshman year I first learned of those dynamic 19th-century black women and it was then that I decided to write my thesis on Frances Harper.

The culmination of this avenue of my intellectual curiosity was the conception and organization of the first Radcliffe Conference on the Study of Black Women in American History. With Janet Bixby, a political white feminist, I dreamt, lobbied and helped to bring into fruition a two-day conference that drew on scholars from the entire country. Our greatest resource was past and present Bunting Institute fellows. Here were the models for whom I had been searching. They weren't visible at Harvard, so with financial assistance from Radcliffe, Education for Action, the Harvard Foundation for Race Relations, and the Radcliffe Union of Students, and with the support of my mentors, Professors Huggins and Sollors, and Radcliffe's Dean Phillipa Bovet, Janet and I imported them.

In short, the contradictions of Harvard taught me "to make a way out of no way." That was one of the most valuable lessons I learned during my four years in and around Beantown. It was reiterated in black hairshops in Roxbury, Mattapan, Dorchester, Medford and the now gentrified South End. The second most valuable lesson was taught me by five sister/roommates. We were as different as could be in demeanor, opinion and economic status. Some of our common threads were our blackness, our femaleness and Harvard. We were six spoiled little divas who had always been the stars in somebody's world, suddenly thrown together and forming what would become possibly the most important relationship of our lives. For eighteen years we had been the "Only." Suddenly, we were forced to recognize that there is no "only"; there are always more smart, talented, black girls out there. We also grew to understand that there was no threat in our newly discovered numbers, just strength and to some extent a certain degree of power.

These two lessons of my Harvard years prepared me in unexpected ways to meet a world full of contradictions where equilibriums are always on the brink of destruction. Now I simply paraphrase Aaron Copland's "New York": If I made it there (in Cambridge) I'll make it anywhere—provided, of course, I find a little music-filled black hairshop.

(1988)

JUDITH JACKSON

Judith Barbara Jackson was born in Chicago on 3 November 1965, and prepared for college at the University of Chicago Laboratory Schools. At Harvard she won several scholarships, participated in black organizations, served for two years as a freshman prefect, and held posts on the business board of the *Harvard Crimson*. In 1987 she received her A.B. in Literature *magna cum laude*. Following graduation she began work as a financial analyst for Morgan Stanley & Co. in Chicago before embarking on graduate work in English at Princeton University.

Trying to Break Out of the Isolation

I came to Harvard thinking I could become as much a part of this environment as anyone else. I envisioned myself maturing intellectually, personally and socially in Cambridge. I had attended white schools—public, private and parochial—all my life and had excelled. I worked hard and was admitted here. Why, I thought, should Harvard be so much different from my previous educational experiences? After four years, I realize the biggest joke I ever played on myself was thinking that I could in fact become as comfortable in this place as an Eliot or a Cabot or an Agassiz.

I arrived here freshman year with some very unrealistic expectations. I thought, or at least I had been told, that college would be filled with compassionate roommates and friends, an active social and extracurricular life and enlightened intellectual pursuits. My first slap in the face came from my two white roommates (both from suburban, middle-class families). They obviously felt uncomfortable with me and

Judith Jackson in 1987

the fact that we were now equals, peers even, since Harvard Admissions had given us all their stamp of approval. I think it was the first time they had encountered someone black who was from a similar family background and was smart enough to get in here. We all went our separate ways when May rolled around.

My next blow occurred when I stepped into the offices of the *Harvard Crimson*. I worked on both the newspaper and yearbook in high school. I felt prepared. Nothing could have been further from the truth. I had never met so many uptight people until I decided to "comp" business. My peers on the news and editorial staffs were amazed that I knew what the *New Republic* was and that the *New York Times* did indeed come all the way to Chicago. I interacted with "Crimeds" who had problems dealing with me since it is possible that the only other black woman they had previously encountered was a maid. I began to doubt myself for wanting to join a staff where there were so few blacks or women or anyone who acted reasonable. My love-hate relationship with the paper continues. The work can be exhilarating, though the people usually are not. I wish in many ways that I had been able to recruit more minorities here, but maybe my inability (or unwillingness) speaks for itself. Why did I need to bring people of color here for them to be listened to only when an editorial needed a "minority" perspective?

My third slap in the face came when I sought out members of my own racial community. I naïvely thought that the blacks I had been unimpressed by in high school would be miraculously transformed into together, committed people in college. Needless to say, the Black Students Association meetings freshman year were long, boring, repetitive and poorly attended. I stopped going when the supposedly wise upperclassmen officers starting asking us what they were supposed to be doing. How was I to know when I had just arrived? I turned to the better-organized Association of Black Radcliffe Women instead and later became a steering committee member.

Looking back, I wonder why I thought everyone else should be together if I was confused, too. As my expectations have moved from hopelessly idealistic to relatively realistic during the last three years, I have become less and less ambivalent about my place in the black community. It is the only home any of us have amid the cultural storm of an isolating Harvard world, and if I do not try to make it better, who will?

My fourth blow came when I tried to take an English course

offered by the Afro-American Studies Department. An adviser told me in no uncertain terms that the department was on shaky ground and their courses were not successful. I was learning fast that Harvard was not providing me with the haven that all my other schools had and some innocent expectations crumbled before my eyes. I was between a rock and a hard place, finding no institutional support from my adviser, and having little camaraderie with my roommates or cultural support from the black community. I finally stopped listening solely to my expectations and heard myself for the first time during the winter of sophomore year. I left my initial concentration in the social sciences for the humanities.

Literature provided me not only with a safe haven and some theoretical tools, but also a way to discover the depths and breadth of Afro-American literature after finding the courage to ignore my adviser's earlier statements about the department and its offerings. Harvard may have attempted to squelch my interest in a discipline that it has only grudgingly recognized in the last twenty years, but it was only after I shrugged off my adviser's advice that my brain started functioning.

It is no wonder that I have since realized that I can only be *in* this place, not *of* it. After freshman year and the intellectual, personal and social successes and failures of the next three years that tempered it, perhaps it should not surprise anyone that I sometimes think that maybe, just maybe, another school might have served me just as well as, if not better than, these hallowed New England halls. What is even more frightening than this initial realization is the memory of how committed I was and how I nearly fought to come here when I could have gone to a Howard or a Spelman or a Fisk or a Hampton, predominantly black colleges that offer a nurturing environment in which to grow intellectually, personally and socially. They are the schools where those friendships for life are made that my parents (alumni of black colleges themselves) always brag about.

So now I wonder why I deluded myself into thinking that Harvard would pander to my needs when instead I could have attended a smaller, more supportive institution in which the flashes of intellectual brilliance I experienced here might have metamorphosed into sustained sunlight. I wonder why I kidded myself when I could have been a part of an active social life like the one in which my older sister matured at Fisk. I wonder why I fooled myself when I could have graduated from a college where being black and *summa cum laude* were not mutually exclusive events. I wonder why I chose Harvard when I could have gone to a school were my personal views would not always be taken as gospel and therefore "representative" of my entire race. I wonder why I attended this university when I could have gone South to a college where white students in black literature courses would not seem to take so much obvious pleasure in being able to say "nigger" because it was written in the assigned reading.

Yet, for as much as I berate myself and the bitter side of my experience, I know that there must have been something reasonable and logical in my original decision to come to Cambridge instead of Washington. D.C. or Nashville or Atlanta. I am obviously ambivalent about this place and my accomplishments and failures here, but now I wonder if that ambivalence is a lesson in itself or maybe I am just rationalizing. Harvard has a monopoly on whatever it is they have been trying to teach for the last 350 years. I both enjoyed and suffered through four years of that curriculum and now understand a little of what Harvard is all about as well as the culture in which it was created.

My lessons of the last four years include the never-ending story that dominant culture—which to my mind is predominantly white and male—tells about itself and its members taught from its own point of view. It is the tale of Western civilization from Homer and Cicero to Jesus Christ to the Crusades to the founding of the New World to the Founding Fathers to Ralph Waldo Emerson to T.S. Eliot and beyond. It is also, more specifically, the Harvard story of Phillips Exeter and the Delphic Club and Collegiate and L.L. Bean and Brooks Brothers and The Game and the Eastern Sprints and a 350th birthday party.

I have learned a vocabulary completely alien to my native environment, but one that enables me to function in a place that I am in, but not of. The isolation I experienced at Harvard will not go away, not if I want to function in society where the rules are written by someone else. Coming here gives me invaluable insights about those rules and how I can better comprehend my own alienation. I am better able to figure out ways to shield the black organizations I am involved in from being tagged "separatist," though we congregate to find support just as actors and athletes and journalists do. I begin to understand how dominant culture views me and others in my community. Harvard has been my first complete taste of life in the fast lane of white, Judaeo-Christian America.

Though it is tempting, I cannot directly compare my Harvard/-

college experience to anyone else's whether here or at a black college. And realistically speaking, I know that being an alumna of Harvard and Radcliffe will not hurt and will probably help me in whatever I want to do. But if this place has taught me anything, I understand that in any of my attempts to comprehend dominant culture I cannot afford to forget the black community that I am both always in and of. Even after four years here, Harvard Yard is not a place I can call home.

Harvard Crimson (1987)

SHANNAH V. BRAXTON

Shannah Vanessa Braxton was born on 25 August 1966 in Staten Island, New York, where she attended Curtis High School. At Harvard she was active with the Third World Student Alliance and the Harvard Foundation on Race Relations, also serving as president of the Black Students Association in 1986-87. A concentrator in government, she wrote a thesis on housing and received her A.B. *cum laude* in 1988. She then began work in Boston as public relations officer for Elizabeth Stone House, a center for battered and mentally ill women.

Painting with Fresh Strokes

Historically, members of the Asian, Black, Mexican, Puerto Rican, and Native American—minority—communities at Harvard-Radcliffe have claimed that the university fails in its responsibility to provide the setting for satisfactory racial understanding and constructive racial interaction. This allegation has resurged in the 1980s.

Since 1980, Harvard has created numerous committees and undertaken many studies of race relations on its campus. Although the administration has made these efforts to explore racial tensions, they have succeeded in little more than constructively discussing a potentially explosive problem.

To "work toward fostering a better understanding of the issues that are of vital concern to minority America and the global societies of the Third World" (as written in the Brown University Center's manifesto), several universities have established Third World centers and incorporated them into their academic communities. Brown, Yale,

Shannah Braxton in 1988

Princeton (even Princeton!), Dartmouth and Stanford all have Third World Centers or Afro-American Student houses, usually equipped with offices, lounges, and kitchen space, and full-time directors. Other universities have established "theme dorms," such as Cornell's Ujaama, and MIT's Chocolate City (even MIT!) to provide Afro-Americans with the space necessary for extensive activities and planning, and the centrality that allows distraught individual members to find support from the group. Residence in these dorms is voluntary, competitive and not limited to minorities.

Whether or not one likes the idea of minority student centers or theme dorms, it is undeniable that the institutionalization of such entities—with central location and university resources—has served to create stronger minority communities, and to complement the ethnically diverse college community in general.

Harvard also neglects the available academic means to encourage racial awareness and understanding. The Core Curriculum, as it now stands, practically endorses notions of racial and cultural inferiority of minorities by virtually excluding the study of their history, literature and art.

If Historical Studies A is to offer "broad ranging courses" to study "through history some of the great issues . . . of our modern world," then what does it mean when the historical experience of today's American minorities that could "explain the background and development of major aspects of the modern world" and their current situations are virtually overlooked? Do not topics such as Racism and U.S. Conquests, the History and Legacy of Slavery, or the History of U.S. and British Colonization qualify as "great issues" and "major aspects" that could help students better comprehend the dilemmas plaguing minorities today?

If Historical Studies B courses sharply focus on periods when "the way in which individual aspirations and individual decisions have interacted with circumstances—economic, cultural, political—to shape a significant portion of the world," how can the Mexican Revolution or *The Strange Career of Jim Crow* possibly not qualify?

If Literature and Arts B (my favorite) includes courses that study "the relation of the arts to the social and intellectual contexts that gave them birth," then isn't it incomprehensible that courses on the Jazz Tradition, Ragtime, Reggae, 'Geisha Girls,' or Salsa and Merengue are not included?

Is it not ironic that minorities culturally and racially discriminated against and oppressed for centuries are nowhere dealt with in the Moral Reasoning section of the Core? The topic of Racism and Rational Man warrants a most extensive study of moral reasoning (or lack thereof) in the U.S. and elsewhere.

What message is sent when particular minorities or Third World groups have their history and culture not regarded as "indispensable to undergraduate education," though they compose over 20 percent of the student body? (Keep in mind that American minorities are not "Foreign Cultures," and should not be placed in that category of the Core.)

The only way for minorities to use the Core to define their own modern experiences—one of the stated purposes of the Core—is by relying on the Western traditional thought that floods the Core. This thought fostered the racism and oppression that put these groups and cultures at the disadvantages that still oppress them today. The message directed toward minorities is that, as a course must "conform to faculty guidelines," so should minorities conform to majority faculty and student thought and preference.

We must address the lack of minority faculty. I will not bombard you with numbers and percentages to prove a point; rather, let me just inform those of you who do not already know that Harvard has no (zero, zip, zilch) tenured Black women professors, nor any Mexican-American or Puerto-Rican senior faculty. The minority junior faculty is equally pathetic in terms of numerical representation, etc., etc. . . .

There are two crucial points to make when discussing the need for increased minority faculty representation. First, the fact is that other Ivy League schools mysteriously overcome the constraints of what Harvard claims is the small pool of minorities from which to choose in academics. Second, the plea for more minority faculty is not based on naïve claims that they will know more about minority courses and cultures, but on the argument that Harvard needs to commit itself to diversity in the real world: that of hiring and tenuring faculty members who could relate to minority students and possible enlighten majority students and faculty prone to ignorance.

What conclusion can anyone draw from all this? Well, ask yourself, where does a minority student go once victimized by verbal racial attacks? What racism or forms of racist expression warrant a registered complaint, followed by disciplinary action on the administration's part?

How do you convince a faculty member that you insist on writing "Black," not "Negro," and with a capital 'B' (so he or she will stop wasting that God-forsaken red ink on your papers!)?

How do you convince a department that bringing a top Puerto Rican historian to Harvard once a month for a half-credit, full course seminar at a mere one thousand dollars, *total* cost, is the bargain of the century?

Finally, what do you do when you want more than the 5.33 friends that would just squeeze into your Mem Hall sub-basement office to attend your organization's two-hour semester planning meetings of general discussions?

These dilemmas constantly taunt and tease many minority students at Harvard. The students could fundraise, beg, borrow or steal to get centers, courses, or visiting professors (and oh, have we ever!). But is it not Harvard's responsibility to prevent Currier House "strike force" double agents from multiplying before they attack? You should start asking yourselves how you are going to function as responsible, representative leaders, parents and educators in the future if you maintain the same level of racial ignorance you had on Day One.

Harvard has the money, the clout, the connections and the resources to establish those institutionalized bodies that have improved the lot of minorities and educated general student communities at schools comparable in status. Why has it not even developed its own Course Catalogue to meet the challenge of cultural diversity in the latter part of this century? Cannot higher education at least mean a lower level of that ignorance from which racism grows?

Harvard Independent (1987)

Martin Kilson in 1969

MARTIN KILSON

Martin Luther Kilson Jr. was born on 14 February 1931 in East Rutherford, New Jersey and educated in a small town in Pennsylvania. He entered Lincoln University (Pennsylvania) in 1949, and became class valedictorian, receiving his B.A. *magna cum laude* in 1953. At Harvard he earned an M.A. in 1958 and a Ph.D. in political science the next year. He started teaching at Harvard as lecturer in government in 1962, was assistant professor of government, 1964-68, and was appointed professor of government in 1969. He was named to the Frank G. Thomson chair in 1988. In 1970 he was elected a Fellow of the American Academy of Arts and Sciences and of the Black Academy of Art and Letters, and has served as consultant to the Fulbright exchange program and the Ford Foundation. His writings cover the fields of political development, American urban politics, Black African politics, and Afro-American intellectual patterns. He is without doubt the Harvard faculty's champion writer of letters-to-the-editor.

Harvard and the Small-Towner

I came to Harvard first as a graduate student (1953-1959), returned in 1961—after a year and a half researching in West Africa—as a Research Fellow at the Center for International Affairs, started teaching in 1962 as a Lecturer in Government and later (1964-1968) as Assistant Professor of Government, and became tenured professor in 1969 (the first Afro-American to teach as full professor in Harvard College). During the 1950s and well into the 1960s the number of Afro-American students here was never enough to constitute a critical-mass—a self-conscious stratum capable of generating claims of its own within the wider Harvard community. But this would all change with a vengeance by the late 1960s and early 1970s. By 1970 some 10% of the 11,176 freshmen offered admission to the fifteen elite colleges in the East were Black. Yale's freshman class, for example, was 12% Black; Princeton's 16%; Barnard's 22%; Radcliffe's 17%; and Harvard's 10%. This enormous infusion of Blacks into the White world of elite WASP colleges occurred, moreover, simultaneously with the political and ideological upheaval in the civil rights movement that eventually broke the back of legalized racism in American life, South and North, and laid the basis for the more protracted struggle to smash behavioral racism in American institutions (in firms, schools, colleges, government, etc.) and in individuals' actions.

This then is the raw boundary-of-fact that delineates my entry to Harvard in the early 1950s and my professional career here since. What shaped my character and thus much of my professional identity and ethnic identity prior to my long Harvard sojourn is my small-towner background—a background that clearly influenced so much of how I have conducted my Harvard journey. In general, American small-towners differ from American big-towners, especially in regard to being less given to fashion and more circumspect toward establishment-pretenders, whether old ones like Harvard or new ones like the neo-conservative or Reaganite intellectuals and elites. Of course, small-towners have no monopoly on this attribute; some big-towners possess it too—though less frequently—and those who did numbered among my graduate school buddies (among them Everett Mendelsohn, Arthur Rosenthal, Robert Moses).

Ethnically or racially, the Black small-towner at the Harvard of my day—the 1950s—was caught between competing establishment-pretenders. First, there was the mainstream establishment-pretender, made up of the typical graduate student (and undergraduate, too) entering Harvard, seeking knowledge preparation and status-pecking preparation for a careerist entry to some institutional or power niche (university, law firm, bank, multinational, government, etc.). Ethnically this category was WASP-skewed and comprised mainly of WASPs and the careerist-minded high-achieving White ethnics (Jews, Irish, a few Italians). In addition, there were secondary establishment-pretender networks—e.g., among first generation elite-college-going Jewish students, among similar Irish students, and among big-city upper-middle-class Blacks, often light-skinned and linked to Greek-letter fraternities.

In fact, many Afro-Americans at the Harvard of my day wished full-fledged entry to the first category of establishment-pretenders. But, alas, the mainstream establishment-pretenders were not much different in their neurotic embrace of racist habits from the rest of the country. So I don't remember any Black among the 25 or so in graduate schools (FAS, School of Education, Law School, Business School) and the nearly 20 in the College who gained status-pecking entry to mainstream establishment-pretender category. Though a few certainly had at least a friendship-nexus to this category—among them, if I recall correctly, were Andrew Brimmer (economics grad student), Clifford Alexander (undergraduate student), Nathan Huggins (history grad student), Lila Fenwick (law student), Harold Scott (undergraduate student) and Gail Jones (undergraduate student—Lena Horne's daughter).

For myself, my native skepticism toward American establishment-pretenders precluded even contemplating the careerist route to these ranks. My roots are deep in the Black variant of smalltown American skepticism, starting from late 18th-century or early 19th-century free-Negro lineage (both maternal and paternal). Initially located in eastern Maryland, the Kilsons-Martins-Lees-and-Laws were yeoman farmers, carpenters, teachers, and the clergyman (my great-great-grandfather) who founded the first African Methodist Episcopal Church in Kent County, Maryland. My maternal great-grandfather, Jacob Laws, left Philadelphia in the 1850s for smalltown Pennsylvania (Ambler, in Montgomery County) where he was a housebuilder and stalwart of a breakaway denomination from the African Methodist Episcopal Church that was called African United Methodist Protestant (formed around 1812), locating a branch in Ambler and building its church with his own hands shortly after returning from the Union Army (Pennsylvania division of 24th Regiment of U.S. Colored Infantry).

This small-townerism surely helped me keep my distance from both the mainstream and secondary establishment-pretenders at Harvard in the 1950s, and thus tilted me toward the intellectual and ideological deviants, namely, leftist graduate students, foreign graduate students (especially African, Indian, and Latin American students), and civil rights activists among Black students. This deviant skewing of my self-definition in graduate school meant, among other things, that my White and Black networks were concentric. They included intellectual Marxists like A. Norman Klein (anthropology grad student), leftist and pacifist activists like Everett Mendelsohn (history of science grad student) and Robert Heifetz (architecture grad student), and civil rights activists like Wally Carrington (law student), J. Max Bond[1] (architecture grad student), and Kenneth Simmons (architecture grad student). The latter three, all Black, had the same small-town background I did—Carrington was from small-town Massachusetts, Bond from small-town Kentucky, and Simmons from small-town Oklahoma. We shared the skeptical view of establishment-pretenders in American society—whether old ones or newcomers—and thus sought anti-mainstream networks at Harvard. With some progressive White students like Michael Tanzer (economics undergraduate) we joined forces to form an NAACP chapter at Harvard, though because of Harvard rules on organizations we called it the Harvard Society for Minority Rights.

My graduate student years at Harvard closed in 1959 when, after marrying a White graduate student in anthropology (Marion Dusser de Barenne), I went on the first of many research trips to Africa. My professional career at Harvard begins in mid-1961, following my return from Africa. It can be treated in two phases—1962-1969; 1969-present. These two periods couldn't be more different. I was one of two Black junior faculty members teaching at Harvard in the 1960s until the Afro-American Studies faculty was put together in 1969. The other was Alvin Labat, an assistant professor in Romance Languages and Literature. Professionally, I decided to reject several invitations from liberal Democratic administrations in Washington under Presidents Kennedy and Johnson to assume policy-making posts. I was aided in this rather difficult decision by my graduate school faculty advisor and intellectual mentor and job-broker Rupert Emerson, professor in the Department of Government and a quiet but keen progressive.

I therefore turned with total attention to teaching, scholarship,

---

[1]The Bond clan's anti-establishment skepticism overlapped my own at several points—during two years in graduate school Max Bond's brother George Bond, an anthropology student at Boston University, was my roommate; and during my undergraduate years at Lincoln University (1949-1953) Max's and George's uncle, Horace Mann Bond—Julian Bond's father—was president of Lincoln and one of my intellectual mentors.

and especially to sharpening an intellectual identity and style for myself. The latter task involved a five-year endeavor to help a small group of Black undergraduate students shape for themselves an intellectually valid approach to the emergent Black-ethnic awareness and solidarity activism surfacing nationally. Aided by a couple of Black graduate students—especially Archie Epps, a theology student—and several undergraduate students (Lee Daniels, Charles Beard, Ayi Kwei Armah, Charles J. Hamilton) I helped to form the Harvard-Radcliffe Afro-American Students Association, acting as faculty adviser. The Afro-American Students Association also launched a magazine, the *Harvard Journal of Negro Affairs*, edited by Lee Daniels, Charles Lovell, Henry Binford and others and financed heavily from my small assistant professor salary.

Curiously enough, this bid to give vigorous intellectual formation to students' Black-ethnic awareness got shanghaied at two points in time, the early period—1963-1965—and the later period—1968-1972. In the early period, a leading figure among the Black establishment-pretenders who wrote for the *Harvard Crimson*—Herbert Denton, now on the editorial board of the *Washington Post*—argued against the founding of the Afro-American Students Association and its journal. His grounds were that the association's purposes were mainly Black, not trans-ethnic, and thus, in this pristine viewpoint, they were undemocratic. I wrote numerous defenses of our association and journal in pieces to the *Harvard Crimson*, arguing that while clearly Black-skewed, the Afro-American Students Association and the journal were progressively Black-skewed, open to trans-ethnic contributions, not ethnocentrically Black-skewed. We won this battle with Denton. In fact, this victory netted me something I didn't seek (and still don't) as a Black intellectual—popularity among rank-and-file Blacks. As a Black intellectual of small-towner skeptical outlook, I've always considered myself firmly insulated against popularity-grubbing—whether for Black-solidarity purposes or for power-grubbing among national power structures.

In the late period—1968-1972—the trauma among Black students emanating from Dr. Martin Luther King's assassination in the spring of 1968 produced another kind of criticism of the Afro-American Students Association. While not open enough to Whites for Herb Denton we became too open to Whites for the new Black-solidarity militants who quickly gained leadership of the Association of Afro-American Students between late 1968 and the summer of 1969, the summer the Afro-American Studies Department was put together.

I figured sizably in the militant Black students' opposition to the old format of the Afro-American Students Association, owing to the independence and pragmatism I applied to my role as the only Black faculty member involved in the faculty committee that designed the Afro-American Studies Department. The militant students wanted lots of political activism in the operation of the Afro-American Studies Department and were disdainful of rigorous intellectual and scholarly values ("Whitey values," some called them). I, on the other hand, favored no ethnocentric militancy in the character of the Afro-American Studies Department and stood firm for the highest intellectual and scholarly criteria. I lost out, as did the Rosovsky Committee's original design for the Afro-American Studies Department. The militant students also won control of the Afro-American Students Association and its journal, though to this day no comparable Black students' journal has emanated from the ranks of the militants.

Since the mid-1970s I have argued often in the pages of the *Harvard Crimson* that the militant students' cathartic ethnocentrism produced a dreadful intellectual malaise among Black students generally. Many have academic performance well below their potential. Recently my viewpoint on this matter—for long a minority viewpoint—gained support from two members of the Black ethnocentric elements at Harvard College in the early 1970s—Jeff Howard and Ray Hammond, now psychologist and physician respectively. In an article in the *New Republic* (September 9, 1985) Howard and Hammond reveal their metamorphosis out of the infantile ranks of Black ethnocentrism and into a more pragmatic viewpoint. They describe the widespread intellectual malaise among Black students and attempt to account for it. I like their characterization of the malaise but question their explanation. They claim that racist rumors of Black inferiority are internalized by Black students, crippling their intellectual agility.

My disagreement with this explanation does not mean I doubt the existence of vicious racist rumors but the importance Howard and Hammond give to such rumors. They forget that such rumors were even more pervasive in the 1920s-1950s era, an era when Black students at Harvard and other top-level colleges performed at and above their potential. If the rumors-of-inferiority hypothesis is correct, Black students in the 1920s-1950s era should have performed even worse than during the current malaise among Black students today.

Thus, what the Howard-Hammond argument misses is that during the late 1960s to early 1970s era, *something happened* to the willingness of Black students to take academic and intellectual pursuits seriously, and this *something* occurs in a period of declining, not increasing racism. What happened was in large part of Blacks' own making, or rather making of Black ethnocentrists who convinced themselves and other Blacks that the catharsis associated with mau-mauing "Whitey's values" was preferable to a pragmatic employment of ethnic militancy.

Howard and Hammond once favored this dead-end cathartic ethnocentrism. They backed the shortsighted attacks of militant Black students—led at one point by Ernest Wilson, now a political scientist at University of Michigan—against the Rosovsky Faculty Committee's proposals for the Afro-American Studies Department. (These proposals integrated the Afro-American Studies curriculum with established departments and faculty.) That these two men have found their way back from the ethnocentric abyss, as it were, reflects a new era of pragmatic approaches to Blacks' presence at Harvard University. Latent racist patterns surely still prevail around Harvard—among which I count the Harvard administration's refusal to divest its investments in the vicious South African economy. But I still believe, as I did 15 years ago, that a progressive pragmatic response to these latent racist patterns is the more effective response, and along with it is the progressive cosmopolitanizing of Black students' lifestyles and networks.

(1986)

Eileen Southern in 1975

EILEEN SOUTHERN

Eileen Jackson Southern was born on 19 February 1920 in Minneapolis, Minnesota. She attended public schools in several midwestern cities, completing high school in Chicago. Scholarships enabled her to attend the University of Chicago, where she earned a B.A. in 1940 and M.A. in 1941. Owing to institutional racism and discrimination in northern colleges at that time, she was obliged to seek employment at historically black institutions in the South, where from 1941 to 1951 she taught at Prairie View State College, Southern University, Alcorn College, and Claflin University while also concertizing as a pianist. Deciding to curtail performing, she moved to New York City in 1951, and embarked on graduate work at New York University, financing her studies by teaching in the public schools. In 1961 she became the first black recipient of a Ph.D. in musicology from an American institution. She began teaching at Brooklyn College in 1960, transferring in 1968 to York College, where she set up and headed the music program until 1975. She then came to Harvard, from which she retired as Professor of Afro-American Studies and of Music at the end of 1986.

She has published widely in the areas of Renaissance and Afro-American music. Her *Music of Black Americans: A History* (1971; 1983) and *Biographical Dictionary of Afro-American and African Musicians* (1982) have become standard references. In 1973 she and her husband Joseph founded the scholarly journal *The Black Perspective in Music*, which they edited until it suspended publication in 1990.

A Pioneer: Black and Female

In 1975 I became the first black woman to be appointed a full professor with tenure at Harvard. My position on the Faculty of Arts and Sciences (FAS), a joint-professorship in the departments of Afro-

American Studies and Music, brought me immediate membership into two highly select, though unorganized groups. The first, which might be designated the "black presence" on FAS, consisted of four males, one of whom was a member of Afro-American Studies. The second group, which might be called the "female presence" on FAS, was composed of a dozen or so women, of whom two were in the Music Department. Neither group paid much attention to my presence as a new member; indeed, the attitude of the black men (including two or three administrators) generally was that of indifference, shifting at times to outright hostility. Considering that FAS had about 350 tenured professors in 1975-76, it is obvious that Harvard hardly was committed to attracting minorities to its faculties. And to me, as a newcomer, it seemed that the minorities already at Harvard did not welcome the idea of being joined by others. It was as if they were reluctant to lose their status of being "the only one." It should be observed that while the number of tenured women on Harvard's FAS has increased dramatically during the past decade, there were only three tenured black professors, all males, when I retired in 1986.

It did not help matters that my first appointment at Harvard was to chair the highly controversial Afro-American Studies Department. I found the students and junior faculty of the Department to be almost paranoid in their position against "outsiders"—that is, those at Harvard who disapproved of the Afro-American Studies program and were committed to its dissolution. As a lecturer in the Department in 1974-75 and the Fall term of 1975, I had been vaguely aware of the controversy, but had not been involved. The concentrators and junior faculty fought me bitterly from the beginning; they wanted Ewart Guinier ['33] to continue as chairman, even though his retirement was imminent. My first hard decision was to defer my appointment until January 1976, when Guinier would take a sabbatical leave prior to beginning the retirement process, because I felt there would be too much tension in the Department with both of us present.

The situation worsened with the passage of time. The concentrators and junior faculty had been allowed to exert much more power over departmental actions than was permissible in other departments (as a member of the Music Department, I knew how governance was handled elsewhere), and they resented any suggestions for change. But of course changes had to be made! The department curriculum did not measure up at all to Harvard standards, the requirements for concentration were much too low, and there were no links to the "outside" Harvard world, such as joint concentrations, for example, or course offerings in the General Education program. Library holdings over the campus were meager in the area of Afro-American Studies, and the AAS Reading Room in Lamont Library was closed. One librarian informed me that no black-studies books would be ordered for her library because she expected the Department to disappear within a year or so. Even the Department's physical facilities needed attention; the general attitude seemed to have been, "Why bother to attend to the building, even though there was a budget, when soon it would no longer be in use?"

Eventually, of course, changes were made in the curriculum, belligerent concentrators graduated, hostile junior faculty left for other institutions. At times the going was rough: I had confrontation after confrontation, some of them quite intense, even violent, with students, the administration, and faculty members. But by 1979, the last year of my three-year tenure as chairman, at least some good results could be seen. Our concentration requirements were respectable; the Reading Room was open and stocked with the important books in the field; we offered a Gen Ed course, Hum 7 (Afro-American Folk Arts), that attracted good enrollments; and the number of concentrators had increased from about seven or eight in 1976 to more than thirty.

I cannot say that there were no fun times in all this. I really enjoyed meeting with students to explain our program; working with the junior faculty to improve the Department and interviewing candidates for appointments; buying furniture, installing carpet, storm windows, and air-conditioners; and testing my powers of persuasion in trying to get others to allow us time to develop. One black professor, for example, regularly attacked the Department in the *Crimson*, but not once did he ever offer suggestions for improvement. Another wrote slashing critiques to the Administration, of which copies eventually came across my desk, but he said nothing to me personally.

In the Spring of 1979, I took a much-needed leave in order to recuperate from three stressful years. When I returned, the junior faculty seemed to have gone berserk, and the Department was in chaos. Looking back, I realize the situation probably resulted from efforts being made to observe the tenth anniversary of the black-student uprisings at Harvard, but at the time I was dumbfounded. The events of that hot spring and summer were too complicated to recount here: I should simply state that, before it was all over, not only had the Administration become involved but also the Department's Visiting Committee and eventually the Board of Overseers—to say nothing of the media all over the nation. After meeting with various committees through the summer, I reluctantly concluded that my contribution to the governance of Afro-American Studies was no longer wanted or needed. In effect, my withdrawal (in spirit if not in physical presence) lasted until my retirement in December 1986, and it was not totally voluntary on my part. At least one good thing, however, came out of the chaos: the Administration decided to appoint three full professors to Afro-American Studies, thus giving the Department a full complement of four professors. When I left in 1986 the Department had one black and one white professor; two slots remained to be filled.

As I reflect on my years at Harvard, I have to admit that, despite the ever-present racism and sexism, which I gradually learned simply to endure, my "minority status" at times brought special dividends. In the first place, if there had been no Afro-American Studies program, it is doubtful that Harvard would have offered me a tenured professorship despite my high qualifications. Some honors came, in my opinion, not only because I was qualified, but also because as a black woman I was highly visible: for example, election to Faculty Council, appointment to the General Education Committee and other important committees, election to the prestigious faculty Shop Club, election to Phi Beta Kappa, and appointment as a Commencement Faculty Aide (I hosted [NAACP Executive Secretary Roy] Wilkins through the two-day ceremonies when Harvard gave him an honorary degree in 1978). My husband and I were invited to glamorous dinner parties and receptions, where we met the great leaders of our time, the celebrated and the obscure. But these were the high points; I had to live each day at a time.

When from time to time I became too depressed with having to cope with Harvard, I would turn to my role model, W.E.B. Du Bois, and reread his account of his days at Harvard. Like him, I went to Harvard because it was a great opportunity for me as a black female scholar, and I accepted the reality of racial and sex discrimination. In its role as nurturer of scholars, Harvard never let me down! I could feel myself growing from year to year, almost from month to month—not only because I had access to those wonderful libraries, particularly the Widener stacks, and the enthusiastic cooperation of the Interlibrary Loan Office, but also because of the many other kinds of assistance given to Harvard professors. There were grants to encourage innovative teaching when I wanted to introduce a new course, teaching fellows to relieve the drudgery parts of teaching, and student research assistants. Then, when I decided to go for the "big one," an NEH grant of over $100,000.00 to develop Research Tools in my field, Harvard gave me every conceivable support. In the later years of my tenure, enterprising colleagues had begun to organize interdisciplinary seminars for faculty, which, in addition to the long-established Music Department seminars, offered me more opportunities for professional contacts. Because of Harvard's nurturing, I published dozens of articles in the major professional journals and dictionaries during my tenure, and completed the research for five major books, three of which were published before I left.

My only regret about my "Harvard Experience" is that it came so late in my career; what couldn't I have done with ten more years?

(1988)

Nathan I. Huggins in 1981

NATHAN IRVIN HUGGINS

Nathan Irvin Huggins was born in Chicago on 14 January 1927. The University of California at Berkeley conferred on him an A.B. in 1954 and an M.A. in 1955. At Harvard he received a second M.A. in 1959 and a Ph.D. in history in 1962. He taught at California State University at Long Beach (1962-64), Lake Forest College (1964-66), the University of Massachusetts at Boston (1966-69, during which period he was also president of the American Museum of Negro History), and Berkeley (1969-70) prior to his tenure as professor of history at Columbia University (1970-1980). In 1980 he returned to Harvard as the W.E.B. Du Bois Professor of History and of Afro-American Studies as well as director of the Du Bois Institute— holding both posts until he succumbed to pancreatic cancer at his Cambridge home on 5 December 1989. He had been a Fulbright lecturer in France, a visiting professor at the University of Heidelberg, and had held Ford Foundation, Guggenheim, Noyes, and Whitney fellowships. His book *Harlem Renaissance* (1971) became the standard work in its field.

Two Decades of Afro-American Studies at Harvard

The year 1989 marked twenty years of Afro-American Studies at Harvard. Born in the tumultuous days of the takeover and "bust" at University Hall and the "strike" that followed—when the air was freighted with charges, claims to principle, and non-negotiable demands—the Afro-American Studies Department is one of the few recognizable survivors of the "student revolution" of the 1960s. As it presently stands, it would hardly be recognized or perhaps approved of by its original student advocates. Its survival, in fact, has been due to modifications and adaptations of those "demands": the nurturing of that germ within the students' concept which had sufficient legitimacy within the University to root itself and take hold.

The student demand for Afro-American Studies was essentially an extension of the civil rights movement, which had by the late 1960s come out of the South and set itself to expose and attack racism endemic in American society and institutions. Those students who would not go on a "freedom summer" in the South could attack racism in the colleges and universities where they were. Universities were attractive targets for good reason. They pretended to be better, more rational, more tolerant, more liberal than the rest of the society. They were more ready than most segments in the society to be publicly embarrassed and apologetic for the historical racism they shared with other American institutions, but they were no more ready than others to change in more than superficial ways.

Harvard, like most American colleges and universities, was willing to open its admissions to a broader social spectrum that might increase the numbers of blacks and others from the inner-city. The numbers of black undergraduates did increase in most major institutions by the end of the sixties, and with larger numbers came different expectations, problems, and tensions. In earlier years, when there were seldom more than six blacks in any Harvard class (one or two at Radcliffe), expectations of "fitting in" encouraged black students to suffer any racial problems privately. With larger numbers and with fundamental changes in national sensibilities about race, however, even personal malaise could be taken as symptomatic of the broad, social pathology.

Certainly, black students of the fifties and earlier decades would have noticed that Harvard offered little about black Americans, or other non-whites for that matter. Very little scholarly attention was paid to Africa, Latin America, or what we now call the Third World.[1] Western Europe and the United States were the hub of Harvard's universe, and everyone seemed satisfied that was as it should be.

---

[1]In this particular regard, Harvard has hardly improved in the past thirty years. Africa and Latin America were better represented in the fifties than they are in the eighties. A strong and important tradition in Asia (China and Japan) guarantees Harvard continuity and leadership in that region.

Harvard was little different from other universities in these regards; ubiquity fed complacency. The newly enrolled undergraduates in the late sixties, however, had little reverence for an order and tradition that seemed to them to be part of the problem, defining the world and civilization so as to sustain and encourage genteel bigotry and even racism. They would demand changes in curriculum so as to make their education "relevant" to their lives. That would require focusing on black people and issues affecting them in ways few scholars in the United States were interested (or equipped) to do.

The painful irony was that the gesture of the colleges toward greater inclusion and uplift was met not only with little gratitude but with hostility and non-negotiable demands. It is little wonder that faculty at Harvard and elsewhere recoiled at the thought of undergraduates, hardly any from college-educated households, presuming to challenge the fundamental principles of liberal arts education. It seemed as if some were saying that Langston Hughes was as important to read as Shakespeare, Eldridge Cleaver as important as Machiavelli. Doubtless, some said as much; reasonableness was nowhere in great supply. But the central issue was the shattering of the complacency of the "hub," that self-created and self-sustaining center of the universe which was exclusively white and male, all else being relegated to the margins.

Harvard responded positively to the need and the demand. A faculty committee led by Henry Rosovsky (which included students as non-voting members) issued a report that recommended a "program" of study in Afro-American Studies. That program would call upon the various departments to provide courses and appoint faculty.[2] The report also recommended increased graduate fellowships for black students and a variety of measures to improve black student life on campus. The student members of the Rosovsky Committee were unable to win for the report the general approval of Harvard's black students. Nevertheless, the report was adopted by the Faculty and a committee was established to implement it.

In two months, however, unrelated matters of the University Hall sit-in, the bust and the strike radically changed the political atmosphere, and the Association of African and Afro-American Students

---

[2]The model was similar to one later adopted by Yale, which for over a decade exemplified the best of Afro-American studies programs.

was emboldened to make new demands. It wanted Afro-American Studies to be a *department* rather than a *program*, and it wanted a student voice in the selection and appointment of its faculty. On April 22, 1969, the faculty were asked to vote on these propositions without altering them. Although deeply divided, the faculty voted for the changes the students demanded.

It was a bitter decision, many of those voting in favor doing so under a sense of intimidation. In that mood of crisis and perceived threat, the department was born. It would suffer, during its first ten years, from the lingering doubts and resentments harbored by faculty never fully convinced of Afro-America as a legitimate field of study, doubtful of it as a "discipline," and suspicious of what often appeared to be separatist tendencies on the part of its advocates.

Adding to the problem was a general confusion of aims by student advocates. There seemed to be three underlying (not necessarily compatible) expectations.

1. *To Have Something That Is Ours*: Ironically, the larger number of black undergraduates seemed to increase or intensify their feeling of isolation. The institution in all its aspects—courses, student activities, facilities—could easily be divided into "theirs" and "ours." Black students could call little of what normally existed at Harvard as "ours." Among a range of other demands for reform, that for black studies was a demand for legitimacy of place. In such a view, the traditional curriculum in the liberal arts—excluding non-whites and non-western culture with scarcely a thought—was "theirs." It was assumed that courses on African and Afro-American history, litera-ture, etc. would be the answer. Some advocates cared about the content of those courses; others cared mainly that the College make room for them, that they appear in the catalogue. For the former, it would not matter much who taught the courses. For the latter, it was often of great importance that the subject matter be taught by blacks. In both senses, however, black studies was a matter of defining "turf" in the university community.

2. *Quest for Identity*: Ironically, it was the very liberalization of America—residential desegregation, greater prospects of upward mobility—that threatened black identity. In the past, all blacks had been pretty much in the same boat, regardless of class and education. Now, prospects for the fortunate few seemed to include admission into the best colleges, positions in corporate America, and escape from the ghetto. Did a step along this road to an "integrated" and

mainstream future mean the abandonment of one's people and one's past? Increased mobility made the question, "Who am I?" all the more compelling. The identity crisis was exacerbated in white colleges where little if anything was taught about blacks, and where teachers would announce without embarrassment that William Faulkner was the best delineator of "Negro character" in American literature. Too often, however, the quest for identity intended the discovery and veneration of black heroes and heroines, the celebration of black people's "contributions," running counter to the recognized scholarly values of disinterested analysis.

3. *Field of Study*: Too often lost in the rhetoric was the idea that Afro-American life, history, and culture constituted a legitimate field of study independent of the demands of the time. Few of the student advocates would have known about the lifelong commitment to the promotion of that field by such major figures as W.E.B. Du Bois, Carter G. Woodson, Arthur Schomburg, J. Saunders Redding, Benjamin Quarles, and John Hope Franklin. The central idea was that the Afro-American experience was worthy for what it told about black people and their history in America and for what it tells, through refraction, about American history and culture. It should be studied by scholars, like any other area of human experience, and it should be drawn from the remote edges, from oblivion, to the center of American studies. That was a concept different from what most students advocated, and it is interesting to note that respected black scholars, such as John Hope Franklin, were more than a little suspicious of the programs that were being created in the name of black studies.

As we enter the twentieth year, much of the dust has settled. Afro-American Studies seems an established fact at Harvard. Arguments about its legitimacy as a field of study or a suitable field of concentration for undergraduates are no longer heard. Its students, in course enrollment as well as concentrators, are remarkably racially balanced. Its faculty contribute to the Core and to other university-wide offerings. There is every reason to believe that the department will remain at about its present strength for some time into the future.

Although it was created in an atmosphere of crises, with confusing and conflicting justification, the present ground on which the department stands is solid and rather conventional. It represents and advances Afro-American life, history, and culture as an important field for scholarly inquiry and study. And it is sustained in this by a remarkable growth of interest in the field over the past two decades. Increasingly, the field has been recognized in the United States and throughout the world. A glance at any of the major professional journals in the humanities and the social sciences will reveal a growing scholarly interest in problems and questions centered in what we now call Afro-American studies. Students of American life in Europe as well as in the Third World have increasingly turned to topics of Afro-American history and literature.

One sees the changes (often clumsy and insufficient) in textbooks of American history or literature. In literature the "canon" is being challenged and opened to include black writers among others. Course content in American history and American literature are beginning to reflect the change. And interdisciplinary programs such as American Studies and Comparative Literature are often leading the way for the mainstream disciplines.

Problems remain, nevertheless. The most difficult task we will have in the future is the recruitment of young people to become scholars in the field, and the identification and appointment of the best of a very small group to faculty positions. For the past decade and more, the best and the brightest of undergraduates have chosen law, medicine, and business over academic and scholarly careers, and that has been an even more exaggerated trend among minority students. At the same time, the demand for scholars in Afro-American studies has been growing as new schools and programs establish themselves.[3] An additional problem of recruitment is that all too often institutions see appointments in Afro-American studies as a way to address affirmative-action needs. That is to say, good white scholars are likely to be rejected even if a black scholar cannot be found. The Harvard department has stressed that we are interested in making the best possible appointments, regardless of race, and that the University's legitimate affirmative-action goals be met through university-wide recruitment.

Our strength into the future will be a measure of our meeting the challenges: to maintain an unwavering focus on our principal

---

[3]Demographic factors will be important. California, for instance, expects that in the 1990s it will become a state with a majority of its population non-white. Its state colleges and universities are reconsidering and reinvesting in a variety of ethnic studies programs, including Afro-American studies.

responsibility—the development and enrichment of our field of study; to maintain the highest standards of teaching and scholarship; to explore the intriguing frontiers of interdisciplinary scholarship.

(1989)

NOTE ON THE TEXTS

The original places of publication of the selections appear in the section below. In many cases the editors have compared the documents to variant printed versions or original manuscript sources. Some passages were omitted, usually to avoid duplication in this volume. Some errors were silently corrected or noted in brackets [ ]. Except for the Malcolm X sketch, the short biographical introductions to the selections were drafted by Caldwell Titcomb, who also assembled the readings. The editors wish to thank Beth Pinsker, who helped to research, prepare, and proofread this volume; Lauren Gwin who provided superb editorial and technical assistance and supervised the assembling of the index; Despina Gimbel for copyediting the manuscript and making many valuable suggestions; and Kay Shanahan for typing and designing the camera-ready copy of the text. We are grateful to Robert Kiely for awarding the project a grant from the Hyder E. Rollins Publication Fund at Harvard University to pay the permissions fees. *Blacks at Harvard* originated in a much shorter 1986 collection titled *Varieties of Black Experience at Harvard*, a work underwritten by the President and Fellows of Harvard College for the university's 350th anniversary.

CITATIONS AND ACKNOWLEDGMENTS

Caldwell Titcomb, "The Black Presence at Harvard, *350 Years: Historical Notes on Harvard* (Harvard University News Office, 1986), 49-51. Revised version. Rptd. by permission. Phillis Wheatley, "To The University of Cambridge, in New-England," rptd. in *The Poems of Phillis Wheatley*, revised and enlarged edition, ed. with an introduction by Julian D. Mason, Jr. (Chapel Hill and London: University of North Carolina Press, 1989), 52. Theodore Parsons and Eliphalet Pearson, "A Forensic Dispute on the Legality of Enslaving the Africans, Held at the Public Commencement in Cambridge, New-England, July 21st, 1773," is excerpted here without the accompanying notes. (Boston: Thomas Leverett, 1773; New York: Reader Microprint, 1985), 3-8, 21-24, 35-42, 46-48, Houghton Library, Harvard University. "Trouble Among the Medical Students of Harvard University," *Boston Medical and Surgical Journal* 43 (18 December 1850): 406. Petition to the Medical Faculty of Harvard University, November-December 1850, from the Countway Library, Dean's File, Harvard Medical Archives. Philip Cash, "Pride, Prejudice, and Politics," *Harvard Medical Alumni Bulletin* 54 (December 1980): 20-25. Rptd. by permission of the *Harvard Medical Alumni Bulletin* and by permission of Philip Cash. Martin R. Delany, "The Slave Factory," ch. 49 from *Blake; or, The Huts of America*, with an introduction by Floyd J. Miller (Boston: Beacon Press, 1970), 214-217. "For Good Government & Urban Politics: The Career of R. T. Greener '70," *Harvard Alumni Bulletin* 67 (12 December 1964): 266-268; no author or sources cited. Copyright © 1964 *Harvard Magazine*. Rptd. by permission. Richard T. Greener, "The White Problem," *Lend a Hand: A Record of Progress* 12 (May 1894): 354-367. Richard T. Greener, Speech at the Harvard Club of New York, excerpted in George Washington Williams, *A History of the Negro Race in America*, vol. 2 (New York: G. P. Putnam's Sons, 1883; rpt. New York: Bergman Publishers, 1968), 442-444. "Harvard's Negro Orator," *New York World*, 21 October 1889, p.1. C. G. Morgan, "Class Day Oration," from the booklet for the *Class of 1890 Baccalaureate Sermon, Baccalaureate Hymn, Class Day Oration, Class Poem, Ivy Oration, Ode, Class Song* (Cambridge: William H. Wheeler, 1890), 19-25. Harvard University Archives, HUD 290.04.6. W.E.B. Du Bois, "A Negro Student at Harvard at the End of the 19th Century," *Massachusetts Review* 1 (May 1960): 439-458.

[Monroe Trotter], "Negro Delegate Tells of His Work," *Christian Science Monitor*, 25 July 1919, p. 14. W.E.B. Du Bois, "William Monroe Trotter," *The Crisis* 41 (May 1934): 134. Booker T. Washington, *Up From Slavery* (1901), in *Three Negro Classics* (rpt., New York: Avon Books, 1965), 189-194; we have substituted the fuller (and annotated) version of "An Address at the Harvard University Alumni Dinner" rptd. in Louis R. Harlan et al., eds., *The Booker T. Washington Papers*, vol. 4, 1895-98 (Urbana: University of Illinois Press, 1975), 183-185. Booker T. Washington, "Principal Washington at Harvard University," 12 March 1907, vol. 9 and "Extracts from an Address at Harvard University," 4 February 1914, vol. 12 from Louis R. Harlan et al., eds. *The Booker T. Washington Papers* (Urbana: University of Illinois Press, 1975), 229, 434-435, respectively. William H. Ferris, "Douglass as an Orator," *Champion Magazine: A Monthly Survey of Negro Achievement* 1 (February 1917), 296-299. Leslie Pinckney Hill, "[The Place of] Religion in the Education of the Negro," *Harvard Advocate* 75 (24 June 1903): 128-130; full title from original manuscript in the Harvard University Archives. Leslie Pinckney Hill, "To William James," in *The Wings of Oppression* (Boston: The Stratford Co., Publishers, 1921), 61. Alain Locke, Two letters to his mother from Harvard [7 December 1905 and 15 December 1905], Alain Locke Papers, Moorland-Spingarn Research Center, Howard University. Alain Locke, "Youth Speaks," *Survey Graphic* 6 (March, 1925): 659-660. Alain Locke, "Sterling Brown: The New Negro Folk-Poet," in Nancy Cunard, ed., *Negro: An Anthology* [1934], ed. and abridged with intro. by Hugh Ford (New York: Frederick Ungar Publ. Co., 1970), 88-92. William H. Ferris, "The Myth of the New Negro," *Spokesman* 2 (July-August 1925): 9-10. Edward Smyth Jones, "Harvard Square," in *The Sylvan Cabin* (Boston: Sherman, French, & Co., 1911), 86-95. Eva Beatrice Dykes, Conclusion to *The Negro in English Romantic Thought or A Study of Sympathy for the Oppressed* (Washington, D.C.: Associated Publishers, Inc., 1942), 153-155, 183. Preface to *Readings from Negro Authors*, Otelia Cromwell, Lorenzo Dow Turner, and Eva B. Dykes, eds. (New York: Harcourt, Brace and Co., 1931), iii-v. Caroline Bond Day, Selections from *A Study of Some Negro-White Families in the United States*, Varia Africana V, Harvard African Studies, Vol. X, Part II (Cambridge, Mass.: Peabody Museum of Harvard University, 1932), 31-32, 39, and accompanying plates (34, 35, and 50). Caroline Bond Day, "The

Pink Hat," *Opportunity: A Journal of Negro Life* 4 (December 1926): 379-380. Caroline Bond Day, "Race Crossings in the United States," from *The Crisis* 37 (March 1930), 81-82, 103. John M. Fitzgerald and Otey M. Scruggs, "A Note on Marcus Garvey at Harvard, 1922: A Recollection of John M. Fitzgerald," *Journal of Negro History* 63 (April 1978): 157-160; rptd. by permission of Karen A. Robinson, Executive Director of the Association for the Study of Negro Life and History, Inc. Raymond Wolters, *The New Negro on Campus: Black College Rebellions of the 1920s* (Princeton, NJ: Princeton University Press, 1975), 324-331. Copyright ● 1975 by Princeton University Press. Rptd. by permission of Princeton University Press. "Colored Students at Harvard," *Harvard Alumni Bulletin* 25 (18 January 1923): 456-457. "Attacks Harvard on Negro Question. J. Weldon Johnson Denounces the Exclusion of Negroes from Its Dormitories," *New York Times*, 13 January 1923, p. 5. "Negro Graduate Protests. Says University Forsakes Freedom for Race Oppression," Ibid. Raymond Pace Alexander, "Voices from Harvard's Own Negroes," *Opportunity: Journal of Negro Life* 1 (March 1923): 29-31. W.E.B. Du Bois, "Harvard," *The Crisis* 25 (March 1923): 199. Charles W. Chesnutt to Roscoe C. Bruce, 10 April 1923, Charles W. Chesnutt Papers, Western Reserve Historical Society, Microfilm Edition, 1972, ed. Olivia J. Martin. "Charles Chesnutt and Harvard" [our title for excerpt] from J. Noel Heermance, *Charles W. Chesnutt: America's First Great Black Novelist* (Hamden, Conn.: Archon Books, 1974), 86-87. "No Racial Discrimination at Harvard," excerpted from *Harvard Alumni Bulletin* 25 (12 April 1923): 826-827. "Negroes in the Freshman Halls," *Harvard Alumni Bulletin* 25 (12 April 1923): 830. Marita O. Bonner, "On Being Young—A Woman—And Colored," *The Crisis* 31 (December 1925): 63-65. Rptd. by permission of Joyce Flynn, Literary Executrix. Sterling A. Brown, "I Visit Wren's Nest," *Phylon* 6 (1945): 225-226. Rptd. by permission. From *Collected Poems of Sterling A. Brown* (New York: Harper & Row Publishers, 1980), selected by Michael S. Harper, "Southern Road," copyright ● 1980 by Sterling A. Brown; rptd. by permission of Harper & Row Publishers, Inc. From *On These I Stand* by Countée Cullen, "The Shroud of Color," copyright ● 1925 by Harper & Row, Publishers, Inc., renewed 1953 by Ida M. Cullen; rptd. by permission of Harper & Row Publishers, Inc. From *The Medea and Some Poems* (New York and London: Harper & Brothers, 1935), 43-47, excerpt from "The Medea of Euripides," copyright ● 1935 by Harper & Row Publishers, Inc., renewed 1963 by Ida M. Cullen; rptd. by permission of Harper & Row Publishers, Inc. Ralph Bunche, "The Virtue of Color-Blindness" [originally titled, "Human Relations In World Perspective"], in Philip S. Foner, ed. *The Voice of Black America: Major Speeches by Negroes in the United States, 1797-1971* (New York: Simon and Schuster, 1972), 882-888. Rptd. by permission. William H. Hastie, "The Black Mystique Pitfall," *The Crisis* 78 (October 1971): 243-247. Rayford W. Logan, "The

Confessions of an Unwilling Nordic," from *The Negro Caravan: Writings by American Negroes*, selected and edited by Sterling A. Brown, Arthur P. Davis, and Ulysses Lee, with an intro. by Julius Lester (New York: Dryden Press, 1941; rpt. Arno Press and the *New York Times*, 1970), 1043-1050; rptd. from *World Tomorrow* 10 (July 1927): 297-300. Kenneth B. Murdock to John A. Lomax, 18 January 1935, Eugene C. Barker Texas History Center, University of Texas at Austin Center for American History; special thanks to Jerrold Hirsch. "Negro Who Sung Way Out of Southern Prisons Wins Two Harvard Audiences," *Boston Globe*, 14 March 1935, p. 12. Excerpts from John Hope Franklin, "A Life of Learning," rptd. as "John Hope Franklin: A Life of Learning," in *Race and History: Selected Essays 1938-1988* (Baton Rouge: Louisiana State University Press, 1989), 277-291; 282-285, 288-291. Copyright ⊚ 1989 Louisiana State University Press, rptd. by permission. Muriel Snowden, "Right to Participate," *Radcliffe Quarterly* 72 (September 1986): 32-33. Copyright ⊚ 1986 Radcliffe College. Rptd. by permission of *Radcliffe Quarterly*. "Miss Radcliffe," *Newsweek* 35 (21 June 1948), 25. Elizabeth Fitzgerald Howard, "Three Generations of a Black Radcliffe and Harvard Family," *Radcliffe Quarterly* 70 (September 1984): 11-13. Copyright ⊚ 1984 Radcliffe College. Rptd. by permission of *Radcliffe Quarterly*. Harold R. Scott, "Harvard and the Performing Arts: 'How Long, O Lord . . . ?'" *Harvard College Class of 1957 20th Anniversary Report* (Cambridge: Crimson Printing Co., 1977, printed for the class), 25-27. Rptd. by permission. William Melvin Kelley, "Black Power," *Partisan Review* 35 (Spring 1968): 216-217. Rptd. by permission of the *Partisan Review* and the author. William Melvin Kelley, "My Next to Last Hit by C.C. Johnson" appears here for the first time and is printed by permission of the author. Archie C. Epps III, "Africans and Afro-Americans," *Harvard Crimson*, 9 May 1963. Herbert H. Denton, Jr., "Afro-Americans," *Harvard Crimson*, 14 May 1963, p. 3. "The Leverett House Forum of March 18, 1964," from *Malcolm X: Speeches at Harvard*, rev. ed. by Archie Epps (New York: Paragon House, 1991 [New York: Morrow, 1968]), 131-160; 189-190. Copyright ⊚ Betty Shabazz. Special thanks to Archie Epps. James Alan McPherson, "On Becoming an American Writer," *The Atlantic* 242 (December 1978): 53-57. Copyright ⊚ by James Alan McPherson; rptd. by permission. Lawrence E. Eichel, "The Crisis of 1969" [originally titled "The Eighth Demand"], from *The Harvard Strike*, by Lawrence E. Eichel, Kenneth W. Jost, Robert D. Luskin and Richard M. Neustadt (Boston: Houghton Mifflin, 1970): 261-288. Copyright ⊚ 1970 by Lawrence E. Eichel, Kenneth W. Jost, Robert D. Luskin and Richard M. Neustadt. Rptd. by permission of Houghton Mifflin Co. Excerpt from the "Rosovsky Report," in the "Faculty of Arts and Sciences, Harvard University: Report of the Faculty Committee on African and Afro-American Studies, January 20, 1969," pp. 33-34. Harvard University Archives. Faculty Vote of April 22, 1969, Appendix I in the

Kilson, Southern. By permission of Harvard Yearbook Publications, Inc.: Braxton, Denton, Griffin, J. Jackson, Nickens, Otuteye, Wilson; special thanks to photo editor Juha P. Maijala '93 for reproducing the Yearbook photographs. By permission of the Radcliffe College Archives: Bonner, Day, Dykes, Snowden (photo by Judith Sedwick). By permission of the Radcliffe Office of Public Information: Howard, Spence (photo by Lillian Kemp). By permission of the Photographs & Prints Division, Schomburg Center for Research in Black Culture, The New York Public Library (Astor, Lenox and Tilden Foundations): Cullen in 1920. By permission of Robert C. Hayden and the Boston Public Library: Trotter in midcareer. By permission of photographer Hugh Bell, New York City: Cullen's gravestone. By permission of photographer Timothy G. Carlson '71: students leaving meeting, 1969. By permission of Scurlock Studio, Washington, D.C.: Brown, Logan. Wm. J. Simmons, *Men of Mark* (1887): Delany. National Park Service (Booker T. Washington National Monument): Chesnutt, Washington (both). *Who's Who in Colored America* (1927 ed.): Ferris; ibid. (1950 ed.): Alexander. Frederick Douglass, *My Bondage* (1855), frontispiece: Douglass. United Press International: Bunche, Garvey, Malcolm X. *Colored American* magazine: Johnson. New York Daily News: Cullen in 1932. *Leadbelly Songbook* (1962): Leadbelly. *Negro Almanac*, 1st ed. (1966): Kelley (photo by Edward N. Barnett). Dustjacket of *Hue and Cry* (1968): McPherson (photo by Bill Troyer). Dustjacket of *Sarah Phillips* (1984): Lee (photo by Steven Olivier Cojot Goldberg). Christopher Edley: Edley. Caldwell Titcomb: cover, *Up From Harvard* (1969), Scott (both). Source unidentified: Franklin.

READINGS

(Some general and miscellaneous works are listed, followed by a sampling of books by or about contributors to this anthology. In the case of works by black Harvard alumni who are not represented by selections in the body of this collection, the Harvard affiliation has been indicated. For reasons of space, articles are not included.—C.T.)

General

Aptheker, Herbert, ed. *A Documentary History of the Negro People in the United States*, 3 vols. (Secaucus, N.J.: Citadel Press, 1951, 1973).

Bailyn, Bernard, Donald Fleming, Oscar Handlin, and Stephan Thernstrom. *Glimpses of the Harvard Past* (Cambridge, Mass./London: Harvard University Press, 1986).

Ballard, Allen B. [A.M. 1957, Ph.D. 1962]. *The Education of Black Folk* (New York: Harper & Row, 1974).

Bardolph, Richard. *The Negro Vanguard* (New York: Holt, Rinehart, 1959) [reprint New York: Vintage, 1961].

Barksdale, Richard [A.M. 1947, Ph.D. 1951], and Keneth Kinnamon, eds. *Black Writers of America: A Comprehensive Anthology* (New York: Macmillan, 1972).

Beckham, Barry, ed. *The Black Student's Guide to Colleges*, 2nd ed. (Providence: Beckham House, 1984).

Bell, Bernard W. *The Afro-American Novel and Its Tradition* (Amherst: University of Massachusetts Press, 1987) [Includes sections on Martin Delany, Charles Chesnutt, W.E.B. Du Bois, James Weldon Johnson, Countée Cullen, and William Melvin Kelley].

Bond, Horace Mann. *Black American Scholars: A Study of Their Beginnings* (Detroit: Balamp, 1972).

_____. *The Education of the Negro in the American Social Order*, 2nd ed. (New York: Octagon, 1966).

Brawley, Benjamin [A.M. 1908]. *The Negro Genius* (New York: Dodd, Mead, 1937; reissued 1966).

_____. *A Short History of the English Drama* (New York: Harcourt Brace, 1921).

Brignano, Russell C. *Black Americans in Autobiography*, rev. ed. (Durham: Duke University Press, 1984).

Campbell, Dorothy W. *Index to Black American Writers in Collective Biographies* (Littleton, Colo.: Libraries Unlimited, 1983).

Chambers, Fredrick, comp. *Black Higher Education in the United States: A*

Selected Bibliography (Westport, Conn.: Greenwood, 1978).

Clark, Edward. *Black Writers in New England: A Bibliography* (Boston: National Park Service, 1985).

Cunard, Nancy, comp. *Negro: An Anthology* (London: The Author, 1934) [reprint, ed. & abridged, with an introduction, by Hugh Ford, New York: Frederick Ungar, 1970].

Davis, Allison [A.M. 1925]. *Leadership, Love and Aggression* (New York: Harcourt Brace, 1983) [Deals with Frederick Douglass, W.E.B. Du Bois, Richard Wright, Martin Luther King, Jr.].

Davis, Arthur P. *From the Dark Tower: Afro-American Writers 1900-1960* (Washington: Howard University Press, 1981) [Includes chapters on W.E.B. Du Bois, Alain Locke, Countée Cullen, and Sterling Brown].

[Epps Report.] *A Study of Race Relations at Harvard College*. Committee on Race Relations, Harvard College, May 1980.

Ferguson, Jeffrey [A.B. 1985]. "Black Student Identity at Harvard and the Rising Black Elite." Senior thesis, Afro-American Studies Department, Harvard University, 1985.

Fine, Elsa Honig. *The Afro-American Artist: A Search for Identity* (New York: Holt, Rinehart & Winston, 1973) [reprint New York: Hacker Art Books, 1982].

Fleming, Jacqueline [Ph.D. 1974]. *Blacks in College: A Comparative Study* (San Francisco: Jossey-Bass, 1984).

Foner, Philip S., ed. *The Voice of Black America: Major Speeches by Negroes in the United States, 1797-1971* (New York: Simon & Schuster, 1972).

Foreman, Christopher H., Jr. [A.B. 1974; A.M. 1977; Ph.D. 1980]. *Signals from the Hill: Congressional Oversight and the Challenge of Social Regulation* (New Haven: Yale University Press, 1988).

Gatewood, Willard B. *Aristocrats of Color: The Black Elite, 1880-1920* (Bloomington: Indiana University Press, 1990).

Gossett, Thomas E. *Race: The History of an Idea in America* (Dallas: Southern Methodist University Press, 1963) [reprint New York: Schocken, 1965].

Greene, Harry Washington. *Holders of Doctorates Among American Negroes* (Boston: Meador, 1946).

Greene, Lorenzo J. *The Negro in Colonial New England* (New York: Columbia University Press, 1942) [reprint New York: Atheneum, 1968].

Hayden, Robert C. *African-Americans in Boston: More Than 350 Years* (Boston: Boston Public Library, 1991).

Jaynes, Gerald D., and Robin M. Williams Jr., eds. *A Common Destiny: Blacks and American Society* (Washington, D.C.: National Academy Press, 1989).

Johnson, Charles S. *The Negro College Graduate* (Chapel Hill: University of North Carolina Press, 1938) [reprint College Park, Md.: McGrath Publishing Co., 1969].

Kallenbach, Jessamine S., ed. *Index to Black American Literary Anthologies* (Boston: G.K. Hall, 1979).

Katz, William Loren. *Eyewitness: The Negro in American History*, rev. ed. (New York: Pitman Publishing Corp., 1971).

Kellner, Bruce, ed. *The Harlem Renaissance: A Historical Dictionary for the Era* (Westport, Conn.: Greenwood Press, 1984) [reprint New York: Methuen, 1987].

Lamar, Jake [A.B. 1983]. *Bourgeois Blues: An American Memoir* (New York: Summit Books, 1991).

Lerner, Gerda, ed. *Black Women in White America: A Documentary History* (New York: Pantheon, 1972).

Lipset, Seymour Martin, and David Riesman. *Education and Politics at Harvard* (New York: McGraw-Hill, 1975).

McMillan, Terry, ed. *Breaking Ice: An Anthology of Contemporary African-American Fiction* (New York: Penguin Books, 1990) [Includes William Melvin Kelley and James Alan McPherson].

McPherson, James M. et al. *Blacks in America: Bibliographical Essays* (Garden City: Doubleday, 1971).

Meier, August, and Elliott Rudwick, eds. *The Making of Black America: Essays in Negro Life and History*, 2 vols. (New York: Atheneum, 1969).

Miller, Elizabeth W., comp. *The Negro in America: A Bibliography*, 2nd ed. (Cambridge: Harvard University Press, 1970).

Page, James A., and Jae Min Roh. *Selected Black American, African, and Caribbean Authors: A Bio-Bibliography* (Littleton, Colo.: Libraries Unlimited, 1985).

Peterson, Marvin W., Robert T. Blackburn, Zelda F. Gamson et al. *Black Students on White Campuses: The Impacts of Increased Black Enrollments* (Ann Arbor: Institute for Social Research, University of Michigan, 1978).

Pierson, William D. *Black Yankees* (Amherst: University of Massachusetts Press, 1988).

Porter, Dorothy B., comp. *The Negro in the United States: A Selected Bibliography* (Washington: Library of Congress, 1970).

Robinson, William H. [Ph.D. 1964]. *Black New England Letters* (Boston: Boston Public Library, 1977).

Roses, Lorraine Elena, and Ruth Elizabeth Randolph. *Harlem Renaissance and Beyond: Literary Biographies of 100 Black Women Writers 1900-1945* (Boston: G.K. Hall, 1990) [Includes Marita Bonner, Caroline Bond

Day, and Eva Dykes].

Rush, Theressa G., Carol F. Myers, and Esther S. Arata. *Black American Writers Past and Present: A Biographical and Bibliographical Dictionary*, 2 vols. (Metuchen, N.J.: Scarecrow Press, 1975).

Sammons, Vivian Ovelton. *Blacks in Science and Medicine* (New York: Hemisphere Publishing Corp., 1990).

Shockley, Ann Allen, and Sue P. Chandler. *Living Black American Authors: A Biographical Directory* (New York: R. R. Bowker, 1973).

Singh, Amritjit et al., eds. *The Harlem Renaissance: Revaluations* (New York/London: Garland, 1989) [Includes essays on W.E.B. Du Bois, Alain Locke, Sterling Brown, and Countée Cullen].

Snowden, Frank M., Jr. [A.B. 1932, M.A. 1933, Ph.D. 1944]. *Before Color Prejudice: The Ancient View of Blacks* (Cambridge, Mass.: Harvard University Press, 1983).

Sowell, Thomas [A.B. 1958]. *Black Education: Myths and Tragedies* (New York: David McKay, 1972).

_____. *Choosing a College: A Guide for Parents and Students* (New York: Harper & Row, 1989).

_____. *Ethnic America* (New York: Basic Books, 1981).

Spradling, Mary Mace, ed. *In Black and White*, 3rd ed., 2 vols. (Detroit: Gale Research Co., 1980) [Bibliography of 15,000-plus black individuals and groups].

Synott, Marcia Graham. *The Half-Opened Door: Discrimination and Admissions at Harvard, Yale, and Princeton, 1900-1970* (Westport, Conn.: Greenwood, 1979).

Tate, Merze [Ph.D. 1941]. *The United States and Armaments* (Cambridge, Mass.: Harvard University Press, 1948) [reprint New York: Russell & Russell, 1969].

Thorpe, Earl E. *Black Historians: A Critique* (New York: William Morrow, 1971).

Turner, Darwin T., comp. *Afro-American Writers* (New York: Appleton-Century-Crofts, 1970) [A bibliography].

Wesley, Charles H. [Ph.D. 1925]. *Neglected History: Essays in Negro-American History* (Washington: Association for the Study of Negro Life & History, 1969).

Whitlow, Roger. *Black American Literature: A Critical History* (Totowa, N.J.: Rowman & Allanheld, 1984) [Includes Martin Delany, W.E.B. Du Bois, Countée Cullen, and William Melvin Kelley].

Wintz, Cary D. *Black Culture and the Harlem Renaissance* (Houston: Rice University Press, 1988).

Woodson, Carter G. [Ph.D. 1912]. *The Education of the Negro Prior to 1861*,

2nd ed. (Washington: Association for the Study of Negro Life and History, 1933) [reprint New York: Arno, 1968].

_____. *The Mis-Education of the Negro* (Washington: Associated Publishers, 1933) [reprint New York: AMS Press, 1972].

Wright, Nathan Jr., ed. [S.T.M. 1951, Ed.D. 1964]. *What Black Educators Are Saying* (New York: Hawthorn, 1970).

Derrick Bell

Bell, Derrick. *And We Are Not Saved: The Elusive Quest for Racial Justice* (New York: Basic Books, 1987; enlarged ed. 1989).

_____. *Faces at the Bottom of the Well: The Permanence of Racism* (New York: Basic Books, 1992).

_____. *Race, Racism and American Law* (Boston: Little, Brown, 1973; 2nd ed. 1980).

_____. *Shades of Brown: New Perspectives on School Desegregation* (New York: Columbia University, Teachers College Press, 1980).

Marita Bonner

Flynn, Joyce, and Joyce Occomy Stricklin, eds. *Frye Street & Environs: The Collected Works of Marita Bonner* (Boston: Beacon Press, 1987).

Sterling A. Brown

Brown, Sterling A. *The Collected Poems*, ed. Michael S. Harper (New York: Harper & Row, 1980).

_____. *The Negro in American Fiction* (Washington: Associates in Negro Folk Education, 1937) [reprint New York: Atheneum, 1969].

_____. *Negro Poetry and Drama* (Washington: Associates in Negro Folk Education, 1937) [reprint New York: Atheneum, 1969].

Brown, Sterling A. et al., eds. *The Negro Caravan: Writings by American Negroes* (New York: Dryden Press, 1941) [reprint New York: Arno, 1970].

Ralph J. Bunche

Bunche, Ralph J. *The Political Status of the Negro in the Age of FDR* [1940], ed. Dewey W. Grantham (Chicago: University of Chicago Press, 1973).

_____. *A World View of Race* (Washington: Associates in Negro Folk Education, 1936 [reprint Port Washington, N.Y: Kennikat, 1968].

Edgar, Robert R., ed. *An African American in South Africa: The Travel Notes of Ralph J. Bunche* (Athens, Ohio: Ohio University Press, 1992).
Kugelmass, J. Alvin. *Ralph J. Bunche: Fighter for Peace* (New York: Julian Messner, 1952; reissued 1962).
Mann, Peggy. *Ralph J. Bunche: U.N. Peacemaker* (New York: Coward, McCann, 1975).
Rivlin, Benjamin. *Ralph Bunche: The Man and His Times* (New York: Holmes & Meier, 1990).

Charles W. Chesnutt

Andrews, William L. *The Literary Career of Charles W. Chesnutt* (Baton Rouge/London: Louisiana State University Press, 1980).
Chesnutt, Charles W. *The Colonel's Dream* (New York: Doubleday Page, 1905) [several reprints, 1968-1977].
————. *The Conjure Woman* (Boston: Houghton Mifflin, 1899, 1929) [several reprints, 1968-1977].
————. *Frederick Douglass* (Boston: Small Maynard, 1899) [reprints, 1970, 1977].
————. *The House Behind the Cedars* (Boston: Houghton Mifflin, 1900) [reprints, 1968, 1969].
————. *The Marrow of Tradition* (Boston: Houghton Mifflin, 1901) [several reprints, 1968-1977].
————. *The Wife of His Youth and Other Stories of the Color Line* (Boston: Houghton Mifflin, 1899) [several reprints, 1967-1977].
Ellison, Curtis W., and E.W. Metcalf Jr. *Charles W. Chesnutt: A Reference Guide* (Boston: G.K. Hall, 1977).
Heermance, J. Noel. *Charles W. Chesnutt: America's First Great Black Novelist* (Hamden, Conn.: Archon Books, 1974).
Keller, Frances Richardson. *An American Crusade: The Life of Charles Waddell Chesnutt* (Provo, Utah: Brigham Young University Press, 1978).
Render, Sylvia Lyons, ed. *The Short Fiction of Charles W. Chesnutt* (Washington, D.C.: Howard University Press, 1981).

Countée Cullen

Baker, Houston A., Jr. *A Many-Colored Coat of Dreams: The Poetry of Countée Cullen* (Detroit: Broadside Press, 1974).
Cullen, Countée, ed. *Caroling Dusk: An Anthology of Verse by Negro Poets* (New York: Harper & Row, 1927; reissued 1974).
————. *On These I Stand* (New York: Harper & Row, 1947).

Early, Gerald, ed. *My Soul's High Song: The Collected Writings of Countée Cullen* (New York: Doubleday, 1991).

Ferguson, Blanche E. *Countée Cullen and the Negro Renaissance* (New York: Dodd, Mead, 1966).

Perry, Margaret. *A Bio-Bibliography of Countée P. Cullen, 1903-1946* (Westport, Conn.: Greeenwood, 1971).

Shucard, Alan R. *Countée Cullen* (Boston: Twayne, 1984).

Caroline Bond Day

Day, Caroline Bond. *A Study of Some Negro-White Families in the United States* [with foreword and notes by Earnest A. Hooton] (Cambridge, Mass.: Peabody Museum of Harvard University, 1932).

Martin R. Delany

Delany, Martin R. *Blake; or, The Huts of America* [serialized 1859-1862] (Boston: Beacon Press, 1970).

_____. *The Condition, Elevation, Emigration, and Destiny of the Colored People of the United States* (Philadelphia: The Author, 1852) [reprint New York: Arno, 1968].

Delany, Martin R., and Robert Campbell. *Search for a Place: Black Separatism and Africa* (Ann Arbor: University of Michigan Press, 1969).

Ellison, Curtis W., and E. W. Metcalf, Jr., eds. *William Wells Brown and Martin R. Delany: A Reference Guide* (Boston: G. K. Hall, 1978).

Griffith, Cyril E. *The African Dream: Martin R. Delany and the Emergence of Pan-African Thought* (University Park: Pennsylvania State University Press, 1975).

Rollin, Frank A. [pseud. of Frances Rollin Whipper]. *The Life and Public Services of Martin R. Delany* (Boston: Lee & Shepard, 1868) [reprint New York: Kraus, 1969].

Sterling, Dorothy. *The Making of an Afro-American: Martin Robison Delany, 1812-1885* (Garden City: Doubleday, 1971).

Ullman, Victor. *Martin R. Delany: The Beginnings of Black Nationalism* (Boston: Beacon Press, 1971).

W.E.B. Du Bois

Aptheker, Herbert. *Annotated Bibliography of the Published Writings of W.E.B. Du Bois* (Millwood, N.Y.: Kraus-Thomson, 1973).

_____, ed. *Contributions by W.E.B. Du Bois in Government Publications and Proceedings* (Millwood, N.Y.: Kraus-Thomson, 1980).

_____, ed. *The Correspondence of W.E.B. Du Bois*, 3 vols. (Amherst: University of Massachusetts Press, 1973, 1976, 1978).

Broderick, Francis L. *W.E.B. Du Bois: Negro Leader in a Time of Crisis* (Stanford: Stanford University Press, 1959).

Du Bois, W.E.B. *Against Racism: Unpublished Essays, Papers, Addresses 1887-1961*, ed. Herbert Aptheker (Amherst: University of Massachusetts Press, 1985).

_____. *The Autobiography of W.E.B. Du Bois*, ed. Herbert Aptheker (New York: International Publishers, 1968).

_____. *Book Reviews*, ed. Herbert Aptheker (Millwood, N.Y.: Kraus-Thomson, 1977).

_____. *The Souls of Black Folk* (Chicago: McClurg, 1903) [frequently reprinted].

_____. *Writings*, ed. Nathan Huggins (New York: Library of America, 1986) [Contains *The Suppression of the African Slave- Trade, The Souls of Black Folk, Dusk of Dawn*, and selected essays].

Foner, Philip S., ed. *W.E.B. Du Bois Speaks: Speeches and Addresses* [1890-1963], 2 vols. (New York: Pathfinder Press, 1970).

Lester, Julius, ed. *The Seventh Son: The Thought and Writings of W.E.B. Du Bois*, 2 vols. (New York: Vintage, 1971).

Logan, Rayford W., ed. *W.E.B. Du Bois: A Profile* (New York: Hill & Wang, 1971).

Marable, Manning. *W.E.B. Du Bois: Black Radical Democrat* (Boston: Twayne, 1986).

Paschal, Andrew, ed. *A W.E.B. Du Bois Reader* (New York: Macmillan, 1971).

Rampersad, Arnold [A.M. 1969, Ph.D. 1973]. *The Art and Imagination of W.E.B. Du Bois* (Cambridge: Harvard University Press, 1976).

Rudwick, Elliott M. *W.E.B. Du Bois: A Study in Minority Group Leadership* (Philadelphia: University of Pennsylvania Press, 1960) [reprint New York: Atheneum, 1968].

Walden, Daniel, ed. *W.E.B. Du Bois: The 'Crisis' Writings* (Greenwich: Fawcett, 1972).

Weinberg, Meyer, ed. *W.E.B. Du Bois: A Reader* (New York: Harper & Row, 1970).

Eva B. Dykes

Cromwell, Otelia, Lorenzo D. Turner [A.M. 1917], and Eva B. Dykes, eds. *Readings from Negro Authors* (New York: Harcourt, Brace, 1931).

Dykes, Eva B. *The Negro in English Romantic Thought* (Washington: Associated Publishers, 1942).

William H. Ferris

Ferris, William H. *The African Abroad; or, His Evolution in Western Civilization*, 2 vols. (New Haven: Tuttle, Morehouse and Taylor, 1913) [reprint New York: Johnson Reprints, 1968].
_____. *Alexander Crummell, An Apostle of Negro Culture* (Washington, D.C.: American Negro Academy, 1920) [reprint New York: Arno Press, 1969].
Martin, Tony, ed. *African Fundamentalism: A Literary and Cultural Anthology of Garvey's Harlem Renaissance* (Dover, Mass.: The Majority Press, 1991) [Contains 15 articles by W.H. Ferris].

John Hope Franklin

Anderson, Eric, and Alfred A. Moss, Jr., eds. *The Facts of Reconstruction: Essays in Honor of John Hope Franklin* (Baton Rouge: Louisiana University Press, 1991).
Franklin, John Hope. *The Emancipation Proclamation* (New York: Doubleday, 1963).
_____. *The Free Negro in North Carolina, 1790-1860* (Chapel Hill: University of North Carolina Press, 1943) [reprint New York: W.W. Norton, 1971].
_____. *From Slavery to Freedom: A History of Negro Americans*, (New York: Knopf, 1947; rev. eds. 1956, 1967, 1974, 1978; 6th ed. with Alfred A. Moss, Jr., 1987).
_____. *George Washington Williams: A Biography* (Chicago/London: University of Chicago Press, 1985).
_____. *The Militant South, 1800-1861* (Cambridge: Harvard University Press, 1956, 1970 with new Preface).
_____. *Race and History: Selected Essays, 1938-1988* (Baton Rouge/London: Louisiana State University Press, 1989).
_____. *Racial Equality in America* (Chicago: University of Chicago Press, 1976).
_____. *Reconstruction: After the Civil War* (Chicago: University of Chicago Press, 1961).
_____. *A Southern Odyssey: Travelers in the Antebellum North* (Baton Rouge: Louisiana State University Press, 1976).
Willie, Charles V. [hon. A.M. 1974]. *Five Black Scholars: An Analysis of*

Family Life, Education, and Career (Lanham, Md.: University Press of America, 1986) [Chapter 2, "John Hope Franklin: The Historian Who Understands"].

Marcus Garvey

Burkett, Randall K. *Black Redemption: Churchmen Speak for the Garvey Movement* (Philadelphia: Temple University Press, 1978).

Clarke, John Henrik, ed. *Marcus Garvey and the Vision of Africa* (New York: Random House, 1974).

Cronon, Edmund David. *Black Moses: The Story of Marcus Garvey and the Universal Negro Improvement Association* (Madison: University of Wisconsin Press, 1955; reissued 1969).

Davis, Lenwood G., and Janet L. Sims, comps. *Marcus Garvey: An Annotated Bibliography* (Westport, Conn.: Greenwood, 1980).

Essien-Udom, E[ssien] U[dosen] and Amy J. Garvey, eds. *More Philosophy and Opinions of Marcus Garvey* (London: Frank Cass, 1977).

Fax, Elton C. *Garvey: The Story of a Pioneer Black Nationalist* (New York: Dodd, Mead, 1972).

Garvey, Amy Jacques. *Garvey and Garveyism* (Kingston, Jamaica: The Author, 1963).

Garvey, Amy Jacques, ed. *Philosophy and Opinions of Marcus Garvey*, 2 vols. (New York: Universal Publishing House, 1923-1925) [2nd ed., 2 vols. in 1, London: Frank Cass, 1967; reprint 2 vols in 1, New York: Atheneum, 1974].

Garvey, Marcus. *Message to the People: The Course of African Philosophy*, ed. Tony Martin (Dover, Mass.: The Majority Press, 1986).

_____. *The Poetical Works of Marcus Garvey*, ed. Tony Martin (Dover, Mass.: The Majority Press, 1983).

Hill, Robert A., ed. *The Marcus Garvey and Universal Negro Improvement Association Papers*, 7 vols. (Berkeley: University of California Press, 1983-1991).

_____, ed. *Marcus Garvey: Life and Lessons* (Berkeley: University of California Press, 1987).

Lewis, Rupert. *Marcus Garvey: Anti-Colonial Champion* (Trenton, N.J.: Africa World Press, 1988).

Lewis, Rupert, and Patrick Bryan, eds. *Garvey: His Work and Impact* (Trenton, N.J.: Africa World Press, 1991).

Martin, Tony. *Literary Garveyism: Garvey, Black Arts and the Harlem Renaissance* (Dover, Mass.: The Majority Press, 1983).

_____. *Marcus Garvey, Hero* (Dover, Mass.: The Majority Press, 1983).

Sewell, Tony. *Garvey's Children: The Legacy of Marcus Garvey* (Trenton, N.J.: Africa World Press, 1990).
Smith-Irvin, Jeannette. *Marcus Garvey's Footsoldiers of the Universal Negro Improvement Association* (Trenton, N.J.: Africa World Press, 1989).
Stein, Judith. *The World of Marcus Garvey: Race and Class in Modern Society* (Baton Rouge/London: Louisiana State University Press, 1986).
Vincent, Theodore G. *Black Power and the Garvey Movement* (Berkeley: Ramparts Press, 1971).

Richard T. Greener

Class of 1870: Report VI (1895), pp. 25-28. Harvard University Archives.
Greener, Richard T. *Charles Sumner: The Idealist, Statesman and Scholar* (Columbia, S.C.: Republican Printing Co., 1874).

William H. Hastie

Chadbourn, Erika S. *The High Mountain: William Henry Hastie* (Cambridge, Mass.: Manuscript Division, Harvard Law School Library, 1984).
Chadbourn, Erika S., Lynne Hollyer, and Richard McNally, comps. *William Henry Hastie: An Inventory of His Papers in the Harvard Law School Library* (Cambridge, Mass.: Harvard Law School Library, 1984).
Hastie, William H. *The William H. Hastie Papers* (Frederick, Md.: University Publications of America, 1988) [107 microfilm reels and two printed guides].
Ware, Gilbert. *William Hastie: Grace Under Pressure* (New York: Oxford University Press, 1984).

Leslie Pinckney Hill

Hill, Leslie P. *Toussaint L'Ouverture: A Dramatic History* [verse drama] (Boston: Christopher, 1928).
_____. *Wings of Oppression and Other Poems* (Boston: Stratford, 1921) [reprint Freeport, N.Y.: Books for Libraries Press, 1971].

Elizabeth Fitzgerald Howard

Howard, Elizabeth Fitzgerald. *America as Story: Historical Fiction for Secondary Schools* (Chicago: American Library Association, 1988).
_____. *Aunt Flossie's Hats (and Crab Cakes Later)* (New York: Clarion Books, 1991).

_____. *Chita's Christmas Tree* (New York: Bradbury Press, 1989).
_____. *The Train to Lulu's* (New York: Bradbury Press, 1989).

Nathan I. Huggins

Huggins, Nathan I. *Afro-American Studies* (New York: Ford Foundation, 1985).

_____. *Black Odyssey: The Afro-American Ordeal in Slavery* (New York: Pantheon, 1977; reprint New York: Random House, 1990, with a new preface by the author).

_____. *Harlem Renaissance* (New York: Oxford University Press, 1971; several reprints, 1973–).

_____. *Protestants Against Poverty: Boston's Charities, 1870-1900* (Westport, Conn.: Greenwood, 1971).

_____. *Slave and Citizen: The Life of Frederick Douglass* (Boston: Little, Brown, 1980).

_____, ed. *Voices From the Harlem Renaissance* (New York: Oxford University Press, 1976).

Huggins, Nathan I., Martin Kilson, and Daniel M. Fox, eds. *Key Issues in the Afro-American Experience*, 2 vols. (New York: Harcourt Brace, 1971).

James Weldon Johnson

Fleming, Robert E. *James Weldon Johnson* (Boston: Twayne, 1987).

_____. *James Weldon Johnson and Arna Wendell Bontemps: A Reference Guide* (Boston: G.K. Hall, 1978).

Johnson, James Weldon. *Along This Way* (New York: Viking, 1933; reissued 1968).

_____. *The Autobiography of an Ex-Colored Man* (Boston: Sherman, French, 1912) [reprint New York: Hill & Wang, 1960].

_____. *Black Manhattan* (New York: Knopf, 1930) [reprint New York: Atheneum, 1968].

_____, ed. *The Book of American Negro Poetry*, rev. ed. (New York: Harcourt, Brace, 1931; reissued 1959).

_____. *God's Trombones: Seven Negro Sermons in Verse* (New York: Viking, 1927; reissued 1969).

Levy, Eugene. *James Weldon Johnson: Black Leader, Black Voice* (Chicago: University of Chicago Press, 1973).

Edward Smyth Jones

"Invincible Ned" [E. Smyth Jones]. *The Rose That Bloometh in My Heart and Other Poems* (Louisville: The Author, 1908).
Jones, Edward Smyth. *The Sylvan Cabin and Other Verse* (Boston: Sherman, French, 1911).

William Melvin Kelley

Kelley, William Melvin. *Dancers on the Shore* (Garden City: Doubleday, 1964) [reprint Washington: Howard University Press, 1984].
_____. *dem* (Garden City: Doubleday, 1967) [reprint New York: Collier, 1969].
_____. *A Different Drummer* (Garden City: Doubleday, 1962) [reprint Garden City: Anchor, 1969].
_____. *A Drop of Patience* (Garden City: Doubleday, 1965).
_____. *Dunfords Travels Everywheres* (Garden City: Doubleday, 1970).

Martin Kilson

Cartey, Wilfred, and Martin Kilson, comps. *Africa Reader* (New York: Random House, 1970).
Emerson, Rupert, and Martin Kilson. *Political Awakening of Africa* [1965] (Westport, Conn.: Greenwood, 1981).
Hill, A. Cromwell [Ph.D. 1952] and Martin Kilson, eds. *Apropos of Africa: Sentiments of Negro American Leaders on Africa from the 1800's to the 1950's* (London: Cass, 1969).
Kilson, Martin. *African Diaspora: Interpretive Essays* (Cambridge, Mass.: Harvard University Press, 1976).
_____, ed. *New States in the Modern World* (Cambridge, Mass.: Harvard University Press, 1975).
_____. *Political Change in a West African State* (Cambridge, Mass.: Harvard University Press, 1966).
Kilson, Martin, and Robert I. Rotberg, eds. *The African Diaspora* (Cambridge, Mass.: Harvard University Press, 1976).

Huddie (Leadbelly) Ledbetter

Asch, Moses, and Alan Lomax, eds. *The Leadbelly Songbook* (New York: Oak Publications, 1962).
Garvin, Richard M., and Edmond G. Addeo. *The Midnight Special: The*

Legend of Leadbelly (New York: B. Geis, 1971).

Jones, Max, and Albert McCarthy, eds. *A Tribute to Huddie Ledbetter* (London: Jazz Music Books, 1946).

Lomax, John A. *Adventures of a Ballad Hunter* (New York: Macmillan, 1947).

Lomax, John A., and Alan Lomax. *The Leadbelly Legend* (New York: Folkways, 1965).

———. *Negro Folk Songs as Sung by Leadbelly* (New York: Macmillan, 1936; 3rd ed. 1959).

Andrea Lee

Lee, Andrea. *Russian Journal* (New York: Random House, 1981) [reprint New York: Vintage, 1984].

———. *Sarah Phillips* (New York: Random House, 1984) [reprint New York: Penguin, 1985].

Alain LeRoy Locke

Butcher, Margaret Just. *The Negro in American Culture* ["Based on Materials Left by Alain Locke"], 2nd ed. (New York: Knopf, 1972).

Harris, Leonard, ed. *The Philosophy of Alain Locke: Harlem Renaissance and Beyond* (Philadelphia: Temple University Press, 1989).

Linnemann, Russell J., ed. *Alain Locke: Reflections on a Modern Renaissance Man* (Baton Rouge: Louisiana State University Press, 1982).

Locke, Alain. *Critical Temper and Aesthetic Vision: Selected Essays*, ed. with Jeffrey C. Stewart (1940; reprint New York: Garland, 1981).

———. *Negro Art: Past and Present* (Washington: Associates in Negro Folk Education, 1936) [reprint New York: Arno, 1969].

———. *The Negro and His Music* (Washington: Associates in Negro Folk Education, 1936) [reprint New York: Arno, 1969].

———, ed. *The New Negro* (New York: Boni, 1925) [reprint New York: Atheneum, 1968, and (with new introd.) 1992].

Locke, Alain, and Montgomery Gregory [A.B. 1910], eds. *Plays of Negro Life* (New York: Harper, 1927).

Locke, Alain, and Bernhard J. Stern, eds. *When Peoples Meet: A Study in Race and Culture Contacts*, rev. ed. (New York: Hinds, Hayden & Eldredge, 1946; reprint 1977).

Rayford W. Logan

Logan, Rayford W. *The African Mandates in World Politics* (Washington, D.C.: Public Affairs Press, 1948).

———, ed. *The Attitude of the Southern White Press Toward Negro Suffrage,*

1932-1940 (Washington, D.C.: Foundation Publishers, 1940).

———. *The Betrayal of the Negro* (New York: Collier Books, 1965) [A revision of *The Negro in American Life and Thought: The Nadir, 1877-1901* (New York: Dial, 1954)].

———. *Diplomatic Relations Between the United States and Haiti, 1776-1891* (Chapel Hill: University of North Carolina Press, 1941; reprint Millwood, N.Y.: Kraus, 1969).

———. *Haiti and the Dominican Republic* (New York: Oxford University Press, 1968).

———. *Howard University: The First Hundred Years, 1867-1967* (New York: New York University Press, 1969).

———. *The Negro in the United States* (Princeton, N.J.: Van Nostrand, 1957).

———. *The Senate and the Versailles Mandate System* (Washington: The Minorities Publishers, 1945; reprint Westport, Conn.: Greenwood, 1975).

Logan, Rayford W., and Irving S. Cohen. *The American Negro: Old World Background and New World Experience* (Boston: Houghton Mifflin, 1967, 1970).

Logan, Rayford W., and Michael R. Winston, eds. *Dictionary of American Negro Biography* (New York/London: Norton, 1982).

McNeil, Genna Rae, and Michael R. Winston, eds. *Historical Judgments Reconsidered: Selected Howard University Lectures in Honor of Rayford W. Logan* (Washington: Howard University Press, 1988) [Includes contributions by three black Harvard alumni: John Hope Franklin, Ph.D. '41; Nathan I. Huggins, Ph.D. '62; and Frank W. Snowden Jr. '32, Ph.D. '44.].

Malcolm X [Malcolm Little]

Breitman, George, ed. *By Any Means Necessary: Speeches, Interviews and a Letter by Malcolm X* (New York: Pathfinder, 1970).

———. *Last Year of Malcolm X* (New York: Merit, 1967).

———, ed. *Malcolm X Speaks* (New York: Merit, 1965).

Carson, Clayborne. *Malcolm X: The FBI File* (New York: Carroll & Graf, 1991).

Clarke, John Henrik, ed. *Malcolm X: The Man and His Times* (New York: Macmillan, 1969).

Davis, Lenwood G. *Malcolm X: A Selected Bibliography* (Westport, Conn.: Greenwood, 1983).

Epps, Archie, ed. *The Speeches of Malcolm X at Harvard* (New York: Morrow, 1968; 2nd ed. with new preface, New York: Paragon House, 1991).

Gallen, David. *Malcolm X As They Knew Him* (New York: Carroll & Graf, 1992).

Goldman, Peter. *The Death and Life of Malcolm X* (New York: Harper & Row, 1973; rev. 1979).

Johnson, Timothy V. *Malcolm X: A Comprehensive Annotated Bibliography* (New York: Garland Publishing Co., 1986).

Karim, Imam Benjamin, ed. *Malcolm X: The End of White Supremacy—Four Speeches* (New York: Arcade Publishing, 1989).

Malcolm X and Alex Haley. *The Autobiography of Malcolm X* (New York: Grove, 1965; expanded ed., New York: Ballantine Books, 1992).

Perry, Bruce. *Malcolm: The Life of a Man Who Changed Black America* (Barrytown, N.Y.: Station Hill Press, 1991).

Randall, Dudley, and Margaret G. Burroughs, eds. *For Malcolm: Poems on the Life and Death of Malcolm X*, 2nd ed. (Detroit: Broadside, 1969).

Wolfenstein, Eugene V. *The Victims of Democracy: Malcolm X and the Black Revolution* (London: Free Association Books, 1989).

Wood, Joe, ed. *Malcolm X: In Our Own Image* (New York: St. Martin's Press, 1992).

James Alan McPherson

McPherson, James Alan. *Elbow Room* (Boston: Little, Brown, 1977).

_____. *Hue and Cry* (Boston: Little, Brown, 1969).

McPherson, James Alan, and Miller Williams. *Railroad: Trains and Train People in American Culture* (New York: Random House, 1976).

Harold R. Scott

Ross, Lillian and Helen Ross. *The Player: A Profile of an Art* (New York: Simon and Schuster, 1962; reprint New York: Limelight Editions, 1984) [Chapter "Harold Scott," pp. 326-333].

Eileen Southern

Southern, Eileen. *Anonymous Pieces in the MS El Escorial IV.a.24* (Neuhausen-Stuttgart: Hänssler Verlag, 1981).

_____. *Biographical Dictionary of Afro-American and African Musicians* (Westport, Conn.: Greenwood, 1982).

_____. *The Buxheim Organ Book* (Brooklyn: Institute of Medieval Music, 1963).

_____. *The Music of Black Americans*, 2nd ed. (New York: Norton, 1983).

_____. *Readings in Black American Music* (New York: Norton, 1983).

Southern, Eileen, and Josephine Wright, eds. *African-American Traditions in Song, Sermon, Tale and Dance, 1600-1920s: An Annotated Bibliography of Literature, Collections and Artworks* (Westport, Conn.: Greenwood, 1990).

Wright, Josephine, and Samuel A. Floyd Jr., eds. *New Perspectives on Music: Essays in Honor of Eileen Southern* (Warren, Mich.: Harmonie Park Press, 1992).

William Monroe Trotter

Fox, Stephen R. *The Guardian of Boston: William Monroe Trotter* (New York: Atheneum, 1970).

Trotter, William Monroe, ed. *The Two Days Observance of the One Hundredth Anniversary of the Birth of Charles Sumner* (Boston: New England Suffrage League, 1911).

Booker T. Washington

Harlan, Louis R. *Booker T. Washington: The Making of a Black Leader, 1856-1901* (New York: Oxford University Press, 1972).

_____. *Booker T. Washington: The Wizard of Tuskegee, 1901-1915* (New York: Oxford University Press, 1983).

Harlan, Louis R. et al., eds. *The Booker T. Washington Papers*, 14 vols. (Urbana: University of Illinois Press, 1972-1988).

Hawkins, Hugh. *Booker T. Washington and His Critics* (Boston: Heath, 1962).

Mathews, Basil J. *Booker T. Washington: Educator and Interracial Interpreter* (Cambridge: Harvard University Press, 1948).

Scott, Emmett J., and Lyman Beecher Stowe. *Booker T. Washington: Builder of a Civilization* (Garden City: Doubleday, Page, 1916).

Smock, Raymond W., ed. *Booker T. Washington in Perspective: Essays of Louis R. Harlan* (Jackson, Miss.: University Press of Mississippi, 1988).

Spencer, Samuel R., Jr. *Booker T. Washington and the Negro's Place in American Life* (Boston: Little, Brown, 1955).

Washington, Booker T. *Character Building* (New York: Doubleday, Page, 1902).

_____. *The Future of the American Negro* (Boston: Small, Maynard, 1899) [reprint New York: Negro Universities Press, 1969].

_____. *My Larger Education* (Garden City: Doubleday, Page, 1911) [reprint Miami: Mnemosyne, 1969].

_____. *The Negro in Business* (Boston: Hertel, Jenkins, 1907) [reprint Chicago: Afro-American Press, 1969].

_____. *The Story of the Negro: The Rise of the Race From Slavery*, 2 vols.

(New York: Doubleday, Page, 1909) [reprint New York: P. Smith, 1940].

_____. *Up From Slavery* [autobiography] (New York: Doubleday, Page, 1901) [frequently reprinted].

_____. *Working With the Hands* (New York: Doubleday, Page, 1904).

Phillis Wheatley

Mason, Julian D., Jr., ed. *The Poems of Phillis Wheatley*, rev. ed. (Chapel Hill/London: University of North Carolina Press, 1989).

Renfro, G. Herbert, ed. *Life and Works of Phillis Wheatley* (Washington, D.C.: Robert L. Pendleton, 1916; reprint Miami: Mnemosyne, 1969).

Richmond, Merle A. *Bid the Vassal Soar: Interpretive Essays on the Life and Poetry of Phillis Wheatley and George Moses Horton* (Washington, D.C.: Howard University Press, 1974).

Robinson, William H. *Critical Essays on Phillis Wheatley* (Boston: G.K. Hall, 1982).

_____. *Phillis Wheatley and Her Writings* (New York/London: Garland Publishing, 1984).

_____. *Phillis Wheatley in the Black American Beginnings* (Detroit: Broadside Press, 1975).

Phillis Wheatley. *The Collected Works*, ed. John C. Shields (New York/ Oxford: Oxford University Press, 1988).

Ernest J. Wilson III

Kemezis, Paul, and Ernest J. Wilson III. *The Decade of Energy Policy: Policy Analysis in Oil Importing Countries* (New York: Praeger, 1984).

INDEX